Indonesian RELIGIONS
—*in*—
TRANSITION

Indonesian
RELIGIONS
—*in*—
TRANSITION

Rita Smith Kipp
Susan Rodgers
EDITORS

The University of Arizona Press / Tucson

About the Editors

RITA SMITH KIPP, associate professor of anthropology in the Department of Anthropology and Sociology at Kenyon College in Gambier, Ohio, has studied Karo Batak kinship, ritual, and village social organization. Her current interests include the anthropology of Christian missionary activity in Indonesia and the study of Islam in Karo culture.

SUSAN RODGERS is associate professor of anthropology in the Department of Sociology and Anthropology at Ohio University in Athens, Ohio; she is also a member of the Southeast Asia Studies faculty there. Her primary research interests include Angkola-Sipirok Batak ritual, kinship, and cultural change, as well as the transition from oral culture to literacy.

THE UNIVERSITY OF ARIZONA PRESS

Copyright © 1987
The Arizona Board of Regents
All Rights Reserved

This book was set in 10/12 202 Electra
Manufactured in the U.S.A.

Library of Congress Cataloging-in-Publication Data

Indonesian religions in transition.

Papers from the tenth Annual Indonesian Studies Conference, held at Ohio University in August 1982.
Bibliography: p.
Includes index.
1. Indonesia—Religion—Congresses. I. Kipp, Rita Smith. II. Siregar, Susan Rodgers. III. Conference on Indonesian Studies (10th : 1982: Ohio University)
BL2110.I52 1987 291'.09598 86-30742

ISBN 0-8165-1020-2 (alk. paper)

British Library Cataloguing in Publication data are available.

Contents

Acknowledgments

*A*S EDITORS OF THIS BOOK on Indonesian religion, we owe our largest debt to the many Indonesian citizens who shared their time and conversations with us during our fieldwork and who graciously allowed us to observe their rich religious heritage. Another major debt is owed to the American students of Indonesia who have convened the annual Indonesian Studies Conference in conjunction with the national summer Indonesian language institute since 1973 at the several universities that offer Indonesian language instruction. Most of the articles in this volume were first delivered at the tenth annual Indonesian Studies Conference, held at Ohio University in August 1982 on the topic, "Religion in Indonesia." As editors and co-chairs of that conference, we particularly wish to thank the directors of the 1982 Indonesian Summer Studies Institute for their encouragement and administrative support throughout the process of conference organization and editing. William Frederick of Ohio University's History Department and Richard McGinn of Ohio University's Linguistics Department and Indonesian language program urged us on with good cheer and good advice throughout the entire project. Ohio University's Southeast Asia librarian Lian The-Mulliner also provided invaluable help in the editing process, and Carolyn Spurlock of that university's Department of Sociology and Anthropology provided accurate, tireless secretarial support.

We also wish to thank our departments at Kenyon College and Ohio University for their support for this project since 1981.

Rita Smith Kipp
Susan Rodgers

vii

Contributors

JANE M. ATKINSON is an associate professor of anthropology at Lewis and Clark College in Portland, Oregon. Her current research focuses on shamanism and gender concepts in Wana.

JOHN BOWEN is an assistant professor in the Department of Anthropology, Washington University, St. Louis. His principal research interests are Gayo kinship, ritual, and social structure, comparative Indonesian social structure, and economic change at the village level.

ERIC CRYSTAL, program coordinator for the Center for South and Southeast Asia Studies at the University of California at Berkeley, has studied on Toraja social organization, religion, and social change. Crystal's recent research includes work in ethnographic film and studies of Toraja modernization, tourism, and village art.

JESSICA GLICKEN works for Allshouse and Glicken, Inc., in Albuquerque, New Mexico. Her current research interests include issues of language, literature, and social structure in Sunda.

BASYRAL HAMIDY HARAHAP is a sociologist employed at the Indonesian LEK-NAS research agency, associated with the Lembaga Ilmu Pengetahuan Indonesia. His recent research focuses on Batak urbanization and Batak literature.

PATRICIA B. HENRY, is assistant professor of Indonesian language and literature in Northern Illinois University's Department of Foreign Languages and Literatures. Among her research interests are Javanese and Indonesian literature.

DAVID HICKS, an anthropologist and a student of symbolic systems in eastern Indonesia, is professor of anthropology at the State University of New York at Stony Brook. His recent work concerns kinship, ritual, and myth in the Tetum area of Timor and the Manggarai area of Flores.

JANET HOSKINS, assistant professor in the Department of Anthropology, University of Southern California, received her Ph.D. in anthropology from Harvard University in 1983. Her recent research concerns comparative social structure in eastern Indonesia, and ritual, gender, and kinship in Sumba.

MAHADI, a professor of law at the University of North Sumatra, in Medan, Indonesia, is a specialist on the interaction of national Indonesian law, Islamic law, and *adat*.

ANNA LOWENHAUPT TSING, an anthropologist in the Women's Studies Program at the University of Colorado at Boulder, did fieldwork in Kalimantan for her Ph.D. from Stanford University. Her current research interests include gender ideas, social organization, and the interaction of local and national Indonesian culture among Dayak cultures in Kalimantan.

TOBY VOLKMAN is a student of Toraja ritual and social change. After work with the Documentary Educational Resources ethnographic film company, Volkman is now staff director for Southeast Asia at the Social Science Research Council. Her recent research on the Toraja concerns modernization, tourism, and religion.

JOSEPH WEINSTOCK, an agricultural consultant in West Java, has a doctorate in Development Sociology from Cornell (1983). He has done research in tropical agronomy in Java and Kalimantan, and his current interests are in forestry and farming systems in Indonesia, as well as regional planning and community development.

SHINJI YAMASHITA, a cultural anthropologist teaching at Hiroshima University in Japan, is a specialist on Toraja culture in Sulawesi. Much of his work concentrates on ritual.

INDONESIA

CAMBODIA – Country Name

HAINAN – Island Name

Aceh – Ethnic Groups

Southeast Asia

Introduction:
Indonesian Religions in Society

*J*NDONESIA IS A STARTLINGLY VARIED PLACE and a country of exceptional social complexity. It has over three hundred ethnic groups
whose members often speak their own languages in addition to Indonesian,
the national tongue, and cultivate their own *adat* (their own local, "ancestral" customs) with varying degrees of enthusiasm and political success.
In many of these ethnic societies, the concept of *adat* itself, despite disclaimers by its loyal supporters, is less ancestral than exquisitely contemporary: *adat* is often a system of symbols created through the interaction of
small minority societies, their ethnic neighbors, colonial administrations,
the national governments, and the world religions, Islam and Christianity.

Indonesia's social complexity derives in part from historical experience.
The chain of islands that became the independent Republic of Indonesia
in the national revolution of 1945 – 49 is situated along a number of
ancient trade routes which linked India and China, and, in more recent
times, Europe and the Spice Islands (the Moluccas of Eastern Indonesia).
The spice trade was first dominated by Portuguese ships in the 1500s after
the fall of Malacca, and then by the Dutch East India Company from 1602
to 1799. Hoping to turn the region into a cornucopia of plantation crops
and best her British and French colonial rivals in Asia, the Netherlands
government controlled large portions of the Indonesian archipelago until

1942. At that point, Japan quickly commandeered the colony in its World War II effort to forge a Greater Asian Co-prosperity Sphere that would include many of the European possessions in Asia. The years since 1949 have brought an independent Indonesia into closer political contact with mainland Southeast Asian nations, with modern India, China, and Japan, and with the Western capitalist societies, now keenly attracted to Indonesia's mineral and petroleum wealth. As a nation, Indonesia has experimented with parliamentary democracy, state-controlled, leftist theories of government, and, since 1965, a military-run regime of technocrats emphasizing rapid economic development.[1]

Indonesia's social complexity also derives from its geography and agricultural patterns. A vast archipelago of over 13,000 islands stretching from the Indian Ocean to Melanesia, Indonesia has the usual Southeast Asian division into mountain regions and lowland plains and valleys. A spine of volcanically active mountains runs down the west coast of Sumatra and through Java, while other mountain chains bisect Kalimantan and Sulawesi and course eastward from Bali toward Timor. In addition to this lowland and highland division, however, Indonesia is also organized around a fundamental polarity between the densely populated old state societies of Inner Indonesia (Java, Bali, Madura), which have long histories of intensive wet rice cultivation and now support about half of the nation's population, and the less populous, more ethnically diverse islands of Outer Indonesia (the bulk of the country's land area, in Sumatra, Kalimantan, Sulawesi, the Moluccas, and Nusa Tenggara Timor, east of Sumbawa). Indonesia's social history has been a long drama of interaction between the less politically centralized and more economically fragile minority societies in Outer Indonesia and the periodically expanding and contracting state societies of Inner Indonesia, south Sumatra, and south Sulawesi. Inner Indonesian court societies came under strong Indic influence from the seventh to the tenth centuries, and later formed the axis of Dutch colonial control in an often rebellious and politically fragmented archipelago.[2]

Indonesia today continues this history of political and social change and realignment, but at an especially rapid pace. A satellite system spanning the archipelago brings television broadcasts, often filled with heavily nationalistic fare, into previously remote areas. The urban-based mass media supplement the national public school system, which also extends into the farm villages. After almost forty years of independence, Indonesia's population is about 64 percent literate. (In the late 1970s, according to UNESCO figures, the literacy rates were 45 percent for women and 70 percent for men.) The urbanization of significant numbers of Javanese and Sumatrans in the same time period has led to new concepts of social identity (national as well as ethnic) and a strong emphasis on "escaping the village" for prestigious salaried work in the country's bloated government bureaucracies. In President Suharto's New Order regime established in 1965, swift economic development has been the national priority, and the central government has extended its influence in a number of outlying ethnic homelands through irrigation projects, miracle rice projects, massive road-building, and joint-venture companies in petroleum, lumber, and minerals with American, European, Australian, and Japanese firms.

Indonesia's religious complexity is as startling as its social diversity. Paradoxically, in the statistical yearbooks published by the national government in Jakarta this would not seem to be so. In those official handbooks, Indonesia's population is listed as being 88 percent Muslim, 5.8 percent Protestant Christian, 2.9 percent Catholic, 2 percent Hindu, and 0.9 percent Buddhist (Buku Saku Statistik Indonesia 1982:172). In addition, small numbers of nonconverted peoples live in largely Muslim or Christian areas, while others participate in "special religions," recognized as such by the government. These neat statistical summaries, however, belie the actual religious variety of the country today; they also disguise the shifting, changing quality of contemporary Indonesian religious life. The various ethnic societies often maintain thriving ritual systems touching on birth, marriage, agricultural increase, and death. These societies often profess beliefs in multitudinous spirit worlds, morally charged cosmic forces, and supernaturally potent ritual objects. These same societies, however, are often Muslim or Christian, some combination of the two, or in the process of conversion thanks to Christian missionary efforts or pressures to conform to an overwhelmingly Muslim national government and national culture.

Today, the "local ethnic religions," so to speak, are in important part *social creations* of the interaction of world religions and village ritual, for before intense contact with Islam or Christianity, local rituals in many ethnic homelands may not have been conceptualized as components of a distinctive and systematic domain. Moreover, "religious belief" may not have been an entity separate from the rest of knowledge.

In the same process, Islam and Christianity have been redefined and reinvigorated in a number of social contexts throughout the archipelago. Islam, for instance, is seen to exist in a fundamentally creative tension with ethnic *adat* practice in the Minangkabau homeland in West Sumatra (Abdullah 1966). In some regions, what outsiders may see as *"adat,"* members of the local society see as Islam. Some Southern Batak, for example, consider formulaic "good luck speeches" part and parcel of good Muslim marriage ceremonies. By contrast, Islam sometimes becomes *adat*. In Java, for instance, the communal meal called the *slamatan*, ostensibly held to control a universe of spirit forces, is sometimes matter-of-factly seen as part and parcel of ancient Javanese custom, although the form of the ceremony may owe much to the Islamic *kenduri* rituals (communal commemorative ceremonies). Perhaps the best way to put the situation is to say that *adat* and Islam mutually define each other.

A similar process is at work in Indonesian Christianity. In the Angkola Batak area of North Sumatra (a region now about 10 percent Protestant and 90 percent Muslim), the Batak translation of the New Testament gives readers the impression that Jesus Christ and his disciples lived in a world of kinship relationships filled with ritually subservient wife-receiving lineages and ritually superior wife-givers—just as the Angkola themselves do.

In other parts of Indonesia or in other social contexts, Muslims and Christians guard the purity of their monotheistic faith from "compromises" with local *adat*. Likewise, some Indonesians "who do not yet have a religion" speak of *adat* and religion as conflicting alternatives, as if to convert to a world religion would require them to abandon *adat*. Miles (1976) relates that the Ngadju Dayak use the phrase *"masuk* Malayu" (to become Malay) to express conversion to Islam, implying that conversion is at once an ethnic as well as a religious change. Similarly, a missionary to Eastern Kalimantan noted that the Kenyah invariably describe non-Christian Kenyah as *"adat* people," and, although people seem "perfectly cognizant" that Kenyah Christians do, in fact, continue to conform to *adat* in many ways, the conventions of speech imply that at some level Christianity and Kenyah *adat* contrast with each other (Conley 1976).

As we explain below, in Indonesian cities and in some of the mass media, Islam and nationalism are joined together in heady efforts of mutual legitimation. But, at the same time, a relatively small group of Muslim purists criticize the national bureaucracy in Jakarta for a lack of true faith. Islamic fervor and popular interest in the idea of a Darrul Islam, or the Islamic state, varies considerably from area to area.

This profusion of religiously charged political alignments and situations makes Indonesia a superb place for anthropologists and other students of religion to investigate the relationships between religion and society and, indeed, to explore the very definition of religion. Indonesian experience calls into question a number of comfortable assumptions sometimes made in the study of religion in other world areas. The Indonesian material asks: Is it productive in all cases to see religion as something counterpoised to social structure, and ultimately "generated" by it, as social scientists in Durkheim's lineage would have us believe? Do all religions everywhere necessarily consist of ritual and belief, as so many standard anthropological definitions of religion aver—or is the component of "belief" an artifact of interaction with the literate and highly systematized world religions (as Hopkins suggests, in this volume)? How should we understand the syncretism of diverse religious traditions of historically different backgrounds? Might not syncretism be more a symbolic conversion in specific social contexts and individual lives than some large-scale social structural phenomenon resulting in a carefully negotiated amalgam of "contrasting traditions"? Some Javanese pride themselves on their capacity to accommodate diverse ideas into a single, seamless vision of the world. Such *toleransi* seems to be less a simple mechanical combination or systematization of contrasting traditions than a reflection of a fundamental philosophical assumption that things in the world can take different manifest forms at different times. Just what is this *toleransi* so celebrated in Indonesian self-concepts? What does it tell us about syncretism as a general phenomenon?

What of the process of conversion itself? What does it mean to say that society X in Kalimantan was 15 percent Muslim in 1960 but is 40 percent Muslim now? Do distinct ethnic cultures "have religions" in such statistical senses? In fact, is the very notion of distinct Southeast Asian ethnic cultures a productive one? If not (as Edmund Leach has been warning Southeast Asianists since the publication of his 1954 book *Political Systems of Highland Burma*), what does it mean to say that Indonesia has many religions? What does it mean, moreover, to say that Indonesia's religions demonstrate a variety of forms, including trance, prayer, meditation, animal sacrifices, monument construction, communal meals, blessing speeches, verbal duels, and so on? How do Muslim and Christian ritual practices relate to these forms?

Questions such as these prompted American Indonesianists to convene the tenth annual conference on Indonesian Studies on the topic, "Religion in Indonesia." All but one of the chapters in this volume are based on papers originally read at that conference held at the Indonesian Studies Summer Institute at Ohio University from August 3 to 5, 1982. Most speakers were anthropologists; of the fifteen authors who presented papers, thirteen were in that discipline, one was a professor of law (Professor Mahadi), and another a sociologist (Basyral Harahap). The papers were almost universally focused on concrete ethnographic situations painstakingly recorded through extended fieldwork in the local language and Indonesian. Many authors self-consciously attempted the sort of "thick description" advocated by Clifford Geertz (1973b). Although the authors deal with quite diverse ethnographic subject matter in societies ranging from the Gayo-Alas in Sumatra to the Tetum in Timor, all are united in conceptualizing religion as something created and in fact continually refashioned in actual Indonesian social contexts.

This idea is explored from a number of directions in this volume. The essays fall into two basic groups: examinations of Indonesian religions and their transformations (the first division of this book) and considerations of the political aspects of the world religions (the second division of the book). We discuss these divisions in turn, giving short introductions to the different chapters as we go.

Indonesian Religions and Their Transformations

Several authors in this volume suggest that religious phenomena in different Indonesian cultures may be helpfully seen as *transformations* of each other and perhaps of other, seemingly nonreligious domains of culture. They also suggest that religious phenomena shift form (from trance to meditation, for example) as one goes from Indonesian culture to culture or as an ethnic religion takes on the symbolism of Islam or Christianity. This idea has also been applied to the study of Indonesian cultures as a whole, beyond religion, and is a useful perspective on the country's ethnic diversity. We can briefly discuss this approach here, with particular reference to the Dayak cultures, Nias, and Bali—three seemingly very different sorts of cultures that may, however, profitably be seen as transformations of each other in different historical and ecological contexts. Their religious systems, too, and what might be called their village arts, may also be caught up in a transformational system. Art itself is actually a close symbolic cousin of religion in these cultures, although in modern Indonesia the two have sometimes separated from each other. This short excursion into Dayak, Nias, and Balinese ethnography will set the scene for introducing the eight papers in the first part of the book.

Indonesian ethnic variety has been simplified into a number of ambitious anthropological and historical frameworks to make the archipelago's cultural diversity amenable to study and comparative analysis. One of the most popular of these frameworks, which divides Indonesia into the Inner and Outer Islands, has already been mentioned.[3] This approach draws on ecological distinctions as well as history, for Inner Indonesia's Java, Bali, and Madura not only have longer histories of intensive wet rice cultivation and state-level organization but also have had more intensive interaction with Indic civilization than most of the Outer Islands. One drawback for the Inner Indonesia/Outer Indonesia schemes, however, is that it obscures

·the fact that large trade states flourished in South Sumatra (Srivijaya near Palembang) and South Sulawesi (Sampaga). These mercantile societies developed through close political and trade interaction with Inner Indonesian societies (and with Malay states), and probably spread their own religious and political influence far inland into Sumatra and Sulawesi. In contemporary Indonesia, moreover, wet rice agriculture is practiced on a large scale in parts of Sumatra and Sulawesi and these areas now support dense populations.

Other schemes for sorting out Indonesian ethnic variety have been based on religion itself. One of these plans asserts that Indonesia is made up of unconverted hill peoples (a group decreasing in population size); Christian or Muslim ethnic minorities in the Outer Islands; Inner Indonesian ethnic groups from old Hindu-Buddhist court states that are now largely Muslimized areas; and peoples living in mercantile coastal societies such as Bugis or Minangkabau, now strongly Muslim. This approach seems partly based on the history of the introduction of Islam into the Indonesian islands. In brief summary, Islamization was intimately linked to commercial ventures and the control of ports. Two small Muslim trading kingdoms, called Sumadra-Pasai and Perlak, had been established in northern Sumatra by the end of the thirteenth century. Foreign traders crossing the Bay of Bengal came to trust these over the less stable non-Muslimized ports, which were more subject to pillage by pirates. These two kingdoms were important in the development of the Sumatran pepper and forest products trade until the rise of Malacca in the early fifteenth century. By the end of that century local Muslim princes controlled harbor kingdoms on the north coast of Java while other small Muslim entrepôts dotted the coastal regions as far east as Ternate and Tidore in the Moluccas. These harbor kingdoms were sometimes minor centers of Islamic scholarship. In some areas, such as Aceh and Minangkabau, Islam spread inland and led to the formation of forthrightly Muslim mercantile societies. These cultures have remained self-consciously pious today. The relationship between the Muslimized coastal areas of Java and the Javanese interior regions was tenser and more unpredictable. Some Javanese courts came to accept Islam only on their own terms, while the religion established itself in the countryside through mystical texts, the attractions of Arabic as a secret language, and Islam's offer of messianic hopes.

Dividing the archipelago into "more Islamized" and "less Islamized" areas has one major drawback: it encourages a "layer cake" imagery of religious diversity. With an eye toward the historical introduction of various religions at set sequential times in Java, for instance, the observer is easily tempted to view contemporary Javanese religious thought as segmented into strata of ancient village animism, Hindu-Buddhist belief and practice, and Islam. The authors in this volume suggest that this may be too mechanistic a view and instead favor a social processual and holistic perspective.

An alternative framework for understanding Indonesian cultures is based not on ecology, history, or religious doctrine but on what might be called folk epistemology. Students of Indonesian cultures sometimes portray ethnic differences in terms of a society's relative attention to hierarchical versus egalitarian organizations; or inner space versus outer spaces of houses, villages, and the universe itself; or centers versus peripheries. Folk ideas for conceptualizing history and power are generally crucial in these analytical schemes.[4]

Looking at Indonesian cultures and religions as transformations of each other is somewhat different from all these frameworks, for it aims to draw attention to underlying similarities rather than to divide Indonesian cultures into distinct categories. We can get a sense for this approach by exploring some of the cultural continuities among three seemingly quite distinct cultures: Dayak, Nias, and Bali.

First, the Dayak. There are at least twenty different Dayak societies in the island once called Borneo and now divided into Indonesia's Kalimantan provinces, Malaysia's Sarawak and Sabah, and newly independent Brunei. Located far upriver from the Muslimized port towns, Dayak societies generally practice shifting agriculture, supplemented with hunting and gathering forest products. All these societies have certain common social organizational features. Traditional villages were composed of multi-family longhouses; village political leadership was ephemeral, dissolving typically in a welter of competing loyalties; true class stratification was absent. High ritual status, if not class status, was often established through the accumulation of sacred house heirlooms (old beads or Chinese jars, obtained through trade with the coast). In pre-national times, taking enemy heads and displaying them in the home village was a major means for men and their families to increase their prestige. Women welcomed their warrior husbands back to the village after a successful raid and received the captured heads in special textiles that they had woven. Similar textiles were used to receive and cradle babies, and in a sense enemy heads were the symbolic, male equivalent of women's living babies. Men went into the forest and came back with severed heads to replenish the life forces of the village; such activity was thought necessary to regenerate the cycles of human and agricultural fertility in the village sphere.[5]

A number of other complementary oppositions were set out in Dayak myth and ritual. The Upperworld was juxtaposed to the Lowerworld and sometimes united by a Cosmic Tree; the Cosmic Tree itself was sometimes portrayed via a ritual assembly of fine textiles draped on swords, a device which united masculine (hard metal) and feminine (pliable cloth); the mythic inhabitants of the Upperworld and the Lowerworld came together to create the contents of the world. Shifting political alliances followed the fortunes of different families as they sought to control the powers that could be released by temporarily uniting Upperworld and Lowerworld, cloth and metal, village and forest, and so on.

Nias, off the west coast of Sumatra near Sibolga, is ostensibly quite a different sort of culture than the Dayak. In pre-national times Nias was a fervently hierarchical society. South Nias, where political centralization was apparently strongest, was organized into high villages ruled by chiefs, who controlled the farm labor services of commoner families and slaves. Nobles lived in tall *adat* houses at the elevated centers of villages, while commoners lived in smaller dwellings along the village periphery. Slaves lived in veritable huts far from the power centers of villages. South Nias settlements were somewhat like little mountains jutting out of the countryside and were approached by long flights of cut stone stairs. Pathways in the village were narrow near the village rim but broadened out as one approached the noble, powerful central plaza, ringed by the high *adat* houses of the aristocrats. The plaza was the site for ceremonies and was paved with closely fitted stones (Nias produced some of Indonesia's most magnificent megalithic architecture). It was filled with vertical and horizontal stone monuments. Each of these had been erected by noble families in their efforts to raise their social standing by hosting communal rituals.[6]

The aristocrats dedicated these megaliths to the memory of their ancestors but such artistic activity was also part of a continual cycle of ritual displays that nobles used to defeat their fellow aristocrats. They vied with each other through the construction of *adat* houses, monuments, wooden sculpture, and ornaments. The construction of a fine *adat* house was a central event in such competition. A chief was obligated to progress through several stages of ritual activity in order to gain permission to dedicate a new house. These ritual works included erecting stone slabs in the village plaza and hosting a number of village feasts where pork and specially commissioned gold jewelry were distributed.

Such largesse was thought to spring from the very nature of aristocrats. They staked their claim to high status via a cosmological belief system that associated power with an extended list of qualities and things that went considerably beyond ideas of height and centrality. Nobles were contrasted to commoners according to the following plan (adapted from Suzuki 1959:43):

Nobles	Commoners
height	lowness
gold	"false gold" (alloys)
yellow	red
silk	cotton flannel
wisdom	ignorance
strength and decisiveness	indecision
beneficence	receptivity
spiritual blessings	physical protection
masculinity	femininity
village	forest

The good order of the universe flowed from the measured *combination* of elements of the two sides, and it was thought to be in the very nature of commoners to work for the benefit of their aristocratic counterparts. Slaves fell entirely outside the system, beyond human society per se.

This schema was part of a larger conceptualization of cosmic structure and the place of humankind within it. Power flowed from temporary, tense unions of complementary opposites. Such ritual activities were controlled by the nobles with the help of priestesses. A typical "power-releasing" and controlling ritual involved carving images of forest animals such as monkeys and then introducing them into the *adat* houses. In taking a creature of the forest and inserting it through human agency into the house (the sphere of humanity and *adat*), wood carvers and their noble sponsors were uniting society and wilderness, human and animal. Such humanized animals helped empower and protect the house and its inhabitants.

Many similarities to Dayak culture are already evident: the idea that complementary opposites unite to release cosmic powers; the association of height with rank; the division of the cosmos into an Upperworld and a Lowerworld that are inhabited by contrastive animals and deities; the idea that male and female were aboriginally one, and, although now divided in everyday life, they unite again occasionally under ritual control. The symbolic concordances go much further than this, however. Recall that Dayak villages were "reinvigorated" by infusion of new heads brought back from the forest. In traditional Nias, too, when a fine *adat* house was dedicated, the owner had to empower it by planting heads under the house posts and displaying them on racks. Death and heads were also used to control dangers: the heads of slaves were buried underneath special poles on which new gold ornaments were displayed, in an effort to neutralize the gold's dangers.

Rivalry between South Nias chiefs eventually filled up the village plazas with *adat* houses, megaliths, and wooden sculptures. Through the late 1800s, an infusion of gold from the slave trade fueled this efflorescence of ritual activity, and indeed Nias's case is a somewhat special one in Outer Island Indonesia. A small, ecologically variable island, Nias's political situation and feverish artistic activity was probably only rivaled by East Sumba. However, it is possible to see South Nias as a Dayak-like culture pushed into overdrive, so to speak, by particular ecological and historical circumstances.

In Kalimantan, rivalry between men was phrased in a language of ritual warfare and head-taking, with a relatively modest accumulation of house wealth. In Nias, chiefs turned the island's surplus into lavish feasts and village architectural activities. In the traditional states of Bali, what may perhaps have been a related symbolic system resulted in a ritual life of unparalleled extravagance involving palaces, fancy court costumes, dances and orchestras, complex theories of government and cosmology, and nearly continual ceremonial activity. Bali's highly productive wet rice subsistence system and its court-based traditional culture are familiar from a number of studies.[7] It could be that traditional Bali was a sort of Nias located in an unusually productive subsistence situation (producing a huge surplus that could be converted into ritual activities) and in a particular contact situation with Indian theories of cosmology and government. Certain basic systems of ideas, such as complementary opposition or the accumulation of prestige through ritual activities, gained new meaning when Balinese courts adopted Indian religious themes. In other words, Balinese religion became *transformed* into new forms as historical circumstances changed.

It could be that transformation takes place at a more limited level as well, affecting such seemingly discrete phenomena as trance, meditation, food display, sculpture, megalithic activity, oratory, prayer, and so on. The chapters in the first section of this book, "Indonesian Religions and Their Transformations," show these various processes in detail.

David Hicks's chapter, "Space, Motion, and Symbol in Tetum Religion," is basically a definitional inquiry. How does one delimit the domain of religion in Indonesian cultures? Hicks suggests that story-telling in that Timorese culture is a crucial constituent of folk cosmology. As a consequence, the analysis of Tetum culture should not be artificially broken down into folklore studies versus religious studies versus kinship studies and so on. Tetum story-telling is religion-telling in a specific sense. Tetum narratives take two forms. In one, events take place along a vertical axis of heaven and earth; in the other, events take place along a horizontal axis on the ground. These two axes intersect at certain places, and these points of "origin," mentioned in both narratives, reveal Tetum notions of their beginnings and the sources of life. Tetum culture is shot through with complementary oppositions such as masculine and feminine, sky and earth, out and in, and village and forest, familiar from other cultures in Eastern Indonesia (Fox 1980). The culture also has the expected fascination with ideas of creativity springing from the union of complementary opposites. Hicks's article points Eastern Indonesianists toward the study of metaphors of space and story-telling in their studies of local cosmological systems.

Eric Crystal and Shinji Yamashita's "Power of the Gods: *Ma'bugi'* Ritual of the Sa'dan Toraja" deals with concepts of trance and purification ritual. The Toraja material suggests that comparative students of the two phenomena might profitably see one as the transformation of the other. At one level, the authors provide detailed ethnographic information about the *ma'bugi'* trance dances and related rituals documented in Eric and Catherine Crystal's 1973 film, "*Ma'bugi'*—Trance of the Toraja." At a second level, they deal with the methodological question of using different types of performances in analyzing a single genre of ritual. At a third level, a crucial one for this volume, Crystal and Yamashita hold that complex events like the *ma'bugi'* can only be understood through a sort of triangulation of analytical frameworks. Here, the authors use a combination of Victor Turner's symbolic approach to ritual and Clifford Geertz's interpretive perspective, set out in "Deep Play: Notes on the Balinese Cockfight" (1972b) and "Thick Description" (1973b).

In "Kaharingan: Life and Death in Southern Borneo," Joseph Weinstock deals with those favorite categories, the sacred and the profane, in his study of a Central Kalimantan Dayak religion. This is a case where interaction with the Indonesian nation and its official concepts of what constitutes a valid religion has shaped indigenous Dayak ideas. As minority populations dominated by the Jakarta government, several Dayak groups (Luangan, Ngaju, Ot Danum, Maanyan) have in essence created a new religion for themselves in counterpoint to the *agama*, the world religions, recognized by the Indonesian state. Importantly, these Dayak peoples have moved toward a separation of the sacred and the profane in the process of defining and systematizing certain of their traditions as *agama*. Rituals to promote life and health and to respond to death were the chief occasions drawing large groups together. These rituals, and the beliefs associated with them, are now termed Kaharingan, Indonesia's newest officially recognized religion. A political movement affected this recognition and focused the ethnic identity of the region's peoples. While apparently carving out a realm of the sacred, Kaharingan has come to stand not for an easily separable realm of the holy, but for an entire way of life. The Dayak material presents a fine illustration of the slipperiness of the sacred in Indonesian cultures and demonstrates the mutual development of political and religious identities.

Patricia Henry's "The Religion of Balance: Evidence from an Eleventh Century Javanese Poem" takes the discussion for the first time into Javanese religion, with all its attendant problems of interpretation and function. Henry presents a courtly poem of the *kakawin* genre, the *Arjuna Wiwaha*, as a text that illuminates Javanese religious philosophy for both outside observers like ourselves and for the Javanese themselves. Specifically, it illustrates the interaction of two congruent systems: trance, a pan-Indonesian and presumably very old practice, and *tapa*, the Javanese version of austerities and meditations. Evidencing the blend or compatibility of these two systems, a section of the poem exemplifies the symbolic mechanics of this blending process and suggests that the poem's philosophy also replicates some strikingly diverse expressive forms: *candi* (temples), dance, and puppetry. Like Crystal and Yamashita's paper on Toraja trance and purification ritual, Henry's essay suggests that such "distinct" cultural phenomena may be best seen as transformations of one another.

The mutual interaction of *adat* and Islam has been particularly vigorous in Sumatra, the frontier of the Islamization of Indonesia starting in the late thirteenth century. In such Muslim Sumatran societies as Aceh, Gayo-Alas, the southern Batak societies, and Minangkabau, *adat* and Islam seem to outsiders to persistently collapse into each other. It is common to find Islamic ritual styles defined as "ancient ancestral *adat*" and local custom lauded as part of Allah's plan for his human world.

The relationship between local ritual and Sufism is the subject of John Bowen's "Islamic Transformations: From Sufi Doctrine to Ritual Practice in Gayo Culture." Early Aceh's Sufism metamorphosed in Gayo into a theory and practice of ritual. The Gayo, a mountain people, most probably became Muslim through the influence of itinerant Sufi mystics some centuries ago. Transformed by Islam, the Gayo in turn transformed it. What had been a contemplative basis for mystical union (the relation of Creator to created) developed into the ontological grounds for ritual practice. The sixteenth century poetry of an Acehnese mystic, Hamsah Fansuri, exhibits the same ideas of being and creation that appear in the Gayo's contemporary cosmogony and in their practical, ritual approaches to healing.

Indonesian culture's transformation into Christian communities follows some of the same patterns found in the process of converting to Islam. A small number of Indonesian mountain peoples and groups in isolated

interior regions and small eastern Indonesian islands have been converted
by European missionaries to Protestantism, or on Flores and Timor, to
Roman Catholicism. Janet Hoskins examines the effect Christianization
efforts had on Kodi culture and its concepts of the supernatural in her
chapter, "Entering the Bitter House: Spirit Worship and Conversion in
West Sumba." She argues that attempts to define religion have not given
due attention to the fact that its two aspects—belief and practice—may be
differently weighted in different religions. When confronted with Christian
missionaries, Sumbanese did not possess a consciously articulated "religion," understood as a set of beliefs. Their spirit worship existed most
consciously as practices, and it was these practices through which the
Sumbanese first drew conceptual parallels with Christianity, interpreting
Christian rituals through their own rituals. Only later, with the growth of a
self-conscious concern with "religion" as something separable from the rest
of life, did the dialogue between Christianity and the traditional religion
come to focus on doctrinal issues of belief.

Toby Volkmann's "Mortuary Tourism in Tana Toraja" recognizes the
important role played by international contacts in the development of
Indonesian religions. Contacts with missionaries around the turn of the
century and with tourists in recent years have changed the Toraja people's
understandings of ritual practice and of ritual in general. Through a quirk
of history, tourists began flocking to see the traditional rituals of this Sulawesi society at precisely the moment when Toraja, for reasons of their own,
had begun to argue over "authenticity" and over the proper place and scale
of rituals in the modern world.

Indonesian religions are constructed in interaction with Islam, the majority religion, and with the national state, as some of these papers have
already illustrated. The chapters in the second section of the book look at
this process in more detail.

The Politics of Agama

The Indonesian word *agama* translates roughly as the English word
"religion," and so the papers in the second section of the book explore the
politics of religion in Indonesia. That phrase calls to mind the ways people
use religious rationales to build unity and loyalty within a polity, to explain
conflict, and to legitimate authority. In some cases, people consciously use
religion to achieve political goals, but in other cases, perhaps most cases,
they do not. Rather, people practice a certain religion and interpret their

lives through its assumptions, and these practices and assumptions have unintended political consequences. The politics of religion, then, may be conscious or merely consequential. In either case, the political implications of religion should not exclude our attention to religion itself and to the recognition of religious motivations in human life.

This is especially so in the study of Indonesia. Ruth McVey (1981), reviewing some social scientific views of Islam in Indonesia, criticizes those who see religion only as "a vehicle for the ambitious and a figleaf for other aims." Keeping motivation, intention, and meaning conceptually separate from the social consequences of religious behavior has always challenged the social scientific study of religion. Remembering that conversion, faith, and the search for meaning are as real and as irreducible as are power, legitimacy, and conflict, in this section we turn our attention to religion's political implications and to the political context of Indonesian religious life.

The politics of religion has a long history in Indonesia. By the late seventh century, Srivijaya, the earliest of the "Indianized" kingdoms of Indonesia, exerted influence over part of southern Sumatra and Java. It is not clear to what extent South Indians actually colonized Srivijaya and similar states that rose and fell in the region during the next eight centuries, or merely served these states as courtly advisers, but Hindu-Buddhist culture and the Sanskrit language were certainly "the civilization of the elite and not that of the whole population" (Coedes 1968:16). The Indianized kingdoms were the first state-level polities of Indonesia, drawing their legitimacy from an imported, theocratic ideology. The kings were gods incarnate, and a "graded spirituality" according to distance from the king determined succession to the throne and to many political offices (Hall 1976). Supernaturally sanctioned oaths bound the king's subjects to him. According to one historian of this period, Hinduism offered the early Indonesian states, "both a projection and a legitimation of monarchical order" (Legge 1964:35).

The last of such Indianized kingdoms, Majapahit, ended in the early sixteenth century, and by that time, as noted, Islam was well established at many points throughout the archipelago, especially in coastal areas and trading ports. The north coast cities of Java, linked commercially to the Muslim entrepôt of Malacca, began to resent their subordination to Majapahit. Legge (1964:44) notes,

> When the harbor principalities, caught up in the activities of a new commercial power, sought to establish their independence from Madjapahit, Islam served as a useful ideological weapon in

their struggle, as it was later to be for Indonesians in general against the European. Islam's contribution to this struggle was twofold. It offered certainly a symbol of resistance, but more fundamentally it constituted an alternative to the whole Hindu view of the world. In bringing man face to face with God without the necessity of a mediating priesthood or a complicated ritual, it implied a doctrine of equality which could offer a powerful solvent for the hierarchical order of Madjapahit.

To the consternation of the Dutch, Islam seemed to spread in the Indies along with the expansion of the pax Neerlandica and colonial rule. By the end of the nineteenth century, when the Netherlands began to tighten its hegemony over the whole archipelago and to incorporate interior regions that had remained independent until that time, a clear "Islampolitik" had emerged. Fearing the power of Islam to transcend ethnic divisions and to inspire resistance, the Dutch hoped to stem the spread of Islam where they could. Officials were cautious about allowing Christian missionaries in Muslim areas where their evangelizing might incite the ire of local Muslim leaders, but the government permitted and at times encouraged missionaries in non-Muslim areas in order to create Christian enclaves or "buffers." The Dutch believed that the tribal religions of formerly independent peoples would not withstand the forces of change and that, as these religions disappeared, people would seek modern replacements. Unless Christian missions offered an alternative, the available replacement would be Islam—and the Dutch did not want to see the peoples of the Indies united in the community of Islam. Some civil servants used "Islampolitik" more forcefully than others, easing the penetration of Christian missionaries while stifling the spread of Muslim merchants and schools.

If any Hollander required a reason for this politik, the war with Aceh provided it. The most costly resistance in Dutch Indies colonial history, the Aceh War flared intermittently for over twenty-five years, fueled by an ideology that defined the struggle against the Dutch as a Holy War, and one which promised reward in the afterlife to those who died fighting for the cause (Siegel 1969). The Hollanders' fear and suspicion of Islam proved prophetic. The first truly nationalistic movement to gain wide following was a Muslim movement, Sarekat Islam.

After independence, the official stance on religion in the new republic emerged as a compromise between proponents of a Muslim state and those who opposed this idea (although they were self-identified Muslims as well for the most part). The compromise entailed making Indonesia an expressly religious nation without making any particular faith the religion of the state. Atkinson (this volume) calls the result of this policy a "civil religion." The men who wrote the Indonesian constitution made the nation stand officially on a common belief in God, who was called, in the language of compromise, Tuhan (Lord) rather than Allah (Boland 1971:36). The men who shaped Indonesia's nationhood hoped to pull its diverse and dispersed peoples together by identifying common values and then fostering strong commitment to these. The new nation's unity was to spring from five summative principles, called the Pancasila. These principles are, in order, the Belief in One God, Nationalism, Humanism, Democracy, and Social Justice. The Belief in One God occupies first place, and, according to official interpretation, "inspires" (mendjiwai) the other four principles (Pendidikan Moral Pancasila, Departemen Pendidikan dan Kebudayaan, n.d.). The term for God in the Pancasila, Tuhan yang Maha Esa, has engendered various translations—the One and Only God (Boland 1971), the Absolute Lordship (Hadjiwijono 1967), and All-Embracing God (Mahadi, this volume). Scholars have also debated whether this term for God represents a "de-confessionalized" Muslim concept (Niewenhuisje 1958), or a neutral (although monotheistic) concept for God (Sidjabat, cited in Boland 1971).

The first of the Pancasila tenets is elaborated in two statements in the Indonesian constitution, sections one and two of Article 29. Section one merely elaborates earlier parts by stating, "The State shall be based upon belief in the all-embracing God." Section two adds that "The State shall guarantee the freedom of the people to profess and exercise their own religion" (Mahadi, this volume). These official pronouncements, and the government structures and policies that grew out of them, have become part of the context in which the religious life of all Indonesians must be understood.

Those who actively espoused an Islamic state in 1948 were a minority, but one that could not be easily ignored, considering the statistical preponderance of those who, regardless of other measures of devotedness, simply identify themselves as Muslim. Muslim leaders speak as an "active minority—within a numerical majority" (Emmerson 1981). Perhaps 20 to 30 percent of Indonesian Muslims are modernist or reformist Muslims, but the political power of reformist Islam has an important economic underpinning as well: long associated with commerce and long-distance trade in the Indonesian islands, reformist Islam has been nurtured by (and possibly nurtured in turn) a middle range mercantile sector (Geertz 1956). Today most Indonesian Muslims have given up talk of an Islamic state, but not all have given up hope (Jones 1981).

Political parties in the new nation coalesced partly along religious fis-
sures, with Muslims split in two main parties, Masyumi, appealing generally to reformist Muslims and drawing most of its power from non-Javanese
areas, and Nahdatul Ulama, a Java-dominated party that appealed to traditional Muslims. The Republican governments, however, have been almost
as wary of Muslim political power as were the Dutch. Even during the fight
for independence against the Dutch, a Muslim separatist rebellion, Dar Al
Islam, sprang up in the Sundanese area of West Java and continued at
some level until the early 1960s. The present government, hoping to di-
minish the sectarian dimension of party politics, has banned the original
reformist party, Masyumi. Now there is only one legal Muslim party, the
Development Unity Party (PPP), the name of which does not even allude
to Islam. Like other parties, PPP cannot easily compete with the government party, Golkar (Emmerson 1981).

In the 1960s, Muslim student leaders began to question the religious
legitimacy of sectarian-based political struggle. Although committed fully
to Islam, they aimed to separate religion from politics (Boland 1974). Traditionally, Muslims have understood submission to God to mean working for
a morally just society such that church-state separation, to use the Western
phrase, is hardly conceivable (Smith 1957:16 – 17). The Renewal Movement, calling for the "secularization" of politics, created a storm among
those Indonesian Muslims who believe that politics, no less any other part
of human life, must be guided by religious motives. The Renewal Movement did not aim, however, to compartmentalize religion and politics in
any simple imitation of the West (e.g., Majid 1979:153). (For references on
the Renewal Movement, see McVey 1981:284.)

The issue of secularization is much larger than party politics. The law
and the courts are another realm in which Islam competes with Western
notions of secular statehood. There is perhaps no more legalistic religion
than Islam, and, although Islam has never been the only source of law for a
country, many Muslims claim that Islam meets all human need for law
(Lev 1972). However, as the chapter (this volume) by Mahadi shows, the
legal situation in Indonesia is historically complex. There are several legitimate bases for Indonesian law: the multitude of customary, often unwritten, legal traditions in the various ethnic groups; a national constitutional
law modeled on Dutch codes; and Islamic law, of the Sjafi'i variety. Mahadi, a professor of law, notes in his paper, "Islam and Law in Indonesia,"
that the Dutch exhibited ambivalence toward Islamic courts and laws—at
times hostile toward them and at other times protective. Indonesian constitutional law has inherited some of this ambivalence. Today, Mahadi con-

tends, the separate Islamic courts primarily hear the marriage and family disputes of Muslims, and the national courts and laws generally aim to parallel and supplement, rather than to compete with, the Muslim legal institutions. As Nancy Tanner (1970) showed some years ago, Indonesians use these different sources of law for their own advantage, benefiting from the flexibility of such a system. She described how the Minangkabau, one of Indonesia's few matrilineal peoples and a people also proud of its long history in the world community of Muslims, argue their legal cases (for example, inheritance disputes) at times from principles of *adat*, but at other times from either the laws of Islam or the civil code of the nation.

The major event of Indonesian history since independence was the accession to power in 1965 of the present, military-backed regime. The Suharto government instituted a so-called New Order (Orde Baru). At that time, the nation's economy was rapidly sliding into disaster. As noted, the New Order took economic development as its dominant theme. Using the mass media, the government now promotes and celebrates new factories, agricultural improvements, and family planning. The New Order has aimed, too, to stem the people's once-strong attraction to communism. The purge that followed 1965, a true bloodbath, took hundreds of thousands of lives, primarily of those suspected of having been communists. Thousands more were imprisoned. This purge sometimes provided a new rationale for old racial resentments, and many Chinese Indonesians, suspected communist sympathizers, lost their lives.

What was the place of religion in this political upheaval? During the purge, religion, or to be precise, *agama*, became the refuge against accusation, imprisonment, or execution. Communism was seen as antithetical to *agama* and, conversely, religious devotion was seen as incompatible with communism. Consequently, people sought to become identified as practicing devotees of one of the *agama*, one of the organized world faiths. In some areas (for instance, the Karo Batak highlands), observers reported mass conversions to Christianity (Grothaus 1970). Many converts or people who suddenly showed a revived interest in their *agama* lapsed again into their previous behavior when the political climate cooled. Even so, Christian churches have continued to grow in the last twenty years, just as Islam and the other organized religions have also gained strength. (The number of Karo Batak Christians has climbed steadily, especially among urban migrants but also in rural Karoland.) The number of mosques has also expanded dramatically throughout the nation in recent years. Similarly, the numbers of persons registered as Hindus and Buddhists have grown, and Buddhist followers now enact rituals in the monumental splendor of the newly restored Borobudur.[8] It is important to note, however, that the restored temple suffered partial damage in a bomb explosion on January 21, 1985—an explosion possibly arranged by anti-government groups.

Leaders in both the New Order and the old have used religion to legitimize or to attain their goals (Majid 1979; Emmerson 1981). Leaders in the newly independent nation needed to unify a diverse array of peoples spread over great distances; the "technocrats" of the New Order want to increase Indonesia's wealth and its standard of living. Both have limited or been suspicious of the political potential of Islam, and yet both have had to mollify powerful religious minorities by injecting a religious commitment into national rhetoric and goals. Although the government enjoys general endorsement of its development goals, some Indonesians worry about the concomitants of economic change—for example, rock videos, nightclub entertainments, Western-style dress, and enormous disparities of wealth. The Islamic world has always viewed modernity and Western technology with ambivalence. Contemporary Muslim intellectuals wonder how to encourage economic development and adopt Western technology without taking Western aesthetic values and standards of morality, Western secularism and capitalism in the same package (Stoddard et al. 1981). The official government rhetoric in Indonesia must, therefore, answer these doubts as well. A recent collection of Suharto's speeches called "Religion in National Development" (*Agama dalam Pembangunan Nasional*, 1981) is full of assurances to the Indonesian public that the country remains committed to being a *religious* nation, that growth and development must focus on moral and religious development, not just obvious technological change, and that religiosity and modernity can and must go hand in hand. The government is quick to defend itself against accusations that it is secularizing Indonesian life. A series of articles and rejoinders dealing with the concept of secularism appeared in Indonesian newspapers in the summer of 1983. One of these (Abdulgani 1983) argued that the term grew out of the very specific situation of the history of the Catholic church in Europe and that it carried connotations of atheism and materialism. Neither this history nor the connotations of the word could apply to Indonesia, Abdulgani argued.

In Indonesia's courts and elsewhere, then, a balancing act takes place. Not an Islamic state, and yet not an entirely secular one either, Indonesia guarantees freedom of religion (*agama*) and at the same time promotes the belief in an all-embracing God. This sets up a logical tension that has surfaced in a number of conflicts. In some of these, arguments about terms and definitions have been central, with a stress on what *agama* is and whether a particular practice, cult, or belief is or is not *agama*. The world's named religions—Hinduism, Buddhism, Christianity, Islam, Judaism, and so on—present no definitional problems. Disputes arise, rather, over how to regard beliefs and ritual practices that fall outside these named categories. Two ambiguous situations arise. First, there are "people who do not yet have a religion," i.e., peoples whose religions are unnamed and uncodified, and who usually live in relatively isolated regions. A second ambiguity arises from people who belong to one of the recognized religions but also carry out practices or hold beliefs that others of the same faith judge heretical at worst and superfluous at best. The practice of *kebatinan*, mysticism, exemplifies this second situation and will take us into the politics internal to Islam. We examine these two ambiguities in turn.

INDONESIANS WHO "DO NOT YET HAVE A RELIGION"

Indonesians speak of those who do not belong to any organized religious community as *orang belum beragama*, people who do not yet have a religion. This category includes those Dayak, Toraja, Karo Batak, and others who continue to follow traditional ways of venerating ancestors and placating the spirits of nature. As Atkinson notes in her chapter, "Religions in Dialogue: The Construction of an Indonesian Minority Religion," the word *belum*, "not yet," implies an inevitability about the future of these peoples. The term *agama*, as noted, usually translates as the English word "religion." However, the term *agama* actually covers a somewhat narrower range than does the English term, under which ancestor worship and animism usually fit as readily as do Hinduism and Islam. Atkinson traces the historical development of the term *agama*. A word that in Sanskrit denotes traditional precept or doctrine, or in fact anything handed down by tradition, *agama* also names the manuals that prescribe the ritual procedures appropriate to Shivaite temples of South India (Fuller 1982.) Historically, then, its meanings overlapped considerably with what Indonesians now term *adat*, tradition or custom. Atkinson suggests that in the context of the term's diffusion into the early Indic kingdoms of Indonesia, it acquired other connotations as well. *Agama* came to be seen as "an attribute of a rich and foreign civilization." The arrival of both Islam and Christianity reinforced these connotations, adding to them an implied connection with literacy and progress. In contrast, Indonesians term the uncodified, tribal religions *kepercayaan*, "beliefs," or simply *adat*, "tradition." Sometimes the practitioners themselves, however, give these religions their own proper names—Perbegu, Aluk Ta Dolo, Kaharingan— usually in response to contact with people who practice an *agama*.

Rather than join the established faiths, some Indonesians have attempted to elevate their own faith as *agama*. Geertz (1973a) called this process on Bali "internal conversion," describing a Weberian process of rationalization that had begun to transform Bali's concrete, ritually embodied religion into a new form that seemed "self-conscious and worldly-wise" by comparison with the old. The traditional aristocracy, the priesthood, and youth had all begun to search for reasons and doctrines that on the one hand explained ritual and social practice and, on the other hand, made explicit sense of life in general. New publications of ancient texts appeared. At the same time, "ecclesiastical" changes occurred. A local "Ministry of Religion" aimed to classify the myriad temple organizations of Bali and to supervise and edu-cate the priesthood. The Ministry and others began to argue, too, that the traditional religion of Bali was a variant of the venerable faith of Hinduism, fully equal to Islam or Christianity in moral weight and equally deserving of official recognition. Bali's effort to win governmental recognition of its religion as a fully legitimate *agama* eventually succeeded.

Geertz suggested that Bali's internal conversion reflected the same pro-cess by which great historic religions came to be and that, by paying attention to what happens on Bali, "we may gain insights into the dynamics of religious change of a specificity and an immediacy that history, having already happened, can never give us" (Geertz 1973a:179). Bali's self-impelled "conversion," it turns out, was not idiosyncratic but, rather, an early example of a process that has happened elsewhere in Indonesia. Several of the contributors to this volume describe a process similar to that which occurred in Bali. As noted, Weinstock introduces his description of the Dayak religion, Kaharingan, by describing the politics of its inception; the politics, that is, of its inception as a named, self-conscious religion, conceptually distinct from the community life and other traditions of Dayak peoples. Similarly, Atkinson reports that, "The Wana . . . have been engaged in a debate among themselves, with their neighbors, and with government authorities over what constitutes a religion." Unlike Geertz, however, she distinguishes the Wana's religious transformation from the genesis of the historic religions, emphasizing that the Wana's rationaliza-tion of their faith has come out of interaction with a powerful nation state in which a "civil religion" occupies an obvious place. Perhaps, Atkinson suggests, the Wana, Bali, and Dayak examples represent a "third possibility" to the contrast between traditional and historic religions: "local cultural traditions in dialogue with world religious systems." In "The Voice of His-tory: A Rhetoric of Centers in a Religion of the Periphery," Anna Lowenhaupt Tsing asserts that most minority Indonesian religions can no longer be comprehended as self-contained systems, closed to influences from other religions and to phenomena such as regional and national politics. A new religion and a new ethnic consciousness emerge in the teaching of an extraordinary Meratus woman who draws on the symbols of power and knowledge from regional and national centers and from sources such as Islam. She leads a nativistic movement that links her backwater area to centers of power, while at the same time imbuing local traditions with a new authority.

The Indonesian Republic, like the Dutch colonial government, has been more willing to allow Christian missionaries to work among peoples without *agama* than to permit proselytization in Muslim areas. In fact, a law dating to 1979 prohibits Christian missionary activity among Muslims. (See Sidney Jones 1981:318 for references to the decrees in question.) Muslims have also begun to engage in mission work or *da'wah*, a term that covers both proselytizing to non-Muslims as well as education and renewal among those already Muslim. *Da'wah* proceeds under the auspices of private organizations such as the reformist Muhammidiyah and also under the Ministry of Religion. This Ministry, for example, has spent some 25 million U.S. dollars to print the Qu'ran and "improve religious education," (Dewan Kemakmuran Masjid Indonesia, n.d.).

Although the peoples who do not "yet" have *agama* do not face coercive pressures to convert, the government's messages about religion surely do encourage conversion. Religious education is part of the public school curriculum; thus, beginning in elementary classrooms, texts and lectures convey the idea that *agama* is progressive (*maju*) and a requisite of good citizenship. By an implicit logic of opposites, the official endorsements of *agama* make those persons without *agama* appear to be disloyal national citizens, uncommitted to the values of the Pancasila, not to mention intellectually and morally backward. The current pressures to take up an *agama*, then, are most usually subtle ones encouraging dignity and national loyalty. However, the nightmare following 1965 is still a fresh memory, and, although people no longer convert to keep from going to prison, everyone knows the government still views people without a legitimate religious affiliation with some suspicion. Official identity cards usually specify religion. Teachers and other civil servants feel that identification with an *agama* helps them attain and keep a position as employees of the government. It is not surprising that membership in almost all the organized religions has increased in the last two decades.

As those people "without religion" begin to convert, they undergo a conceptual sorting out of *agama* from *adat*, and both of these from national loyalty. This sorting out process divides life into compartments that correspond, at least in part, to Western compartments of religion, tradition, and politics. The process entails circumscribing religion as one part of life, related but separate from other parts, i.e., it entails what Weber described as a process of religious rationalization. We can briefly trace this process historically for the Karo Batak of Sumatra who today are predominantly Christian, but among whom a sizable minority still practice the traditional religion, Perbegu, with a small minority following Islam.

Many Karo Batak who migrated to the Sumatran East Coast in the 1800s assimilated into the Malay culture of the lowland sultanates. Others remained ethnically Karo, even if politically subordinate to the sultans. At this time, becoming Muslim and becoming Malay were synonymous. Muslim and Karo Batak were mutually exclusive identities. Karo ate pork, spoke a Batak language, and were divided into patrilineal clans. Malay eschewed pork, spoke Malay, and reckoned kin bilaterally. If one became a Muslim-Malay, one was no longer a Karo Batak. Dutch Christian missionaries entered the region in the late nineteenth century, along with a colonial plantation economy. The missionaries employed indigenous Christians from Menado as helpers and teachers. The Europeans and Minahassa missionaries confounded the old ethnic markers between Batak and Malay. For example, the Minahassa teachers spoke Malay in the beginning, and they had no clans, but they did eat pork. "You too are a Batak," a Karo man told one of the Minahassa teachers who expressed a taste for pork (Tampenawas 1894).

The Karo were not very interested in the missionaries' message at first. They especially feared that becoming Christian would mean becoming Minahassa, or Dutch, or, at any rate, something other than Batak (Tampenawas 1894; Joustra 1896). The first conversions occasioned a great deal of discussion among Karo lowlanders, some of whom assumed that baptism would exempt the converts from the authority of the village headmen, or perhaps would mean they were to be drafted as soldiers to fight with the Dutch against Aceh. The missionaries labored to be understood as the messengers of a new *religion*, but the Karo understood conversion as evidence of a new ethnic or political loyalty. During the Indonesian Revolution, Karo Christians feared, too, that their religious identity would mark them as Dutch loyalists.

Only after independence, when the missionaries withdrew to a helping role and the Karo Batak Protestant Church (GBKP) became an independent church under indigenous leadership, did the number of Christians begin to increase significantly. Karo no longer question, moreover, whether Christianity is compatible with an identity as a Karo Batak. The GBKP, the single largest organization of the Karo Batak, cultivates Karo language and *adat*, in part from self-interest: the various Protestant churches of Indonesia divide along linguistic and cultural differences as often as differences of doctrine. There would be no distinctively Karo Batak Protestant Church were there no distinctive Karo Batak. The church tries to open new congregations wherever a small number of Karo Batak families take up residence in urban areas. In those settings, the church becomes a way to bring Karo families into contact with each other (Pdt. A. Ginting-Suka, personal communication). In the cities, the church is the only public context in which people use the Karo language, and in some urban Karo families where Indonesian has become the language of the home, the church has become the only context in which children regularly hear the Karo language.

Into an either/or situation between Karo and Malay identities, then, the new Christian *agama* introduced a compromise position. The Karo could take up an *agama*, with all its implications of modernity, literacy, and good citizenship, and still keep a great many *adat* traditions. For the Karo, these traditions include pork eating and exogamous patrilineal clans, both of which many Karo see as incompatible with Islam. If Islam once stood as the counterpoint to Karo *adat*, Christianity now stands as a counter counterpoint. People nowadays contrast Islam with Christianity more readily than they contrast either of these religions with *adat*. In the process of sorting out *adat*, *agama*, and national loyalty, Karo *adat* has become increasingly secular. The Karo use both their sense of a distinctive, secular ethnicity, and their adherence to a minority religion, to mark themselves apart from the Muslims who make up the dominant majority surrounding them.

THE POLITICS OF ISLAM

A minority status defines the political situation of Indonesians "who do not yet have a religion," but the Muslim majority of Indonesia is not a politically seamless whole. We must consider, too, the politics internal to Islam and internal to those ethnic groups that define themselves as Muslim. The Dutch Islamicist Snouck Hurgronje saw Islam as an overlay on top of the local varieties of Indonesian *adat*. In this view, Islam competes with and opposes these older layers of *adat* and of other religions (Siegel 1969). Basyral Harahap's chapter, "Islam and Adat Among South Tapanuli Migrants in Three Indonesian Cities," reflects this common point of view, arguing that "religious loyalties, locally conceptualized as somewhat antagonistic to local ethnic customs, are stronger than *adat* consciousness." *Adat* and Islam, sometimes competing and sometimes complementing each other, shape the lives of South Tapanuli migrants in Medan, Jakarta, and

Bandung. The urban setting accelerates what has been happening in the Sumatra homeland for some time—an increasing cultural ascendancy of Islam over *adat*. Harahap looks at different ritual practices as indices of the shifting balance of *adat* and Islam. For South Tapanuli Batak who migrate to urban areas, Islam becomes increasingly a source of individual and family guidance and the impetus around which social relations form. Migrants draw more closely around the activities of the mosque than do their country cousins, yet like their cousins, continue to sponsor the life-crisis rituals prescribed as *adat*. The wealth of the migrants and the greater emphasis on Islam, as well as the exigencies of urban life, all modify the traditional ritual practices.

Although from one angle Islam appears as an urbanite's substitute for the traditions and values of the home region in Sumatra, from another angle this opposition is false. Families in the home region, too, identify strongly as Muslims, and parents urge their children who migrate to the cities to "be a real Muslim" above all. It is clear, too, that South Tapanuli urban migrants combine religious devotion with ethnic pride and identity, forming associations with other South Tapanuli migrants on the basis of religion, as well as of common origin from village, district, and region. When 7,000 South Tapanuli migrants met together in Jakarta in 1982 to celebrate the end of Ramadhan, hear a religious leader, and also perform the traditional songs and dances of their homeland, South Tapanuli *adat*, ethnic identity, and Islam must have seemed at least momentarily unified. A strong commitment to Islam has become part of the *adat*, so to speak, of a large majority of those who trace their roots to South Tapanuli. Taufik Abdullah has made a parallel argument about the relationship of *adat* and Islam among the Minangkabau. Arguing that Islam effected qualitative changes in *adat* and to some extent has become absorbed in *adat*, Abdullah prefers not speak of the recurrent conflict between *adat* and Islam in Minangkabau history as a conflict between two opposing value systems, one overlaid on the other. He argues rather that Islam and *adat* are "pillars" or parts of a single system, Alam Minangkabau, and that the conflicts between them have formed a "spiral" or dynamic force in the history of this people (Abdullah 1966, 1972).

The dividing line between those who have *agama* and those who do not may appear more sharp to those who do not have it than to those who do. Indonesian Muslims divide among themselves along a continuum of syncretism and reformism. At one end of the continuum, some Indonesians combine Islam with religious practices deriving from cultural sources other than Islam, and at the other, the followers of Mohammed attempt to reform or purify their faith of all extraneous addenda. This continuum of difference has always been part of Indonesian Islam, indeed, of Islam in general. Since the Revolution, however, these differences between Indonesian Muslims have become increasingly politicized.

In 1955, scattered mystical "schools," primarily Javanese, met to form the Badan Konggres Kebatinan Indonesia (BKKI). The BKKI aimed to enhance the legitimacy of mystical practice (*kebatinan*) as religion and as "one of the foundations on which a nation can be built" (Hadiwijono 1967: 3). The BKKI hoped to have *kebatinan* named as one of Indonesia's official religions with representation in parliament, but the Ministry of Religion resisted, defining the attributes of a religion (a holy scripture, a prophet, a belief in the absolute lordship of God, a system of law for its followers) in a way that precluded mystical practice. Following the attempted coup of 1965, executions or forced disbursement decimated many mystical groups which were thought to have been infiltrated by communists, but *kebatinan* has continued to flourish under the New Order. Without gaining official status as a religion, *kebatinan* nevertheless attracts many of the country's military and government leaders (Mulder 1978; Emmerson 1981).

Reformism, the effort to purify Islam of admixtures, has surged periodically throughout the history of Islam in Indonesia (e.g., Dobbin 1977), but it has gained special strength in this century (Peacock 1978). The banning of Masyumi has dampened the importance of sectarian differences in national party politics, but the political conflict between reformists and other Muslims takes place also outside party politics, and at local levels as well as national ones. Cederoth (1981) describes one local expression of this conflict that helps put the papers in this volume in wider perspective.

The Sasak of Lombok divide between factions called *wetu telu* and *waktu lima*. The latter faction follows a form of Islam that is relatively more reformed than that of the former, but Cederoth feels that both factions are at least partly syncretic in their religious practices. In *wetu telu* political traditions, a hereditary aristocracy occupies a redistributive pinnacle from which the privileges of their status obligate them to provide feasts focused on ancestor propitiation and the maintenance of sacred groves. *Waktu lima* Sasak claim, in contrast, that Muslims are equal before God and so do not recognize the aristocracy's social prerogatives. The reformists also decry the syncretic beliefs and other backward ways of the traditionalists. The politico-religious division has an economic basis. *Wetu telu* Sasak, agriculturalists, look on trade as a pariah's practice, but many *waktu lima*, some of them in fact immigrants to Lombok from other islands, engage unabashedly in profit-oriented commerce. Cederoth describes the gradual material and numerical ascendancy of the *waktu lima* faction over the *wetu telu*, an ascendancy that threatens the agrarian livelihood of the traditionalists and that has brought sporadic outbreaks of violence and destruction.

The politics of religion concern not only maneuverings in a religiously plural society but also the way a religion articulates with the authority structure of a nation or a particular locale. Two papers in this volume, each dealing with Indonesian Muslims, document the way the concepts of Islam fuse with values and social structure in particular places. Jessica Glicken, in "Sundanese Islam and the Value of Hormat: Control, Obedience and Social Location in West Java," examines the way the doctrines of Islam and Sundanese concepts and values transpose each other. The Sundanese express an emphasis on *hormat*, knowing and fulfilling one's proper position in society, through the use of a language which marks out status differences with three levels of politeness. Glicken argues, however, that learning to behave with appropriate *hormat* is also "a religious struggle—the triumph of *akal* over *hawa nafsu*," i.e., the struggle to make reason triumph over egotistical desires. Glicken focuses on the communication of these religious and cultural concepts in Islamic schools where children learn to memorize the Qur'an in Arabic. Less the content of the text than the way it is used ("The emphasis is on correct pronunciation and copious memorization"), religious instruction impresses children with the authority of holy words and of the teacher. "Pupils' respect and obedience to the teacher manifest their respect and obedience to the community and to Islamic (social) laws." Glicken's focus on the bases of Sundanese authority complements Jackson's (1980) study of the Dar Al Islam Rebellion in the same region. Jackson, trying to determine why men did or did not participate in this rebellion, found that individuals' religious convictions were of less predictive value than individuals' life histories. Men participated in the rebellion if they had a personal allegiance to a religious or village leader who persuaded them to do so.

Conclusion

Indonesian concepts of self, society, and sanctity of the sort just outlined make it clear that the anthropology of religion in these cultures must command a conceptual vocabulary of exceptional subtlety. What we first expect to constitute religious phenomena—spirit beliefs, rituals, and cosmologies—here seem endlessly refractable into other forms—megaliths, marital exchanges, puppet theater, and notions of social status. Religion, a definitively bounded subject to the Western eye, loses its familiar shape.

Religious transformations do not run wild, however, and are not random, kaleidoscopic changes of pattern. Taken one at a time, as the papers in this volume do, and placed in the context of particular histories and particular socio-economic conditions, transformations of this sort make sense. They do not, in fact, make sense any other way.

These Indonesian materials ask us to rethink the received scholarship about religion. Some symbolic and structural approaches to Indonesian religion have come under fire recently for not paying sufficient attention to the full political and social context in which symbols are used (e.g., Rosaldo 1980; Asad 1983). Geertz, it happens—as the premier American student of Indonesian religion—has borne the brunt of this criticism. Asad, for example, criticized Geertz for treating religion as if it had no connection to material conditions and social activities. Asad's critique focused almost exclusively on Geertz's programmatic essay, "Religion as a Cultural System" (1966); however, Asad largely ignored the ethnographic work that embodies Geertz's theoretical program. *Religion of Java* (1960), "Ritual and Social Change" (1957), and *Islam Observed* (1968) are not simply descriptions of religious *consciousness*. These accounts do give readers a sense of what the symbolic universe is like in Java and Morocco but also provide a sense of how symbols shape people's everyday lives. Geertz's ethnographic work shows people using and fashioning symbols, through meditation, prayer, and miracles, to be sure, but also while making a living, participating in town meetings and in national elections, and raising families. Taken in its entirety, Geertz's work perhaps best exemplifies the balance of attention to cultural analysis and social context that the study of Indonesian religious change requires.

As Asad understood it, Geertz's programmatic essay aimed to set forth a "universal, a-historic definition of religion," (1983:238) but Geertz has elsewhere stated that definition per se is not the issue (1968:1). His definition was a vehicle toward a new approach to religion. Geertz aimed to compensate for a style of studying religion that had forgotten to deal directly with the subject itself. At the time Geertz wrote, anthropologists typically looked past religion to focus almost entirely on the social forms in which religious behavior was embedded. Now that the pendulum has swung the other way such that symbolic approaches are the more prevalent, it does appear that some of these works suffer from a kind of myopia that does not look far enough beyond the boundaries of symbolic systems. Surely both cultural analyses and attention to social structure and social processes must coexist in the study of religion, especially if we aim to understand how religions and religious symbols change through time—that is, if we hope to comprehend subjects such as conversion, the gradual ascendancy of world religions over tribal religions, and the fact that religious symbols change form and meaning across time and space.

We suggest several approaches for future work. First, those who concentrate on structural or symbolic studies should attend at some point in their work to the existence of symbolic systems within social contexts of varying scope. As the papers in this volume show, in Indonesia that social context is national and international, not just local. This is true even in the remote reaches of the archipelago. At the local level throughout Indonesia, religious qualities often infuse and legitimate local power structures. Hicks's description of how Tetum origin myths explain asymmetrical alliance, and Glicken's account of the authority of religious teacher/leaders in Sunda provide two illustrations. At the national level, the government embraces religion in the generic, but no religion in particular, both to legitimize its exercise of power and also to mollify those who resist the idea of a wholly secular state and society. The government and perhaps most Indonesians define "religion" as *agama*, placing those who do not "yet" have such a religion in a position where they must either defend their religions as *agama*, convert to one of the recognized world religions, or else create new candidates for the label *agama*. Only by taking account of these politics do the contemporary transformations of religion in Indonesia begin to become intelligible (the attraction to reformism on the part of many Muslims, for example, or the increasing salience of Islam in the lives of South Tapanuli migrants to the city). These politics shed light, too, on the shift of attention from ritual practice to doctrine in Sumbanese religious thought, on the appeal to "history" in a religious movement among the Meratus, a people who have no written history, and the Wana's construction of their religion as morally equal to any *agama*.

Other political vectors were presumably at work shaping past transformations of Indonesian religions. Bowen's chapter describes a transformation from doctrine to ritual form, a transformation that reverses that described by Hoskins, reminding us that the direction of the changes we see enveloping Indonesian religions are not, in every case, one way. In the contemporary context, the process Hoskins describes is the more frequent. Literacy and the spread of academic learning cannot but reinforce the concern with doctrine that is a hallmark of modern religions. The Gayo's adaptation of Sufi ideas into curative rituals reflects, however, the prestige of Islam in an earlier period and its association with the state-level polities of coastal Sumatra. The very transformative blending described by Bowen reflects, too, the limits of those state polities and the more orthodox, self-contained forms of Islam that they nurtured.

A second line of approach entails cooperative scholarship. Groups of scholars of a single region can look for symbolic transformations and socio-historical differences as potentially co-variant entities. Finally, those who choose to attend to the sociopolitical contexts of religion should not lose sight of the power of religious symbols from the insider's perspective. Attention to the sociopolitical contexts of religion should not mean reducing religion to the desire for political legitimation. We must move toward a more balanced, holistic view of our subject that is neither so near-sighted that it misses the forces of change impelling people to refashion their symbolic worlds nor so far-sighted on the tumultuous social plane that it misses seeing religion itself.

Part One
Indonesian Religions and Their Transformations

I. *Space, Motion, and Symbol in Tetum Religion*

David Hicks

*T*HE GENERAL INTENT OF THIS ESSAY is to suggest how religion can find accommodation with notions of space in the characteristic Indonesian art medium of story-telling. I shall analyze two narratives and relate their form and contents to the religion of the people who tell them, the Tetum of Timor. Although the evidence adduced for the coordination of topology, religion, and art is culled from a single case study, this conjunction is a local instance of a style of thinking widespread throughout Indonesia, as the work of Clamagirand (1980), Judith Becker (1979), A.L. Becker (1979), and others indicates.

More specifically, I will show how certain beliefs in Tetum religion find expression in two contrasting genres of narrative, which the Tetum people themselves distinguish verbally. The first type explicitly identifies these beliefs and gives literal revelation of them. By most criteria of classification, they would be regarded as religious texts, in the same way that Biblical myths of genesis are classified as explicitly transmitting "messages," or stating convictions of dogma, that belong unequivocally to matters of religion. The Tetum cosmos is divided into an Upperworld and an Underworld; consistent with dual division, we find myths depicting the relationship between these two worlds along the plane of a vertical axis. The other type of narrative also depicts the relationship between the two worlds, but does so by projecting this duality onto a horizontal axis and by expressing meta-phorically whatever references there are to the cosmic natures of either world. Tales of this genre are allegorical narratives rather than straightfor-ward religious texts; they can be recited without the listener necessarily being made aware of the religious (and, for that matter, social) dogmas they enclose. These two axes may be said to serve as literary coordinates for religious ideas in other Indonesian societies. By empirically substantiating their operation in the religion of one population in the archipelago, I hope to reinforce my suggestion that their presence here is not a parochial phenomenon but may serve instead as a model for the comparative inves-tigation of religious ideas elsewhere in Indonesia.

The Vertical Axis

The Tetum hold the belief that human existence is cyclical. Human beings leave the sacred womb of the Great Earth Mother (symbolized by their mothers' womb) at birth.[1] They live their lives in the secular world as humans. At death, they return to the sacred world (symbolized by the grave). This is what I have elsewhere termed "The Tetum Cycle of Human Existence" (Hicks 1976:24). The cycle replicates the original pattern of existence depicted in a myth of origin (Hicks 1976:22). After the island of Timor had been created, two brothers, Rubi Rika and Lera Tiluk, and their sister, Cassa Sonek, were born from the womb of the earth mother *(rai ina)*. They left her body by clambering out of a vent in the limestone surface of Caraubalo princedom *(suku)*, an opening known as Mahuma and referred to as the "vagina" *(fono)*[2] of mother earth. On the surface of the earth, a secular domain, they founded the princedom of Caraubalo, lived out their lives, and at death returned to the sacred womb of their earth mother to become the original ancestral ghosts of the princedom. Here, they live today, in the company of a variety of different spirits with whom, by ritual offerings, their human descendants living in the secular world try to maintain a condition of cooperative harmony and cosmic balance.

The secular world includes also the sky, in whose firmament dwells the masculine deity, *maromak*, sometimes identified with the sun *(loro)*. He created the first human beings by copulating with mother earth, inseminat-ing her with rain, and then retreating back to his sky abode.

By this account, the Tetum of Caraubalo regard the geography of their cosmos as consisting of three strata related by the spatial contrast, up *(leten)*/down *(kraik)*: sky, earth's surface, earth's interior. Dyadic and triadic interfusion is commonly found in the symbolic classifications of the eastern Indonesians, and in Tetum symbolism occurs most prominently in the architecture of the house, in the segmentations of descent groups, and in oral prose. In these cultural fields, as in that of cosmic geography, Hocart's observation that, "In the few cases where we seem to catch the triple organization in the act of forming itself it is by the splitting of one of the components into two" (1936:282), holds true.

The most frequent mode of dividing up their cosmos typical of the Tetum villagers is dyadic. As they picture it, the cosmos's primary division is into the Underworld and the Upperworld, that is, into a world that is sacred *(lulik)*, spiritual *(klamar)*, feminine *(feto)*, and alien *(foho)*, and one that is secular *(sa'un)*, human *(ema)*, masculine *(mane)*, and familiar *(tetu)*. The Upperworld incorporates both the earth's surface and the sky. As such, it is that cosmic moiety which "splits into two." The sacred moiety, the Underworld, remains irreducible, as diagramed in Figure 1.1. Here, the letter "A" represents the place of birth and death, the "vagina" of mother earth and (by analogy) that of human women, and the grave in which corpses are deposited and thereby returned to the sacred womb. The Mahuma vent is centrally located on the vertical axis between the masculine sky and the feminine womb. This place of transition between them is known as *wé*. Transitional points in their symbolic classification are often termed *wé*, or *matan*, or compounded as *wé matan*, by the Tetum.[3] Since I have previously given a full gloss on the term *matan* (Hicks 1978b), I shall simply register the fact here that it includes among its referents "center," "source," and "origin." *Matan* is also the Tetum term for "eye"; it occurs in Bahasa Indonesia as "eye," "center," "core," "nucleus" (Echols and Shadily 1963:240) in the form *mata*, which, according to Dempwolf (1938), is its original form. It is often used in combination with *wé* in formal speech at rituals. A *wé matan* is a spring, a stream, or the "source of a princedom," namely, the Mahuma vagina. In myths of origin, transformations from secular to sacred by creatures that are ambiguous typically occur at *wé matan* (see van Wouden 1968:50; Hicks, 1976:77−78). *Wé matan* may itself be combined with another compound, *ahi matan* (*ahi* = "fire"; *ahi matan* = "hearth," "descent group"), which is also used in ritual language to convey the idea of the source of an individual's cultural existence, that is to say, his descent group. This corporation is his link with the ancestral ghosts and the sacred world from which he emerged at birth and to which he will return at death. Among the referents of *wé* are "liquid," "water," "source," "origin," so that its connotations overlap with those of *matan*.

David Hicks

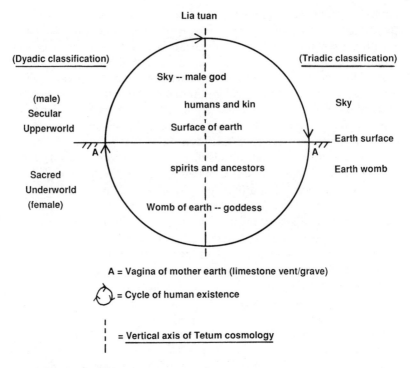

Figure 1.1. Vertical Axis of Tetum Cosmology

Both *wé* and *matan*, either separately or conjointly, find ready employment in ritual and literary contexts where the notion of origin or transformation is evoked. A difference between them is that *matan* suggests the notion of fixity; *wé* conveys the suggestion of movement or flow. What Endicott (1970: 136, 144) remarks of Malay magical thinking applies equally to Tetum collective thought. Water and other substances (such as blood, coconut milk, and betel chew) weaken the boundaries between many kinds of categories, facilitating passage between them. When put into the service of symbolism, they function as communicators and mediators between human beings and spirits—and also between groups of humans themselves; for instance, between wife-giving descent groups and wife-taking descent groups. On the other hand, in some cases, and according to context, water can act as a symbolic barrier between humans and spirits, and between different human groups.

In this model of human existence, then, the Tetum characterize the cycle of life as a vertical motion, up – down – up, beginning in the sacred world, moving through the secular world, and returning to the sacred world, via a center point which serves as a source of entry/exit to the worlds. This version is what we might call "religious" and, as noted earlier, is formulated relatively explicitly by the people themselves. The alternative version is allegorical and must be educed from its literary hypostatizations.

In other words, religious ideas find revelation in explicit myths of origin whose stock elements or narrative elements (e.g., themes, incidents, plots, diction, imagery, motifs, scenes, and *dramatis personae*) are organized in a manner consonant with a vertical axis. As we see from the text analyzed below, narratives that express these doctrinal ideas in allegorical form organize these elements along a horizontal axis.

The Tetum themselves distinguish these two types of narrative (Hicks 1973). *Lia tuan* (*lia* = "word," "language," "speech," "term," "to speak"; *tuan* = "old," "ancient," "venerable," "worthy of respect," "important"), "the ancient stories," are myths purporting to explain, justify, and interpret the origins of things—human, topographic, social, and cultural. They lie along the vertical axis. *Aiknananoik* (*aik* = "tree," "wood"; *nananoik* = "narrative," "story," "tale"), "folktales," are so-called because of the practice, common in some parts of the Tetum regions of Timor, of an orator reciting his tales under spreading branches of a tree (Sá 1961:8). The tale set out below is one such *aiknananoik*.

The Horizontal Axis

The axis we have just discussed may be regarded as a vehicle for conveying certain ideas concerning the metaphysical tie between human beings and spirits. Since an important category of spirit is that of ancestral ghost, by implication the axis connects a contemporary population with ghosts of people who are now dead but who in life were of the same community. By contrast, the horizontal axis stresses the differences (expressed through the ideas of exogamy and marital exchange) between human populations that are contemporary with one another: between "us" (*tetu*) and "them" (*foho*).

This is one of a series of complementary oppositions that appear in the text. The two principles of logical constraint, complementarity and opposition, cooperate with four other constraining principles in weaving the stock elements typical of *aiknananoik* into coherent form: exchange, analogy, inversion, transformation.

I shall here be analyzing a Tetum narrative, which, on the surface, bears no resemblance to the myth of origin referred to above, apparently telling nothing about the cycle of human existence.

Before tackling its exegesis, we need to make a brief excursus around the cardinal points of the local compass. In the horizontal plane, the Tetum nominally acknowledge four cardinal directions. "North" is either *foho* (also "alien," "savage," "mountain") or *tassi feto* ("the woman's sea"). "South" is either *tetu* (also "us," "familiar," "civilized," "plain") or *tassi mane* ("the man's sea"). "West" is *loro monu* ("the place where the sun sets"). "East" is *loro sa'e* ("the place where the sun rises"). North and west are linked with the sacred, femininity, alienation, the unknown, and death. South and east are linked with the secular, masculinity, Tetum civilization, the familiar things of human existence, and life.

With the spatial coordinates of the secular world at the earth's surface thus established, let us now consider our narrative.[4]

A very long time ago, some princes of Samoro princedom left for Wé Hali to obtain the Wé Hali princess as a wife for their Samoro prince [Fig. 1.2]. When they arrived in Wé Hali they found there people of many kingdoms who had a like intention. The crafty people of Wé Hali attractively dressed their aristocratic girls in a fine way, and introduced them to the emissaries so that they might select the one most suited to them.

Before they entered the royal palace, the Samoro men chatted in friendly fashion with the king's servants in an attempt to discover which among the girls was the real princess. The servants replied that none of the girls was the true princess, but that a girl who was in the kitchen, dressed like a maid, was. Thus, when the Samoro men entered the palace to choose their queen they did not decide on any of those that Wé Hali presented for their inspection, but claimed the maid working in the kitchen. The Wé Hali men, realizing what had happened, did not agree. The Samoro men, knowing the men of Wé Hali would not satisfy their wishes, decided to abduct the princess, and secretly informed her through her handmaids. The daring ruse thrilled her, so the girl agreed. Then exactly at midnight, when all were asleep, the Samoro men, making use of their magic, seized the princess and fled at once that night, travelling without a break till they had reached the Wé Hali frontier sometime before dawn. In this way they arrived upon the [western] bank of a river known as the Wé Nunuk [*nunuk* = "lip"].

Suddenly, the river filled with water, and many crocodiles surfaced to defend their princess. Then the girl, being for them the daughter of the Sun, and therefore the lady of all the elements, spoke to them in a friendly fashion, and made the following pact

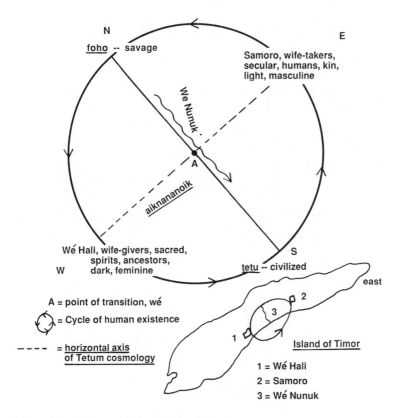

Figure 1.2. Horizontal Axis of Tetum Cosmology

with them. They were to carry her and the Samoro men to the other bank of the river. Once this was done, neither the Samoro men nor their descendants, from one generation to the next, would ever hunt or eat crocodile meat. The crocodiles accepted the princess's proposal and took her to the other side of the river, as well as all who followed in her retinue. After all the Samoro people had passed, the waters of the river began to rise, and still more crocodiles appeared on the surface to bar passage to the Wé Hali men, who pursued the Samoro folk in order to get their princess back. Already on the opposite bank the Samoro men were joyously celebrating the victory they had won that day. So even at the present time they sing the refrain:

'They boasted the Wé Nunuk was carrying much water, but the men of Samoro passed it on foot— dry!'

Because of this tale, the people of Samoro still hold in great veneration the crocodile, never ill-treat it, and always call it, "grandfather." When fording a river which may conceal crocodiles, they say:

'Grandfather, you mustn't do anything bad to us, mustn't bite us. We are your grandchildren.'

Wé Hali lies to the west of Samoro, that cardinal direction associated in Tetum thinking with the land of the dead. But the land of the dead is also a projection onto the horizontal plane of the world of spirits, the sacred world, or sacred womb. The journey begins, therefore, with a passage from east to west; from the secular world (male) to the sacred world (female). This is the inverse cycle to that taken by the infant or the three founding ancestors of Caraubalo. The association between Wé Hali, the feminine, and the sacred is further stressed. Sá (1961:232) notes that the *hali* is a *ficus indica* tree, which grows near water and is regarded as sacred. The term itself is composed of the term for younger sibling: *ali* + *h*. The younger sibling in Tetum classificatory thought is a transitional figure, an ambiguously secular and sacred one. Sá (1961:232) summarizes a myth which describes how a certain "family" *(familia)*, arriving from overseas, landed on the southern coast of western Timor, and there settled down. With them they brought a pitcher *(lolon)* made of green bamboo from a species of *wé hali*. The bamboo was promptly planted; in the course of time it grew and developed many leaves. Under its shade the family also grew in size until it was big enough to be called a village, Wé Hali.

In conjunction with *hali*, the term *wé* conveys an image of a feminine-sacred source of nature and life. Most peoples of Timor practice asymmetric alliance, in which wife-giving descent groups are thought to provide the source of life for their wife-takers (e.g., Clamagirand 1980); in a literal sense they do, for they make it possible for the wife-taking group to recruit new members for the next generation. The Tetum hold the same notion, and in former times the people of Samoro acted as wife-takers to the people of Wé Hali (Sá 1961:235). Since the system was, by definition, asymmetric, Samoro was prohibited from giving women to Wé Hali. Wé Hali, for the people of Samoro, was the sacred source of life.

The Tetum believe that life comes about in the act of creation which occurs when complementary opposites conjoin: male/female, secular/sacred, wife-takers/wife-givers. The terms of each pair—sexual, metaphysical, institutional—complement each other, yet also oppose one another. This is so with the complementary opposition inherent in the characters of the two populations. Wé Hali is associated with the west, femininity, and the sacred. Adjunctive to Wé Hali are the night and darkness (the Samoro people take their departure at midnight). Similarly, the sacred world is thought to be a place of darkness; the secular world a place of light (the term, *naroma*, "light," "clear," may be cognatic with *maromak*) (Fig. 1.2), an alternation of dark and light which recalls to mind Beckett: "They give birth astride of a grave, the light gleams an instant, then it's night once more."[5]

The river [*wé*] Nunuk both unites and disjoins the two places and their populations. It is another *wé*; another "source" or "opening." It is the entrance to Wé Hali in the west, the source of future life for the people of Samoro.

When the travelers reach their sacred, feminine destination they do not find the order which, according to custom, they are entitled to expect. Disorder and confusion reign, as we see from the following four infractions of conventional expectations.

1. The wife-givers of Wé Hali blatantly violate the prohibition against persons of different social classes marrying.[6] This they do by offering to their *royal* wife-takers a girl who, as a servant, comes from the class of *slaves*. Royalty is the highest of the Tetum social classes; the class of slaves is the lowest (Hicks 1983).

2. The princess is transformed not into a woman of the aristocratic or even commoner classes but into a slave—a polar inversion. Yet, the very fact that her royal body is draped with clothing worn by commoners suggests the transformation that has taken place here is not a simple matter of inversion, but one of disorder.

3. Disorder is continued in the clothing worn by the female aristocrats. They are "attractively dressed," a phrase I take to imply that these aristocrats are dressed in superior fashion, appropriate more to women of royal class than to women of their own. We have, incidentally, *three* categories of female emerging in this tale: the princess, the aristocrats, and the slave. They are *related*, though, dyadically, as superior/inferior.

4. The wife-givers, by refusing to hand over the princess, are, in effect, denying their institutional responsibility of providing their established wife-takers with a bride. It might be argued that the men of Wé Hali are being solicited for the hand of the princess by the representatives of many kingdoms, so that they may give the women to whomsoever they choose. On the other hand, these asymmetric alliances were usually established arrangements which bound together descent groups and larger units, such as princedoms, and even kingdoms, for generation upon generation, and Wé Hali and Samoro princedoms are affinal partners.

The case I wish to argue is that disorder has overcome the system of collective representations that cohere into Tetum cosmology, and that it has come about by the local *adat* being undermined by Wé Hali.

In another work (Hicks 1984), I make the point that a central contention of Tetum religion is that disorder can be combated by recourse to a stock repertoire of symbols which express the *leitmotif* of disjunction leading to the restoration of cosmic order. Various ritual practices are then employed to reseparate categories improperly confused—typically, as the result of breaches of Tetum *adat*. Wé Hali has disrupted the traditional system of Tetum ideas; since the story does not include episodes of drastic punishments, illnesses, and deaths, which the onset of disorder brings in its train, it is clear that the impaired cosmic order must have been swiftly restored. Hence, the above narrative would certainly be expected to contain examples of the stock elements I have just mentioned.

And contain them it does. In Tetum symbolism, among the agents responsible for providing discontinuity are rivers (which, of course, in other contexts serve as mediators) and four temporal markers: dawn, sunset, midday, midnight. Cheated out of the right to obtain their bride, the Samoro men kidnap her, and, acting as surrogates for their own royalty, transform the girl back to her proper (royal) status. This transformation restores cosmic order, which is then maintained by the barrier formed by the Wé Nunuk. It repels those who might again threaten disorder. In Tetum symbolic numerology, the number two symbolizes the notion of disjunction, and in this story we find the two antagonistic populations on two opposite banks. On the western bank dwell the wife-givers of Wé Hali in their feminine world of the sacred. On the eastern bank dwell the wife-takers of Samoro in their masculine world of the secular.

The story of the journey to Wé Hali is, by this interpretation, the narrative of a Tetum population that regenerates itself by not only returning *to* the womb of its sacred mother, but returning *with* a human womb of its own. One mytheme recurring in Tetum narratives is the picaresque adventures undertaken by persons from one community traveling to the west or voyaging overseas. These persons from the secular world, in tracing the path taken across the sky by the (masculine) son, or in crossing a body of water, are usually transported in a boat, conveyed in a coffin, or carried by a crocodile.[7] All three vehicles play a part—sometimes a decisive one—in changing the hero from a state of secularity to one of sacredness. They are agents of transformation.[8] According to some myths, the island of Timor itself is likened to a crocodile (Sá 1961:11), an analogy that finds material expression in plastic form in Caraubalo princedom, where buffalo-horn figures of human beings riding on the backs of crocodiles are carved by local sculptors. In one myth of origin, the original ancestors of the Tetum arrived from the west by boat and settled down in Wé Hali. From here the Tetum spread to other parts of the island. Other narratives record the sailing to Timor of the first Catholic priests who came from overseas—i.e., the sacred world (Sá 1961:90). The term for "priest" is *nai lulik* ("sacred lord").

Thus far I have emphasized the alien nature of the group whose duty it is to supply brides. But what, we might ask, is the nature of the woman thus delivered? It could come as no surprise for us to discover that she is herself alien to the group which obtains her.[9] The rules of exogamy see to that. Further, like the group which provides her, a wife is associated with the sacred world. The husband and his descent group are secular. The sexual conjugation of wife and husband in the institutional relationship brought about by the marital exchange symbolizes the union of both cosmic moieties (Hicks 1984).

The source of life for a descent group is the institutional bonds forged and maintained between wife-giving groups and wife-taking groups. From the union thereby created derive new recruits to the wife-taking group, as well as the benefits of political cooperation and cosmic harmony between humans and spirits. This is one of the chief ways by which the local *adat* is observed. It requires that humans and spirits cooperate in ritual, and, if the proper harmony is maintained, babies, peace, and health in the two groups are likely. Wife-givers, wives, and spirits are equated, in a sacred association much in keeping with the world from which they come: the west and Underground. This is the antipode of the eastern, Upperworld domain of those who dwell in the secular world.

The Two Axes

As we have seen, the two axes have polar contrasts. The vertical axis consists of a cycle whose commencement in the myth of human birth begins in the sacred world, ascends into the secular, and then descends into the sacred world once more. In Hicks (1984), I attempt to show that in this sort of cycle, one which begins in the feminine domain, femininity is associated with the concept of the inside, as is so in many eastern Indonesian societies. This is generally true with the Tetum. However, the inner is sometimes linked with masculinity, and one such context appears to be when the commencement point is on the horizontal axis in narratives or in the symbolic configuration of hamlets and the surrounding jungle. When the vertical axis is projected horizontally, the cycle ceases to associate inner

1. <u>Lia tuan</u>	dark female sacred -->	light male secular -->	dark female sacred -->

2. <u>aiknananoik</u>	secular --> male light	sacred --> female dark	secular --> male light

Figure 1.3. The Two Cycles in Contrast

with feminine. The starting (and finishing) point is masculine. The people of Samoro start their journey in the secular world, cross into the sacred, and then return to the secular world once more (Fig. 1.3). The vertical axis opposes humans and ancestral spirits, living and dead, present and past, yet unites members of the same descent group (i.e., kin and their ancestral ghosts): these are conjoined into a relationship of *descent*. The horizontal axis unites human beings; two populations which (as remarked earlier) are contemporaneous. Yet its polar contrasts are wife-taker and wife-giver, separated by descent, united in a relationship of *affinity* (Fig. 1.2).

At the node of reconciliation of the two axes (Fig. 1.4), the Mahuma vagina (vertical axis) and the Wé Nunuk river (horizontal axis) coincide—a finding totally consistent with local ideas associated with wé, origins, and sources.

Conclusions

Lévi-Strauss has convincingly demonstrated that the six logical relations we have adduced from our Tetum data—opposition, complementarity, exchange, analogy, inversion, and transformation—order many of the stock elements in the narratives told by tribes of South America. This finding supports the argument that these logical constraints are innate properties of human thinking. Since the narrative elements, and at least some of the religious features, analyzed above are common to other peoples in Indonesia, it is likely that the coordinate deployment of these two axes in verbal art to convey religious ideas is a device that goes beyond the mere confines of Tetum civilization.[10] As I suggested in my introductory remarks, this possibility could provide a useful point of departure for the comparative study of religion in Indonesia. An inquiry of this nature would also have the wider theoretical interest of putting to the test Lévi-Strauss's argument

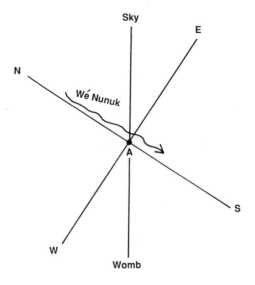

A = node of reconciliation (wé)

Figure 1.4. The Node of Reconciliation

that to be fully understood a myth must be examined in all its variants. The Tetum religious ideas analyzed here might well recur in all manner of guises in other Indonesian cultures. Here, of course, we are not dealing with the transformation of myths themselves so much as transformations of key religious notions, but the theoretical point is the same. The empirical *El Dorado* awaiting the ethnographer for testing this possibility is as expansive as Indonesia itself.

2. Power of Gods: Ma'bugi' Ritual of the Sa'dan Toraja

Eric Crystal and Shinji Yamashita

A SINGLE, CRUCIAL TORAJA RITUAL, *ma'bugi'*, is analyzed here, and a mode of investigating rituals that combines symbolic analysis (Turner 1969) with interpretive approaches (Geertz 1972b,1973a) is proposed. This combined approach is demanded by the complexity of the Toraja material; of the indigenous religions still flourishing in Indonesian societies, that of the Sa'dan Toraja of Sulawesi is among the most varied and intricate.[1]

Scholars have long noted that the artistic traditions (Heine-Geldern 1966:190) and megalithic practices of this region (Heekeren 1958:62) may be representative of a "prototypical" Southeast Asian culture complex long predating Western contact. It would be misleading, however, to portray Toraja culture as static. The great bulk of the Sa'dan Toraja population today resides within the borders of the Tana Toraja Regency, some 300 kilometers to the north of the Sulawesi Selatan capital city of Ujung Pandang. Bordered on the north by forested mountains, the Toraja region is linked to the Bone Gulf and the Makassar Strait by a single motor road. One of the last regions of Indonesia to fall under Dutch control (1906), the Toraja area was subsequently isolated from outside influence after World War II for much of the Darul Islam rebellion in South Sulawesi (1951 – 65). Over the past fifteen years, the pace of social change has quickened with the establishment of secure political conditions, the enhancement of overland communications, and, most importantly, the rise since 1973 of international tourism.[2] Today roughly 60 percent of the Tana Toraja population of 312,000 adheres to Christianity, 10 percent have embraced Islam, and 30 percent of the Toraja people profess loyalty to the faith of their ancestors, *Aluk To Dolo*.[3] In recent years there has been increasing syncretism among formerly rigid Calvinist Protestants; a slow but steady erosion in the absolute numbers of traditionalist *Aluk To Dolo* adherents as older people pass away; and, thanks to tourism, increasing international attention paid to *Aluk* ritual.[4]

Toraja religion is in large part a *ritual* phenomenon, and its analysis demands attention to that fact. Geertz's work is useful here. In advocating a cultural analysis of religion, he once defined a culture as "an historically transmitted pattern of meanings embodied in symbols, a system of inherited conceptions expressed in symbolic forms by means of which men communicate, perpetuate, and develop their knowledge about and attitudes toward life" (1966b:89). This defines, too, exactly the Toraja concept of *Aluk To Dolo*.[5] *Aluk* means "the way of doing" in its broader usages, and is roughly synonymous with Indonesian *adat* (custom) or, in some usages, *kebudayaan* (culture). In a narrower sense, it denotes the "way," suggesting the specific and invariable design of a ritual's performance according to what the ancestors *(to dolo)* have established. In these respects, *Aluk* ritual is a cultural performance to the extent that ceremonialism is a fundamental, not an ancillary, aspect of dogma. Religion here is practiced rather than conceptualized in an abstract manner. The stress in Toraja, as in Bali, is "on the orthopraxy, not orthodoxy—what is crucial is that ritual detail should be correct and in place" (Geertz 1964:177). We must examine ritual practice, then, to understand both the belief and practices of *Aluk To Dolo*, the condensed form of Toraja culture itself.

Geertz's perspective can be set into the larger anthropological literature on ritual. Geertz suggested that through religion people move "beyond the realities of everyday life to wider ones which correct and complete them. . . . In a ritual, the world as lived and the world as imagined, fused under the agency of a single set of symbolic forms, turn out to be the same world" (1966b:112). Turner (1969), following van Gennep (1960), noted that rituals have three phases: separation, margin or limen, and aggregation. Turner places special emphasis on the critical functions of the liminal stage. These two sources of insight—Geertz on religion in general and Turner on ritual—can be usefully combined. A ritual's first stage separates people from the context of everyday life in order to seek deeper understanding of a transcendental reality. In the second stage, the ritual performance, specialists and adepts communicate with shades and spirits through symbolic manipulation. Finally, returning to the everyday world, the community finds itself renewed from its profound if fleeting religious experience (see also Leach 1961b: 134). In this scheme the liminality of ritual is significant only when viewed in relation to the experience of daily life from which ritual starts and to which ritual returns. Ritual performances, then, are attempts to establish the order of orders by re-organizing the "knowledge about and attitudes toward life" into a meaningful reality. This general model of ritual can also apply to a *particular* ritual, such as the *ma'bugi'* examined in this paper.

Toraja rituals, as noted, are quite complex. In the dialectic process that ties ritual to everyday life, ritual, an unwritten "text" (cf. Geertz 1972b: 448 – 53), enhances and enriches mundane life in the community. Like a text, it is interpreted and reinterpreted by religious specialists according to their skills. Unlike a written text, though, the contents of a ritual can be heard, felt, smelled, and tasted. Ritual is a text experienced. The Toraja have a rich and complex oral tradition, too, and unwritten texts parallel the ritual "text," at times, as oral liturgy.

Ritual performances in the *Aluk To Dolo* tradition often involve the full panoply of Toraja song, dance, craft, and textile traditions. The Toraja area is most famous for its elaborate death rituals at which scores of sacrificial animals die and guests attend by thousands. We take up *ma'bugi'* ritual, however, because it is the only ritual in the southern *Tallu Lembangna* districts of Tana Toraja where the power of the *deata* spirits of life and agricultural bounty is said to manifest itself before the assembled village community. Although the Toraja consider *ma'bugi'* only a moderate ritual in terms of economic sacrifice and community participation, local ritual specialists stress that it is crucial.[6] For anthropologists, the *ma'bugi'* can be used as an exemplary lens through which one can view the fundamentals of Toraja religion in general.

As we shall see in detail later, the essence of *ma'bugi'* lies in trance experience. In the anthropological literature, trance phenomena have been discussed chiefly in relation to shamanship. However, in Tana Toraja there are no professional shamans.[7] Rather, everybody in *ma'bugi'* can fall into trance according to the depth of his or her ritual participation. The "depth" depends upon the degree to which a community and individuals are involved in the ritual; also crucial is the particular setting of the performance. In the most general terms, the *ma'bugi'* is locally designated as a trance ritual, but individual performances may or may not actually realize that state. Here again we should recall that the Toraja religion is not a religion of dogma but of practice and that ritual is a performance similar to the

Greek *dromenon*, "a thing done" (Harrison 1951:35). In this perspective, trance in Toraja has much more in common with other Indonesian artistic performances such as the trance drama in Bali (Belo 1960) and the Javanese *wayang* performance in trance (Becker 1979:232 – 33) rather than shamanism in a narrow sense. In fact, it is the collective performance of dance, as we see later, that induces trance in Toraja. The trance performance here, the "game" *(paniogoan)*, is no less dramatic than the famous Balinese trance theater.

In our research, we observed *ma'bugi'* at different times and places and in different modes of performance. In fact, during the earlier stages of our joint work we found ourselves viewing the ritual differently. Our "data" reflected our individual constructions of each performer's constructions, a phenomenon discussed by Geertz in his essay "Thick Description" (1973b:9). Collaborative work per se began when we tried to integrate these differing observations into a single analytical framework. We finally came to the conclusion that our different observations themselves provided a clue for a fuller understanding of the ritual. We examine the "multi-vocality" of ritual contexts and also variation in several *ma'bugi'* performances. Through analysis of the variation, we grapple with a much-ignored question in the anthropology of religion: why trance rituals can also be purification rites, or to put it more generally, why fundamental religious forms are transformed from one to another in certain ritual settings.

Ma'bugi' *Ritual*

The Toraja divide rituals into two rigidly separate kinds: rites of the eastern side *(aluk rampe matallo)* and rites of the western side *(aluk rampe matampu')*. Other binary oppositions—east and west, right and left, life and death, cool and hot, pure and polluted—typically structure Toraja ritual.[8] People propitiate the *deata* spirits only during life-side, *rampe matallo* rituals. These eastern side rituals enhance life, the agricultural harvest, and general well-being. People call on *deata* during all stages of the rice rituals, beginning with sowing and concluding with the harvest's storage. After people store the grain in large granaries, four or five months ensue before rice planting again commences. If a community holds a *ma'bugi'*, they do so just prior to a ritual termed *mangkaro kalo'* or *mangkaro bubun* ("clean the irrigation canals" or a well) that opens the new agricultural year.

Nobele observed a *ma'bugi'* fifty years ago (1926:59–61)[9]; subsequently,

Claire Holt recorded it in the mid-thirties during her "dance quest" to the more remote concerns of the archipelago. Unfortunately, Holt recorded the dance and song outside the ritual context, and these recreations convey little of the ritual's intense emotion and graphic symbolism (1939:50–52). The term *ma'bugi'* has several senses: it is a melodic lullably sung by parent to child; it is a circle dance performed during the large three-day consecration of a family house *(tongkonan)*; finally, the *ma'bugi'* is a curing ritual involving an entire village community and marked by mass trances by both religious adepts and others. Only infrequently, no more often than at three-year intervals, does the "fat" *(lompo)* or true *bugi'* unfold. It requires that all who reside within a given community observe months of food and ritual taboos, weeks of practice dancing, and, in the end, several days of intense emotional experience. At the rite's apogee the world of the gods and that of humans, but for a moment, meet and merge.

In his narration of the film *Ma'bugi'* (produced and photographed by Eric and Catherine Crystal (1974), Tominaa Ne'Ba'du provides an extensive exegetical commentary on the ritual's rationale. According to the *tominaa* (priest of the right, that is, of life), people perform *ma'bugi'* in times of distress and want, "when the children do not properly grow and become strong, when the buffalo and pigs stand diseased in their pens, when the rice plants do not become full with grain." People stage a *ma'bugi'* so that the spirit, *Puang Maruruk*, the "Just Lord," may be inclined to banish illness, misfortune, poor harvest, and other calamities. *Puang Maruruk* resides at the edge of the heavens in a house thatched with red *tabang* leaves. The "Just Lord," in past decades, "sowed the skins of young children with the flakes of gold" (caused smallpox in Toraja villages) because people had not killed enough cocks in sacrificial offerings.

Ma'bugi' is, first of all, a healing ritual. Healing in its broadest sense means not only curing individuals, but also restoring harmony between humans and their environment and between humans and deities. Adults sing the *ma'bugi'* song to young infants to preserve and protect them. *Ma'bugi'* is also like a curing rite of former times, *memaro* ("to go crazy"). Performed during a serious illness, *memaro* induced close neighbors and family members of the afflicted to fall into trance. Finally, for those individuals of sufficient wealth and rank to merit the largest of Toraja seven-day death ceremonies, a rite called *ma'bugi' ma'gandang* concludes the long sequence of funeral ceremonies. This rite, several years after interment, marks a transformation from ancestor (the deceased) into *deata* life-giving spirit. As the sun rises, the ancestor of the left (west) has passed into the realm of the right (east).[10]

Tominaa Ne'Ba'du stressed that villages hold *ma'bugi'* only when things are not right. This is not strictly true, as some villages endeavor to stage a *ma'bugi'* in non-crisis times. Traditional villages hold *ma'bugi'* once every three years, and only a death during the critical planning period may radically alter that timing. All the situations at which people perform the *ma'bugi'* song and dance have as their central theme a celebration of life. Toraja healing thus fits in the broader context of promoting well-being and fecundity, both of humans and of domestic plants and animals. As Hocart noted, "Ritual promotes life by promoting everything on which life depends: crops, cattle, children—and also what these depend on: rain and sunshine" (Hocart 1954:123).

The Performance of Ma'bugi'

The *ma'bugi'*, like almost all Toraja rituals, occurs in several forms. There are variations, too, in elaboration and style, in size and in intensity. Within a single community the performance of *ma'bugi'* may vary considerably from one decade to the next, depending on the availability of ritual specialists and other conditions, and the participants' level of energy and enthusiasm. Throughout Tana Toraja, ritual performances vary from valley to valley, from village to village, and from district to district. Common threads of meaning course through Toraja tradition, however, allowing believers from throughout the Toraja homeland to understand *Aluk To Dolo*.

We observed a number of *ma'bugi' lompo* rituals during our fieldwork in Tana Toraja. The Makale version of the rite as filmed by the Crystals was more elaborate than those performed in Mengkendek district in 1977. We shall call the former version, documented in 1971, the "strong" version and the 1977 performance the "weak" version. We will describe both versions.

THE STRONG VERSION

Although homesteads are scattered throughout the valleys and precipitous rice terraces, each householder identifies with a specific village and looks to the descendants of the putative first settler of the land[11] for leadership in ritual matters. The pioneer agriculturalist of Rantekasimpo village in the Makale district hosted the *ma'bugi'* there in late 1971. His normally placid courtyard became the ritual arena, pulsating with the chants of hundreds of dancers whose movement and song evoked extraordinary behavior.

Many weeks before the event, villagers had gathered nightly at the court-yard to practice the *nondo* dance, moving in the circular "path of the spirits" from left to right. The village leaders had consulted *tominaa* priests of life on the suitability of time and place.[12] Finally, they decided to initiate the food taboos and other restrictions in preparation for *ma'bugi'*. The rite per se begins when people circumambulate the village bearing the offering vessels of four supernaturals. Long textiles, fixed to one another with thin bamboo pins, serve as symbolic mobile borders delimiting the confines of the ritually engaged village. Participants bathe in the waters of the river Sa'dan, purifying body and home territory in anticipation of what lies ahead. Taboos *(pemali)*—such as abstinence from consuming pork, corn, and hot peppers, or the commitment to refrain from direct participation in death rituals—purify the community for the forthcoming encounter with the supernatural. Corn is associated with death and so must not be consumed. People say that hot peppers recall the searing pain of knives piercing flesh, and so they ban peppers from a ceremonial center where the entranced will soon "play with knives."

Some go into trance while circling the limits of the community at the ritual's start. That same day, in the late afternoon, people make offerings to the ancestors, the Lord of the Land, *Puang Maruruk*, and the generalized *deata* spirits, and then consecrate a sacred fireplace of *kapok* logs. At this time a very few participants fall into a somnolent state of possession, directing, in languid tones, a "song of the possessed" to the spirits:

> You must possess me,
> Press on as I feel faint,
> Awareness is ending,
> You drive me quivering to earth.

Now some first bring knives into play. Although the *tominaa* oversees the proper sequence of ritual events, another more specialized adept functions as master of the trance. This is the *to ma'burra*, "the one who spits." Before others may draw their knives and press them in their bodies, the *to ma-'burra* must first cut his tongue and spew blood upon the fireplace. It is he who also determines the "games" which highly skilled trancers will act out at the close of the *ma'bugi'*.

The consecration of the fireplace, the laying of the first offerings, the summoning of the ritual specialists, and the invocation of community-wide taboos signal several additional weeks of nighttime dancing and chanting. People make offerings before each nocturnal gathering, and each evening prepare for the apogee of the *ma'bugi'*, a time when the sacrifice of many scores of chickens, curing rituals, and the participation of many hundreds of people bring the ceremony to a dramatic conclusion. The *ma'tere'allo*, "stabbing in the daylight," is the concluding event. As the final day of the *ma'bugi'* dawns, each household prepares glutinous rice and chicken meat, roasted separately in freshly cut bamboo. After practicing their dancing for weeks, women and girls don gold ornaments, elaborate beadwork, and fancy headgear in preparation for their dancing. Early on this last day, the ceremonial center of the village fills with spectators who come from distant villages to join the "lords of the *bugi'*," the host villagers, to witness the climax. People again make offerings—betel, egg, rice, and chicken meat— and then the elaborately costumed daughters of the village begin dancing, forming a central circle around which others gather to participate or observe.

The large courtyard, laid with smooth river stones reserved for Toraja notables, contains three homes and three large rice granaries. To the northeast of the principal granary is the spirit offering place, and somewhat to the east of this is the sacred fireplace *(kaponan)* consisting of an even number of *kapok* logs. One of the granaries houses the "one who spits" and other trance specialists who come from distant locales. Here they sleep and are provisioned. Far to the northeast lie the headwaters of the life-giving Sa'dan river, origin place of the *deata* spirits. Homes and granaries always face to the north or northeast. The west and the setting sun are associated with ancestors; east is the direction of *deata* spirits, omnipotent in matters of agriculture and fertility. To the southwest is the land of the ghost souls; southwest is crucial in the orientation of death but is of little consequence here.

In the context of the *ma'bugi'*, within its courtyard setting, several planes of cosmological orientation intersect. The *kapok* log fireplace orients to the north, and spirit offering place lies on a plane from the west (where offerings are placed to the ancestors) to the east (where the *deata* offerings are proffered). The fireplace axis, south to north, and the offering place axis, west to east, intersect at the ceremonial center. A third axis soon appears, a transection from terrestrial to celestial planes. Shortly before the ritual's apogee, trance specialists commence work on a long bamboo structure. This is the *eran la'bo*, or ladder of knives. When situated vertically in the middle of the ritual arena, only the most daring adepts climb up it to encounter the gods descending from the heavens.

The *ma'bugi'* ritual summons the *deata* spirits to the village, and, to a certain elect number of participants, the *deata* become visible. As the dance and chanting grow more intense, a group of men split off from the ever-widening circle of dancers, proceeding to the vicinity of the *kapok* log fireplace. Under the direction of the *tominaa* priest, they take a red *tabang* leaf in hand and begin to call the *deata*. Chanting as one unit they move north toward the sacred fireplace and then back as the melodic counter-point of the *nondo* circle dance continues close by. The male chanters review in *gelong* (special *ma'bugi'* verse) the offerings of preceding weeks; they implore the spirits to approach; they speak in metaphorical terms of the "tumbling of stones under rushing waters," anticipating the onset of trance. The chanters summon *deata* from the Underworld, where they have scales and fins, and also from the sky, from whence they descend to prominent mountaintops before journeying en masse to the ceremonial center. Chanting and dancing continue until suddenly a lone woman spins rapidly out of the group from the circle dance. With long black hair flying, she prances from one end of the ceremonial ground to the other. Simul-taneously, one of the male chanters near the fireplace becomes violently possessed, his limbs thrashing in the air and his face contorted in expres-sion of profound ecstasy. A number of others fall into spontaneous trance as dancers and chanters withdraw rapidly to merge with the large crowd of spectators. For perhaps half an hour, possessions occur under the careful observation of community leaders. Trancers are closely guarded to protect participants and observers alike from inadvertent harm. In time, the energy ebbs and performers fall into dissociated, quiescent states.

As trancers fall back to the periphery, ritual specialists call on the chron-ically ill and weak to come forth. An adolescent girl has narrowly escaped death by lightning. She suffers severe psychological stress from this calamity which claimed her father's life. Young children with no appetite, who for years have not grown or become robust, and old people suffering from manifold disabilities come forward to be healed. Trance doctors (practi-tioners known for their healing skills) are among the first to become pos-sessed and now move rapidly from one patient to the next. Massaging their patients with premasticated bits of *tabang* leaf, rubbing them with blood extracted from their own bodies, and sometimes whirling young children over their heads, these spirit-endowed healers apply therapy available only during the *ma'bugi'*. Healers or parents may now bring young children near the fireplace to be touched lightly by the flames. Healers also now use the waters from the ritual "well" (a *kandian lau'* gourd containing bits of iron, leaves of red *tabang*, the soothing *darinding*, and the cooling *passake* plants) to heal the bodies of the afflicted. People believe that the heat of the ritual fire combined with the cool waters of the "well" have especially curative effects in this special context of a supernatural presence. At the close of the ceremony, some even gather the charred remains of the fireplace to reserve as medicine for everyday illnesses. The charcoal is mixed with water, and makes a tonic for stomach pains, headaches, and the like.

Ma'bugi' curing happens at the close of the initial stage of spontaneous possession. The ritual concludes with what might best be termed "professional" trancing. Some performers here have participated in stylized trance roles for many years. The "one who spits" leads this group: acting in accordance with personal inspiration, a few days before the apogee of the ritual he designates a scenario to be followed by trance adepts. At Rantekasimpo in late 1971, the principal "game" *(paningoan)* was to be the ascent of a ladder of knives. Ancillary activities were to include dancing upon the taut skin of drums, self-mortification with daggers, dancing upon hot coals, and standing upon clusters of sharpened bamboo stakes. In the western Toraja districts, additional tests of faith occur at *ma'bugi'* rituals: rolling upon a bed of sharp cactus-like spines, lying upon sharpened bamboo stakes arranged in fence-like fashion five feet above the ground, and spinning heavy wooden drums gripped by a short cord held between the teeth. The Makale district is particularly known, however, for its techniques of "playing" with steel. Here, as in all other professional trance activities, the intervention of the spirits prevents harm. Self-inflicted knife wounds are rendered instantaneously harmless with the light touch of a red *tabang* leaf. Similarly, the blades of the ladder of knives do not injure the feet of the possessed as one after the other the climbers ascend to the pinnacle. The thorns of the *duri bangga* plant and the razor-sharp bamboo stakes cause no harm to the trance adepts because, it is believed, the benevolent powers of the *deata* spirits intervene between the men and the natural consequences of their daring.

Much as the community as a whole endeavors to right the imbalance of natural forces by undertaking the dangerous *ma'bugi'* ritual, individual participants place their faith in the life-sustaining *deata* spirits and perform extraordinary feats of endurance and agility. The *ma'bugi'* strives to restore the balance of nature, allows for individual catharsis in trance, and revitalizes community belief in the normally unseen supernaturals which here alone manifest their power before the community.

When the *ma'bugi'* ritual finally concludes, people usher the controlling supernatural, *Puang Maruruk*, beyond the community boundary. A final "sweeping of the red leaves" out of the courtyard and the resumption of participation in the annual round of death rituals finalizes the end of another cyclical *Ma'bugi'* ritual. The providential results of the trance rite endure long past its conclusion, though. The fields now will produce in abundance, the pigs and water buffalo will multiply and become strong, children and adults will remain free from illness. When misfortune again visits the village, people will once again summon the *deata* spirits to the ceremonial center to renew faith and well-being.

THE WEAK VERSION

The *ma'bugi'* performance of the Mengkendek district can be characterized as "weak" in comparison with the one from Makale, especially in terms of the trance performance. Although trance is thought essential in Mengkendek, too, the numbers who actually fell into such a state were very limited. In two *ma'bugi'* performances staged at Tinoring village in late 1977, we saw only two spontaneous trance performances in the first and no trance at all in the second, where even invited trance "specialists" failed to become possessed. People commented that other villages "like" trance much more than they do. In addition, we did not find the sacred fireplace or ladder of knives so important in the Makale area *ma'bugi'*. By contrast, *ma'bugi'* in Mengkendek stresses purification or religious cleanliness, and sacrificial offerings to the supernaturals. Although these motifs also exist in the Makale area, our attention there is naturally drawn to the more dramatic possessions. A comparative description of the two rituals enhances our understanding of this significant Toraja rite.

Both rituals in the Mengkendek district were five-day events. On the first day, the people prepare the ritual space for the *ma'bugi'* at the corner of the rice barn. In contrast to the situation in Makale, this space is the rice granary of the *to bunga' lalan* (overseer of rice rituals who determines when work should begin at the start of the agricultural year), rather than that of the village chief and descendant of the first settler of the land, the *to bara'*. The rice barn, supported by pillars, shelters an elevated floor, used for receiving honored guests. In this space, especially the northeastern corner, people welcome the *deata* spirits. The northeast is the most auspicious, because it overlaps the east and the north, the directions of life-promotion. Here people also place bamboo containers (*suke bugi'*) with *tabang* leaves on top, palm wine, areca nuts and a *kandian lau'* gourd container for holding "cooling" plants. A sacred *maa'* cloth hangs around the pillars of the rice barn to ward off evil influences. Green bamboo containers hold rice softened with water. This is food for the *deata* spirits which the "mother and father of *ma'bugi'*," the *indo'* and *ambe' bugi'*, will share. This couple is selected from among local villagers who are "clean"— that is, who have no outstanding sacrificial obligations to their deceased relatives. They eat, sleep, and reside on the floor of the rice barn for the duration of the five-day ritual. They may not eat "hot" foods *(tangkande malassu)*; instead they eat "cool" foods such as raw soaked rice, cold water *(woi sakke)*, and palm wine. As was the case in Makale, people dance the *ma'bugi'* at the eastern side of the rice barn every day during the ritual, and sometimes throughout the night until dawn.

On the second day the villagers walk in procession around the border of the community, stopping at the four corners of the village road to perform the *ma'bugi'* dance while shaking the *maa'* cloth. This rite, termed *marimba*, "warding off evils," cleanses the community. The priest of rice *(to bunga' lalan)*, who leads the procession, holds the gourd container in his hand, sprinkling water with a whisk of the cooling plants. This purifies the community and helps it remain "cool" during the intense ritual which follows. While the *marimba* ritual aims to purify the community, the ritual on the third day (termed *mendio'*, "bathing") purifies each responsible member of the community. All go in procession to a stream which is the natural border with a neighboring community. At the stream "father of *ma'bugi'*" *(ambe' bugi')*, along with the *tominaa* priest, pray jointly, calling the *deata* spirits. They face east, the direction associated with *deata*, holding a bundle of *tabang* leaves. After the prayer, all the participants wash their faces and hands while murmuring that the water will ensure their good health. The fourth day, termed *allo datu*, the "day of king," is a holiday without any ritual or, to be more precise, a day of abstention from work.

On the final day *(la'pa')*, the ritual center moves from the rice barn to the ceremonial field termed the *pa'bugiran*. In Makale, the courtyard of the first settler or village chief serves as the *pa'bugiran*, while in Mengkendek this site is outside the hamlet in an open field. At the northeastern corner of this ceremonial field stands a large sandalwood *(sendana)* tree, a tree of life for the Toraja, and a symbol of prosperity. At the base of this tree, villagers hang a *maa'* cloth, a *kandian lau'* gourd, the four bamboo tubes holding glutinous rice, betel nut, and a large number of *tabang* leaves. Here, too, villagers offer chickens to the supernaturals. To the people of the southern Toraja districts of Makale, Sangalla', and Mengkendek, the coloration of sacrificial chickens is especially important.[13]

Sacrificial chickens are first purified with water and then given some uncooked rice to eat. Holding the chicken in his hands, the *tominaa* makes a short prayer and then cuts its throat with a small knife. He inspects the liver to see whether it contains white juice, a good omen, or yellow, a bad omen. If the omen is bad, they sacrifice another bird. After cooking the chicken parts in a bamboo tube over an open fire, they place some meat from the left side on a banana leaf along with rice and betel nut. This offering occurs four times, once for each of four supernaturals.[14] After the offering to the four supernaturals, villagers may begin to eat their own rice and chicken which they have prepared at home and brought to the ceremonial ground. Then, the *nondo* circle dance commences.

Analysis

We have so far described the *ma'bugi'* ritual with special heed to the difference between the Makale (strong) and Mengkendek (weak) versions. These "data" already reflect actors' as well as observers' interpretations, because, as we mentioned earlier, they are "our own constructions of other people's constructions" (Geertz 1973b:9). Therefore, our task in this analytical section is not a matter of "we observe, we record, then we analyze" but rather a "thickening" of the description (cf. Geertz 1973b:20) which we have already presented. In this effort, our anthropology of religion is basically an interpretive one. We do use symbolic and structuralist approaches as part of this effort, insofar as they help us understand the ritual. We examine how fundamental Toraja religious ideas, symbols, and actions are manipulated and interpreted in the particular ritual at hand.

Variation in ritual performances is of key importance in fully understanding the ritual. The question should be viewed in two ways. From the actor's point of view, variants of a ritual provide him with different experiences. In the final analysis the *ma'bugi'* may be experienced by the Mengkendek people as a purification rite, and by the Makale people as a trance performance. Two people, two communities, and two performances have their own "true" interpretations of a single ritual. From the analyst's point of view, however, it is not necessary to assume that one of these variants is somehow "truer" than the other. Or, to borrow the structuralist assertion, any variant is a "true version," and the myth [read ritual!] consists of all its versions (Lévi-Strauss 1955). This viewpoint is actually shared among the actors of ritual, too, in their recognition of *"lain desa, lain adat"* (different village, different customs).

In other words, both versions of *ma'bugi'* are, in interpretive terms, the "commentary" to each other. Our analysis, then, uses both variants of the ritual to achieve a more complete understanding than either variant alone could provide.

Purification stands out as the theme of the Mengkendek *ma'bugi'*; trance dominates the Makale version. Placed together as a continuum, purification appears to be a "weak" or elementary form of trance. Purification is certainly a prerequisite for trance; trance is the most purified state in which the power of gods manifests itself. In what follows we analyze the basic elements of the ritual in a continuum from the weak to strong forms. First, we view *ma'bugi'* as a purification ritual; then, we attend to the major symbols of the ritual; and finally, we examine the meaning of trance, the strong manifestation of both purity and the power of gods.

PURITY AND ORDER

The *penanian* or *bua'* is the community which stages a *ma'bugi'*. This ritual community traces its origin to a putative first settler of the land; associated households unite to carry out ritual obligations in common. In the contemporary administrative system, this community corresponds roughly to the present *kampung* as a subdivision of the *desa*, an administrative village.[15] In Mengkendek, the *ma'bugi'* functions to purify the traditional community. It removes the pollution which constantly accumulates during the course of everyday life. Both the ceremonial circumambulation of the village borders (*marimba*) and the participants' ritual bathing (*mendio'*) reinforce this point. *Ma'bugi'* clearly delimits the sacred and/or purified space of the interior as against the profane and/or polluted world of the outside. To regain an evanescent purity for however brief a period of time, the Toraja people stage a *ma'bugi'* approximately at three-year intervals. Poor rice harvests, ill domestic animals, sickly children, and such are all external signs that the accumulation of pollutants has become burdensome.

The Toraja concept of *masero* compares to our concept of purity, although it is also used in somewhat different contexts. In a physical sense, the word describes, for example, a clear sky (*maserona langi'*), clean water (*maserona woi*), or a glowing gas lamp (*maseromo tu lampu gas*). In the phrase *masero indanna*, it has an economic sense: the debt is wiped clean. *Rara masero*, "clean blood," refers to nobility who suffer no mixture of blood with lower status people. Finally, a ritual called "holding clean" (*untoe' sero*) is the final rite of the death ritual; after *untoe' sero*, people are freed from taboos relating to death and may once again eat rice. Thus, the concept of *masero* covers a wide range of ideas about purity and cleanness.

The opposition of pure and impure, furthermore, parallels the symbolic opposition of "cool" and "hot." As in other parts of Indonesia, the Toraja concept of "cool" *(sakke)* is associated with what is good, healthy, and calm, as opposed to the state of being "hot" *(makula')*, which signifies anger, emotional distress, sickness, and that which is bad. Therefore, the food taboos of the *indo'* and *ambe' bugi'* demand that they consume only "cold water" *(woi sakke)*, palm wine, and uncooked rice. The putative "owners" of the *ma'bugi'* ritual thus keep themselves and all others in the village (their "children") in a cool and safe state. The cooling plants in the *kandian lau'* gourd form a whisk for sprinkling "cool-making water" on ritually superheated space. First the *deata* space at the northern corner of the rice barn is cooled; then, the water is used to cool ill people at the height of the *ma'bugi'*. At the very center of the event, ritual space has been especially cooled, cleansed, and purified.

The *maa'* cloth which is hung about the rice barn is also important for a purification purpose. Like the Batak *ulos*, a life-giving cloth, it is believed to have magical powers of protection from evil spirits. As a mobile purifier, it is used as well in the *ambe' bugi'*'s prayer for *deata* spirits (the celebrant puts on the cloth). It is used as well in the ritual circumambulation of the village border (the processionists dance *ma'bugi'* at the village corners while shaking the cloth), and in the chicken sacrifice at the bottom of the *sendana* tree located at *pa'bugiran*, a ritual ground (the cloth is hung about the tree). The *maa'* cloth usually has its own name suggesting a heavenly origin (e.g., *Doti Langi'*, Heavenly Cross.). The cloth is also counted as a form of inheritance termed *mana'* *(pusaka* in Indonesian) and in that way is similar to spears, *keris*-swords, beadwork, et cetera. In rituals the *maa'* cloth is taken out from the storage and used to keep the ceremonial space purified.

In Mengkendek, the choice of the rice barn of the "rice priest" as a ritual center is itself instructive. First, to the Toraja, rice is of heavenly origin, a symbol of life as well as the staff of life. The production of this all-important grain relies in large measure on the beneficence of the powerful *deata*. Exactly because of this association, the core members of the deceased's family then observing mourning obligations may not eat rice during the death rituals. At that time they eat the corn (which in turn is tabooed in life rituals as an "unclean food," suggesting death). Second, in daily social intercourse, hosts do not receive guests in the house proper, but at the rice barn. There, they sit, relax, and often take a meal in common with their hosts. It is a prestigious place where *deata* spirits, in *ma'bugi'* contexts, stay as the "divine guests."

One major difference between the Makale and Mengkendek rituals is that in Mengkendek the height of the *ma'bugi'* *(la'pa')* is performed at a sacred ground *(pa'bugiran)* situated far beyond the homestead of the priest of rice. This in fact is normally the case in other Makale villages as well, but at Rantekasimpo village, the home of the chief and the *pa'bugiran* are one and the same.[16]

In Makale the process of cooling, cleansing, and purifying can occur only after the performances of some of the "hottest," most dangerous, emotionally intense, and potentially harmful activities have taken place. Here fire *(kaponan)* is also a principal cleansing element. Ill adults and parents of sick children climb atop the heavy *kapok* logs above the flames. In Makale, therefore, not only cool water but also hot flames are ritually used for cleansing or curing purposes. In the death ceremonies people cook food furtively at small fires behind the ceremonial huts or under the temporary dwellings. Conversely, fire is central at the other "eastern side rituals" of promoting life (for example, at the *ma'sulo tedong* closing the old ritual year, and at the *ma'bua' pare*, the large fertility cult of rice). In daily contexts, a fireplace *(dapo')* is always set at the eastern side of the house.

Mary Douglas once argued that the concept of purity is deeply related to that of order (1966). This view can be aptly maintained in the case of the Toraja *ma'bugi'*. In Toraja the concept of purity *(masero)*, we have seen earlier, covers a wide range of ideas: the *masero* is the state in which every physical, economic, social, and religious burden is wiped "clean." "To hold clean" *(untoe' sero)* is the most fundamental force driving the Toraja people to the rituals. Social status *(rara* = "blood") is also almost always discussed in reference to "purity." To the Toraja ordinary man, especially in the hierarchical villages in southern Tana Toraja, there are more "pure-blooded" persons above him and less "pure" persons below him. In other words, Toraja social hierarchy is based on the degree of "purity" of blood of the high nobles *(puang)*, who are said to have a "white blood," and are situated on top of the hierarchy.[17] The "whiteness," again, is the major attribute of *deata* spirits, the purest being.

To purify is, then, to establish and re-establish, if but momentarily, an order in opposition to the darkness of disorder by invoking the ultimate force, the *deata*.

Importantly, the order thus achieved is conceptualized as the prerequisite for vitality. In *ma'bugi'*, the *indo'* and *ambe' bugi'* (the ritual couple) confine themselves during the five days of the ritual to the purified space of the rice barn. We interpret this ritual cohabitation as a sacred marriage before divine guests—the *deata*. Indeed, local informants stressed that persons who play this role do so in the hope of being granted additional children in the future. What we see here is a parallel between human productivity and agricultural abundance, a parallel played out in terms of vitality.

TWO KEY SYMBOLS OF LIFE: PLANTS AND CHICKENS

Two key symbols are deeply connected with the Toraja conception of life: plants and chickens. These are also to the fore in *ma'bugi'*.

Rice, as noted, symbolizes the life-promoting principle, and a group of "cooling" plants symbolically restores the purity of ritual space. There are two other plants which play an important role in the ritual. One is the red-leaved plant termed *tabang (Cordiline Terminalis)*. People plant *tabang* around a homestead to keep away evil spirits. In the *ma'bugi'* ritual, the *tabang* leaves indicate the presence of the *deata* spirits. Actually, the *gelong* (verse) text depicts the *deata* arriving through the *tabang* leaves (Veen 1979:112). "To tear up the *tabang* leaves" is a metaphorical expression referring to the performance of *ma'bugi'* (Veen 1965:144). Healers use it particularly in the curing of the sick. According to Nooy-Palm (1979:225), this plant's impressive red color associates it with blood and, therefore, with life and vitality.

The *sendana* (sandalwood) tree which stands at the northeastern corner of the Mengkendek *pa'bugiran* is a Toraja version of the tree of life (cf. Nooy-Palm 1979:219). In ritual verse, it is always called the *sendana sugi'*, "rich sandalwood tree." Indeed, it symbolizes richness, abundance, and fertility, and at the *pa'bugiran* of Mengkendek one informant, looking up at the *sendana* tree, commented: "This big old tree has witnessed many *ma'bugi*'s of our ancestors. The rich branches of the tree symbolize those numerous performances." In the rituals termed *merok* and *ma'bua'*, the two largest life-promoting rituals, participants plant a young *sendana* tree. Finally, the metaphor of the tree with many branches expresses the genealogy of a family, especially its richness in descendants.[18] The *sendana* tree represents, then, a concept of "life" much broader than an individual human life.

Plants in Toraja rituals symbolize a general concept of life and its continuity: paddy repeats a cycle of death and rebirth; a tree outlives many human generations. The Toraja's concept of *lolo* means at one and the same time, "the young sprout of a plant," and "the umbilical cord of human beings." As a great tree with many branches grows from a small sprout, so a family or a kin group with many descendants grows from an ancestral sprout.

Chickens represent life, too, but aggression and dynamism as well. In folktales, a cock frequently appears as the magical animal that has a power to revive the dead hero.[19] Toraja use the work *kurre* both to call chickens and to call a soul.[20] In wood carvings, the cock is always portrayed on the top front of the *adat* house and the rice barn, together with the *barre allo*, the sun motif. In the latter case the cock is associated with the Upperworld, and especially with the sun, the source of vitality and light. The cockfight is deeply related to the Toraja masculine ethos. In former head-hunting forays, the *tominaa* priest crowed like a cock before an expedition party departed (Kruyt 1923–24:312).

Interestingly, the ancestor of chickens is called *Puang Maro*, the "Lord of Madness or the Possessed." The ancestors of chickens were mad because they ate each other and pecked each other (Veen 1965:95; 1976:412). There are two interpretations of this "madness." Nooy-Palm suggested that hyperactive pecking is "neurotic," a state comparable to trance, and "during this feast certain individuals become possessed just as *Puang Maro* once was" (1979:209). Alternatively, Veen, following his informant, suggests that the expression "to eat each other and to peck each other" is a metaphor of copulation or incest (1976: 427). If so, *ma'bugi'* is a story about an "original sin" and rationalizes the use of chickens as atonement. For this most serious offense, chickens, the descendants of *Puang Maro*, take respon-sibility. Humans sacrifice chickens to purify an original sin. The chicken is, then (to mix metaphors) a sort of "scapegoat" in this purification drama. Conversely, the chicken is sometimes a symbol of righteousness (cf. Nooy-Palm 1979:211). In fact the cockfight, too, is said to have originated as a form of divine judgment.

In *ma'bugi'*, we have seen four kinds of chickens die, and the dis-tinguishing criterion among them is color: (1) the black-legged; (2) the red-necked: (3) the yellow-legged; and (4) the white-legged. These fowl are of-fered respectively to the ancestors, to the master of earth, to the evil spirits, and to the *deata* spirits. They are set, one to four, from the south to north (or the left to right) as the sacrifice is made facing east. Structurally, therefore, the four colors, the four supernaturals, and the four directions (the combination of the north/south and the east/west axes, which also parallels the right/left and the heaven/earth[21]) correspond to each other, suggesting the same structural principle of conceptual order. The chicken sacrifice, then, relates to Toraja concepts of cosmic order, the number "four" representing the All.

In daily consciousness, a plant is a plant, a chicken is a chicken, and they are nothing mystic. In the framework of ritual, however, these daily objects are placed within intricate "texts" of symbols. Here the plant is not just a plant, the chicken is not just a chicken: they become something different from, and something more than, those objects as viewed in everyday con-texts. The ritual performances in this way "momentarily make explicit what is otherwise a fiction" (Leach 1954:16). In other words, in the ritual people attempt to transcend the discrepancy between "just a thing" and "just a fiction" through the manipulation of ritual symbols. In this sense, the two key symbols, plants and chickens, function as the root metaphors on which the Toraja concept of life is founded. The mundane, transformed, becomes the entry way to the transcendant.

TRANCE AND THE POWER OF GODS

Unlike classic shamanic performances, in Tana Toraja the *tominaa* priest of life does not himself fall into trance. Instead he leads a ceremony of mass or community possession in which paroxysms of apparently "wild" trance behavior lead to curing and the performance of *paningoan* games. Everyone who dances the *ma'bugi'* dance and feels the power and presence of the *deata* spirits faces the possibility of falling into a trance. The *ma'bugi'* dance is a circle dance, accompanied by the song *(gelong)*. The circle goes slowly to the right-hand side, the direction of the *deata* or life-promotion. The dance's circularity may represent the harmonious relations between humans, and between humans and supernaturals as well. The *gelong* verse describes the coming of the *deata* spirits who are summoned to the ceremonial place. From the performer's point of view, however, the emotions that arise from singing and dancing are much more important than the content of the *gelong* text. Singers stress the importance of singing in *unison:* the song must be sung as if it were one voice. Therefore, it usually takes a long time to tune up the voices, through simply harmonizing with meaningless words such as "ei, ei, ei. . . ."[22] It is this feeling of "oneness" the performers enjoy so much.

As the performers get excited, they begin the jumping step, *nondo',* sometimes executing it very violently. To borrow the words of Holt, the dance and song "end with an outburst of ecstatic nature on the part of one or more dancers" (1939:73). Even when only a few actually fall into trance, all the community is drawn toward intense involvement in the ritual. Urban-dwelling sons and daughters join the dancing despite Calvinist strictures to the contrary. Neighbors from surrounding villages actively participate in song, dance, and trance, thus sharing in its benefits.

Trance is a state in which "awareness ends," when union is effected with the *deata* spirits who have come to the ceremonial place. This is the state termed *mentama deata,* meaning "the *deata* spirits enter." One explanation of trance is that the *deata* spirits enter into the body of the possessed. The other explanation is that this phrase refers not to the *deata* entering the human body but to the *deata* entering the village community. According to the latter, the *deata* who have come to the ceremonial place control the action of the entranced.[23] In both interpretations, the *deata* and the possessed become one, and humans are made to act abnormally according to the will or control of the *deata* spirits. What is proclaimed here is, to quote Lewis, "not merely that God is *with* us, but that He is *in* us" (1971:204; Lewis's emphasis).

The *deata* spirits are not sharply delineated in terms of individual personalities. The invocations stress that *all* the *deata* come down together. In other words, the *deata* are not the gods with well-articulated personalities but rather an unnamed life-giving energy. Therefore, the people in trance do not know which *deata* take them (cf. Zerner 1981:107). The *deata* come from outside of the village community at the beginning of the ritual, and at the end of the ceremony they are asked to leave it. The *deata* seem to be divine strangers. Coming and going, then, is a fundamental characteristic of the *deata*, and so the *deata* symbolize fluid, not static, power. The *deata* also represent "outsideness," i.e., a power external and macrocosmic, a power that cannot be judged from the standard within the earthly village community. When the *deata* arrive, the external and fluid energy penetrates everything and all becomes superanimated, as if it were a charged battery. Trance takes place in these "ecstatic"—in the original sense of the word, "ex-status"—circumstances.

In Makale's ecstatic drama, the motif of climbing the ladder of knives quite theatrically recalls Eliade's theme of the "eternal return," of the unceasing human desire for reunion with a once approachable cosmos irretrievably distanced by the primal transgression of mythological times (1957:106–7). Within sight of Rantekasimpo village where the *ma'bugi'* of Makale was staged, there are certain limestone bluffs termed Sarira; Toraja say these are vestiges of the celestial ladder once joining the Toraja people with their high god. After a long era of easy communication between humans and gods, an evil human stole the golden fire flint of the high god, *Puang Matua*, who then wrathfully sundered the ladder of the sky *(eran di langi')*. Ascending the ladder of knives and also climbing a tall bamboo pole strongly suggest the momentary reunification of terrestrial (human) and celestial (supernatural) planes of existence. The actions of trance performers are allegorical. Just as the stab wounds they inflict upon themselves will fail to penetrate the skin, and the chronically ill will certainly be cured, so the community as a whole will be protected by the *deata* spirits. For a brief moment spirits descend to the center of the village community, are met between earth and sky by trance adepts seated above a high ladder of knives—a ladder which recalls the link that once assured easy access between humans and the gods. The spirits appear to the entranced who described them as miniature yellow-haired men who speak, encouraging them to perform normally impossible feats. *Ma'bugi'* both renders and manifests the cosmos and yet transcends it. Trance ratifies, however briefly, the capacity of humans and spirits to join as one. Trance in Toraja allows for the restoration of prosperity, the renewal of fundamental cosmological principles, and the momentary reunification of humans with the realm of the gods.

Belo writes about the Balinese that they are "a people whose everyday behaviour is measured, controlled, graceful, tranquil" (1960:1). This describes the Toraja, too, who calmly live their everyday lives within a structured social hierarchy. There remain, however, uncertainties, areas over which humans have little control. Sickness, misfortune, and death occur capriciously, throwing normal patterns into disarray. The mass trance and particularly the extraordinary actions of trance adepts deviate markedly from the control required in daily life. On the sociopsychological plane, the trance rite provides an opportunity for prominence for deviant or underclass individuals who normally enjoy little import in the highly stratified, tightly ordered Toraja social universe. Directly experiencing the power of gods, participants renew their faith in the ultimate principle beyond humans.

Conclusion

If ritual is an experienced text, then what kind of experience does *ma'-bugi'* provide? We suggest that what is experienced, in the final analysis, is the power of the gods. Participants experience this power in the process of purification, in the sacrifice of chickens, and, in particular, through trance. The *ma'bugi'* as a whole is the dramaturgy, or symbolically constructed mechanism by which participants—performers and observers—experience the power of gods. By experiencing this power, then, we have seen that the *ma'bugi'* ritual is concerned with the renewal of order on the one hand and vitality on the other. An important point is, therefore, that the Toraja sense the "order," the "vitality," and the "power" in a single ideological set of continua.

The Toraja are not unique in this respect, of course. Similar instances can be taken from the other religious traditions of Indonesia and the Southeast Asian world. For example, Anderson pointed out in his insightful essay on the Javanese idea of power (1972) that power in that culture is *concrete*, whereas in the West the idea of power is conceptualized in more abstract terms. He argues this as "the first and central premise of Javanese political thought," and writes: "It [power for the Javanese] is not a theoretical postulate but an existential reality. Power is that intangible, mysterious, and divine energy which animates the universe. It is manifested in every aspect of the natural world, in stones, trees, clouds, and fire, but is expressed quintessentially in the central mystery of life, the process of generation and regeneration" (Anderson 1972:7). Power thus exists simultaneously in the fertility of human procreation, in the abundance of agricultural products, in the prosperity of the society, and in the vitality of the state: in a word, power is "the ability to give life" (1972:19). The power thus conceived is exactly the same kind that we have discussed in this paper through the lens of the Toraja *ma'bugi'* ritual. Power is, for the Toraja as well as the Javanese, life, and life is power. The power of gods is nothing but that of promotion of life.

It is beyond the scope of this paper to relate this fundamental Toraja idea of power to the various cultural dimensions of Toraja politics as Anderson did in his brilliant essay about Java. We can, however, point out that the term *bugi'* of *ma'bugi'* is said to have originated from the name of the coastal people of Sulawesi, the Bugis, and that in this view the first *ma'bugi'* ritual was held in order to defeat the evil invader, the Bugis (cf. Radjab 1952:153; Kennedy 1953:28). Historically, the Bugis tried to take over the Toraja land several times. One might therefore presume that the images of the invader Bugis and the evil spirits which bring misfortune overlap.[24] Enemies—both actual and spiritual—can be defeated by invoking the power of gods. A parallel can be found even in contemporary Toraja political life: in the campaign of the 1977 Indonesian General Election, the Mengkendek sect of *Golkar* performed the *ma'bugi'* dance against the enemy parties, to ensure their victory.

In this context, the belief in the ritual's "efficacy" is by no means an illusion. "Ritual action," Leach says, "serves to *express* the status of the actor vis-à-vis his environment, both physical and social; it may also serve to *alter* the status of the actor" (1968:525; emphasis added). We should recall here again that the rituals of Toraja in the *Aluk* tradition mean "the proper ways of *doing*," and that *ma'bugi'* is a "healing" ritual in its fullest sense. Through its involvement in the life-giving power, the *ma'bugi'* ritual of Toraja attempts to "alter" the state of the existence—of the people, of the land, and of the society—toward such powerful images of life as the sunbeam or the burning fire, the root images of the Toraja concept of *masero* ("cleanness").[25]

In the analysis of *ma'bugi'* ritual, special attention has been paid to the variation between the Mengkendek (weak) and Makale (strong) versions. We discovered that two dominant religious themes—purification and trance—can be viewed in a single continuum. A parallel of this can be taken, though in somewhat different form, from the Balinese harvest rituals discussed by Boon (1977:107–12). The Balinese harvest festival is celebrated alternately as *ngebekin* and *ngusaba*. The former has the character of an offering to the demons while sometimes inducing trance; the latter, primarily a festival of thanksgiving to the deity, is more elaborate than the *ngebekin* which is also called the "little" festival (Boon 1977:108–9). Thus, in Bali the harvest ceremony oscillates as it were in weak-strong beats, between the little and elaborate rites, and between the rites "of potential demonic influence with rice production" and "of divine benevolence in bestowing abundant harvest" every alternate Balinese year. An important point here is that both variants of ritual format are two aspects, "negative" and "positive," of the same reality. Although these alternate mechanically regardless of the actual current harvest, Boon(1977:109) argues further, "they can be more accentuated in certain environmental extremes." In the *ngebekin* harvest of 1972 in an extremely rich area in southwest Bali, he observed "the *ngebekin* ritual keyed with actuality insofar as the harvest festivals served as the occasion for intense trance activities and demonic possession," because that year the peasants "who were acknowledging in a demonic register a bountiful wet-year harvest were also currently experiencing a severe drought which bade ill for the next crop." In this way, the difference that appears as the regional variation in Toraja seems to be manifested in what Boon called "the complex temporal dimensions of the rice cult" in Bali.

The contrast of purification and trance can be explained again in another way. Leach once pointed out that ritual stylization tends to distort the everyday norm in either of two directions: "the emphasis may be ascetic, representing the intensification of formal restraint, or ecstatic, signifying the elimination of restraint" (1968:526). In the case of *ma'bugi'*, we have found both of these ritual distortions: It is "ascetic" in the sense that purity is achieved only by observing numerous taboos *(pemali)*; it is "ecstatic," of course, because of trance. Or, if both of these are taken together, we would say that the ritual which begins with asceticism (purification) ends with ecstasy. Even in the Mengkendek version of *ma'bugi'*, the dance performance on the final day has an ecstatic character. The contrast of "ascetic" and "ecstatic," and of purification and trance, shows the two different modes of a ritual transformation of everyday reality.

The scope of the present paper was limited to a single Toraja ritual, but we believe this rite is crucial for giving shape to the Toraja's experience of religion and, therefore, for understanding their entire religious tradition. Settings vary from place to place—even within Tana Toraja, as we have seen—so that what is true of the particular performance need not hold anywhere else. However, as Geertz notes, "anthropologists don't study villages (tribes, towns, neighbourhood . . .); they study *in* villages" (1973b:22; Geertz's emphasis). We believe, therefore, that our investigation is of more than regional significance.

3. Kaharingan: Life and Death in Southern Borneo

Joseph A. Weinstock

$\mathcal{F}$OLLOWING THE DUTCH ADMINISTRATIVE PATTERN, the independent Indonesian government created a single province of Kalimantan in 1953, but within three years regional pressure forced its subdivision into three separate provinces (Legge 1961:66). Originally divided topographically, the Indonesian portion of the island of Borneo became the provinces of East Kalimantan (Kalimantan Timur), including the watersheds of the Mahakam and all other rivers flowing east; South Kalimantan (Kalimantan Selatan), covering the watersheds of all southward flowing rivers, such as the Barito and the Kahayan; and West Kalimantan (Kalimantan Barat), including the watersheds of the Kapuas and other westward flowing rivers. For the provinces of East and West Kalimantan this topographical distinction still holds true, but not so in the case of the watersheds of the southward flowing rivers. (See Fig. 3.1.)

Numerically and politically superior, the Moslem Banjars quickly dominated the province of South Kalimantan. After the failure of parliamentarian efforts to create a Great Dayak territory separate from the predominately Banajarese South Kalimantan, an open rebellion, known as the movement of the Cutlass and Shield Pro Panca Sila (GMTPS), broke out along religious lines. The predominately Ngaju Dayak group began raids in late 1956 on various government installations within the province.

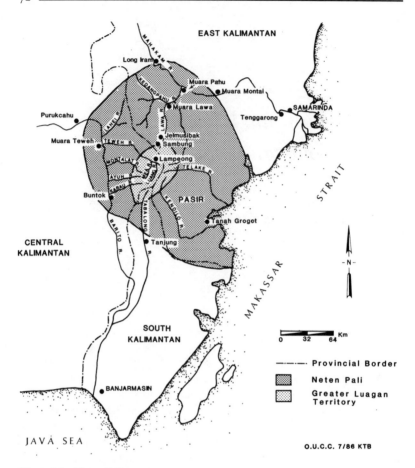

Figure 3.1. Neten Pali

Its objectives were the recognition of the Dayak religion under the Pancasila and the creation of an autonomous province of Central Kalimantan. According to the Pancasila, or five principles, every citizen of the republic is guaranteed religious freedom. Sukarno, aware that religious strife could sunder the fragile structure holding together the thousands of islands which comprised the Republic of Indonesia, and faced with potentially more dangerous armed rebellions across the archipelago, acceded to these demands and signed an emergency decree in May 1957 whereby the autonomous province of Central Kalimantan came into existence (Miles 1976:121). Granting regional autonomy to the Islamic fundamentalists of

Aceh in northernmost Sumatra and creating the Dayak province of Central Kalimantan (Kalimantan Tengah) were two of the most visible actions taken by Sukarno to maintain religious harmony.

Secure with a province of their own, the Dayaks ceased to oppose the central government, but the events of the mid-1960s proved the position of their religion less secure. The abortive Communist coup and subsequent rise of the "New Order" regime of Suharto changed the complexion of religious freedom. Lack of religion or atheism was equated with Communism, expressly outlawed in the "New Order." Complications ensued as indigenous religions, such as those in Kalimantan, Sulawesi, and even Java, were recognized only as *kepercayaan*, beliefs, rather than *agama*, religion. Caught in a catch-22 situation, the Dayaks were told that they did not have an *agama* and thus became suspect in the anti-Communist fever of the late 1960s. By the early 1970s, negotiations began between Central Kalimantan and the national government over recognition of the indigenous religion of the peoples of the province. This culminated in official recognition in 1980 of Kaharingan as an *agama* (Weinstock 1981).

Agama *and the Sociological Concept of Religion*

Until the mid-nineteenth century, the Luangan and other Dayaks of southern Borneo maintained themselves relatively detached from the outside world.[1] Basically self-sufficient in food production, they traded minor forest products such as rattan and damar resin for the salt and cloth they needed. Except in the Pasir and Banjar regions, the spread of Islam was insignificant; thus, the traditional system of beliefs was left relatively undisturbed. Perceptual distinction of religious and non-religious activities was not made; there existed a unitary cultural system integrating subsistence and spiritual activities.

Increased interaction with the outside world, both in the form of Islam and Christianity as well as in the form of Indonesian national culture, brought with it adoption of a perceptual dichotomization of *adat*, tradition, as distinct from *agama*, religion. Practices and beliefs directly related to the spiritual realm have become categorized as *agama* following the definition of this term in the Indonesian national language, Bahasa Indonesia. Practices and beliefs dealing with the more mundane aspects of life, such as agricultural and economic activities, have become categorized as being within the realm of *adat* following the definition of this term in Bahasa Indonesia. Thus, where religion was once a facet of the cultural system, it has become perceived as a bounded, and ultimately extractable, aspect of that cultural system.

From the perspective of the Indonesian government, demarcation of what is and what is not religion and religious activity is necessary. Separation of the state from religion is necessary in a country where more than one religion flourishes. Where cultural diversity is extensive, as within the national boundaries of Indonesia, there exists a need to distinguish between what is religious and under the authority of the church, and what is secular and potentially within the jurisdiction of the state. Hence the perceptual dichotomy of *adat* and *agama*, while not necessarily distinct in the minds or lives of the people, is very real and critical to the functioning of the state.

For a people like the Luangan, this situation posed minimal problems prior to the late nineteenth century since they were only nominally integrated within any higher order political structure beyond that of the tribe.[2] At the tribal level of sociocultural integration there was cultural unity. Speaking a common language and holding a common set of beliefs, the Luangan did not perceive a separation of *adat* and *agama* for they had no need for such a division. With intrusion of the state in the form of the Dutch East Indies government of the late nineteenth and early twentieth century came the issue of separation of the religious from the secular. This issue was to form the basis for politicization of the Dayaks of southern Borneo as they increasingly faced forced integration with the state structure.

How has religion as a sociological concept been defined and used? The best-known work on the subject has been that of Durkheim ([1915] 1965). The product of an integrated state society, Durkheim accepted as a universal phenomenon the separation of the sacred and the profane into mutually exclusive realms. For him religion, be it primitive or modern, only pertained to the sacred realm. As has been discussed, the perceptual dichotomy of a sacred and a profane in societies of a lower order of sociocultural integration (that is, bands and tribes), may not exist. The development of such a perceptual dichotomy in the case of the Luangan came about through integration into a higher order of sociocultural integration—the state. Thus, separation of sacred and profane perceptual realms is not a social universal, as Durkheim would have us believe, but is a product of political evolution.

Where does Kaharingan stand? Kaharingan as a formal label for the belief system of the Luangan, Maanyan, Ngaju, and Ot Danum is a political feature of the Indonesian state. It represents religion in the Durkheimian (1965:62) sense of a "... system of beliefs and practices relative to sacred things . . . ." But for its followers the definition of Kaharingan is not so restrictive. Forced at least superficially to accept a perceptual distinction between *adat* and *agama*, the secular and the profane, in reality the people operate as though no such dichotomy exists. For them Kaharingan is the embodiment of their cultural system.

Durkheim (1965:22) found the most basic characteristic of religion was that it was eminently social. He noted that, "Religious representations are collective representations which express collective realities; the rites are a manner of acting which take rise in the midst of the assembled groups and which are destined to excite, maintain or recreate certain mental states in these groups." Kaharingan, as a body of beliefs, functions in such a manner among the Luangan. It is a critical, integral facet of Luangan identity, even among those individuals who have come under the influence of other religions (i.e., Christianity or Islam). Kaharingan rituals, as collective representations, are the central structural feature which creates the community out of otherwise disparate households. One might say that the Luangan are the people but that Kaharingan is the community.

Kaharingan: Origins of the Term and to Whom It Applies

Initially the belief system of the peoples of southern Borneo had no formal name, for it was perceived as inseparable from the totality of their cultural system. With increasing integration with the state came adoption of the perceptual dichotomy of *adat* and *agama*, the secular and the religious. Conceptualization of *agama* as something separate from *adat* caused problems; the people had no name for something called religion. Among the plethora of names used by the people, many simply meant "the religion" *(Gama Ono)*, or "ancient religion" *(Agama Kuno, Agama Helu)*. [3] Names attached to it by Christians and Moslems often were derogatory, such as heathen, *hiden*, and infidel, *kapir* (Kertodipoero 1963:13; Usop and Mihing 1979:164). In the mid-1940s a non-derogatory, widely accepted name for this religion was formalized—Kaharingan.

Kaharingan is said to originate from the root *haring*, which means self-existent, source, or vitality. One use of *haring* is *parey haring*, which means "padi (rice) which grows spontaneously." Another use of the term, coming in ritual chant of the shamans, refers to "a drop of water with self-existent life, the river current carries the breath of life" (Usop and Mihing 1979:164). Schwaner (in Roth [1896] 1968:clxxii), in describing the creation story of the inhabitants of the Barito River Basin, refers to a *Danum Kaharingan Belom Baninting Aseng* as the heavenly "water of life" which contained the germs of all plants. Parallels between life and water also showed up in explanations of the meaning of the name Kaharingan which were provided to me by Luangan villagers: "the source (water) of life" and "water so pure you can bathe a baby."

It should not be assumed that the religion of the southern peoples of the island is radically different from the belief systems of northern Borneo peoples. Nor should one believe that the term *kaharingan* only occurs in the southern half of the island. Use of the word *kaharingan* and its cognates appears widespread, although precise definitions vary. Among the Tempasuk Dusun of British North Borneo (Sabah), *Kenharingan* or *Kinorohingan* is the male Supreme Deity who, with his wife, created the world (Evans 1922:152; 1953:17).[4] Many particular religious forms are similar across the island, such as the practice of secondary mortuary rites and curing rituals, but the corpus of religious beliefs now formally known as Kaharingan belongs only to the peoples of the southern part of Borneo. This covers the greater ethnic groups known as the Luangan (Lawangan), Maanyan, Ot Danum, and Ngaju (see Fig. 3.2).

Kaharingan and the Luangan

For the Luangan, possibly more so than for the Ngaju or Maanyan, Kaharingan is the community. The traditional settlement pattern of the Luangan has never been one of strongly nucleated villages as typically observed among "longhouse" dwelling peoples elsewhere on the island. Large single-room houses with attached kitchens, scattered across a territory are still the norm in many Luangan areas. Each structure is occupied by an extended family and is situated among the various parcels of land used by its residents. Pressured by the Dutch colonial administration and more recently by the Indonesian government, the Luangan have built formal villages along major rivers, although often they are occupied by only a minority of the residents of the region. What molds the scattered households into a community is Kaharingan, for it is primarily at times of ritual that they coalesce.

Among the adherents of Kaharingan there is no set religious leader, nor is there a fixed abode for ritual presentation. Specific ceremonies are held as needed in the home of those sponsoring the event. Ritual is performed by anyone possessing the training appropriate for the required ceremony. It is not unusual even for a community of two hundred to have a dozen or more individuals who are shamans of life or death ritual, or both. Except

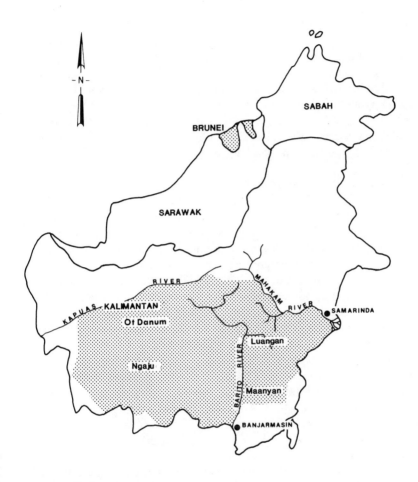

SABAH

BRUNEI

SARAWAK

KAPUAS RIVER

KALIMANTAN

Ot Danum

MAHAKAM

RIVER

SAMARINDA

Luangan

BARITO RIVER

Ngaju

Maanyan

BANJARMASIN

KM
0   100   200

O.U.C.C. 7/86 KTB

for prohibition on female death shamans, knowledge and training in ritual are available to anyone desiring them. Among the Luangan, separation of the secular and the profane in Kaharingan is minimal, for even the language of ritual is identical to that of daily speech.

Kaharingan has no formal written texts nor has it a fixed religious calendar. Basic religious principles, as embodied in ritual, are maintained through oral tradition. There is no routinized form of worship, for worship of deities, unitary or multiple, is not part of the religion. A degree of seasonality influences the timing of certain ritual activities, most obviously those of agriculture; otherwise, Kaharingan can be said to adhere to no calendric timetable. Ceremonies are held when they are needed, such as holding a curing *balian* when someone is ill, or they are held when the sponsoring parties can afford it, as is the case with secondary mortuary rites.

Kaharingan has been characterized as being both a monotheistic and a polytheistic religion. Although there is a sole Supreme Deity, creator of the universe, there are also many spirits permeating the world in which humans live. Schärer (1963), in his well-known work on Ngaju religion (i.e., the Ngaju version of Kaharingan), acknowledges this spirit multitude and discusses at great length the spirits, or deities as he refers to them, which he assigns to an Upperworld and an Underworld. Even though he cites Hardeland[5] as noting that the Supreme Deity does not play a major part in worship, and despite his own infatuation with the elaboration of multitudinous spirits, Scharer tries to deny the relative insignificance of the monotheistic aspect of Kaharingan. True to his Christian missionary zeal, he sees the central feature of Dayak culture as their conception of a Supreme God. The thesis of his work is that "...the idea of God runs through the whole culture and religion like a scarlet thread, and that it is the focus of life and thought" (1963:6). Clearly, this is not the case. For the Kaharingan practitioner, it is the multitude of spirits inhabiting the nether world of humans who are of central concern, not the ethereal world of a Supreme Deity.

At no time, ritually or otherwise, is a Supreme Deity worshiped. Rarely is reference to a Supreme Deity encountered, so rarely that there is no agreed upon name. Often multiple names are given—*Lahtala Diu'us Tuha, Ranying Mahartara Langit*, or *Lalunganing Singkor Olo*—which are descriptive in nature with such meanings as "God in the Sky." The most commonly used names are a series of cognates—*Latala, Lahatala, Mahatala, Mahatara, Hatala, Alatala* (Riwut 1958:305; Kertodipoero 1963:32; Dyson 1979:119; Usop and Mihing 1979:164). These names are probably not indigenous but rather cognates of the Islamic *Allah Ta'ala*, or from the Hindu term *maha* meaning "great." In the upper Teweh River, ancestral homeland of the Luangan, the name *Tunggal* is given as the oldest known name for the Supreme Deity, who is considered to be both male and female, as well as omnipresent.

Humans are perceived as existing in a world filled with spirits. They are in the sky and under the earth, inhabiting the mountains and special trees. They exist in the water as well as in persons, and certain spirits are believed to dwell in the meter-high jars known as *guci*. Acknowledgment of a Supreme Deity as creator of the universe occurs in oral mythology, but it is the various spirits who exist in, and interact with, the human world who must be addressed. Enumeration of how many spirits exist and of their dwelling places varies considerably. Kertodipoero (1963:29) cites mythological accounts of 8,888 spirits, but most shamans would claim considerably less.[6] What previously has never been noted is that there are two parallel, and yet overlapping, realms of spirits in Kaharingan cosmology. One realm is that of spirits of the human soul, both of the living and of the dead, while the other realm is of spirits which are nonhuman. This division is not absolute but rather a continuum; spirits of the former may overlap into the realm of the latter, especially in the case of curing rituals.

During life each individual has a single soul which among the Luangan is known as *iu'us* or *du'us*.[7] The soul of a living individual is susceptible to sickness; thus, a person must be constantly on guard. It is believed that sickness is carried in the air and can "fall" upon the soul. Particularly dangerous times to be out-of-doors are when it is *hujan panas* (raining while the sun shines) and the period around sunset and early evening when sickness is believed to be prevalent.[8]

Kertodipoero (1963:31) and Hudson (1966:30) interpret sickness as being perceived as a loss of the soul, or at least part of it, from the body. Hence, ritual restoration of the soul to the body is all that is necessary. Although it is true that the Luangan and Maanyan believe that all, or part of, the soul has left the body of the stricken individual, the soul did not just wander off leaving a void; rather, it was displaced by the miasma of sickness. With the assistance of certain curing spirits, the shaman must first draw the sickness out of the body of the afflicted. When this has been accomplished, the shaman snatches the soul out of the air and restores it to its rightful place in the body.

When an individual dies, there is a transformation of the soul. Upon death, bifurcation of the soul occurs, *ju'us* divides into *kelalongan* and *liau*. *Kelalongan* is the "refined" soul of the head/brain.[9] It goes to live in *Tenangkai* (*Senangkai*), an abstract heaven located in the sky. *Liau* is the "coarse" soul of the body/shadow.[10] It goes to live on Gunung Lumut (moss

Joseph A. Weinstock

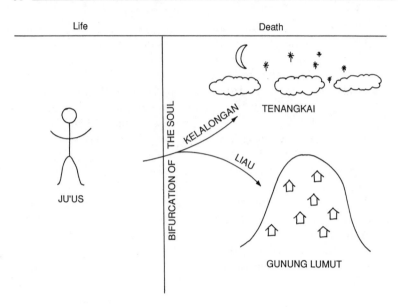

Figure 3.3. Journey of the Soul

mountain), a real mountain located near the headwaters of the Mea River, a tributary of the upper Teweh River in Central Kalimantan (Fig. 3.3). The afterworld of *liau* is not perceived as a single village, but rather as a district containing a number of villages. For example, the *liau* of a woman who dies in childbirth goes to live in the village of women who have also died in childbirth; the *liau* of an old man who drowns goes to the *liau* village of people who have drowned.

An alternate but less widespread version of the journey of the soul after death maintains unity of the soul. Upon death the soul does not bifurcate but simply changes into *liau* and goes to Gunung Lumut to live. After the proper secondary mortuary rites have been held for the deceased by the relative, the soul changes from *liau* into *kelalongan* and travels from Gunung Lumut up to *Tenangkai*, the heaven in the sky (Fig. 3.4).[11]

The living coexist not only with the spirits of the dead but also with a whole array of nonhuman spirits as well. The latter are not ancestor spirits but are spirits of nature. No two individuals would agree as to precisely how many individual spirits exist, what their names are, or even where they all live, but there is agreement as to the categories to which they all belong. Among the Luangan, all of these spirits fall into one of three categories: (1) *Naiyu*, (2) *Gaib*, and (3) *Mulung*.

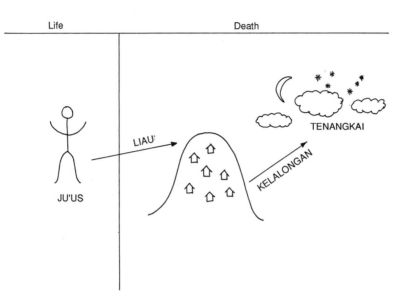

Figure 3.4. Alternate Journey of the Soul

It is believed that humans are inherently good and would not, under normal circumstances, harm another human being. Only when persons fall under the influence of certain spiritual forces do they desire to harm another person. *Naiyu*, bloodthirsty spirits, cause people to take such actions. Because they like to drink blood and eat red food, blood from the sacrificial animals and red rice are used in rituals to propitiate them. *Naiyu* are invisible but are said to make noises in the night. Although they can be dangerous, more often they are used for protection, rather like a patron spirit. By regularly feeding certain *naiyu* animal blood and red foods during ritual times, an individual can expect to call upon them in times of need, such as combat.[12]

There is a general class of spirits which inhabit certain plants and animals, as well as special items, like the meter-high ceramic jar (*guci*). These spirits are collectively known as *gaib*, or *ganan*. Basically good-natured, these spirits can cause sickness should they become annoyed. If a villager cuts down a specific tree which is believed to contain a *gaib*, he may become ill, only to recover after he has propitiated the offended spirit through an offering of food. One of the strongest among such spirits is that which dwells in the wood of the *ulin* tree (*Eusideroxylon zwageri*). Known in English as ironwood, it is used for structural beams, shingles, and sometimes floorboards of houses. It is also used for a number of ritual items, including the carved poles (*blontang*) used for carabau sacrifices, grave houses, and the ossuary of secondary burial. The spirit of ironwood is considered to be stronger than the spirit of man, for items made from the wood often last a century or more. Often one sees during curing rituals open bamboo trays (*ancak*) hung in the ironwood rafters of the house. They hold food offerings to propitiate the *ulin* spirit.

The most important category of spirits are those known as *mulung*. It is in this category that the human and nonhuman realms of spirits overlap; most *mulung* are spirits of nature, but certain human spirits can also become *mulung*. Even those *mulung* who are of nonhuman origin may be given anthropomorphized attributes. Dwelling in the sky, as well as on and below the earth, *mulung* are the good spirits who assist the shamans in curing, aid the midwives with the birth of a child, and protect the crops.

Most often called at times of sickness, the *mulung* help the shaman exorcise sickness from the body of the afflicted. Individual shamans are acquainted with different *mulung* upon whom they may call during a curing ritual. Aside from calling natural spirit *mulung*, such as the *mulung* of water, the shaman may request assistance from the refined soul spirits, *kelalongan*, of well-known shamans of the past. In particular, he will call upon the now deceased shamans who were once his teachers, and famous legendary figures like Ayus, Silu, and Kilip. In such cases, human spirits— the refined soul spirits of past shamans—cross over into the realm of the nonhuman, or natural, spirits and become *mulung*.

Among the large number of possible *mulung*, there are at least three who are common among all Luangan. These are the spirits of rice (*Luing*), the earth (*Tonoi*), and water (*Jewata*). *Luing* is both the creator and the patron spirit of rice. Since *Luing* is identified as female, offerings to her play upon her female vanity. "Luing, being female, likes pretty things," was the villagers' explanation for the planting of *gerronggong* flowers (*Celosia cristata*) along the borders of all swidden rice fields. The second commonly known *mulung* is *Tonoi* (*Tondoi*), the spirit of the earth. According to the Kaharingan creation story, God formed the first man out of the clay of the earth; for this reason, *Tonoi* is considered to be the patron spirit of newborn babies. At the baby ceremony, *Ngulas Bidan* (*Palas Bidan*), held a few months after birth, thanks are offered to the midwives (*bidan*) who attended to the birth and to *Tonoi* for the creation of the baby. The third common *mulung* spirit is that of water, known as *Jewata*, or a cognate thereof.[13] Since the Luangan are a river-based society, the spirit of water is quite important. *Jewata* is considered to be especially important for children so that they will neither fear the river nor drown. As a sort of patron spirit of children, *Jewata* is often one of the *mulung* called upon by the shaman to assist in drawing sickness out of the body of a child.

I disagree with Schärer's thesis that a monotheistic conception of God is central among adherents to Kaharingan, but I am in agreement with his belief that "Dayak (i.e., Nagiu or Luangan) culture is a unity, that is in the sense that life and thought coincide and are defined by a common focal point through which they must be interpreted and to which they constantly refer" (Schärer 1963:3). That this common focal point is the conception of a sole Supreme Deity, or even a polytheistic conception of spirits, is erroneous. It is Kaharingan cosmology as a whole which provides cultural unity. The intertwining of elements of what might be called religion with the greater cultural system is so extensive as to become inextricably merged.

Life and Death: Ritual and Shaman

As has been seen in the previous section, the Kaharingan perception of the universe is dualistic in nature. On one side there is life and on the other there is death. All ritual activities follow in accordance with this dichotomy; there are those dealing with life processes and the living, and distinctly separate are those dealing with death and the dead. Likewise, there are two distinct sets of shamans and shamanistic ritual.[14] The body of ritual and the shamans dealing with life processes are known as *balian*.[15] The body of ritual and the shamans dealing with death are known as *wara*.[16] Through apprenticeship, individuals take training quite separately in either life or death ritual. Some may become expert in both sets of ritual, hence becoming both a *balian* and a *wara* shaman. Others may study just one set of ritual, or become proficient in only a single ceremony, such as the simplest curing ceremony.

Reinforcing the life-death dualistic perception of the universe are several sets of binary oppositions. These are even/odd, white/black, and down/up. With the exception of very short rituals held for three days (nights) or less, all major life rituals must be held for an even number of days. Death ritual, without exception, must always be held for an odd number of days. White cloth represents the refined soul, which helps the *balian* shaman in curing ritual; black cloth represents the coarse soul, the soul of prime concern to *wara* shamans and of mortuary rites. Down on earth and downriver are where living man makes his home; up in the sky and upriver on the mountain are where the bifurcated souls of the deceased make their abodes. Elaboration of these sets of binary oppositions can be seen in the ensuing descriptions of various life and death rituals.

There are three types of life ritual: (1) curing *balian*, (2) thanksgiving *balian*, and (3) family ritual. In the first two, trained *balian* shamans must officiate, but the last may be conducted by nonspecialists. Among the Luangan, either males or females may become *balian* shamans, although male shamans tend to predominate. The same does not appear true for all Kaharingans. Among some groups, most notably the Maanyan, female shamans predominate.

Sketched below are the primary forms of life ritual. Often specific names for ceremonies vary regionally, as well as the precise format in which ceremonies are performed, but basic ritual content tends to remain constant. Principal sources of the material herein provided are the Taboyan of the upper Teweh River, the people most often cited by other Luangan as originators of much Kaharingan ritual.

The simplest form of curing illness is a *Balian Luangan*. Other common names for this ceremony are *Balian Toraia* and *Balian Dusun*. This *balian* is characterized by a single shaman wearing ordinary dress but marked with stripes of lime on cheeks, arms, and chest, and wearing a wrapped head cloth (*laung*). Typically, someone of the house in which the ceremony is taking place will assist the shaman in preparing the various "ingredients" necessary for the ceremony.

Like all curing *balian*, *Balian Luangan* are held only at night, generally beginning about an hour after the sun has set. It is left to the shaman to determine how long the ceremony will last, but typically *Balian Luangan* will end by midnight, at which time the guests are fed. Depending upon the seriousness of the patient's illness, and upon the family's willingness to defray the expense of the ceremony, a *Balian Luangan* may be held one or more consecutive evenings. For each night that the ceremony is held, at least one chicken must be slaughtered and all attendant guests fed.

Balian Bawo is a more powerful curing ceremony. In cases of serious illness, especially when the afflicted has vomited blood, a *Balian Bawo* will be chosen by the family. It also will be used for an individual for whom a *Balian Luangan* has been unsuccessful. As a higher level ritual, a *Balian Bawo* requires the sacrifice of at least one pig and a minimum of two shamans to perform the ceremony. A *Balian Bawo* is performed for two or more consecutive nights.

As with a *Balian Luangan*, a *Balian Bawo* requires various "ingredients." These are similar to those used for a *Balian Luangan* but are more numerous. Dress of the *Balian Bawo* shamans consists of a special decorated sarong of individual design, a belt with long sashes hanging down each side, a *luang* headcloth, and lime stripes similiar to those of a *Balian Luangan* shaman. Most important of all is a set of *ketang*, heavy (approximately a half-kilo apiece) metal bracelets made of a mixture of silver and old broken gong metal smelted together. They are formed with an open hollow center so that when they are worn, two on each wrist, they can be jangled together to produce a pleasant ringing.

One of the two or more shamans is the head *balian* and always leads the chants. An additional person, often but not always female, assists the shamans. This person is known as a *pa'mapat*. It is the role of the *pa'mapat* to prepare the bowls of burning incense wood, beeswax candles, and other "ingredients" during the course of the ceremony. More important, it is the *pa'mapat's* responsibility to determine the illness of the patient. Once she or he has been told by the spirits the type and cause of illness, the *pa'-mapat* informs the shamans by chanting to them. Like the *Balian Luangan* shaman, the *Balian Bawo* shamans call the curing spirits, *mulung*, to assist them in treating the patient. They do so with the use of the broad *biyowo (sawang)* leaf (*Cordyline terminalis*) and the notched *ringgit* palm leaf (*Cocos nucifera*), the first being the symbol of the paddle the spirits will need to get to the ceremony should they have to travel by canoe and the latter being the symbol of the jungle knife necessary should they find they must traverse the jungle. Waving the *biyowo* and *ringgit*, the shamans beseech the curing spirits to descend the *penyemba*, a piece of cloth and long palm fronds hung from the rafters of the house, and to accept the offerings laid out below. During the course of the *Balian Bawo* the shamans dance around the offerings, jangling their *ketang* bracelets. The last item, dancing for the spirits, is one of the most important differences between a *Balian Luangan* and a *Balian Bawo*.

Balian Luangan and *Balian Bawo* are the oldest *balian* for curing. According to mythology, they were created and first practiced by the ancestors in *Neten Pali*. The ritual language used for *balian* is the same as the dialect of the upper Teweh River, or the original Luangan dialect.[17] These forms of *balian* are the only curing rituals used by the Central Kalimantan Luangan, but an additional form has arisen among the East Kalimantan Luangan.

Balian Sentiew is relatively new, with its origins dating only to around the beginning of the twentieth century. The Pahu branch of the Luangan are generally given credit for its creation. It and its variant, *Balian Kenyong*, do not use the Teweh River dialect of *Bahasa Luangan*, but an admixture of the Pahu dialect of *Bahasa Luangan* and the Kutai dialect of Malay. This in itself is quite interesting since *Balian Sentiew* appears to have developed simultaneously with the Pahu people's conversion to Islam. Pigs, taboo in Islam, are not sacrificed during this ceremony; goats are the important sacrificial animal. Although the Moslem Pahu today deny their Luangan Kaharingan origins, there are reports of some Pahu people who still perform this ceremony. Their neighbors, the Benuaq and Tunjung subgroups of the Luangan, regularly use *Balian Sentiew* ritual. It is easily distinguishable from other *balian* in that the shamans performing the ceremony wear *junung*, ankle bracelets which have small silver bells. The *Balian Sentiew* shamans, of which there must be two or more, dance to call the curing spirits, producing a tinkling sound from the *junung* as they do so. Unlike *Balian Luangan* and *Balian Bawo*, in which the spirits are called to cure "natural" sickness which has fallen on the afflicted from the air, *Balian Sentiew* calls the curing spirits to deal with illness caused by the forces of black magic.

Many names are given for specific *balian* curing ceremonies, but all fall into one of three forms described here. Differentiation of ritual forms is based upon several criteria, but for the Luangan layman, dress of the shaman and dancing are used to determine which form of *balian* is being performed.

1. *Balian Luangan:* A simple ceremony performed by a lone shaman who neither dances nor wears wrist or ankle bracelets.
2. *Balian Bawo:* The ceremony is performed by two or more shamans wearing special dress, including *ketang* wrist bracelets, who dance for the spirits.
3. *Balian Sentiew:* The ceremony is performed by two or more shamans wearing special dress, including *junung* ankle bracelets, who dance for the spirits.

Hence it is easy to determine that the simple ceremony called a *Balian Toraja* in the upper Teweh River is actually a variant of the *Balian Luangan* ritual form. Likewise, what is called a *Balian Kenyong* by the Benuaq and Tunjung is identifiable as a variant of the *Balian Sentiew* ritual by the *junung* worn on the ankles of the shamans.

Aside from curing, *balian* are held to give thanks to the spirits for the recovery from illness of family members, and/or for a bountiful harvest. Thanksgiving *balian* often are interlinked with other rituals, either curing or death, which have been held previously. Family ritual also may be held in conjunction with thanksgiving *balian*. Among some communities the celebration of certain such events is calendric while in others it is not. Traditionally, thanksgiving *balian*, like curing *balian*, are individualized proceedings, with ceremonies sponsored by extended families. Owing to the potentially enormous expense of specific thanksgiving *balian*, particularly *Balian Buntang* (*Gugu Tahun*), members of some villages today may jointly sponsor a single, village-wide event.

Ritual forms used for thanksgiving *balian* parallel those used for curing—i.e., the *luangan* and *bawo* ritual forms. One slight variation is *Balian Buntang*, the special ceremony traditionally held only after an exceptionally abundant harvest. Although of the *luangan* ritual form, its length and elaborateness make it ritually distinct. To be able to perform a *Balian Buntang*, a shaman must undergo special apprenticeship.

Kerwaiyu is a thanksgiving *balian* held in conjunction with the beginning of harvest. Normally a single-night family ritual is held by each household to eat the first meal of new rice, but when this activity is combined with thanksgiving to the curing spirits for the recovery of sick family members during the past year, the ceremony becomes a two-night *balian*.

When an exceptionally bounteous harvest has filled the rice bins to the brim and all family members have survived the year in good health, the decision may be made to hold a *Balian Buntung* (*Gugu Tahun*). This is no small undertaking; a *Buntang* must be at least four days and nights of continuous ceremony. Should the family desire to sponsor a ritually complete *Buntang*, or one which is "sampai kerbau" (until a carabao), the ceremony must last for eight days and nights since it is ritually prescribed that anything less is insufficient for a carabao sacrifice. Often two or more families will pool their resources to sponsor a *Buntang*. Traditionally, this ceremony is not regularly held, although some communities strive to make it an annual post-harvest event.

As in the *luangan* ritual form, dancing is not performed for the spirits, nor are any type of bracelets or anklets used, but the *buntang* ritual form is more elaborate. Four or six shamans with two or four assistants jointly perform the ceremony under the leadership of the senior shaman. During the four, six, or eight days of the *Buntang*, the shamans must properly recite the chants and execute all ritual without any sleep. Rest breaks are taken to smoke and eat, and they may go to the river to bathe and refresh themselves, but the shamans must stay awake until the final night's feast— the eating of the sacrificial carabao in the case of an eight-day *Buntang*, or the pigs in lesser *Buntang*.

Balian Longan Bulau is another thanksgiving *balian*. It is made to uphold a promise made to the curing spirits during an earlier *Balian Bawo* curing ritual. Being also of the *bawo* ritual form, a *Longan Bulau* requires two or more shamans, each of whom are outfitted with a set of *ketang* bracelets and special *bawo* dress. There is also a *pa'mapat*, who assists the shamans during the ceremony. As with a *Kerwaiyu* or a *Buntang*, the curing spirits are called to partake of the festivities given in their honor. At least one pig must be slaughtered on the final night of the two- or four-night affair. In many ways a *Longan Bulau* is like a scaled-down *Buntang* ceremony with the addition of elements of the *bawo* ritual form, particularly that of the shamans dancing for the curing spirits.

The final type of thanksgiving *balian* is a *Sapu Ipar* ceremony. This is a special one-day affair held immediately following a secondary mortuary rite. *Sapu* means to sweep, and the purpose of a *Balian Sapu Ipar* is to cleanse the house of any vestiges of death lingering after the secondary mortuary rite has concluded. The ceremony is conducted by a lone shaman with a single assistant, using the *Luangan* ritual form.

Certain simple life-process events are primarily family affairs and do not necessitate the services of a ritual specialist, hence they are generally not formal *balian* ceremonies. These family rituals, as I have chosen to call them, include agricultural rituals, baby rituals, and marriage. Typically attended only by members of the extended family and possibly by a few neighbors, these events will sometimes be expanded to become formal *balian* ceremonies, or they will become incorporated into an already scheduled *balian*. Expanding family harvest ritual into a short, two-day, thanksgiving *balian* is an example of the former, while incorporation of a wedding into a large thanksgiving *balian* is an example of the latter.

Agricultural production is a function of the household, as are rituals of the agricultural cycle. Silently praying to the padi spirit, *Luing*, to make the padi fertile and bountiful, a member of the household or extended family ceremonially plants the first rice seeds in the new swidden garden. When the fields have turned golden yellow and the grain has nearly reached maturity, it is time for each family to hold a *Pesiwa*, the ceremonial eating of the new year's rice. Often a small affair attended only by household members, it may be expanded into a small thanksgiving *balian* which, as mentioned earlier, is called a *Kerwaiyu*. If it is a simple, single-night ceremony, it is properly called a *Pesiwa Sesutik*, whereas a two-night *balian* is formally known as a *Pesiwa Kerwaiyu*. In either case, some form of *Pesiwa* must be held by each individual household before full harvest is initiated.

One to several months after a baby's birth, the family holds a small ceremony to thank the midwives (*bidan*) who attended to the birth, and also to honor *Tonoi*, the earth spirit, for the creation of the baby. Known as, *Ngulas Bidan* (*Palas Bidan*), it is attended primarily by family, with a senior member officiating. Payment to the midwives is made at this time and tiny bits of food are flicked into the air by senior household members as symbolic payment to the earth spirit.

The marriage ceremony, in and of itself, is not a *balian,* but it is frequently combined either with an already scheduled thanksgiving *balian,* or a special thanksgiving *balian* will be added to signify the joyousness of the event. There appear to be dozens of potential variations in actual weddings depending upon whether or not the bride is already pregnant, if the marriage is approved by the parents or not, whether it is a first marriage, et cetera, but there is a basic ritual form common to all. The *penghulu,* a popularly elected village leader of tradition (*adat*),[18] officiates at all weddings, whether or not they are combined with a *balian.* Seated on gongs, the bride and groom rest their feet on a piece of dried-up bamboo formerly used for cooking (the symbol of death) and a young banana trunk (the symbol of life); they are ritually "sewn together" by the *penghulu* who runs a threaded needle through the backs of their clothes.

The other side of Kaharingan ritual dichotomy deals with death and the dead. Death is considered absolute for the physical body; the human soul is believed to be eternal. Actual disposal of the physical remains of the deceased is relatively insignificant. Far more important is the journey of the now bifurcated soul, and the liminal phases through which it must pass before becoming permanently settled in the afterworld. Liminality here denotes the transitional nature of the successive phases of death. The separation of the deceased from the world of the living is not immediate but takes place in three phases. Until the bifurcated soul has gone through all three transitional phases of death, it does not relinquish its earthly attachments. Prior to the soul's passage through the final liminal phase of death, the deceased's estate can be neither sold nor divided and a surviving spouse cannot remarry.

Kelalongan, the refined soul, is not of overly serious concern to the living. A bit of food will be offered to the *kelalongan* of deceased ancestors during times of ritual, but their needs are slight. Living in the abstract heaven of *Tenangkai,* they have little need for material items. They do not bother the living, and it is therefore unnecessary to propitiate them— although the living will honor the *kelalongan* of their ancestors through symbolic gestures of offering a few grains of new rice at harvest time and small bits of food at ritual occasions. This is done to ensure the assistance of the *kelalongan* spirits of past shamans in curing rituals.

Liau, the coarse soul, is of more immediate importance. The afterworld of *liau* spirits on Gunung Lumut is a replica of the living world; thus, for the *liau* to live comfortably, their living descendants need to supply them with all the appropriate creature comforts. The body of the deceased is placed in a canoe-shaped coffin, representing the means of transportation to the afterworld, and is buried with many of his material possessions, such as pots and pans, for he will need these in his new home. Erected over the grave is a four-post structure with a roof, symbolizing the house in which *liau* will live on Gunung Lumut. Old clothing, a pillow, and even a mattress, if the deceased owned one, are placed under the grave house. Around this are planted specific plants, such as *komatsirang* (*Codiaeum variegatum,* croton) and *biyowo* (*Cordyline terminalis,* ti), the latter being the symbolic paddle and "tree of life."[19] Now *liau* has a complete home in which to live in the afterworld village, but it will need something to eat. This will be provided during the several death rituals marking the liminal stages through which the bifurcated soul passes in the journey of death.

All death ceremonies must be executed by an appropriately trained ritual specialist. Novices learn death ritual through active apprenticeship with established specialists, with several years passing before they become initiated as death shamans. Among the Luangan, it is forbidden for women to become death shamans. This may not always have been the case, for Luangan mythology recounts tales of famous female death shamans. The performance of ritual for five, seven, or more consecutive days and nights without sleep in the secondary mortuary rites has proved fatal for several Luangan female shamans—hence the institution of the prohibition. Interestingly, while death ritual is exclusively a male domain among the Luangan Kaharingan, among the Maanyan Kaharingan it is exclusively a female domain (Hudson 1966:359). Apparently the Maanyan do not perceive women as any more susceptible to succumbing to the demands of death ritual than are men.

Slow resonance of a gong being struck signals to all in the village that death has occurred. Word of who has died and where the corpse lies quickly passes around the community. Relatives and friends gather at the house to prepare for the burial. *Ulunmate* (*Kelangkang*) begins the same day, so that the soul spirits of the deceased can begin their journey to the afterworld without delay. In the past, the body of the deceased was often kept in, or under, the house in a sealed wooden coffin until after putrification of the flesh. Then the coffin would be opened, the bones lustrated and given secondary burial as part of the secondary mortuary rite. This practice was banned by the Dutch, and later by the Indonesian government, for health reasons. According to law, burial is now supposed to be carried out within twenty-four hours of death. With the body becoming odoriferous quite rapidly in the tropical heat, the family has little desire to contravene the law and keep the body in the house any longer than necessary, although they may wait an extra day or two for relatives living far away to arrive.

The seventh night after death, the family holds a small ceremony known as *Nuru Hari (Param Api, Maram Apui)*, the second liminal phase of death. Relatives and friends again gather in the house of the deceased. The two death shamans, chanting alternately, call the coarse and refined souls, *liau* and *kelalongan*, of the deceased to come down from the afterworld where they have been residing since *Ulunmate*. As at the *Ulunmate* ceremony, food is set out for the soul spirits, *liau*'s under a black cloth and *kelalongan*'s under a white cloth. They are invited to eat, smoke, and chew betel since all items consumed by the spirits of the dead and the living alike are believed to follow the souls to the afterworld. Only chickens were offered during the *Ulunmate* ceremony, but at least one pig is slaughtered for the *Nuru Hari* ceremony. The end of the second liminal phase of death finds *liau* comfortably outfitted with a canoe (the coffin), a house (the grave house), clothing, bedding, pots and pans, a moderate amount of rice, chickens, and at least one pig. Other than building up a rice supply, all that is needed to complete the good life in the village of the dead on Gunung Lumut is a carabao.

The final liminal phase of death is the secondary mortuary rite, known among the Central Kalimantan Luangan as *Gombok*.[20] Passage of the bifurcated soul through the first two liminal phases of death is ritually predetermined—*Ulunmate* occurring the night after death and *Nuru Hari* on the seventh night after death. Such is not the case with a *Gombok*, which may be held any time after completion of *Nuru Hari*. Provided that the family has the resources at hand, a *Gombok* can be celebrated immediately, or twenty years might pass before it is held. But it must be held at some time for every adult, male or female, who has died. In the case of children there is some flexibility; if the child had not walked on its own (i.e., probably less than one or one and a half years of age), no *Gombok* is held. For children above this age, but still prepubescent, secondary mortuary rites are optional.

Ostensibly the third liminal phase of death is like the first two, except that the celebration of its passage is much grander. As with the earlier *wara* ceremonies, the coarse and refined souls are recalled from the afterworld and symbolically offered food so that they will not go hungry. Early in the course of the *Gombok*, chickens will be slaughtered. By the ceremony's midpoint, several pigs will have been killed and eaten, with the final evening bringing the running of the carabao, also eventually consumed by the guests. Wearing woven rattan headrings, *beyoyang*, with cloth or bark-cloth tails, the shamans travel around the room *ngerangkau* dancing. *Ngerangkau* dancing is done to honor *liau* and *kelalongan* and to offer them the food which has been prepared. Now the soul spirits must return to their homes in the afterworld for the last time. For *kelalongan* this journey is easy; he need only fly to *Tenangkai* in the sky. *Liau's* journey is more arduous. It requires travel over the real world to reach Gunung Lumut, and assistance will be needed in carrying food home from the festivities.

Through recitation in chanting form, the death shamans travel with *liau* upriver to Gunung Lumut, stopping en route to bathe, pick fruit, fish, and fix meals. In some areas a *limar* (*seleolo*), or ritual canoe, is used to travel to Gunung Lumut with *liau*. This is a life-sized, canoe-like structure with an ornately carved prow and stern, hung from the rafters of the house. Tied to the ritual canoe and also suspended from the rafters is a *ringka jawa*, a large bundle containing tubes of sticky rice, plates of carabao meat, and other food items which *liau* is taking back to his home on Gunung Lumut. The shamans sit in the ritual canoe, rocking forward and back as they recite the journey to Gunung Lumut. Upon reaching Gunung Lumut, *liau* at last passes through the final liminal phase of death and is permanently settled in the afterworld.

Why would anyone feel compelled to sponsor a secondary mortuary ceremony, particularly in light of the enormous expenditure required? The most obvious reason is that the soul spirits are left in limbo if it is not held, but this is not the sole reason. A widow, or widower, is forbidden from remarrying until a proper secondary mortuary rite has been held for a deceased spouse.[21] Such a person is considered ritually unclean until after the appropriate rites have been completed. Tangentially, a widower who is also a *wara* shaman is forbidden from taking part in the secondary mortuary rites for his deceased wife. His services will not be called upon for a *Gombok* held for any deceased individual until he has sponsored the proper rites for his deceased spouse, because it is feared that he may, in his grief, forget the ritual chants and lose the souls on the journey to the afterworld.

Of more general concern are the principles of inheritance with respect to the deceased's estate. After death, the estate of the deceased may be used by members of the family, but division and transfer of actual ownership of the estate can occur only after the bifurcated soul of the deceased has passed through the third, and final, liminal phase of death. Sponsorship obligations for secondary mortuary rites fall heaviest upon those individuals who stand to gain the most from their completion.[22] At the end of the final rites, the village elders gather to discuss and distribute the component parts of the deceased's estate, taking into consideration not only kinship but also assistance in performing the *Gombok*. Individuals unrelated to the deceased but who contributed either financially or with labor for the event will be given remuneration, even if only a plain white ceramic plate with a dab of *iomit* (*Curcuma domestica*, turmeric) paste as a sign of thanks. A relative not helping with the *Gombok* might find his parcenary right to the estate of the deceased reduced, or even denied, by the village elders.

Hierarchical Levels of Ritual

Within the dichotomy of life and death, Kaharingan ceremonies vary in terms of ritual power. Hierarchical levels exist both within and between various ceremonies. Differentiation in hierarchical levels of power is accomplished in several ways. The most obvious differential is that which exists between ceremonies. A *Balian Luangan* curing ritual has relatively low ritual strength. It may be used for a slight stomachache or other common ailment. For an individual suffering febrile delirium, vomiting blood, or afflicted with some other serious ailment, a *Balian Luangan* is insufficient. In such cases one needs stronger measures; thus, the usual choice is a ritually stronger ceremony, like a *Balian Bawo*. If one suspects foul play, then the choice of ceremony would be a *Balian Sentiew*, the *balian* effective in overcoming the effects of black magic.

A second aspect of hierarchical levels of power is expressed by the length, in days and/or nights, of a particular ceremony. Holding a curing *balian* for three consecutive nights makes it more powerful than if it had been held for only two. A *Balian Buntang* which runs for eight days and nights is of greater honor to the spirits than one held for a mere four days and nights.

A third indicator of differential ritual power is expressed through the type and number of animals slaughtered and eaten at the ceremony. For the simplest ceremonies only chickens are killed and cooked. Such is the case of a typical low-level curing *balian* such as *Balian Luangan*. A more complex, and hence a ritually stronger, ceremony like a *Balian Bawo* requires not only chickens, but the addition of at least one pig. At the pinnacle of the ritual hierarchy, ceremonies demand the sacrifice of a carabao, along with pigs and chickens. [23]

The three aspects of hierarchical levels of power are not fully independent but are partly interlinked. For example, a three-day *Gombok* ceremony is only "sampai babi" (until a pig), but a five- or seven-day *Gombok* must always be "sampai kerbau" (until a carabao), with at least one carabao being sacrificed. Here exists a case where the length of the ceremony partly dictates the level of animal offering necessary. Another example of differential levels of power is the interlinking of the type of

Table 3.1.
Hierarchical Levels of Life Ritual

Level of Ceremony	Length of Ceremony	Type of Sacrifice
	Curing	
Balian Luangan	1 day minimum	Chickens
Balian Bawo	2 day minimum	Chickens and pigs
Balian Sentiew	2 day minimum	Chickens and goats
	Thanksgiving	
Balian Kerwiyu	2 days	Chickens
Balian Longan Bulau	2 days	Chickens and pigs
	4 days	Chickens and pigs
Balian Buntang	4 days	Chickens and pigs
	6 days	Chickens and pigs
	8 days	Chickens, pigs, carabao
*Balian Sapu Ipar**	1 day after a *Gombok*	Chickens

*Being a life ceremony, *Balian Sapu Ipar* should logically, in accordance with Kaharingan numerology, be an even number of days. Its attachment to a *Gombok*, or death ceremony, appears to justify its being held for an odd length of time, or a single day.

ritual with the type of animal sacrificed. For a *Balian Luangan* ceremony, one may offer a pig to the curing spirits, but only chickens are mandatory. To perform properly a *Balian Bawo*, the level of animal offering begins with at least one pig in addition to chickens. Likewise, a *Balian Bawo* has to be a minimum of two consecutive nights, while a single night will suffice for a *Balian Luangan* ceremony. Thus we have an instance of partial linkage between type of ceremony and length of presentation. (See Tables 3.1 and 3.2 for a summary of hierarchical levels of ritual.)

Numerology plays an important role in Kaharingan ritual. Even numbers represent life, odd numbers represent death. The exception to this are curing ceremonies, since they are typically held for only one, two, or three consecutive nights. Longer ceremonies, including all thanksgiving *balian* and all *wara* ceremonies, strictly adhere to this division. As a life ceremony, *Balian Buntang* may be held for four, six, or eight days but may never be held for five or seven days. Likewise, *Nuri Hari*, being a death ceremony, is always held the seventh night after death, not the sixth or the eighth night.

Table 3.2.
Hierarchical Levels of Death Ritual

Level of Ceremony	Length of Ceremony or Time After Death	Type of Sacrifice
Ulunmate	At death	Chickens
Nuru Hari	7th night after death	Chickens
Secondary Mortuary Without Secondary Burial		
Gombok	3 days	Chickens and pigs
	5 days	Chickens, pigs carabao
	7 days	Chickens, pigs, carabao
	9 days	Chickens, pigs, carabao
	2x7, 3x7, etc.	Chickens, pigs, multiple carabao
Secondary Mortuary With Secondary Burial*		
Gombok with *Nyelemat*	2x7, 3x7, etc.	Chickens, pigs, multiple carabao

*The Family has the choice of sponsoring a secondary mortuary rite either with, or without secondary burial. Should they so desire, the family may hold a *Gombok* without secondary burial and later hold a second *Gombok* with *Nyelemat* (secondary burial).

Secondary mortuary rites, *Gombok*, must be held for an odd number of days. If a five-day *Gombok* is considered insufficient by the family to honor a deceased relative, they must expand the celebration to a seven-day event. Should the family be wealthy and truly wish to honor the deceased, they might double the length of the ceremony, Such a *Gombok* would actually be fourteen days long, an even number, so it is simply referred to as being two times seven days. The supreme form of honoring one's deceased is a *Gombok* with *Nyelemat*. This is a secondary mortuary rite held at least two times seven days which ends with secondary burial *(Nyelemat)*. The lustrated bones of the deceased may be put in a *guci* jar kept in the house or buried, put in a *guci* jar on a tall *ulin* wood pole *(Talo* or *Talung)*, placed in a carved *ulin* wood ossuary on a single post *(Keriring)*, or joined with the bones of other deceased family members in a large carved *ulin* wood ossuary mounted on two posts *(Tamblah, Tamplak* or *Salung)* or in an *ulin* wood ossuary with four posts *(Sandong)*.

Kaharingan as Religion

Returning to Durkheim (1965:62), we have, "A religion is a unified system of beliefs and practices relative to sacred things, that is to say, things set apart and forbidden—beliefs and practices which unite into one single moral community called a Church, all those who adhere to them." I have taken issue with the first half of this definition with regard to Durkheim's rigid dichotomy of the sacred and profane. Durkheim's analysis of religion dwells upon the sacredness of ritual, a religious realm separate from a secular realm. Although separation of sacred and profane may occur in some societies, it is not a fundamental aspect of religion for it is not true of all societies. The Luangan are a case in point. The language of ritual is that of daily life, and ritual activities of the shamans are neither secretive nor restricted to a religious elite. Ritual activities are open and understood by most laymen, with shamanhood open to all.[24] The latter is evident by the large percentage of individuals in some Luangan communities who are trained in Kaharingan ritual to one degree or another. Thus, I am in agreement with Evans-Pritchard's (1965:65) position on Durkheim's dichotomy of the sacred and the profane when he says that ". . . far from being cut off from one another, they are so closely intermingled as to be inseparable."

The rest of Durkheim's definition is useful here. Kaharingan, as a religion, has been shown here to have a "unified system of beliefs and practices," but not just to sacred things. It provides the Luangan with a unified body of values and beliefs encompassing a total world view, but without a rigid dichotomy of sacred and profane. Rather than dividing the universe into a sacred realm under religion, with everything else in a mundane profane realm, Kaharingan encapsulates the entire perceived universe within its internal dichotomy of life and death. As such, Kaharingan does not create social differentiation between religious leaders and laymen.

The last part of Durkheim's definition of religion is particularly relevent here for it deals with the creation of a community. Religion, according to Durkheim (1965:62), provides the ". . . beliefs and practices which unite into one single moral community called a Church, all those who adhere to them." For the Luangan, Kaharingan functions as a "church," by Durkheim's definition, for it provides the pivot around which households coalesce to form and operate as a community.

Flexibility has been the feature responsible for Kaharingan remaining a vital force in southern Borneo. Large ostentatious ceremonies may still be the ideal, but little social stigma is attached to performing abbreviated ones. For much of Kaharingan ritual there is a great degree of latitude with respect to choice of ceremony and of the hierarchical level at which a specific ceremony is performed. Actual prescription in ceremonial presentation is limited. General principles of ritual are prescribed for any specific ceremony, but shamans are allowed a wide range of improvisational freedom. Attendance at, and participation in, ritual is open. Christian Luangan often are present at Kaharingan ritual presentations and local Moslems are welcome, although they seldom attend.[25] Visitors from other regions, Luangan and non-Luangan alike, are always welcome to attend and, if qualified, may participate in ceremonies. On several occasions I have encountered visiting shamans performing curing *balian*, and even secondary mortuary rites, jointly with local shamans.

The Luangan are a highly individualistic, one might even say anarchistic, people. Households work their fields and carry on daily activities independently of their neighbors. Kaharingan reflects this cultural characteristic, while at the same time providing the social focus which creates the community out of otherwise disparate households. Multiple household sponsorship of large ceremonies does occur, but most often the responsibility for specific ceremonies lies with a single household.[26] For the elaborate secondary mortuary rites, extended family and even neighborhood cooperation will be clearly evident, and yet a single individual, typically the head of the household, will be denoted as "the sponsor." Despite the individualistic nature of Kaharingan ritual, it also serves as the primary source of social cohesion for the community. Regularly across the evening breeze one hears drums telling of a curing ceremony in one village dwelling or another. Inside, friends gather to watch the shamans perform and to share the day's gossip while fixing a fishing net or harvest basket. The gong's slow knell announces death, time for people to gather and mark ritually the passage of a neighbor's soul into the afterworld. Planting and harvest bring family and friends together in ritual celebration of the agricultural rites of passage. Birth, marriage, and thanksgiving draw the community together under the sphere of Kaharingan to celebrate life's joyous events. Rather than the concept of a Supreme Deity as the scarlet thread running through the culture and religion as perceived by Schärer (1963), it is Kaharingan which weaves the societal thread that binds the community from life through death.

4. The Religion of Balance: Evidence From an Eleventh-Century Javanese Poem

Patricia B. Henry

*I*SSUES OF RELIGIOUS TRANSFORMATIONS—between India and Indonesia, between Java and Outer Island Indonesian cultures, between meditation and trance, and between different periods of Javanese historical experience—are the subject of this essay. Since my main text is an Old Javanese *kakawin* from the eleventh century, a brief review of Javanese literary traditions will be useful as a preface to the actual textual analysis. The latter will deal with the *kakawin* as a richly ambiguous form which points both in the direction of trance (linking it to pan-Indonesian patterns) and in the direction of meditation, joining this genre to several world religions.

The history of Old Javanese literature begins in the early ninth century with the charter of Sukabumi in West Java. Earlier inscriptions have been found, but they are written in Sanskrit, not Old Javanese (Zoetmulder 1974:3). The Old Javanese literary tradition of *kakawin*, which I will be examining in some detail here, flourished from the tenth to the fourteenth centuries, and it allows a view of Javanese life, ideas, philosophy, aesthetics, and religion in a historical depth unique in the Indonesian world.

As concrete evidence of the civilizations and cultures of the past, these writings have played an important role in the evolution of Indonesian national identity—especially, of course, as interpreted by Javanese. The national motto, *"Bhinneka Tunggal Ika,"* is taken from a fourteenth-century Old Javanese *kakawin*, the *Sutasoma*; as such, it is emblematic of the historical reality of the ancient kingdom of Majapahit. It is often translated as "Unity in Diversity"; a more literal translation would be "the multiplicity (of) that *(bhinneka = bhinna ika)* is the oneness (of) that *(tunggal ika)*." It expresses an idea with many levels of relevance: today it declares the national unity of Indonesia's many ethnic groups; for the civilization that produced it, it expressed the Buddhist and Hindu truth that an essential oneness underlies the illusory variation perceived by the senses. The older meaning is given new political significance in its present context, but at the same time its antiquity gives it the pre-colonial legitimacy that is part of its power as a national motto.

The process by which these words have spanned the centuries is a complex one which I shall only touch on here. It is ironic, given the role of Old Javanese materials in the nationalist movement, that it was primarily Dutch and Dutch-trained scholars who made many of the manuscripts accessible in print (Supomo 1979:180). Furthermore, while these writings are seen as very much a part of ancient Javanese civilization, the palm-leaf manuscripts *(lontar)* on which the Old Javanese *kakawin* are written owe their existence to the efforts of the Balinese scholars and scribes who continued to copy and recopy them after the Javanese courts converted to Islam at the end of the fourteenth century. Finally, although the imagery of this ancient civilization has contributed heavily to the Java-centrism with which modern Indonesia must contend (see, for example, Lowenhaupt Tsing, this volume; Reid 1979; Supomo 1979), the writings which allow us to perceive it are testimony to the tremendous influence on Java by Indian and Sanskritic culture.

In the case of *kakawin*, for example, we are dealing with a script that was adapted from Indian writing systems, and with a genre of poetry directly traceable to that of Sanskrit *kāvya*. *Kakawin* are written to comply with rules of Sanskrit prosody, which is no simple task given that Old Javanese and Sanskrit do not even belong to the same language family. The problem is somewhat mitigated by the high proportion of Sanskrit words used in the *kakawin* (estimated by Gonda at 25 and 30 percent; see Zoetmulder 1974:8), in itself a noteworthy matter. As Zoetmulder (1974:7) observes:

> There are two points about Old Javanese which strike the casual observer at first glance: on the one hand the all-pervading presence of words of Sanskrit origin, and on the other, the fact that, despite this tremendous influence of a foreign language belonging to an entirely different linguistic family, Old Javanese has remained in its entire structure and all its essentials an Indonesian language.

Patricia B. Henry

Moreover, the subject matter with which the *kakawin* concern themselves, like that of the *kāvya*, is primarily taken from the Sanskrit epics; it tells of heroes and gods—such as Arjuna, Indra, Shiva—which would be recognized by any Indian audience. Many of the stylistic devices, metaphors, and tropes would be equally familiar. Nonetheless, the Javanese poets are creating Javanese poems which comply with the rules of Sanskrit *kāvya*, not translations or imitations of Sanskrit works in Old Javanese.

This essay will examine in some detail a particular Old Javanese *kakawin*, the *Arjuna Wiwāha* (Arjuna's Wedding). The text expands upon a story taken from the Indian epic, the *Mahābhārata*, and tells of successful meditation for supernatural weapons by Arjuna, one of the famous Pāṇḍava brothers. It was composed in the early eleventh century, by the poet Mpu Kaṇwa, in the East Javanese court of King Erlangga. As one of the earliest works from Java which have survived to the present, it is frequently celebrated for the beauty of its language and its literary merit (see Zoetmulder 1974:234—49; Poerbatjaraka 1926; Berg 1938). As a *kakawin*, it also articulates much about the religious philosophy of its time, which will be my main focus here. I am especially interested in exploring the relationship between the Indic tradition of *tapa* or meditation (from Sanskrit *tapas*), with that of the trance rituals found throughout Indonesia. My argument is that both of these systems contributed directly and indirectly to the belief system articulated in *kakawin* generally and in the *Arjuna Wiwāha* in particular.

Before comparing the two traditions, it is necessary to outline in a general sense what, in the context of this essay, I mean by each. In the case of *tapa*, the aim of the adept is to achieve detachment from the world of the senses through meditation or *samadhi*. A description of the setting and the result of this meditation is found in Canto III of the *Arjuna Wiwāha* (AW 03.06 and 03.07) (text: Poerbatjaraka 1926; translation based on Henry 1981). The hero, Arjuna, is meditating in an isolated cave on Mount Indrakīla, when he is approached by the celestial women who intend to test his powers of concentration. The goal of his meditation is to meet the "god within," to become one with the Absolute or undifferentiated reality (as opposed to the differentiated reality of the phenomenal world):

03.06a lwir tanpa wwang ikang gihāluru pamūrṣitanira
        hana kuṇḍa nisprabhā
03.06b tīstīs tan hana wuryyaning sapu magātra wahu
        mĕtu dukutnikang natar
03.06c sakwehning wiwudhānggana sĕḍĕng awor unĕng
        iriya lawan raras hati
03.06d kāshcaryyān pangungang katon kadi lingir
        kanaka shashāngka pūrṇṇama

03.07a āpan sāmpunikāng anāshraya-samādhi
        tinĕmunira sang hane dalĕm
03.07b lekan rakwa sirān pasāmpunan angarccana
        kumĕñar ikāng prabhāngadĕg
03.07c rūpanyān pashilā tĕhĕr kumisapu ng
        tangan apatitis agra nāsika
03.07d līna ng sukṣma sharīra māri karĕngö
        praṇawa huwus apiṇḍa niskala

03.06a The cave was as if uninhabited, wilted were
        [Arjuna's] flower offerings, there was a fire-
        pot without fire.
03.06b The grounds were silent, there were no traces
        in the dirt of the patterns made by stickbrooms,
        grass was already starting to grow.
03.06c All of the celestial women were disturbed at
        that point; they were drawn to the cave,
        feeling the bitter pain of love.
03.06d As they looked inside they were amazed; what
        they saw was like a shining golden statue, like
        the brilliant full moon.

03.07a Having completed that isolated meditation,
        he [Arjuna] had met the Inner One.
03.07b For months, they say, he had perfected his
        worship, blazing like an upright flame.
03.07c His appearance was as follows: seated cross-
        legged, his hands in his lap, his eyes fixed
        on the end of his nose.
03.07d Vanished was the soul; the sound of the sacred
        syllable "om" had reverberated into silence,
        he was at one with Nothingness.

Once this state has been achieved, it conveys power or *sakti* (Skt. *shakti*) to
the adept. As in the passage above, the adept is frequently described as
shining or blazing with light. This metaphor of fire can be extended to the
actual generation of warmth (*tapas* literally means "heat" in Sanskrit), and
this leads to another source of power. We find frequent descriptions, in
both Indian and Javanese works, of someone meditating with such profi-
ciency as to generate an uncomfortable amount of heat; this heat then
disturbs the gods, or other beings in the vicinity, who complain to the gods,
so that they try to disturb and disrupt the meditation of the adept. Failing
to do so, the gods will bribe and/or reward the meditator with supernatural
gifts, weapons, boons, et cetera, in order to get relief from the destructive
force of *tapa*.

The ultimate goal of meditation for the individual is the achievement of release *(mokṣa* or *nirvana)* from the cycle of rebirth, but this removes one completely from the phenomenal world. Between the extremes of total involvement in the world and total release from it is the case, taken as the ideal in the *Arjuna Wiwāha,* of the hero who is meditating in order to obtain power, to be used for the good of others, in this world. The ultimate release is thus postponed; this is especially appropriate for a member of the *kṣatria* or princely caste, such as Arjuna, in his role as a protector of the community. In the opening passage or *manggala* of the *Arjuna Wiwāha,* the poet describes this ideal hero and pays homage to him as a protective entity to ensure the successful progress of the poem:

01.01a ambĕk sang paramārtha-pa.n.dita huwus limpad
sakeng shūnyatā

01.01b tan sangkeng wiṣaya prayojananira lwir
sanggraheng lokika

01.01c siddhāning yashawīryya donira sukāning rāt
kiningkingnira

01.01d santoṣāhĕlĕtan kĕlir sira sakeng sang hyang
jagatkāraṇa

01.02a uṣṇisangkwi lĕbūni pādukanirā sang mangkana
lwirnira

01.02b manggĕh manggalaning mikĕt kawijayan sang
pārtha ring kahyangan

01.01a The consciousness of the scholar of the
highest understanding has emerged from
the stillness of Emptiness.

01.01b His intent is not to seek things pleasing
to the senses which would make him comfortable
in this world.

01.01c The achievement of fame and heroism is his
goal; the happiness of the world is what
he longs for.

01.01d Peaceful, he is content to be separated
by the screen of his material existence
from the Creator of the world.

01.02a I bow to him, my head is at the dust
of his sandals, the one who is thus,

01.02b An assured source of power for the tying
together in verse of the story of Pārtha's
(Arjuna's) victory in heaven.

In the case of trance ritual, a different kind of power transference takes place. Here an individual or a group of individuals goes into trance in order to be possessed by or in communication with the spirits and/or the ancestors. Through this possession and communication, those in trance benefit others in the community, either at the level of the individual, in the case of curing rituals, or at the level of the entire community, when the ritual is intended to purify the village and counteract evil influences that have been causing crop failures, disease, et cetera. As in the case of meditation, it is not seen as necessarily desirable for an individual to remain permanently in a trance state; in fact, this is seen as dangerous and undesirable, and there are rituals and ritual specialists to ensure the safe re-entry of those who go into trance. (See Crystal and Yamashita, this volume, on trance ritual among the Toraja.)

What do these two traditions have in common? First of all, they both are a means of bringing other-worldly power into this world. With *tapa* the power reaches the community through individuals who acquire and use it, but their position as powerful entities brings benefit to those in their circle of influence, in the same way that those who enter trance can benefit those around them. Secondly, both involve an anomalous and ambiguous notion of self. For the adept at meditation, the most important part of the process is the dissolution of ego into the absolute; likewise, those in trance are literally "not themselves"—they have been taken over by the power that enters them. Finally, in both cases the adept who conveys other-worldly power to the community must be able to return to the community. His or her importance as a link to this power demands that there be a balance between involvement in each.

In relating all this to *kakawin* poetry, it is necessary to explore the significance of this literature in the context of the early Javanese courts where it was produced. It was clearly not intended only as secular entertainment. The beginnings and endings of the poems, where the various authors effect a transition between the world outside the poem and the world of the poem, are passages full of religious significance. Especially at the beginning, the poet invokes a divinity as a *manggala*—i.e., a protective entity—to ensure the successful progress of the poem. The entity taken as *manggala* may vary according to the subject matter of the poem, and in some cases the identity of the divinity is not clear, as in the case of the *Arjuna Wiwāha's manggala*, quoted above. As Zoetmulder (1974:175) points out, however,

> it is not so much the identity of the god invoked by [the poet] as the manner of invocation and the aspect in which the deity is viewed that matters. And these appear in most cases to be similar

despite the variety of names. The god concerned is always the god who is present in everything that can be described as *langö*, the god of beauty in its widest sense.

Zoetmulder goes on to elaborate on the concept of "religio poetae" (1974: 173 – 85), in which the poet focuses his energy on the god of his choice by taking him as the *manggala* of the poem, and then worships him and seeks union with the deity through the poem in an act of literary yoga.

There is another aspect of the deeper significance of *kakawin* which is brought out by Zoetmulder in connection with the relationship between the poet and his royal patron (1974: 165 – 73). In the case of the king especially, this patron is the incarnation of a god, and as such may be identified with the deity worshiped as the *manggala* of the poem. In addition, the narrative of the poem itself may in some cases present an allegorical account of events in the life and reign of the god-king. In numerous poems (such as the *Hariwangsha*, the *Shiwarātrikalpa*, the *Rat-nawijaya*, the *Sutasoma*, and the *Hariwijaya*), there are passages in which the poet expresses the hope that his work will contribute to the well-being of the king and the prosperity of the realm (Zoetmulder 1974: 168–69); it may also be the case that the nature of the poem-as-allegory plays an important role in bringing about these effects, in much the same way that Javanese *wayang* shadow plays portray events (such as weddings) that are analogous to and protective of the occasions at which they are performed. (See Robson 1981 for a recent discussion of *kakawin* as allegory, Becker 1979 on *wayang*.)

In the *Arjuna Wiwāha*, we have a *kakawin* which we know from other sources (most notably the Calcutta inscription; see Kern 1917) tells a story closely related to events in the life of the poet's royal patron, King Erlangga of East Java. The poem tells of Arjuna (one of the heroes from the Indian epic, the *Mahābhārata*) and of his successful effort to gain weapons from the gods through meditation. As it turns out, the gods need his help as well, in defeating a demon, Niwātakawaca, who is threatening Indra's heaven and who can only be killed by a human being who has obtained power *(shakti)* through meditation. The gods test Arjuna to make sure that he is sufficiently proficient in meditation and that he is not so detached from earthly concerns as to be unwilling to involve himself in their fight. After passing these tests (the first in the form of seven celestial women who try to seduce him, the second as a philosophical discussion with the disguised Indra concerning the role of meditation in life), Arjuna is granted weapons by the god Shiva, goes to heaven to battle the demon, and is rewarded with seven months as king of heaven, married to the seven celestial women who had earlier tried to distract him.

We know that, like Arjuna, Erlangga also spent time in exile, meditating in the mountains of East Java. He emerged from this exile to conquer his enemies and unite his kingdom. It has been argued by C.C. Berg (1938) that the similarity does not end there, and that Erlangga's marriage to a princess from Sumatra was the occasion for the writing of the *Arjuna Wiwāha*. Berg goes on to hypothesize that the poet's function in writing the poem was as a kind of "priest of literary language," and as such protected the king and ensured the prosperity of the marriage in the same way that the *dalang* (shadow puppeteer) provides a protective performance of *wayang* for marriages, circumcisions, and similar occasions in Java today.

It may be that in the *Arjuna Wiwāha* we have a poem written for a specific occasion; the title, "Arjuna's Wedding," is one supporting argument, and the epilogue of the poem, where the writer Mpu Kaṇwa mentions a forthcoming ceremony *(samara-kārya)* that may be a wedding, is another:

36.02a sāmpun kekĕtan ing katha arjuna wiwāha
        pangarana nike
36.02b sākṣāt tambay ira mpu kaṇwa tumata amĕtu-mĕtu
        kakawin
36.02c bhrānta apan tĕhĕr angharĕp samara-kārya
        mangiring ing aji
36.02d shrī airlangghya namo'stu sang panikĕlan
        tanah anganumata

36.02a Thus completed is the composing of the story;
        "Arjuna's Wedding" should be the name of it.
36.02b In fact, this is the first time that Mpu Kanwa
        has managed to bring forth a *kakawin* poem.
36.02c (He is) confused because shortly he will
        prepare for *samara-kārya* (war/love-feast?)
        in which he will participate with his knowledge
        of sacred writings.
36.02d The great Airlangghya, homage to him, who causes (the
        poet) to wear out his pencil, and who grants
        the blessing of his approval.

(translation based on Zoetmulder 1974:243)

There is dispute about the translation of this epilogue, especially concerning the word *samara-kārya*, which can be interpreted as either "war" or "wedding" (see Zoetmulder 1974:247–49). It may be safer to argue that the parallels between Erlangga's life and Arjuna's story constitute a more general analogy, and that the work was intended as a source of power for

Erlangga's reign by incorporating that reign into the tradition of meditating princes established by Arjuna. In either case, we have evidence for a correlation between events in the king's history and events in the poem, and we also have passages in this and other poems which show that *kakawin* language was perceived as having a beneficial effect on the world. Taken together, these indicate that *kakawin* poetry, as well as being a means of "literary yoga" for the composer, also had inherent power of its own.

In the *Arjuna Wiwāha* itself, we have an indication of the co-existence of *wayang* along with meditation in the eleventh century. Arjuna's *tapa*, as mentioned above, is of major importance in the narrative. When Indra comes to test this *tapa*, he mentions *wayang* specifically as a shadow play, and as a metaphor for life:

    05.09a hanānonton ringgit manangis asĕkĕl
                mūḍa hiḍĕpan
    05.09b huwus wruh towin yan walulang inukir
                molah anugcap
    05.09c haturning wang trĕṣṇeng wiṣaya malahā
                tar wwihikana
    05.09d ri tatwanyān māyā sahana-hananing
                bhāwa siluman

    05.09a "There are those who watch the shadow
                play, weeping and sad in their foolish
                understanding,
    05.09b "Knowing full well that it is really only
                carved leather which moves and speaks.
    05.09c "This is the same situation as those who
                thirst for things of the senses; even
                worse, these are unable to realize
    05.09d "The truth of the illusory nature of
                everything in this deceptively manifest
                world."

Indra is acting here as "nirvana's advocate": he wants Arjuna to disagree, so that the gods can enlist his help against the demon Niwātakawaca, but Indra presents the strongest possible case for total withdrawal from the world to see if Arjuna will be persuaded. Arjuna responds to this by saying that one must avoid both extremes, those of passionate involvement and complete detachment; he specifically links nirvana with death. One must participate in the world as in a game, obeying the rules while realizing the true nature of reality:

05.10a ujar sang paṇḍyārum kamuniwacananbwat kawiratin
05.10b sinambut de sang pārtha rahayu dahat ling
        muniwara
05.10c kunang yan dharmma kṣatriya yasha lawan wīryya
        linĕwih
05.10d yayadwat ring gĕgwan makaputusa sang hyang
        kalĕpasĕn

05.11a apan nora wwang tyāga ri dalĕm i heng yāwat
        ahurip
05.11b ikāng nirbbāṇācintya pati patitisning wang
        irikā
05.11c pangantyantyan tekang suka-wibhawa līlāmĕng-
        amĕngan
05.11d ujar sang pārthāngakṣama sinahuran de muniwara

05.10a (Thus) the words of the scholar (Indra),
        compellingly lovely was his wise pronouncement
        on the nature of Detachment.
05.10b Answered by Pārtha (Arjuna): "Truly wonderful
        are the words of the excellent monk.
05.10c "Nevertheless, in the case of a *ksatriya*, the
        life duty of fame through good works and
        heroism are more stressed.
05.10d "Truly you are mistaken in supporting that
        which is used to achieve Release.

05.11a "Isn't it true that no one should be neglectful
        of either inner or outer reality as long as one is living?
05.11b "It is not possible to imagine Nirvana (while
        alive); death is the (only) target for people in that situation.
05.11c "It is just a way of passing time, that enjoyment
        of power, a delightful game to play."
05.11d (Thus) the words of Pārtha, begging forgiveness
        (for disagreeing); (he was) answered by the
        excellent monk:

In this argument, Arjuna maintains that there should be a balance between inner and outer; he is essentially maintaining the validity of the
latter against Indra's arguments for the former. Earlier in the poem, he was
shown to be equally adept at holding to his meditation despite the whole-
hearted efforts at seduction by the celestial women sent by Indra. Here too
he strikes a balance, maintaining the inner reality against the outer:

04.08b pañcendriyāwĕdi tumon wiṣayanya ngūni
04.08c wruh mangrĕngö wruh umulat juga tan wikalpa
04.08d māryyāngaweṣa ri hĕningnira saprahāra

04.08b His five senses recoiled at becoming involved
　　　　with the things that had just been offered.
04.08c Aware and hearing, aware and seeing, even so
　　　　he is undisturbed.
04.08d (His senses) will refrain from threatening
　　　　his purity even for a moment.

Note that Arjuna is not oblivious to the sights and sounds of the women's temptations; he can see and hear them, but he remains detached nonetheless.

The basis for Arjuna's balanced stance between excessive attachment or detachment is his duty to serve others. When Indra continues to argue that any attachment to the world of the senses is dangerous and will lead to being caught in the circle of rebirth (AW 06.01 – 06.03), Arjuna's response is to maintain that he has no choice, since he must obey the wishes of his elder brother and work to benefit others:

06.04a sahurira tan apañjang singgih shabda muniwara
06.04b nghulun atiki katalyan dening bhakti lawan asih
06.04c hana pinaka kakāngkwān shrī dharmmātmaja
　　　　karĕngö
06.04d sira ta pinatapākĕn mahyun digjayawijaya

06.05a harĕp ayasha mahaywa ng rāt lāwan kaparahitan
06.05b juga raputu mahar.si n pamrih-mrih mataki-taki
06.05c ya tan anumata sanghyang tāde matya tan uliha
06.04d nahan ujarira yekān pendah rūpa muniwara

06.04a His reply was not lengthy: "True are the words
　　　　of the best of monks.
06.04b "(But) this humble servant is bound by loyalty
　　　　and love.
06.04c "There is one who was created as my elder
　　　　brother, Dharma's glorious son, famous.
06.04d "It is for his sake that I practice *tapa*;
　　　　he desires all-encompassing victory.

06.05a "The hope of performing meritorious deeds that
　　　　will bring happiness to the world and further
　　　　the welfare of the people—

06.05b "This alone is the reason your grandson strives
so intensely to practice austerities.
06.05c "If it is not agreed to by the gods, there is
no other choice but to die without returning
home."
06.05d Thus his words; at that the form of the monk
became transfigured in beauty.

Indra reveals his true nature at this point, explains that his arguments (and the earlier temptations of the celestial women) had all been a test which Arjuna has passed with flying colors, and prophesies success for Arjuna's endeavors to obtain weapons. At the same time, the stage is set for the furthering of the gods' plans to use Arjuna to help defeat their demon enemy.

The philosophy of balance emerges as the underlying theme of the entire poem. It is articulated explicitly, as in the argument with Indra, and is implicitly present in the balanced structure of the text. Briefly, the poem can be divided into two sections, the first of which describes Arjuna's control over the inner world of his passions, while the second demonstrates his control over the outer world as he defeats the demon. His detachment in the first half, where he resists the temptations posed by the seven celestial women, is balanced by his involvement in the second half, where he marries them. The character of Arjuna, who has self-control and succeeds, is balanced by that of the passionate Niwātakawaca, who fails because he can't control his lust for the celestial women. Within the first section, the tests given Arjuna balance the inner and outer, as described above, and, on a still lower level, the stanzaic structure of individual verses often exemplifies a balance of opposites. For example, in 05.09, lines a and d oppose the ultimate delusion (people who weep at the shadow play) against the ultimate truth (that the manifest world is illusion); within this frame are set opposing interpretations of the "common sense" mind-set in lines b and c: people know the shadow puppets are not "real" (they're only carved leather) in the same sense that they know things in the ordinary world *are* real (in fact, they're wrong). The content of the poem itself makes numerous references to the idea of balance as well, one of the most striking being a hymn which Arjuna offers to the god Shiva after the latter's test of his strength in battle. To quote part of the hymn:

10.02a wyāpīwyāpaka sārining paramatatwa durlabha kita
10.02b iccāntā ng hana-tanhanāganal-alit lawan hala-
hayu
10.02c utpatti sthiti līṇaning dadi kitāta kāraṇanika
10.02d sang sangkan-paraning sarāt sakala-niskalātmaka kita

10.02a   "Pervading from both the outside and the inside,
the essence of the highest reality, difficult
to apprehend are you.

10.02b   "(According to) your wish there is being with
non-being, rough with refined, and evil with
good.

10.02c   "The creation, maintenance, and destruction
of existence, you are indeed the cause of all
that.

10.02d   "The one from which all originates and to which
all returns in the end, the soul of both
material and non-material are you."

There is no question that the religion and philosophy (as well as the metaphors and many of the words) underlying this concern with balancing inner and outer owes a great deal to Indic and specifically Sanskritic influences. I maintain, however, that it is also part of a tradition underlying both *tapa* and trance in Java. In its most general form, it consists of maintaining communication between these inner and outer forces via a powerful individual who has access to the world of the spirits, gods, and ancestors, and who brings benefit to the community as a result.

The literary yoga of writing a *kakawin*, as well as the yogic ideal described in *kakawin* such as the *Arjuna Wiwāha*, are clearly within the tradition of meditation. The power of the poem to affect its community presents an interesting parallel to the case of trance. The parallel does not exist between the poet and the person who goes into trance; rather, I would argue that the poem itself substitutes for the person entered by a spirit while in trance. Although the notion of something "entering" a poem may seem somewhat abstract, there are many indications that *kakawin* language had a very concrete existence in the perceptions of those who used it. In a recent paper, S.O. Robson (1981) has discussed the oral nature of *kakawin*, pointing out that the present-day Balinese tradition of reciting *kakawin* aloud is likely a continuation of practices existing at the time these works were written. The use of meters in composing *kakawin* is evidence for a concern with the sound of the language as well. In this connection, it should be pointed out that, although there is no evidence that works on the theory of poetics were written in Old Javanese (as they were in Sanskrit), we do have a fifteenth-century work on prosody, the *Wrttasañcaya*, which is a kind of poetic textbook on the use of Sanskrit meters (Zoetmulder 1974:105).

The poem, then, had a physical existence as a particular kind of sound as it was recited aloud. In addition, there is evidence from the poems that they were seen as existing as places. Several poems describe the writing of a poem as the building of a *caṇḍi* or temple for the god invoked as the *manggala*: one of the relevant passages, from the Bhomakawya, reads "May his *caṇḍi* now be erected in the words of the poem, so that it may become a worthy abode for the god of love when manifesting himself" (BK1.1; translation and reference from Zoetmulder 1974:185). In the architectural sense, *caṇḍi* were stone buildings, erected not as places for public worship but for the enshrinement of deceased kings after death had reunited them with the deities of whom they were incarnations on earth. In this way the king could "make his magical power available for the benefit of the world" (Robson 1981: 6–7). The poem that contains a god, of whom the king is an incarnation, is thus analogous to the *caṇḍi* that contains a god previously incarnate as a king, and both are a means of ensuring the well-being of the community around them. In both its writing and the sound of it being read aloud, the poem constitutes a form in which formless power can manifest itself. In the *Arjuna Wiwāha*, furthermore, the story of Arjuna's meditation is preaching what the poem is practicing, as it tells of Arjuna's concern with benefiting his family through his *tapa*.

I see *caṇḍi* as part of a continuum, in which we can see a development from trance on one end to the blend of Hinduism and the god-king cult on the other. In trance it is people who serve as the medium for possession by spirits or ancestors; in this state, they may act out or recite myths of various sorts, to varying degrees. Perhaps more crucial is the role they play in extending the realities of myths into the present, and of articulating the roles to be played by their present audience in the ongoing story (see, for example, Franken 1984:241, 358, for a description of the 1949 festival of *Jayaprana* in Bali). The next stage I see as represented by the *Sang Hyang Dedari* dancers of Bali: especially when trouble threatens the community, young girls enter trance (possessed by spirits of *widyadharis*, celestial women), and dance the stories narrated by a person who functions essentially as a *dalang* (puppeteer) does in *wayang*. In *wayang*, puppets replace people in acting out these stories. The *dalang* is not in trance; rather, he is in a state closer to meditation, in order to control the forces contained in the puppets. The characters these puppets portray are usually from Indian sources, but they have also been incorporated into the ancestry of the Javanese (see Rassers 1959).

With *kakawin* literature, these characters exist in poetic language. The role of the poet, like that of the *dalang*, is to control their existence through the meditative practice of composing the poem. Like those in trance, the poem provides a link to power, and, as in the *Arjuna Wiwāha*, recontextualize the present by identifying the king with an ancestor/hero. Finally, with the *caṇḍi*, the spirit which enters the temple is that of the god who has been incarnate in the deceased king. Here too narrative plays a role, as many of the *caṇḍi* are carved with stories identical to those told in *kakawin* (and in wayang). These stories presumably have relevance to the life of the king of the *caṇḍi*, as the stories told in *kakawin* are thought to do. The link thus established brings prosperity to the realm.

My use of the word "continuum" does not reflect a belief that trance dancers, *wayang*, *kakawin*, and *caṇḍi* necessarily represent stages in a development through time. Since we have evidence of trance ritual in places where Indian influence was not prevalent, and since such rituals as *kuda kepang* (where "hobby horse" dancers enter trance) exist in Java today, we are justified in considering that some such ritual existed in Java prior to the Hindu period. On Java and Bali, however, Indic culture penetrated to such a degree that most of the trance phenomena there shows signs of Indic influence. (For example, the *Sang Hyang Dedari* dancers owe part of their name to Skt. "widyadhari.") *Wayang* too has been heavily influenced by Hinduism and is thought by some scholars (Ras 1976) to have in fact originated in South India. Where there are no physical traces (such as manuscripts or temple reliefs) to guide us, we can only speculate on the nature of trance ritual and *wayang* in early Java. It seems likely, though, that some kind of trance ritual and *wayang* existed side-by-side with the *kakawin* and *caṇḍi* traditions during Java's Hindu period. Evidence from the *Arjuna Wiwāha* itself testifies to *wayang*'s existence in the eleventh century (see the discussion of AW 05.09 above).

In conclusion, the argument here is that there is congruence between the traditions of trance and *tapa* as they existed, and still exist, in Java. Works such as the *Arjuna Wiwāha* should be viewed in terms of such congruence, in order to understand their significance in the culture that produced them. This culture was Javanese, not Indian, and while the extent of Indic influence was very great, the readiness with which Javanese culture absorbed and adapted to such influence may be due in large part to this congruence.

5. Islamic Transformations: From Sufi Doctrine to Ritual Practice in Gayo Culture

John Bowen

*J*N GENERAL, STUDENTS OF RELIGION in theMalayo-Indonesian world have sought out the *asli*, the indigenous system of ideas, values, and rules that will presumably be formally more systematic, phenomenologically more real, and culturally more clearly bounded than the local varieties of the world religions. In many parts of the archipelago this analytical strategy has proven to be a sound one, since the relatively recent and superficial impact of Islam, Hinduism, or Christianity has not yet dislodged the locus of structure from a set of earlier values and traditions. However, such an approach has left the study of Islam (in particular) high and dry in areas of its long and persistent cultural influence. It is as if Islam were treated as more or less "received" (to use the Dutch legal term) into traditional belief systems, but never to have actively transformed those systems.[1] If such a view of Islamic influence since the thirteenth century were true, it would be a unique and fascinating historical case, differing markedly, for example, from the complex interactions that characterized the adoption of Buddhist and Confucian political models in neighboring Thailand, Burma, and Vietnam.[2]

Such a perspective would be particularly misleading in those coastal areas and their immediate hinterlands where Islam was widely accepted by the seventeenth century: the northern ports of Java, the central regions of

Sumatra along both coasts, and above all Aceh. In Aceh, as James Siegel has pointed out, both Islam and traditions *(adat)* were integral to the cultural perspective of each major social group—villagers and religious scholars *(ulama)*, sultan and chieftains.[3] Discordance and miscommunication between these groups were not the result of a fissure between *adat* and Islam—although this was a politically convenient Dutch theory at the time—but rather the result of differing conceptions of what being a "good Muslim" and a "good Acehnese" might mean (Siegel 1969:68–70). Aceh as a state and a society was formed from a number of small, culturally heterogeneous, linguistically diverse, and politically fractious states, drawing on supra-ethnic symbols of Islam and its ideology. As a state, Aceh focused on the Arabic seals of the sultanate, the legends of beneficent Islamic kings, and a burgeoning Malay-language, Persian-derived religious literary culture. As a society, Aceh focused on the village, structured around the dual leadership of the headman and religious leader *(keucik* and *teungku)*, the "father and mother" of the villagers.[4] Aceh would thus appear to provide appropriate material for the study of the historical interaction of Islamic and pre-Islamic doctrinal and ritual forms.

Today, it is likely that the results of this interplay are best preserved in the highland Gayo society of central Aceh. Unlike much of the rest of the former sultanate, the Gayo area has been relatively untouched by later reformist and modernist Islamic movements, except for the northern town of Takengon. In part, the religious stability of the central Gayo area is due to the small role played by trade; in part, it is due to substantial isolation from other areas of Indonesia and from foreign teachers and missionaries. After their inclusion in the fourteenth-century *Hikayat Raja-Raja Pasai* as a people who fled inland from the north coast in order to escape the initial wave of Islamization, there is no mention of the Gayo in any text prior to the late nineteenth century. Although a group of Minangkabau traders brought reformist teachings to the Gayo town of Takengon in the late 1920s, such *kaum muda* teachings remain largely confined to the town itself. Moreover, religious teaching and the transmission of oral traditions in Gayo remain essentially a village activity. Neither *pesantrens* nor their *ulama* acquired the separate institutional and cultural identity that they did in Aceh proper or in Pidie.[5] Within the boundaries of Gayo society, the religion-tradition-leadership mixture appeared and appears more of a piece than in the rest of the province. Thus, one would expect that here, above all, Islamic cultural forms would have received a relatively holistic interpretation; that is, that the penetration of doctrines, values, and prescriptions into the corners of the social and cultural fabric would have been deepest.

I propose here to examine the transformative effect of this religious penetration by tracing the development of a specific, early Acehnese Sufi set of ideas through its persistence and transformation in contemporary Gayo theory and practice. The thesis that I shall develop in this paper is double-edged: that a Sufi theory of being and knowledge was both transforming and transformed as an element in Gayo culture. Without losing its essentially religious focus (the relation of Creator to created) but rather by expanding upon that focal idea, what had been a contemplative basis for mystical union was developed into the ontological grounds for ritual practice. In the sections that follow I shall begin by sketching the argument behind early Acehnese Sufi poetry, then present its transformation into a Gayo cosmogony, and finally trace the relationship between these ideas of being and creation and their practical, ritual application in current Gayo approaches to healing.

Acehnese Sufism and Ḥamzah Fanṣūrī

The weight of currently available evidence, scant as it is, suggests that the first conversations of Indonesian societies to Islam took place sometime in the late thirteenth century. Marco Polo, who stopped in six ports along the Acehnese coast in 1292, remarked that only one of them had adopted Islam and that even in that port (Ferlec, now Perlak) conversion was limited to the inhabitants of the city.[6] The other city-states of the northern coast were converted to Islam over the ensuing century, and by the end of the fifteenth century the religion had been accepted by the north coastal ports of Java as well.[7] The initial conversion process, then, can be said to have taken place from 1300 to 1500.

Although the rough dates of these religious changes may be agreed on, the question of why conversions took place when they did elicits no such convergence of opinion. It appears from the evidence of gravestones, Arabic trade records, and Chinese accounts of travels to the area that there were Muslims in Aceh from the eighth century. Why, then, was a period of five centuries with little or no conversion activity succeeded by a rather sudden and widespread upsurge in Islamization over the following two centuries? One explanation of this "conversion gap," advanced notably by Schrieke, was that the diversion of the international spice trade through Cambay and on to Aden, itself the result of the Crusades and the Mongol invasions, set in motion a fairly clear and resolutely linear series of historical events: Cambay Gujaratis spread out over Sumatra and the Malay peninsula in search of trade, bringing Islam with them; Portuguese competitors (and bearers of Christianity) soon seized control of key ports, notably Malacca in 1511, and set off a race in the name of both religion and trade; Hindu

Javanese traders were displaced from Palembang and converted to Islam in their new port-homes (Pasai in Aceh or Malacca). Schrieke's argument is, in fact, more nuanced than this portrayal allows, but he tended to see conversion to Islam as relatively unproblematic once sufficient numbers of Indian Muslims could be brought into play.[8]

Several difficulties arise with this mode of explanation. First, the early series of conversions to Islam (the north coast of Sumatra beginning in the late thirteenth century, Malacca most likely in 1436) predates the presence of the Portuguese in the area by almost a century, and the initial Islamization of Javanese coastal cities was well underway when the Portuguese captured Malacca. Secondly, it is difficult to see how Gujarati traders could have imparted the specialized knowledge, even scholastic modes of analysis, that were present in the Acehnese and Malay courts in the fourteenth and fifteenth centuries.[9] And finally, the early works produced in this area point to an active process of translation, education, and conversion that demanded highly trained scholars with intellectual roots in Persia, India, and Arabia.[10]

The growth in Islamization over the thirteenth and fourteenth centuries may be more satisfactorily accounted for by the nascent activity of Sufi missionaries. Beginning in the thirteenth century, these proponents of particular religious orders provided the leading edge of Islamic expansion with a flexible and integrative texture. Wandering Sufi teachers supplemented the rather arid Quranic explanations of what man must do with a richer account, often tied to local custom, of how he might do it. In Anthony Johns's (1961:15) apt characterization of the Sufis in Indonesia:

> They were peripatetic preachers ranging over the whole known world, voluntarily espousing poverty; they were frequently associated with trade or craft guilds, according to the order *(tarīkah)* to which they belonged; they taught a complex syncretic theosophy largely familiar to the Indonesians, but which was subordinate to, although an enlargement on the fundamental dogmas of Islam; they were proficient in magic and possessed powers of healing; and not least, consciously or unconsciously, they were prepared to preserve continuity with the past, and to use the terms and elements of pre-Islamic culture in an Islamic context.[11]

The first exposition of Sufi ideas available to us in Malay (or in any other Indonesian language*) is in the works of the late sixteenth-century poet

---

*A note on orthography: Arabic words will be written following standard conventions; however, when these words become Indonesianized, they will be written without diacritics to indicate Indonesian/Malay/Gayo pronunciation. Thus, '*ulama*/*ulama*, *zāhir*/*lahir*, etc.

Ḥamzah Fanṣūrī. Ḥamzah was most likely born in Barus (Fansūr in Arabic, in West Aceh), wrote a number of prose and poetic works in Malay after extensive travels in the Middle East, Siam, and Java, and probably died before the succession of Iskandar Muda to the Acehnese sultanate in 1607.[12] Al-Attas has attempted to reconstruct from Ḥamzah's writings and those of his critics a picture of the religious milieu into which he stepped upon his return from his travels in the West. On the one hand, certain self-styled Sufis taught the "democratization" of mysticism: God can be reached merely by the performance of certain self-denying ritual practices. In Ḥamzah's ridiculing stanza:

> Everyone is "intelligent" and "wise"
> Everyone is hungry and thin, . . .[13]

These local teachers preached what might be termed an empiricist pantheism based on "locating" God in the fontanelle or in the lungs. Ḥamzah's commentary was:

> His Being is pure as limpid water,
> His Attributes are beautiful without compeer,
> He is not in the eyes, the nose, and the brow—
> Don't you gaze there growing giddy![14]

On the other hand, the Acehnese religious establishment (the judges, *qāḍī*, and the acknowledged experts in religious affairs, *'ulamā*) appear to have been actively opposed to these Sufi teachers and practitioners. Teachings such as Ḥamzah's which argued for a subtler form of mysticism were nonetheless included in the doctrines called heretical. The mundane, literal, and legalist readings given by "the Judge," as Ḥamzah refers to this establishment, denied any relation of man to God other than the arid one of mechanical observance of Islamic ritual duties. In a masterly quatrain, Hamzah cites the Quranic passage that God is nearer to man than are the veins in his neck and then ridicules the Judge:

> "Glory be," it is such a wonder,
> He is nearer than the jugular veins;
> Remarkable that the Judge and the Preacher—
> Should be so close and yet so luckless![15]

Rhetorically, Ḥamzah relied on dialectics to convince his readers. By positioning himself between those who saw God as literally "in" all existing objects and those who saw God as a distant, unreachable Creator, Ḥamzah presented his own views as a reasonable, richer alternative.

Ḥamzah saw creation as a process of successive determinations or manifestations *(tajalliyāt)* of a single, eternal, underlying reality. The true relation of man to God can only be understood, in Ḥamzah's view, by comprehending just how man came to be. In his cosmogony Ḥamzah drew on earlier Sufi writings, in particular those of Ibn Arabī, and much of Ḥamzah's work consists of translations of and commentaries on Persian poetry as well as texts of the Quran and Hadith.[16]

Ḥamzah's creation consists of five stages following an indefinite state of indeterminate, unknowable, and nonmanifest essence. The first manifestation of this essence is as four initial qualities and relations: Knowledge *('ilm)*, Being *(wujūd)*, Sight *(shuhūd)*, and Light *(nur)*. These qualities are the first outward aspects *(ẓāhir)* of the pure essence and make possible the first relations. Ḥamzah writes that at this first stage:

> ... the Knower and the Known, the First and the last, the Outward *(Ẓāhir)* and the Hidden *(Bāṭin)* acquire their names (Sharab:15).

This set of initial relations lends attributes and names to the pure essence, and remains an integral part of all subsequent manifestations of being:

> Determinations never cease to occur and are without limit, but Knowledge, Being, Sight and Light are never separate from them all (Sharab:15).

In the second stage of manifestation appear the Fixed Essences or Prototypes of things, perhaps best thought of an exemplars of the phenomenal world. Ḥamzah likens the Prototypes to waves appearing in the ocean which give form to the water without yet separating from it—an image which he develops throughout the exposition of his theory. Ibn Arabī was probably the first to use the term *a'yan* (prototype) in this sense, indicating by it both latent states in the mind of God and future possibilities of existence, states which, in Johns's view, "can only be expressed in terms of the divine names and all the possible relations that hold between them" (1957:20). Ḥamzah calls the spirit of the Prototypes the "relational spirit" *(rūh idāfī)* and identifies it with the Light of Muhammad, created by God after the manifestation of knowledge has permitted the differentiation between the Knower and the Known:

> That is to say, the Knowledge that sees the Known is the Reality of Muhammad (Haqīqat Muhammad). . . . Between the Knower and

the Known, that is when the Light of Muhammad. . . first separates from the Divine Essence (Dhāt) (Asrār:41).

Ḥamzah is drawing on a Sufi interpretation from the early eighth century of the "light verse" (āyat an-nūr) of the Quran. In this tradition, the
light mentioned in this passage pertains to Muhammad, from whose light
in turn came the other prophets (Schimmel 1975:214).
Several quotations from Muhammad are cited by Ḥamzah at this point:

> Further, the Prophet says: . . . "I am from God's
> light and the faithful are from my light.
>
> I was a prophet when Adam was yet between water and
> clay" (Asrar: 42—43).

Moreover, the relation of the Light of Muhammad to God (as Knower to
Known) is reproduced in the creation of all other beings; the rest of Creation then knows Muhammad just as Muhammad knows God. Ḥamzah
cites and interprets a *ḥadīth qudsī* (testament about God's words to Muhammad) with respect to the Light of Muhammad:

> I created all of Creation for your sake; you I created for My sake
> (that is, Creation came into being from the Light of Muhammad,
> and that Light from the Divine Essence) (Asrār: 43).

In the ensuing three stages of creation the Prototypes manifest themselves as spirits *(rūh)*, then as inscriptions, and finally as phenomenal
existents. These stages are likened by Ḥamzah to the cycle through which
water passes under the influence of the sun: the churning waves of the
ocean produce a vapor or cloud that holds the immediate potential of
bringing things forth into the world. This image of pregnant possibility
corresponds to the creation of potential existents with souls or spirits of
three types: vegetable, animal, or human. The cloud is allowed to burst
forth with raindrops at the command of God, "Be!", when the form of
existence of each phenomenal entity is inscribed in the Well-Protected
Tablet *(al-lawḥ al-maḥfūz)*. Finally, the rain falls on the earth. And rivers,
as the inscriptions of form, are made into the empirical reality of things in
the world.[17]
  The movement of manifestation from God to souls to souls-in-the-world
achieves closure when the souls return to the divine sphere after death.
Ḥamzah reinforces his imagery at this point by punning from an Ara-
bicized Aramaic term to Malay: souls return to *Lāhūt* (Divinity) just as the

rain, after its journey through rivers and streams, returns to *laut* (the ocean).[18] Because a cycling of material substance implies an underlying identity of that substance through changes in form and appearance, the image of the ocean gives Ḥamzah just the right vehicle for steering between naive pantheism and its orthodox antithesis. Clouds and raindrops remain identical with the ocean in underlying reality, yet emerge and separate from the ocean. God is seen as both immanent (in reality) and transcendent (in form) to the phenomenal world. Ḥamzah translates a Persian text into Malay to make his point:

> Laut sedia; apabila berpalu menjadi ombak baharu,
> Dikata orang "ombak," tetapi pada haqiqat laut jua.
>
> (The sea is timeless; when it heaves it becomes waves,
> People say "waves," but in reality it is just the sea).[19]

Taken alone, this passage might suggest the naive, substantivist pantheism that Ḥamzah was trying to avoid. Ḥamzah nicely avoids this by superimposing a second image, in which the shadow is distinguished from its corporeal source. The world is presented as the image or shadow of initial possibilities, which appear to God as the Known:

> As to the world, although it is existing it is yet
> nothing but the shadow of the Known (Asrār:77).

The prior existence of God's knowledge of things in this theory leads Ḥamzah by, but not into, the problem of free will. Ḥamzah considers God to work through the actions of men, and passages such as the following seem to imply that God determines men's actions:

> it is He that causes Ḥamzah to move so that he can move. If He
> does not cause him to move, Ḥamzah cannot move, for Ḥamzah
> is but a shadow. If the Possessor of the shadow does not cause him
> to move, how can Ḥamzah move? (Asrār:76–77)

Ḥamzah is less concerned, however, with the possible causes of actions than with turning men's attention toward the ultimate reality of God. In his rhetoric, he emphasizes the shadow image over the self-portrait of man as puppet. It is the image of shadows, and their relations to human action and causation, that other thinkers drew from Ḥamzah and used to buttress a theory of magic.

Al-Attas argues that a key element of Ḥamzah's texts is the new use made of certain Malay words. In particular, Ḥamzah uses the word *ada* (to be, existence) as a technical equivalent to the Arabic *mawjūd*, a term which in contemporary Sufi use referred to both the *ẓāhir*, the outward phenomenal world, and the *bāṭin*, inner hidden reality (al-Attas 1970:195–97). Ḥamzah then loaded onto this single lexical item a complex and novel (in the Acehnese context) theory of being, a theory that attempted to relate these two senses of *ada* largely through a series of concrete images. Ḥamzah encountered both lexical and politico-religious difficulties in his endeavor.

First, the new sense of the term *ada* differed radically from the generally accepted meaning of the word (roughly, "presence of an object"), which implies a relation of container to contained. As al-Attas points out, *ada* is linked to *isi* (contents) in Malay, and the two words are used interchangeably across the Malayo-Polynesian language family (al-Attas 1970:163–72). If Ḥamzah's writings were interpreted in terms of this traditional sense of *ada*, they could be likened to the works of his pantheistic opponents for whom God was contained within man. Such interpretations of his writings did indeed lead to their condemnation as heretical during the reign of Iskandar Thani (1636–1641).

Second, the rejection of Ḥamzah's views (and those of his follower, Shamsu'l-Dīn) coincided with the transition from the strong ruler Iskander Muda (1607–1636) to his relatively weak successor, Iskandar Thani, and the rise of a newly arrived Gujarati religious figure at the Acehnese court, Nur ud-Din ar-Raniri. Lombard suggests that the orthodox reactions against Sufism in Aceh may have been linked to similar changes taking place in India at that time; ar-Raniri's personal role in leading the reaction would strengthen this hypothesis (Lombard 1967:162–63).

Although Ḥamzah's acceptance and prominence in Aceh may have been due to the prior acceptance of Sufi teachings, in general, in fact he succeeded in redefining the field of religious discourse in Aceh. Commonplace Sufi teachings at the time appear to have been concerned with the location of God in man—ironically, a very worldly version of other-worldliness. Ḥamzah attempted to displace the question of God's relation to man from its place in a conceptual scheme defined by the image of a container and its contents (a discourse of location), to a sheme defined by the images of shadow and body, and of the emergence of phenomenal forms from an oceanlike, underlying reality (a discourse of manifestation). Despite the repudiation of his works at the Acehnese court under Iskandar Thani, Ḥamzah's writings had a profound influence both on the subsequent generation of Acehnese teachers (most notably Abd ur-Rauf of Singkel) and on poets elsewhere in the archipelago (including the author of the

Sya'ir Perang Mengkasar; see Lombard 1967:163–64). In the following section I shall suggest that, in Aceh, Ḥamzah's theory provided a new exegetical framework at the village level as well and that Ḥamzah's view has had a profoundly transforming effect on both reflective discourse and ritual practice.

Gayo Cosmogony

The Gayo have led a shadow existence in Acehnese history, appearing only once by name in Acehnese chronicles (and then in a fourteenth-century account of the formation of Pasai). Gayo, a mountain people, have served as the sedentary, ethnically homogeneous, agricultural counterpoint to the Acehnese theme of trade, ethnic admixture, and movement. The traditional political relationship of the Gayo kingdoms to their nominal Acehnese suzerains appears to have been limited to paying an annual tax in return for the conferral of a symbol of legitimate authority, the short sword or *bawar*.

Today there are about 200,000 Gayo living in three regencies in the center of Aceh province. Villages are small, comprising from thirty to a hundred households organized around one or more localized descent lines. Almost all Gayo engage in wet rice cultivation; coffee near Takengon and tobacco in the southern districts are the major cash crops.

Gayo see themselves as one of the original peoples of Sumatra, descending from a son of the king of Rūm (Constantinople). Subsequent marriages and migrations led to links with Karo Batak and Acehnese. Myths about Gayo history and relationships with neighboring groups are told openly and freely. Myths concerning the creation of the world, however, touch directly on esoteric knowledge *(ilmu)* and are therefore only told in connection with the transmission of such knowledge, usually to children or close relatives of traditional healers *(guru)*. This knowledge is usually transmitted orally, although some healers keep small notebooks with spells, religious sayings or letter-symbolic diagrams that are useful for healing.[20]

The following myth of creation was told to me at several separate occasions, with only slight variation, by two knowledgeable men. One of these men was the head of one of the five villages in the Isak complex, a noted healer, and the performer of the ritual described in the following section. The second informant was my major source of stories of all kinds, a very good deer hunter and pretty good healer, and my closest village elder brother. Several other informants have confirmed particular parts of the myth. The myth of creation is told not as a traditional story *(kekeberen)* but rather as an explanatory or exegetical tool; I first heard pieces of the myth when I asked questions about healing. This particular embeddedness of the story in a system of esoteric, practical knowledge is itself of importance as part of the transformation of Ḥamzah's theory into a local exegesis; it also means that the following bits of the myth were recorded one by one and not as a single, continuously told story.[21]

Gayo creation myths begin with the appearance of two lights (Malay *cahaya* or Arabic *nūr*): the Light of God and the Light of Muhammad. One account describes the origin of the two lights as follows:

> In the beginning there was only *kalam Allah* (the word of God) and a single object that was round like an egg. From God came an order and the egg-like object split in two. Half became the Light of Muhammad and the other half became the Light of God....All things on earth were then created from the Light of Muhammad.

In another version of the beginning of the myth, using different imagery, the two lights are described as "the shadow of the *alif* (/) annd the *mīm* (ᶜ)." The *alif*, the first letter of the Arabic alphabet, stands for God (the /a/ in *allahu*), while the *mīm* stands for Muhammad. At this initial stage the two letters were still but shadows of the yet unwritten forms. Then:

> the letter *mīm* was written. Then from this dot (ᶜ), which is the starting point for writing all letters, was written the letter *alif*.

Now, although God had existed in an inner *(batin,* from Arabic bāṭin) form before Muhammad, Muhammad received an outer form *(lahir,* Gayo vocalization of ẓāhir) before God; to make the stroke of the letter *alif* you must first make a dot, the initial touch of pen to paper, and this dot is the initial *mīm*. This disharmony of precedence led to an argument between God and Muhammad. God told Muhammad to recite the confession of faith, with God first, Muhammad second:

> Muhammad refused, saying that it should be the other way around. So God said: "All right, let us each hide and try to find the other." God hid and Muhammad could not find him, because God can disappear; even though God has an object in the letter *alif,* God is not identical to that letter and can exist independently of it.

> Muhammad, however, could not disappear, and so God found him when he tried to hide; he remains *mīm* and always an object. So Allah won, and the confession of faith was set down in the way that God had commanded, and in that way it was taught to Adam.

Relative to God, Muhammad is *lahir*, the initial differentiation from God. Muhammad as objecthood has its sign in the *mīm*; from this letter were then created the Quran and the physical essence *(zat)* of all living things. God as the source of life is signified by the *alif*:

> God then planned in his mind what were to be the contents of the world. He planned all the *ruh* (souls) that would eventually descend to the earth, and then wrote a *lam* (ل) in the *luh mahful* (tablet), the place where all the *ruh* are kept. This *lam* contained all the souls. He planned first, and this was in the *lam*, and then as he created (these things), as they became *lahir*, the *alif* was added so there was a *lam-alif* (ﻻ). The essence *(zat)* of the things was from the *mīm*, but their light, that which gave them life, was from the *lam-alif*. The first is Muhammad, the second is the Light of Allah and the Light of Muhammad.

Three distinct actions of God are described in this passage. First, the things that will eventually exist are planned by God. Second, the souls of potential existents are inscribed in the *luh mahful* (the Gayo vocalization of *Lawḥ al-Mahfūẓ* or the Well-Protected Tablet). The state of inscription is signified by the letter *lam*. Finally, the *alif* of God is added to the *lam* to produce material things[22]; while *mīm* is the sign of objecthood, the double letter *lam-alif* stands for life given by light to the object, God's contribution brought into being. The creation sequence can be seen as an interplay of light and letters, producing a more personalized and concrete parallel to Ḥamzah's cosmogonic schema. I have placed the two systems in correspondence in the following chart:

Stage	Ḥamzah	Gayo
1	Relations: knower-known, *ẓāhir-bāṭin*	Light of God–Light of Muhammad
2	Prototypes, Nur Muhammad	Muhammad inscribed as *mīm*, objecthood
3	Potential existents and their *rūh*	Planning of existents and their *ruh*
4	Inscription of forms in the Tablet	Inscription of souls as *lam* in the Tablet
5	Materialization of things	*Alif* added to *lam*, things are given material existence

The key figures and their order of mention have been preserved from Ḥamzah's cosmogony to the Gayo myth. The account proceeds from the relationship of God and Muhammad to the planning of the *ruh*, their inscription in the Tablet, and their appearance in the phenomenal world. However, the relationship between these elements has been transformed. In Ḥamzah, creation is depicted as successive and progressive manifestations of a substance: waves rise out of the sea to become clouds, and then droplets, and finally rain. In the Gayo myth, creation results from the successive combinations of *batin* with *lahir* elements: the relative pairs God/Muhammad, *alif/mīm*, *lam/lam-alif* form a chain of signs leading to the entry of beings into the phenomenal world. Sometime after he narrated the story of creation to me, one healer in Isak restated the terms of the myth as follows:

> first there was the Light of God, the *lahir* of which God was the *batin*. But this light was still *batin* in relation to an object which was uncreated before God drew the initial dot *(mīm)* and then the line *(alif)*. That is why God was the first *batin*, but Muhammad the first *lahir*.

The *batin/lahir* chain reaches from the Light of God and Muhammad, through the elements of the body, out to the spirits that control hunting and use of the land. The image consistently used both to name and to describe these relations is that of the shadow or reflection *(bayan)* of an object, the same image used by Ḥamzah. Briefly stated, the chain is as follows: The Light of Muhammad has a *lahir* in the human body, called the "white shadow/reflection" *(bayan putih)*. This individualized presence of the Light is the means of spiritual communication among all sentient beings, a power which I shall explore in the following sections. The *bayan* has its *lahir* in turn in a "black shadow/reflection" *(bayan item)*, which provides the basis for destructive conduct. These two *bayan* must remain in balance within the individual, and one object of healing a sick person is to use the white, cooling element to heal the body and the black, destructive element to attack the evil spirits that are threatening the patient's survival.

The chain continues, reaching the corporeal boundary of the body, where the *sebet tungel* (roughly, "solitary companion") serves to guard the body against the entry of spirits. It has a *lahir* counterpart in the visible shadow, referred to here as the *bujang item*. The shadow leads the chain outside the body, although remaining connected to it, and into the world of the guardians of the land. The immediate *lahir* of the shadow is the *pawang tue* (the hunting spirit and descendant of Cain), which has its *lahir* in turn in the *tembuni* (afterbirth), which is buried immediately after birth to initiate the relationship between a lowland person and his upland, hunting counterpart. According to one informant, the *tembuni* has its *lahir* in the *sidang opat*, the four guardians of the land, to whom offerings must be made before any agricultural activity is begun.

In the sections that follow, I shall discuss only the first of these couples, the relation of the Light of Muhammad to the individual through the *bayan putih*. This relation makes possible spiritual communication. Each of these *batin/lahir* relations, however, determines a specific domain of Gayo ritual; together, the chain provides a coherent template for communication across the entire range of beings. Below I have listed the correspondence of each relation to a ritual domain:

Relation	Ritual Domain
Light of Muhammad/	all spells and communication
bayan putih	through *maripet*
bayan putih/bayan item	healing through cooling and exorcism
bayan item/sebet tungel	exorcism of spirits
sebet tungel/bujang item	spells for bodily protection
bujang item/pawang tue	hunting magic and sorcery
pawang tue/tembuni	birth ritual
tembuni/sidang opat	agricultural ritual

Each of these domains deserves separate treatment; for the remainder of this paper I shall focus on the concept of communication through *maripet*. To anticipate, this Gayo concept represents the appropriation of a Sufi concept of gnosis *(ma'rifat)* as a vehicle for ritually entering into and making use of the ontological *batin/lahir* chain. We shall return to Ḥamzah's writings to trace the transformation of this concept before examining its application in ritual.

From Knowledge to Power

Let us return to the initial stage in Ḥamzah's schema, the stage of Relation or pluralities. Ḥamzah calls on images of knowing, seeing, and illuminating in order to present the idea of Relation in concrete terms. Each of these images has been elaborated in Sufi thought: colors and light are key symbols in Iranian Sufism; reflections and mirrors figure in Ḥamzah and Arabic writers.[23] But Ḥamzah attributes to knowledge the motivating role in God's creation of the world. Several *hadīth qudsī* (sayings ascribed to God) are quoted to this effect:

I was a hidden treasure and I desired to be known, so I created creation in order to be known (Sharāb:2).

The term "knowledge" translates the Arabic ma'rifat, which in Sufi usage refers to approaching close to God and thus knowing the world through God. Al-Attas glosses ma'rifat in Ḥamzah's writings as "participation in God's knowledge of things." It is thus a higher state of knowledge than that indicated by the term 'ilm, "everyday knowledge." Ma'rifat is knowledge of God through God's knowledge of the world. Thus, what is ma'rifat for men is but 'ilm for God; the latter word is used in the following passage from Ḥamzah to describe the initial Relation[24]:

But for the Known, God the Glorious and Most Exalted would not have been ẓāhir, and without the Knower, the Light of Muhammad would not have been ẓāhir (Asrār: 42).

Knowledge by God of a Known, a set of potentialities for the world, was the presupposition for creation: in the beginning was Knowledge. In the Sufi view, and in particular Ḥamzah's, man's task is to close this epistemological circle, to know God in the world and thus return to His knowledge of that world. Because man is part of the world, the task of gnosis is best begun with himself. The most often-quoted saying of Muhammad in Sufi writing is a charter for ma'rifat: "whosoever knows himself knows his Lord."[25] The ultimate goal of this process is union with God, wāṣil:

drowning in the sea that has no shore
(Muntahī:126)
like the moth plunging into fire
(Sharāb:71)

In the Sufi system, ma'rifat is the two-way link between bāṭin and ẓāhir. On the one hand, Knowledge was the impetus for the initial emergence of a ẓāhir out of the bāṭin of God, the manifestation of Relation as the first moment of Creation. Knowledge was the objectification of Divinity but demanded a complementary seeking of Knowledge by the final manifestation of creation, man. On the other hand, man feels impelled toward the source of his being. Ma'rifat provides the key to the reversal of the process of manifestation, passing from ẓāhir to bāṭin, stripping away inessential appearance to focus on God. Ḥamzah links this process to fanā (self-extinction) and, more importantly for our concerns here, with effective communication between man and God:

you must cast your vision only upon God's existence with perfect ma'rifat.

annihilate your self from (consciousness in) the worshipper and
the Worshipped.

Prayer is not valid except with *ma'rifat*.[26]

The links between *ma'rifat* and communication, on the one hand, and
the passage from *bāṭin* to *ẓāhir*, on the other, were preserved in the Gayo
concept of *maripet*. Whereas *ma'rifat* refers to knowledge, realization, and
gnosis, I would gloss *maripet* as "powerful depictive concentration." In
everyday life, *maripet* is likened to the art of pictorial memory by the Gayo:

> *Maripet* is like imagining what your village looks like when you
> are not there.

But in its ritual use, *maripet* is the vehicle for crossing from the *lahir* realm
into *batin*, and effecting changes in that domain. Many uses of *maripet* are
to bring around a recalcitrant person to one's own design: to catch the
fancy of a would-be sweetheart, to induce insurmountable feelings of long-
ing, or to soften the resistance of an employer, a parent, or a rival sorcerer.
But *maripet* may also be used to foretell fortune in an upcoming battle
(used during the period of secessionist struggle in the 1950s) or, as in the
following example, to cause a spirit to leave the body of a patient.

The successful use of *maripet*, according to my informants, involves
three elements: imagining an object or person, concentrating on the object, and mentally suggesting a desired outcome. The required level of
concentration must be learned, and some healers have spent periods of
weeks or months meditating in seclusion or reciting *dhikir* chants (the
name of God or the first part of the confession of faith).

> It is like a coconut: there is the husk, and then the meat inside
> that, and then the water inside that, and then the oil on the water.
> You have to think only of the oil inside that coconut. That is
> *maripet*.

The ability to bring about the effects of *maripet* is not an automatically
inherited power, although very often the relevant skills and spells have been
handed down from fathers to sons or mothers to daughters. (Although the
division between kinds of esoteric knowledge is not strictly marked or limited by gender, many domains of this knowledge tend to be distributed to
men only or to women only.) Healers attain a sufficiently high level of
ability through study and practice; its source is in the Light of God and
Muhammad and so equally available to all persons. The healer quoted
above noted how we can cause a quick flash of light to appear in our eyes if

we press in on the lids. This is the Light of God and Muhammad. He then continued:

> This light is also the source of *maripet*, its path between you and someone else. You can see if someone else is still healthy and alive by putting him into your *lam-alif.* If you can call up this as an image and put it together with your own image in your *mar-ipet*, then the person will be healthy; if not, then he or she will be sick or die soon. This is because the *lam* is the place of God's plans, and we can have access to those plans through our *maripet*, through *nur* (light), since this light is our connection with God.

We are now ready to examine the ritual use of *maripet* and its relation to the *batin/lahir* chain of manifestation.

The Efficacy of Maripet

In this section I shall turn to one case of the application of *maripet* in a ritual context, that of a cure to expel an evil spirit *(jin)* from a patient's body. The diagnosis and cure were carried out on February 10–11, 1980, in Isak. I witnessed the cure, but the content of the spells used and the exegesis of the entire process were given to me on the following day by the healer.

Healing may be performed by anyone who knows of a spell, or of a medicinal plant or other object that has proven to be effective in the past. The relatives of a sick person may often try one or more home remedies for an illness, and after achieving little or no success with these may call in one of the four or five well-known healers who live in Isak. The failure of the use of leaves or simple spells to conteract the illness is taken as a sign that a spirit is involved and that the powerful *maripet* and spells of an experienced healer are needed. Today, the failure of the *guru* to remedy the illness may lead to the patient's relatives to turn to either the *mantri*, a local health worker, or to bring him into the hospital in Takengon, a two-hour trip over the mountains.

Prominent healers in Isak work in competition with one another and will admit to doing battle with the help of spirits in order to discredit each other. These competitions as well as the identities of the sorcerers involved remain private, and such *guru* battles are of dubious merit in the eyes of the community. No one will publicly admit to having brought on an illness, nor openly denounce a rival *guru*. But several of these healers pointed out to me that after they had cured a person of his disease by sending back the spirit to its source, a certain rival *guru* in Isak fell ill, presumably from the "returned" spirit.

It was only after I had worked with several of these healers for a year that they began to dictate their spells to me. However, once a *guru* began to teach me his knowledge, he did so with great enthusiasm and a concern that I learn it correctly. In two cases our relationship was a formal one of teacher to pupil, and I made a formal return presentation at the end of the teaching period in order that the magic might continue to be effective thereafter. Such a presentation also allows the pupil to teach the knowledge in turn to others, as a link in the chain of transmission.

In the case in question, a small girl had fallen ill, and efforts by her family to bring her out of the sickness had been to no avail. The *guru* determined that the illness had been caused by a spirit *(jin)* that had been sent by someone else and had entered the body of the girl. In this case he did not tell me who had done the sending, indeed claimed that he did not know and did not need to know, since the spells would send back the *jin* to whoever had sent it in the first place. The cure, then, had two objectives: to remove the spirit from the girl's body (exorcism) and to return it to its sender. These two objectives were attained by two separate segments of the ritual, held over two days.

The vehicle for the exorcism and the return of the *jin* was a small, wrinkled citrus called the *mungkur* (Malay: *limau purut*). This inedible, soapy-feeling fruit is one of the privileged instruments of communication via *maripet* because of its role at the time of Adam and Eve. Gayo say that the *mungkur* carried Adam's soul from heaven to Eden after the first soul had slipped out of Gabriel's grasp and become Satan. Shortly thereafter the fruit was called in once more to clean up the Garden after it had been despoiled by Adam and Eve. At that time it asked God that it be allowed to serve man as a cleanser, healer, and an exorciser of *jin*. God agreed to these three requests and planted the *mungkur* tree on the border of Eden, with one branch reaching into the garden, to cleanse and heal, and one reaching down toward Hell, to perform destructive acts when called upon to do so in the name of God (e.g., returning *jin* to their senders). This relation between man and the *mungkur* has continued until the present day.

In the first segment of the curing ritual the *mungkur* was used to receive the *jin* out of the patient's body and contain it until it could be sent away. This process of removing something from a person's body with an intermediary object is called *seduei*[27]; it was accomplished by waving the *mungkur* around the patient's head seven times, moving counterclockwise (a "loosening" direction), and counting backward from seven to one. This "reverse *seduei*" brings the *jin* out of the body and into the *mungkur*. The circling motion acts as a token *(isyarat)* of the intended effect, which is accomplished by *maripet*. Such external tokens "strengthen your own *maripet*"; they are an outward sign of an inner process of depiction and intention and they also guide that intention. While concentrating on the *mungkur's* appointed task, the healer recites to himself the following spell[28]:

> O citrus, king of the citruses, I know your origins. 'The Light of God' is the name of your soul, 'The Light of Muhammad' is the name of your body, *ruh batin* your real soul. . . .
>
> (followed by an invocation to the *mungkur* to take out the *jin*, and ending with)
>
> Because you came down to earth at the same time as he (the patient), and your original requests come due today and must be put to use.

The *seduei* spell accomplishes three things. First, it identifies the healer as someone who knows the origins, and thus the obligations, of the *mungkur*. This knowledge is in itself powerful, and it operates across the range of Gayo spells: knowing the origin of steel, for example (it was defeated and bent to make man's bones by Gabriel), gives one power over it, a power that was very useful, I am told, in war. Secondly, the spell names the *mungkur* as the Light of God and the Light of Muhammad. Knowledge of names is a second key to ritual power in Gayo spells. Moreover, whereas names are often semantically meaningless to Gayo (the names of steel, for example, are corruptions of Persian words that occur nowhere else in the culture), the two names given to the *mungkur* in the spell refer back to the initial relation of *batin* to *lahir* and, in doing so, index the peculiar power of the *mungkur* to cross that boundary. Finally, the fruit is designated as the outer form of a *ruh batin* and thus capable of acting as the sign of events taking place in the *batin* realm.

As the result of this combination of action, *maripet* and spell, the *mungkur* draws the spirit out of the patient's body and into itself where it can be dealt with in the second segment of the ritual. Names, knowledge, and *maripet* taken together draw on the myth of creation and the origin of the *mungkur* in order to create a field of magical efficacy wherein outward speech will have inward results.

On the following day the healer, the patient, her parents, and I continued the cure on the banks of the Jambo Ayer, the main river running through Isak. With the *jin* now inside the *mungkur*, the healer's task was to send it off, back to the person responsible for the illness in the first place.

Such a "returned *jin*" is said to bring about, at the very least, a period of discomfort for the sender and, possibly, to cause him serious illness. The inability to specify the precise results of the ritual helps the healer to report a positive verification, particularly in a society where most people are complaining of an ailment most of the time. I shall quote here the healer's own description of what he did in this part of the ritual:

> You put the *mungkur* on a rock. The rock is then *imaripeten* (imagined through concentration) to be the moon, the site of Heaven. In this way the *jin* will willingly stay inside the *mungkur* once it is put on the rock. The angels are then ordered to help keep in the *jin* . . .[here he read an appeal to the angels].

> Then you pick up a second rock which you imagine to be the sun. Your arm becomes "God's *alif*" (through *maripet*), and is raised ready to strike the *mungkur* with the second rock. Then the "black movement" *(gerak item)* is ordered to hit the *jin* inside the *mungkur*; the "black movement" is your arm's shadow. You are only the *lahir* that strikes the *lahir* of the citrus. You then say:

>> "O citrus, it is not you whom I hit but rather Iblis Syetan, full of hate and evil. It is not I who strike you, but rather your own conduct that strikes you."

> Then you strike and crush the *mungkur* with the rock and throw away the remains.

In the first segment of the ritual the *mungkur* was identified with the initial relation of *batin* to *lahir*, as the Light of God to the Light of Muhammad. The second segment, however, begins with the immediate, proximate end of the chain of being: on the one hand, the *lahir* of the healer, the *mungkur*, and the two rocks; on the other, their *batin* counterparts (the moon, the sun, the *jin*, and the healer's own shadow as the *gerak item*). Two parallel states of being are thus established. In one, the healer's arm brings down a rock to crush and squash the *mungkur*, and then tosses it away. In the other, shadow state, the shadow strikes the *jin* with the unbearably hot sun, sending it out of the *mungkur* and back to the original sender. At this level of the analysis, each outward object acts as a sign of a *batin* object upon which the intended action, conveyed by *maripet*, falls.

However, the *lahir* objects signify not only their proximate *batin* counterparts but also the hidden reality of God at the opposite end of the chain of manifestation. "God's *alif*" designates the sign of God in the world, his quality of immanence and empirical reality, but also the absolute Knowledge of things that God possesses, Ḥamzah's "the Known," and the *alif* opposed to the *mīm* in the Gayo cosmogony. At this point I would suggest that Ḥamzah's concept of *ma'rifat*, as "participation in God's knowledge of things," best describes the power invoked by the healer. God's *alif* ensures that the *jin* will be returned to whoever had sent it, by virtue of God's knowledge of the sender's actions. Recall the final line of the spell:

> It is not I who strike you, but rather your own conduct that strikes you.

and compare it to Ḥamzah's statement of God's immanence in the world, translating a Quranic verse (8:17) to make his point:

> It was not you who slew them (enemies of Muhammad) but God who slew them (Asrār:37).

It is this feature of *ma'rifat*, the realization of God's immanence in the world, that was retained in the Gayo *maripet*. Expressed in terms of the persistence of images, shadow was retained even while waves were discarded. The healer's arm does cast a shadow, which does the immediate *batin* deed, but this shadow is also the mere reflection of God's reality, just as Ḥamzah presented his own movements as the shadow of God's actions. The critical difference between the two systems is that the Gayo healer has extended the cycle of God—man—God one more half-turn, to bring the state of *maripet* back into the world.

For Ḥamzah, the lesson of verses such as the one cited above was that God is ever-present in the actions of individuals. The historical proof of this was to be found in God's intervention at crucial points in several battles between Muhammad's troops and the forces of the still-unrepentant Mekka. This closeness-in-action is likened by Ḥamzah in subsequent verses to the transparency of a clear wine in a fine glass, or, once again, to the waves and their ocean—in neither case is the one element distinguishable from the other. The point of *ma'rifat* is to become aware of this indistinguishability.

The point of *maripet*, however, is quite different. Knowledge of things in the world as God's signs—and Gayo often pointed out that this is the real meaning of *āyāt*, otherwise translated as verses of the Quran—allows one to manipulate them skillfully to bring about desired results. Desire has been added to gnosis, and the result is magic.

As a result of this shift in focus, the imagery of shadow and body that was developed in Ḥamzah's writings is reversed in the Gayo texts. Ḥamzah's central concern was the effectiveness of God in the world. His imagery of the shadow is thus as the worldly *(ẓāhir)* reflection of an inner reality: "Ḥamzah is but a shadow" of the real Mover, and the world "is but the shadow of the Known." In the Gayo myth and exegeses, however, the central concern is the effectiveness of man's outer actions on inner reality. Shadows are inner images of *lahir* bodies: the arm of the healer casts a shadow that effects change in the *batin* realm; God and Muhammad initially were shadows of their respective letters, the *alif* and *mīm*. A reversal of perspective has led to a reversal of imagery as well.

Conclusions: The Transformation of Religion

We can now return to the problem which began this paper, that of the role of Sufism in the spread of Islam in Indonesia. Johns and others have suggested that Sufi teachers made an otherwise arid and legalistic religion more appealing for communities in the archipelago by presenting a richer picture of man's relationship to God. The contemporary ethnographic evidence would suggest that conversion was fundamentally a process of transforming already existing cultural systems along Islamic lines. Let us retrace the outlines of this process.

Ḥamzah and other writers of the sixteenth and seventeenth centuries were faced with a religious tension between a naively pantheistic Sufism and a politically powerful orthodox reaction to it. Working from an earlier tradition of Islamic mysticism, these writers saw as their task to depict the closeness of man to God without obliterating the distinction between the two. Ontologically, the relationship was portrayed as the development of the world as gradual manifestation of God. Epistemologically, man was urged to know God by realizing how the world is as God knows it, closing the circle of creation through mystic realization. God took on the dual aspect of an ultimate *bāṭin* to the *ẓāhir* of the world and an ultimate Knower to be reached through *ma'rifat*.

This conceptual structure would have been fundamentally altered in a different cultural context. We know little about what this context might have been for the Gayo in the seventeenth century. The evidence of the Pasai chronicle cited earlier suggests that the Gayo existed as a distinct society during the period of initial Islamization, resisted conversion for some period thereafter, but by the early seventeenth century had converted to Islam, either as part of the contemporaneous expansion of the Acehnese empire or as the result of missionary activity before that time. Gayo spirit beliefs in this period would have contained certain elements found in contemporary Gayo and Malay cultures. The *pawang tue* and *sidang opat* included in the list of *bāṭin/lahir* relations presented above also appear in Malay culture, rendered in English by Skeat and others as the "spectral huntsman" and the "Prophet Tap" (from *sidang tetap*) (Skeat 1900:113–20, 238). Whatever the early structure of these elements may have been, they were developed within a transformation of the Sufi framework.

In the first aspect of this transformation the relation of God to the world was elaborated as a general relative pair, *baṭin/lahir*, signified by the letters *alif/mīm*, and generative of a chain of relations between elements, some of which had been part of a prior cultural logic and which were reinterpreted in terms of a new general theory of being. In the second moment of the transformation, the epistemological approach of man to God signified by *ma'rifat* was drawn on to create magical power. *Ma'rifat* was re-presented as vision, drawing its power from the presence of the Light of God and Muhammad in the individual. Furthermore, since *baṭin* had been elaborated into a substratum common to all sentient beings, *ma'rifat* was able to develop into a power of seeing and communicating in that realm. The earlier Sufi ideas were thereby brought into play in a Gayo field of magical efficacy.

6. *Entering the Bitter House: Spirit Worship and Conversion in West Sumba*

Janet Hoskins

*D*EFINITIONS OF RELIGION, both in anthropological writings and in popular usage, have long straddled a rather complex conceptual problem by speaking of the object of study as "a unified system of beliefs and practices," "an institution composed of both creeds and rites," or "a set of symbolic forms and acts which relate man to the ultimate conditions of his existence" (Durkheim 1915, Evans-Pritchard 1965, Bellah 1964). Although such two-in-one definitions do point out the need to integrate study of precept and practice, they beg the question of which of these terms is given cultural emphasis within the context where it is studied, and they give little attention to the ethnographic problem of how religion is perceived (if, indeed, it exists as a concept at all) by the people concerned. Recent efforts to redefine religion in terms of the more encompassing category of symbolic phenomena (Geertz 1966b) do not bring us any closer to solving this particular dilemma because they do not consider to what extent religious systems of symbolic action are also articulated in the more abstract form of doctrine. A key question to be explored in this paper is the relation between belief and practice, or between creed and ritual, as this relation is played out both in indigenous concepts concerning the domain of religion and in the conceptual shift in that domain implied by conversion.

Specifically, I shall examine the redefinition of Sumbanese spirit worship in the mode of a "religion," as the result of a dialogue with both the externally introduced creeds of the Christian church and the Indonesian nation state. On this rather isolated island in eastern Indonesia, we can see how the indigenous system of worship, initially defined as a system of practices and rules of ritual procedure, was later reinterpreted as a system of belief, reflecting a new self-consciousness and concern with doctrine. This process relates to two specific conceptual problems and to two historical moments in the transformation. The first conceptual problem is, as mentioned, the balance of belief and practice in the definition of religion; this investigation will, in fact, cause us to call into question the supposed universality of "belief" as a category of anthropological discourse. The second is how this relates to the more general process of religious rationalization as it has been described in a number of different contexts, in Indonesia and elsewhere. It will be argued that conversion is itself a category of "rationalized religion," expressed in terms of beliefs rather than practices, and thus true conversion is not really possible until the nature of the indigenous conceptual systems has undergone a substantial transformation.

The two historical moments examined in this study are stages in the dialogue between the Sumbanese and significant outside interlocutors. The first dialogue, which was primarily between indigenous spirit worship and the Christian church, occurred during the period of early contact and evangelical activity beginning in 1909. During this period, both the new faith and the traditional one were defined as systems of prohibitions—the one associated with a "bitter house" (entered only on the seventh day), the other with a "bitter mouth" (the ritual silence during planting). The second dialogue, which began in the period after independence and continued during the time of my fieldwork in 1979–1981, was formulated in response to the notion of religion presented by the new Indonesian state. In addition to trying to accommodate their traditional system of worship to notions of monotheism and the authority of the written text, the Sumbanese were encouraged to re-think earlier practices in terms of wider issues like moral discipline, community values, and the ethical distinction between good and evil. The rhetoric of nation-building and New Order pressures for ideological uniformity fostered a new search for the "underlying principles" of the metaphoric imagery of ritual language. Traditional elders were brought together at meetings which re-articulated specific local expressions in terms of abstract values—usually the values proposed as characteristic of Indonesian village democracy. But a further consequence of this re-articulation of belief was that some of these traditional figures also tried to formulate written accounts of spirit worship which would constitute a parallel system of belief rivaling the Christian Bible.

The terms of the dialogue themselves were altered by these historical changes: From a contrast in practices and ritual procedure, it came to be presented in terms of a rigidly demarcated domain of "religion" *(agama)*, which was opposed to categories such as "custom" *(adat)*, "culture" *(kebudayaan)* or "art" *(kesenian)*. I will try to explore here the extent to which these ideological shifts affected the conceptual world in which supposedly "traditional" spirit worship was conducted, as well as the conceptual world of those who were avowedly Christian converts. A degree of reflexivity and self-consciousness which was the product of these changes permitted Sumbanese thinkers to build a new world of relationships between ideas and actions within the old house of ancestral custom.

These questions of ideological transformations and modernization are particularly interesting to examine in the Sumbanese context because of the island's reputation for religious conservatism. In both the eastern and western regencies, roughly 80 percent of the population continue to identify themselves for census purposes as worshipers of the traditional deities. In fact, the Indonesian census cards used on Sumba have a special "sixth column" where—in addition to the officially recognized religions of Protestantism, Catholicism, Islam, Buddhism, and Hinduism—there is a category labeled *agama marapu. Marapu* is a Sumbanese term used to designate the invisible powers resident in the house and garden, village and ceremonial center, as well as deified ancestors who still take an interest in their human descendants. The fact that the indigenous system of spirit worship receives an official recognition on the census card and thus *de facto* acknowledgment provides a rare (and perhaps unique within Indonesia) testimony to the resilience of the traditional ways, despite missionary activities carried out by both the Dutch Reformed Church and the Catholic Church since the turn of the century. My account will proceed through an examination of the indigenous system, the period of early evangelization, the beginnings of conflict between the church and local ritual practitioners after independence, and recent reinterpretations which address the problem of how local spirit worship relates to the Indonesian government category of "religion." This short history of conversion and religious change in West Sumba, and particularly the district of Kodi where I did my fieldwork, should illuminate the more general problem of defining religion in terms of either belief or practice.[1]

The Indigenous System

As was the case in many traditional societies, the religious, political, and economic systems of the Sumbanese seem to have been initially undifferentiated. At the beginning of this century, the code of ritual etiquette and rules for interactions with supernatural beings or *marapu* also served to regulate marriage choices, the division of land, administrative prerogatives, and the exchange of livestock and cloth. Whenever a woman changed hands, whenever a promise was made, whenever a community shifted its residence, the ancestral spirits had to be informed and small offerings had to be made to them. They were the invisible witnesses of all important transactions, and they could hold the partners to their commitment by poisoning the very meat dedicated to them if such commitments were undertaken insincerely. The different domains of social life were so bound together that failure to follow the proper procedures in one domain (such as the performance of a burial rite) would have repercussions in another: failure of the crops, illness in the house, or destruction by fire or lightning. There was no separate "secular" realm where transactions could be carried out which did not concern the ancestral spirits. The relationship between the human community and the invisible world of the deities was one of complementarity and balance. In Sumbanese terms, both the human and the spirit entities were necessary to satisfy cultural ideas of completeness. In the dualistic terms familiar to peoples of the eastern end of the archipelago, they expressed this as the *pa panggapango* or "two-fold nature" of the universe, which was structured by oppositions between inside and outside, male and female, cultural order and natural vitality. *Pa panggapango* relationships did not involve totally discrete categories but rather the contrast between the two halves of the same whole. Major deities, addressed with a double name such as "Elder Mother, Ancient Father," or "Mother of the land, Father of the rivers," epitomized this synthesis of male and female principles and were portrayed as protective parents who defended and nourished their living offspring. This high degree of integration between elements in the system reinforced the dependency of each sphere upon another and made religion difficult to isolate from the social and spatial totality of life.

What was clearest in the traditional system was not its general principles or abstract ideas about the structure of the cosmos but, instead, the rules and procedures which had to be followed in order to deal with the various spirits. Although the universe was described as made up of six levels of land and seven levels of sky (*nomo ndani cana, pitu ndandi awango*), followers of the traditional system did not seem to have any clearly formulated cosmology, with the various deities neatly arranged on separate levels in a wedding-cake – like structure. Instead, they expressed the relations of hierarchy and deference among the various spirits in terms of the names used to address them and the speech etiquette needed. Only the less important spirits of the margins and peripheries could be called on directly, while all of the higher deities had to be approached through spirit deputies and intermediaries, in a complex chain of communication which eventually led back to the Creator. While not very directly involved in everyday events, this double-gendered power (called the Mother Binder of the Forelock, Father Creator of the Crown—*Inya wolo hungga, Bapa rawi lindu*) was the maker and sustainer of human life. Prayers were, however, never addressed to this highest power, who was often referred to as "the one whose namesake cannot be mentioned, the one whose name cannot be pronounced" (*nja pa taki camo, nja pa numa ngara*). Minor entreaties and pleas had to be brought first to the local guardians of the garden hamlet and clan village, the lower-ranking deities who then carried the message up to the Upperworld.

Although the Sumbanese have elaborate mythological traditions concerning the voyages of the ancestors or the history of a particular sacred object, they do not present a detailed vision of life in the Upperworld or of the origins of deities and spirits. These are presented as mysteries which cannot be resolved by ordinary men, and most Sumbanese would agree that it is not appropriate for them to ask such questions. Other familiar themes in Western religious discourse such as the ultimate destination of the soul, the origin of the human race, and the underlying reasons for suffering (beyond case-by-case instances of a given spirit's anger) are also largely ignored in the otherwise very rich body of Sumbanese oral literature. In effect, it appears that their attention was focused on maintaining a developed body of traditional practices—forms of offerings, intricate prayers in a poetic parallelistic ritual language, rules for feasting and building gravestones—but not on explicating them. A primary concern was for ritual correctness rather than cosmological speculation. Although it was important to determine the proper procedures to maintain smooth relations with the spirit world, explanation was always undertaken piecemeal, in terms of the particular context at hand, rather than formulated in the more abstract language of religious dogma or doctrine. Religious specialists saw their own role as repeating the sacred "words of the ancestors," preserved in the paired couplets of traditional verse, rather than devising their own interpretations. Even the oldest and most respected priests would assert that they were only "like small children, grasping the rope on a spinning top, who repeat the words of the forefathers, like little boys, holding onto the net for a discus toy, who stretch out the speech of the ancestors" (*enga pada pokato kalaiyo, kaco pa kadughu ngguni a patera ambu, enga pada lereho kadiyo, kaloro pa lamenda ngguni a paneghe nuhi*). Their role was not to assert or describe the order of the universe but simply to reenact the cosmic system in ritual procedures where the truth of the sacred mysteries would become evident. "We are just the lips told to pronounce, we are only the mouths told to speak" (*ghica pimoka a wiwi canggu tene, ghica pimoka a ghoba tanggu naggulo*), they would repeat humbly.

This attitude of humility and self-deprecation before the unknowable meant that spokesmen for the traditional system often chose to retreat into disclaimers whenever challenges were made to their system of worship. Since it would have been culturally inappropriate to claim a full under-standing of the workings of the *marapu*, they had to stubbornly insist that there was a logic underlying the rites dedicated to the ancestral deities but it lay beyond their own grasp. No single practitioner felt qualified to serve as a prophet of his own tradition, so that there was no formal articulation of doctrine to parallel the teachings of the Christian church.

Period of Early Evangelization

The period of early evangelization in West Sumba was marked by three characteristics: first, a time of recalcitrance and distrust of the first mission-aries; second, the gradual development of an attitude of tolerance, when the new faith was seen as operating in the separate sphere of government service; and third, a mutual redefinition of both systems in terms of a contrast of ritual practices. These three stages formed the necessary pre-amble to the following period, when the dialogue between the Christian church and the indigenous system assumed greater importance and where we can discern the beginnings of a shift from a definition of contrast in terms of practices to the articulation of these differences in terms of belief. Our best accounts of early missionary activity and the initial constitution of the indigenous system come from D. K. Wielenga, the first Dutch Re-formed minister sent to the island to begin systematic evangelization. Be-fore his arrival, there had also been a short-lived attempt by the Catholic Church to establish a Jesuit mission at Pakamandara, in the Laura district of West Sumba, which lasted only from 1889 to 1898. Despite some initial success in converting children who were recruited into Catholic schools, the mission was abandoned after repeated threats and security problems related to the slave trade and regional warfare. Wielenga established himself at the port town of Waingapu, East Sumba, in 1904, and also met with many initial difficulties: His home and church were burned down twice by hostile Sumbanese, and once he was so severely wounded that he had to return to Jakarta for medical treatment (Kapita 1976b:47). After 1907, however, the small church and clinic were finally stable enough for Dr. Wielenga to undertake a trip to the western part of the island to look for appropriate places to open a second mission station. He chose two sites, both of them close to the coast for security reasons and for easier access to supplies. One was at Kalangga, Memboro, along the north coast; the second was in the buildings at Pakamandara left behind from the first Catholic mission. There the first Protestant schools were established to educate the sons of local rulers and noblemen. Consistent with Dutch colonial policy at the time, these schools were seen as places to train future administrators, and admission was thus contingent on a hereditary claim to rank. The first teachers were Christian Indonesians brought from other islands (such as Roti, Savu or Ambon) which had already been more thoroughly evangelized. Soon the Dutch Church had opened up a number of other elementary schools in neighboring districts, so that by 1933 the island had seventy such village schools and four secondary schools, as well as a "theological college" near the original mission station in Karuni where promising students could continue their studies.

The Dutch Reformed Church organized its evangelical efforts through an extensive network of Sumbanese-born religious teachers (*guru injil*) who carried copies of the Malay Bible into the more distant regions. They were given some literacy training, a small salary, a prestigious link to the authority of the church; they were charged with reading selections of the Bible to local people and translating them into the vernacular. For two of the ten Sumbanese languages (Kambera in the east and Wayewa in the west), full translations of the Bible were made by the Dutch linguist Dr. Onvlee and his local assistants. But most Sumbanese linked the use of the written text and Malay language to the practice of Christian religion, and membership in the church came to be expected of anyone who continued his studies to the secondary level or beyond. Those who remained in the villages without any aspirations to government service did not feel especially attracted by the new faith, however. This attitude persists even today. An old woman told me that, though she favored education and had no reluctance at seeing her children and grandchildren enter the church, she felt it was not appropriate for herself: "If I held the Christian Bible in my hand, I would not be able to read it. So why should I hold it if it has no use to me?" In effect, mastery of Malay and of elementary reading skills were seen, however falsely, as the prerequisites for ritual correctness in the new Christian system.

Besides its reliance on the strange magic of book and pen, the Christian church was seen by the local population mainly in terms of the ritual requirement of church attendance on the seventh day of the week. As such, it was designated in local languages as the "house that one enters on the seventh day," or the *uma pa tama lodo pitu.* The seventh day was associated in the Christian system with a series of prohibitions which seemed to parallel the prohibitions of the tenth month of the Sumbanese calendar: It was not proper to sing or dance on Sundays, frivolous activities and feasting were frowned upon, and the violation of these taboos was shrouded with threats of supernatural sanctions. In local Sumbanese languages, the period of prohibitions which lasted through the planting season was designated as the "bitter months," because during these months the young seedlings and sprouts of the fields were declared "bitter" (*padu*) or inedible. In labeling the Christian church as the house that one entered on a day associated with prohibitions, they came to call it the "house of the bitter day," or simply "the bitter house" (*uma padu*). This label did not in itself indicate any hostility or suspicion of the church but was simply an acknowledgment that it had a different demarcation of sacred time. Thus, the Christian church was assumed to parallel the indigenous system in expressing its truths and mysteries indirectly, primarily through a series of rules and procedures which would provide its followers with a method for communicating with and appeasing the higher powers with which it was associated. The two were defined and presented as images of the same sort of conceptual system, expressed in alternate ways which, to the Sumbanese, were consistent with their earlier understanding of the cultural variation already visible between the different districts of the island.

The Catholic Church returned to Sumba in the 1930s and was also assimilated into the native category of the "bitter house." In fact, during its initial years, it seems to have been very difficult for most Sumbanese to distinguish between the two, since both were brought from overseas by European (usually Dutch or German) missionaries. Tensions did exist between leaders of the churches, however, as a result of the 1913 "Flores-Sumba Contract," by which the colonial government made Flores the designated territory of the Catholic Church and Sumba the designated territory of the Protestant Reformed Church (Luckas, n.d.:18). After establishing itself soundly in Flores, the Catholic Church later argued that its history of evangelization in Sumba was as long as that of the Reformed Church, so that it would be unfair to forbid them from "returning" to those converts left behind by the Jesuit departure in 1898. The government relented on this point in order to permit an expansion of the schools and hospitals on the island but maintained a policy that only the Protestants were given government subsidies and the official stamp of approval, since they were seen to be operating within the parameters of a privileged relation to the state.

On their return to the region, however, Catholic priests found that, of the hundreds of children who had been baptized by the nineteenth-century Jesuits, nearly all had returned to their traditional system of spirit worship and many were polygamously married. Most could only be traced through the Christian names which had been given to them on a village-wide basis: Thus, in 1889, sixty-five of the Sumbanese children baptized by Pater Schweits were named Maria, fifty-one Xaverius, thirteen Cecilia, and eighteen Alosius (Luckas, n.d.:11). In 1930, after a new church had been built in Waitabula, a crossroads settlement also in the Laura district, efforts were made to recruit those early "Catholics" back into the church with elaborate Christmas celebrations and the opening of new schools. The extension of social services, especially hospitals, came to be more important in the Catholic Church than it had been for the Dutch Reformed Church. By 1936, two large hospitals had been built (one in Waitabula, the second in Homba Karipit, in the westernmost Kodi district), as well as eleven schools, but expansion during the fifties, sixties, and seventies has now brought the number of Catholic schools to over forty (one-third as many as the Protestant schools). The different histories of the churches have produced different patterns of membership: The Catholics, who made up 6 percent of the population in 1980, are largely concentrated in "pockets" close to the mission stations. Aside from the employees of the schools and clinics, most of them seem to have joined the church in gratitude for the help—in the form of schooling or medical care—which was extended to them. The Catholic priests, who are still largely of Dutch or German extraction and cannot, as a rule, speak the local languages, remain attached to the mission buildings, traveling much less than native Protestant ministers. The Sumbanese describe the Catholic ritual pattern as one of attachment to a sacred center (compared with those traditional priests who rarely leave their own lineage cult houses), while the Protestant ritual pattern is one of active involvement in the outside world, particularly local administration and education. The 11 percent of the population who identify themselves as Protestants are thus much more evenly spread throughout the region and include schoolteachers in isolated villages as well as most town dwellers. The town and a few coastal ports also have small populations of Moslem traders (3 percent of the population), most of whom are descended from sailors and traders who came to the island from Ende three or four generations ago. Although there is no active effort to convert the local Sumbanese to Islam, some conversions do occur as the result of marriages between Moslems and the indigenous population.

The First Dialogue with the Church

The first period of dialogue with the Christian church, in both its Protestant and Catholic manifestations, was marked by the gradual emergence of points of difference, points of conflict, and points of convergence between the two systems. As Christian concepts of what constituted a "religion" became more salient, spokesmen for the integrity of local traditions began to tailor their responses to fit those areas. They also came to see joining the church or remaining outside it in terms of wider social strategies which defined one's relation to the powerful outside forces whose authority seemed to be represented, to the Sumbanese, in Christian iconography. The leaders of the local population differed on whether the new faith and the older system were basically complementary or antithetical. Civil servants, local politicians, and government officials usually took the position that the worship of *marapu* spirits could be seem as "custom" and was not in most cases incompatible with the teachings of the church. This allowed them to continue to attend local ceremonies and rituals, under the pretense that these were simply kinship obligations, while still claiming a prestigious alliance with the forces of progress and the Dutch Church. Ministers, traditional religious practitioners, and the few who had voluntarily left the church took the opposite position. They said that the major content of all traditional activities was their appeasement of spirit powers, so that such activities could not be engaged in without a sincere commitment to the religious principles that they embodied. The Dutch ministers expressed this position by forbidding many of their converts from participating in traditional rituals; the local religious practitioners paralleled this policy by refusing to allow Christian prayers in the context of the ancestral villages. But the hardening of these positions took some time, and it is important for us to try first to trace the trajectory of responses to these challenges and the new definition of religion which these events provoked.

The way in which this question was first articulated for the Sumbanese was in relation to the problem of defining church membership. The church was, in effect, the first voluntary organization that most people had ever encountered, and as such there was much initial ambiguity about whether baptism in itself was sufficient to define one as a Christian, or whether membership also required compliance with the rules and regular participation in church ritual. Since many of the initial converts were schoolchildren, baptism was often misrepresented as a prerequisite for school attendance and, especially, continuation to the secondary level. In fact, few people joined the church unless they had already made a commitment to schooling, government service, and relations with the outside world. The key symbols of the Christian world were the book and pen, instruments to record messages and communicate them to people far away. The Christian Bible could be carried far from one's own home, and it was possible to pray to Christian deities for their protection even when one was far from the traditional village altars of rock and tree. Worshipers of the local spirits had to return each year to the site of their ancestral stone graves bringing the first fruits of the harvest and new entreaties for continued health and prosperity. They could ask for a spirit companion to accompany them on a particular journey, but they could not bring the full protection of their forefathers to the town or university. The Christian, on the other hand, carried his altar with him, so to speak, in the Malay Bible, and it was a protective device as he entered another world, which ordered its appropriate worship schedule around the church gatherings on the seventh day.

Many traditional villagers who were not hostile to the church seem to have seen the relation of their spirit practices to those of the Dutch systems as geographically and socially separate spheres. The church provided a different type of spiritual protection and guidance appropriate for a different setting; thus, it merely extended the circle of ritually mediated interactions to include those that stretched beyond the island itself. As before, Kodi people who traveled outside their traditional domain made token invocations to the deities of the regions into which they ventured, so that their later ventures into Dutch schools, hospitals, and local administration followed this same pattern.

Beginnings of Conflict Between the Church and Local Practice

Points of conflict did not emerge until somewhat later, when the church leadership began to assert its authority to regulate other aspects of the lives of its converts. These differences, although some of them may have surfaced briefly during the first years of the church's evangelical activities, did not really become important until the period after independence.

Burial of the dead became the focus of a controversy which soon drew attention to different interpretations of the destination of the soul after death. For Christians, death itself was seen as the point of transition, the instant when an individual's soul was united with God and freed from its relations with family and kinsmen. For the traditional Sumbanese, on the other hand, the dead continued to be enmeshed in on-going social relations—and, in fact, they grew in a sense more powerful after death than before, because of their new ability to enforce supernatural sanctions and make demands on their descendants.

The church did not initially object to traditional burials in the ancestral villages which line the west coast of the island, but there was a general policy discouraging communication with the dead through divinations. Since dead parents and grandparents seemed to speak through the diviners only to demand new burials and the fulfillment of past ceremonial obligations, their requests were rarely consistent with Christian practice. Once a temporary church structure had been erected in the district capital of Bondo Kodi, some land was set aside to serve as the consecrated burial ground for converts. Schoolchildren were among the first to be buried there, as well as some older people who chose the site (according to local gossip) in order to avoid the high costs of sponsoring a traditional stone-dragging ceremony to erect a megalithic tomb in their own village. As the number of bodies resting beside the small Protestant church grew, however, traditional diviners began receiving messages that some of them were unhappy there.

In the early 1950s, those whose relatives had succeeded in erecting impressive stone graves now asked to be transferred to those more socially prestigious structures. Recurrent illnesses and hardship were explained by local ritual practitioners as a result of the failure to bury these dead in the traditionally appropriate way. Soon the whole lineage and extended kin network began to mobilize itself for the transfer. It would involve moving not only the bones of those buried on consecrated Christian ground, but also those of many younger wives, children, or poor relatives who had received an initial burial in the garden hamlets before stone graves were ready for them. Thus, to most Sumbanese, the Christian burial was treated as only a temporary resting place before an appropriate ancestral site was ready. To the church leadership, however, such a move was unacceptable. They saw it as taking persons committed during their lives to the Christian God and "stealing them back," so to speak, into paganism after their deaths. The church also refused to accept the evidence of traditional divination, in which the spirits concerned were questioned through the medium of a sacred spear and made to reply at the base of the central house pillar. Communications from the invisible world were, ironically, listened to more attentively by local government officials—who sought to avoid conflict by proposing a new use for the disputed land.

But, on this point, the church stood firm. In 1952, after a long and tumultuous debate about the value of the church leadership versus the importance of traditional obligations, a whole group of earlier converts seceded from the local Christian community. They refused to submit to these rules and insisted on returning the bones of their kinsmen to the ancestral village. As a result, they were banned from attending further services and were labeled apostates and betrayers of the true faith (Indonesian *murtad*). The division established at this time between those who had chosen the church and those who rejected it was to become very influential in shifting concepts of church membership from simple adherence to a series of practices (such as attendance at services, or reading from the Bible) to a commitment to the ideas and principles which underlay the belief system. It was through these conflicts concerning practices such as burial, marriage, or feasting that—gradually—differences in doctrine and wider interpretations of the universe began to emerge.

Other points of difference and conflict between the church and traditional practice were less dramatic: The most common reason for someone to be suspended from church membership and forbidden from taking communion was his violation of the polygamy rules. This was in fact fairly common, since the church strategy of evangelization had been to focus on local leaders, encouraging them to draw in their friends and family at large group baptisms. Polygamy, although practiced by only 10 to 15 percent of the grown men, was the mark of a prominent social figure. As a consequence, the rate of polygamy after a generation or so of Protestant evangelizing was actually higher among baptized Christians than among the unconverted. The church, while continuing to condemn the practice, allowed the guilty husbands to continue to attend Sunday worship service but not to take communion. Their multiple wives and children, however, were still welcomed to drink the blood and eat the body of Christ.

When the Catholic Church established itself in the 1930s in Homba Karipit, the German priests were initially stricter than the Dutch ministers had been, barring both men and women from the communion table if they were polygamously married. But a recent re-evaluation of such rules by both churches allows for a final forgiving of the "sin of love" for those older men who agreed not to marry again and seemed in any case rather close to death. This leniency brought back many prominent elders into the Christian community shortly before they died and encouraged their descendants to hope for a final forgiveness themselves.

Participation at feasts, curing ceremonies, and divinations was also initially condemned by the leadership of both churches—but later accommodated under the rubric of family and community obligations. The early Dutch missionaries forbade their converts from eating meat dedicated to the *marapu* spirits, reasoning that this would discourage attendance at feasts with a religious purpose. But since even marriage, funerals, and naming ceremonies required a ceremonial invocation before the slaughter, in fact there was almost no killing of pigs and buffalo which was not preceded by requests for protection from the *marapu*. Christian converts, many of them important people who relished the honors conferred on them by participation in the ceremonial system, objected that the church had in effect forbidden them from eating meat at all. Within a few years, this prohibition was revised to a rule that prayers of consecration could not be pronounced by anyone who called himself a Christian. The rule was absurdly easy to follow, since almost all ceremonial ritual speech was recited by specialists called in from the outside. The emphasis on message bearers and mediated communication with the spirits in the traditional system meant that no man was allowed to be a priest in his own house.

This last regulation also called into question the criteria which could be used to distinguish a Christian ceremony from a *marapu* rite, particularly in the light of the increasingly common practice of holding family rituals with elements of both systems: a Bible reading and Christian blessing in Malay, followed by an invocation in Kodinese ritual language by a traditional elder. A compromise between the two systems was established by dedicating a share of the sacrificial meat to each set of deities, then dividing it among the guests according to their professed religious preference. When policemen or government soldiers from other islands were present, Islamic prayers and sacrifices were also included—creating "feasts of syncretism" which combined elements of all three ritual systems. The local church leadership finally concluded that it was better to accept such mixed ceremonies with an attitude of tolerance, because they provided a forum for people of different persuasions to hear the words of the Christian minister and perhaps ultimately come to benefit from them.

Christian prayer meetings (*pembacaan*, literally "readings") and "thanksgiving celebrations" (*pengucapan syukur*) were often performed on the same occasions as those which traditionally had required the mediation of *marapu* spirits: at times of illness, transitions (shifting residence, marriage, or adoption of new lineage members) or hardship (after a fire, lightning bolt, or crop failure). These meetings were a response, of course, to occasions where there was a perceived need for spiritual counsel and assistance, and they generally followed the same pattern as the night-long *marapu* ceremonies: explanation of the reasons for the gathering, a dedication of the animals to be slaughtered, and the distribution and consumption of food. The only marked differences were in the languages used—Biblical Malay in one, traditional ritual language in the other—and the replacement of the sacred authority of the central housepost with that of the Christian Gospel. But while questions could be asked directly of the housepost in traditional divination rites, with yes or no answers provided by whether or not the diviner's thumb reached its mark at the tip of the spear, the answers provided by the Bible were most enigmatic.

One informant once told me that the major difference between Christian and *marapu* beliefs was that *marapu* divination provided a much more specific explanation of human suffering and misfortune. Although Christian preachers interpreted illness and calamities as signs of divine displeasure, they could not pinpoint either the precise cause or the proper procedures to appease the high god. *Marapu* divinations, on the other hand, allowed the victims to identify the angry spirits by name, to ascertain the chain of events which led to their misfortune, and to find ways to mediate the problem in ritual fashion. For Christians, however, speculation could continue to run wild concerning the causes of an affliction, and there was no way for the human community to know if the ritual compensation offered was an adequate one.

It was this moral and philosophical uncertainty which local religious teachers presented as the consequence of original sin—an obligation to repent and suffer, even without full knowledge of the reasons for this suffering, because of a burden of wrongdoing inherited from the ancestors. Since in a traditional Sumbanese context the living are always laden down with obligations to perform ceremonies and arrange burials because of their duties to preceding generations, the idea of original sin as unfulfilled obligation was both compelling and convincing. Many local religious teachers recast the Biblical story of Adam and Eve in a Sumbanese idiom to expand on its explanatory value for village people. A common consequence was the local perception that the sins of Adam and Eve lay not in eating the forbidden fruit *per se*, but in failing to perform the necessary rites to "cool down" the land on which the apple tree stood, bringing it within the circle of ancestral protection and making its fruit consumable. The sons of Adam were thus condemned to suffer not because of their thirst for knowledge but because of their disrespect for ritual boundaries and the category of bitter foods.

The distinction that the Sumbanese themselves make between the spirits associated with the inner, social world of ancestral authority and cultural control and the outer nature spirits of the wild also came to be reinterpreted in Christian terms. Early religious teachers, trying to convince the people to stop worshiping the invisible spirit powers that they designated as *marapu*, took to translating the term as *setan*. Although early linguist-missionaries and Dutch administrators understood that the term was in fact very complex and multivalent (cf. Lambooy 1937), this gloss was the one most frequently used in village evangelizing. It identified all the members of a complex cosmological structure with malicious, capricious spirits at the periphery, similar to the Moslem *jinn*. When spokesmen for the traditional system protested that spirit beliefs also provided a bulwark for community discipline and personal morality, some members of the church leadership began to distinguish between the "good *marapu*," which they identified as the ancestors (Indonesian *nenek moyang*, Kodi *ambu nuhi*), and the "bad *marapu*" or *setan*, who were the autochthonous inhabitants of the forests and fields, seashore and ocean. The spirits of the natural surroundings were seen as innately evil; those of the culturally established village centers were presented as good. This application of a moralistic, ethical character to an opposition which was in fact rooted in complementary principles of control versus vitality proved difficult to uphold. In effect, death and suffering were much more often attributed to sanctions imposed by the ancestors than to the nefarious activities of the wild spirits. The supposed *setan* of the forests and fields were often the only helpmates and companions that a man had on a long journey, and—in return for small sacrifices—they could also provide him with medicines and magical powers.

As a result, the Christian criticism of *marapu* beliefs stigmatized the worship of only a certain class of spirits—significantly, that class of spirits most often addressed in a private, individualistic context. It allowed the church to take a much more tolerant attitude toward those large-scale rituals which would tend to come to the attention of its leadership and to condemn only those smaller-scale interactions which were harder to observe.

Christian prayers were also often granted a magical efficacy similar to that of the ritual language associated with the ancestral centers. They were used to ward off wild spirits and extend the protection of the social community to newly planted crops. In this respect, the church identified itself with ritual land, bringing it within the realm of cultural control. There seems to have been a deliberate effort to identify the Christian message with the nurturing, protective attitude of the ancestral spirits (addressed as Great Mother, Great Father) rather than the more volatile spirits of the outside. Their power was often compared in Sumbanese ritual language to the flow of cooling waters, and for this reason Dr. Onvlee, the Dutch linguist who translated the Gospel into Sumbanese languages, chose to call it the *li'i amarainginga*, the cooling or salutary words.

He realized, however, the different semantic weight assigned to such terms in Sumbanese languages and has written an interesting and extended account of his difficulties in finding an appropriate translation for the Christian concept of the "holy" (Onvlee 1938). Beginning with efforts to assimilate Christian teachings to metaphorical representations of fertility, prosperity, and well-being (the "cool waters" which are beseeched in traditional prayers to cure fevers), he finally concluded that they could just as properly be identified with the opposing pole: the "hot," spiritually charged category of those objects where divine power was supposed to dwell—such as sacred houses, village altars, or the divination pillar. In effect, the Sumbanese ritual oscillation between hot and cold, bitter and bland, is part of cyclical movement of spiritual energies which does not fit well into Christian theology. It assumes that the bitter, hot, or prohibited nature of certain things is only a transitory stage through which they must pass before they are brought inside the circle of ancestral control where these energies are harnessed to social tasks.

Dr. Onvlee's discussion of the possibilities that he considered further supports an interpretation of the early dialogue between the church and local spirit worshipers as one phrased in terms of practices rather than beliefs: His search for a parallel to the Christian concept of "holy" was only to take him further astray by leading him to other terms which express their degree of "holiness" by their social distance from everyday life. Thus, he also tried using the East Sumbanese word *maliling*, which refers to the stipulations of respect and avoidance which must be observed between specific kin categories, such as father-in-law and daughter-in-law. In suggesting that the church could be described as a *uma maliling* or "respected, separate house," he was associating it with prohibitions and restrictions that made it suitable only to slaves. It is in the *uma maliling* that many of the most sacred objects of the lineage are stored: spirit drums, gold crests, heirloom water urns, and magical weapons obtained from overseas trade. These objects are seen as full of so much spiritual energy that ordinary men are afraid to handle them and will not risk their lives to live near them. Only slaves, who were generally considered "socially dead," are expendable enough to guard this sacred patrimony. Needless to say, it was not very helpful to the cause of village evangelization to define the church as a building so sacred that ordinary men might fear to gather inside it. The West Sumbanese term, *uma padu* or "bitter house," had something of the same sense but was less stringent in its prohibitions, so that the church leadership eventually resigned itself to this label. But its daily use only underlines the irony that Onvlee himself observed in discussing the problem of translation; any term which seemed, in local terms, to define the Christian ritual center as important and sacred also served to set it apart from ordinary life and limit the number of converts who dared to cross its threshold.

Recent Reinterpretations

Although kept at a distance from many of the more remote villages, the influence of the Christian church was still pervasive. Prominent social figures found it convenient to represent themselves as converts of the "bitter house" in the context of government service or administrative office, even if they continued to participate in and sponsor traditional ceremonies at home. Children who were taught by Christian teachers in the elementary schools brought home pamphlets of Bible stories in the vernacular and told their elders about Indonesian nationalism and the principles of the state ideology or Panca Sila. Recent years have seen the conscious rearticulation and reformulation of traditional concepts to fit these models—sometimes in a reflective and insightful fashion, at other times in a largely mechanical justification of prevailing ideologies in traditional terms. Among the latter are several efforts by government officials to "translate" the Panca Sila into Sumbanese ritual language in order to demonstrate Suharto's assertion that Indonesia's "indigenous political system" was one of social democracy. Published statements are largely limited to collections of homilies extolling the value of cooperation, tolerance, unity, and mutual aid (Dapawole 1969), but they have proven an important propaganda tool in gaining the confidence and support of more isolated regions. Sumbanese in general delight in verbal prowess and seem to have been greatly pleased at the sound of the modernizing program of the nation state affirmed in words that imply a mythical ancestral mandate.

More interesting for our own purposes are the reformulations of traditional belief in the mold of "religion," as defined in contrast to the Christian system. The task of writing down the tenets of the traditional system of spirit worship and translating them into Indonesian has now been taken up by several local schoolteachers, most of them Christian converts themselves. Their goals are usually to show the coherence and complexity of local beliefs and to compare them to the principles and events of the Bible. A few, however, who have strayed away from the church and come within the new category of apostates or exiles from the Christian community, have taken a different tack: They have made a record of a number of traditional beliefs and practices in the hopes of constructing a parallel system, which could rival the Bible and present an alternative explanation of the same religious problems. It is to these formulations, and specifically to a rather incredible document produced by one of my best informants, that I now turn.

Maru Mahemba, the author of this piece, was a well-respected and articulate older man who had served both as a Protestant village evangelist and as a traditional ritual speaker. Although he had joined the church in the early 1930s when it was just beginning to spread into the interior, he seems to have been more intrigued with exploring another conceptual system than convinced of its superiority to the traditional system. He worked for a while at convincing others to join him in the church because of the opportunities that it offered for education and participation in the local government, but in 1952 he was among the leaders of those who seceded from the church after the dispute concerning the burial of the dead. At the time of my fieldwork, he proved himself an excellent and very dedicated informant precisely because his concern with traditional spirit worship was not only intellectual but also personal. This "book" of some fifteen pages was compiled on his own and dictated to one of his sons, a schoolteacher, in response to several discussions that he had had with me about the relative status of *marapu* beliefs and Christian dogma. Both its form and its style of argument were shaped by and in opposition to the teachings of the church which he had learned as a young man. But its originality lies in its insights into the differences between the two systems and its attempts to justify the *marapu* system on its own terms.

The book began with a conventional listing of seven classes of spirits in the hierarchy of invisible powers that are worshiped—moving from the Creator, on to the first man and woman, the house deity, clan deity, spirits or mortality, spirits resident in ancestral tombstones, and finally the spirits of the dead in general. It then went on to observe that "the *marapu* religion also has things which are forbidden, as every religion has its prohibitions." Following the Kodi fondness for the sacred number seven, seven "commandments" were then presented, translating into traditional ritual language Biblical-like injunctions against stealing, killing, or deceiving one's kinsmen. The obligations to feed the deities and make offerings at certain points of the year were first negatively phrased (highlighting the dangers of presenting them with impure food), then positively presented in an outline of each household's calendrical obligations. Sensitive to Christian criticisms of the rhetoric of traditional offerings, Maru Mahemba then went on to explain the conventions of humility and apparent deception used in addressing the spirits:

> It is said that the marapu religion[2] is a false one, because it is founded on lies which are contained in its prayers. It is true that the words which are pronounced in the invocations are not always the most direct way of saying things, so that this can be said to be deceiving the spirits—but it is not possible to deceive those fellow men who watch and help in the distribution of ritual foods. It is true . . . even after a large harvest, one must still say that the bag of white rice where the cacatows play is not full, and the sack of foreign rice which we lift up does not burst at the brim. It is true that even if one has many horses and buffalo, dogs and pigs, one must still say in prayers that the pigs are not plentiful and the chickens are not abundant. . . . It is true that, in our religion, even when a man's belly is full and he has had enough to drink, he will still say "I haven't enough rice to fill my belly and I haven't drunk enough water to satisfy my thirst." But this is so because in our religion you cannot make yourself appear rich in front of the spirits; you should not brag or show off before them; you should not display your accomplishments before them. The marapu religion teaches you instead to make yourself seem poor to those above, to belittle yourself in their direction and to make all that you do appear insignificant.

The contradiction that he is addressing here is only partly that of the conventions of pleading with the ancestors and asking them for additional blessings of fertility and prosperity. It is also the crucial difference between the Christian model of personal prayer, with its idiosyncratic formulations of desires and the formalized collective mode of traditional prayer. What Dutch ministers interpreted as deception and lying was integrated into traditional religious practice as an etiquette of respect and deference, defining the appropriate attitudes of men toward the deities and stressing that worldly wealth can never rival the mythological opulence and abundance of the heavenly rain kingdom.

The book continued its elaboration of traditional numerology with an account of the seven holes in the human body that correspond to seven classes of spirits, and of the seven stages of ceremonial accomplishment in the feasting system. Social stratification was represented on the model of the human hand, moving from the thumb which stood for the prominent leader to the little finger for the slave. Rules regulating the performance of certain ceremonies to shift residence or to call back the souls of those who have died a bad death were also included. Then, the argument became once again a defense of traditional practice against Christian criticism, beginning with a plea for tolerance:

> According to the words of the marapu religion, all of the religions in this earth go in only one direction and have only one as the Binder of the Forelock and the Creator of the Crown.[3] Just as there is not a single river that does not flow into the seas, in the same way there is not a single religion on this earth which does not flow in the direction of the Binder of the Forelock and Creator of the Crown. In other words, there is only one mountain that we all wish to climb. There are many paths which one can go up to reach the top. There is not one of those paths which will not take you to the mountain top. They all lead in the same direction, and they all can be followed. In the same way, all of the religions on this earth: They are just different paths which are followed, and they all go back to the Binder of the Forelock and the Creator of the Crown.
>
> The problem with the marapu religion, according to some people who have converted to other religions, is that it was never written down—because schools did not come to Sumba or to Kodi for a long time. There is only the language that was passed down (through the generations) and the speech that was sewn up (into couplets). And it is because of this that the marapu religion has not disappeared up to this day.

The justification then presented for the validity and persistence of *marapu* beliefs took the form of an extended history of some of the oldest Kodi villages and a genealogy which traced the inhabitants of certain lineage houses back seventeen generations. Obviously modeled on Biblical genealogies, this evidence was marshaled to demonstrate the historical depth of Kodi tradition and the fact that the links to the time of the ancestral mandate were still intact. It was also used in what emerged as a defense of the oral transmission of knowledge as the binding force uniting all of the Kodinese in a common form of worship:

> The marapu religion was called a false religion by the followers of the other paths because nothing was written down. This is true, say the followers of the marapu path. . . . But, inspite of that, the sixteen founders of our seven original clans are still known to us, and the seventeen generations which link us back to that time. This is because of what we learned from the language passed down and the speech sewn up, the words of the ancestors which are preserved for us in the marapu religion. To this day, it is these words which bind the children of the ship at the Lyali source and the children of the water at Nyapu.[4]

We should note that the very eloquence of this plea for understanding and tolerance of *marapu* practice is couched with reference to universal principles introduced from the outside. Where this book is in fact an accurate reflection of *marapu* worship is in its cataloging of ritual practices and the rules for conducting ceremonies correctly. Where it ventures into a direct dialogue with Christian critics is precisely where it takes the form of an apologia in their terms, an effort to abstract dogmas and principles from a mode of symbolic action whose logic was until then basically implicit. This text, dictated in the vernacular to a literate son who rarely had the occasion to write in his own mother tongue, is thus a thoroughly anomalous mixture of appeals to a universalist theology and defenses of particularistic practice. It transforms the nature of traditional worship in trying to interpret it, arguing that only by assimilating *marapu* ritual to the categories of Christian belief can its true value be recognized or articulated.

Conclusions

The preceding discussion has concerned the effects of external forces on the Sumbanese conceptual system which concerns spirit worship and, specifically, how these ideas have been transformed in relation to the dilemma of conversion. The two "moments" in the process of religious change that we examined in some detail were structured as dialogues with two different external forces. During the period of early evangelization, the main interlocutor was the Christian church, and both the new church and the traditional system were defined in opposition to each other by contrasting ritual practices. In the period after independence, the most significant outside interlocutor changed from the Dutch Reformed Church to the new Indonesian state, and a new consciousness of ideology and abstract principles of belief caused a redefinition of traditional spirit belief in the mode of a religion. The holistic indigenous world of ritual practices related to the ancestral spirits was broken up into the officially defined domains of custom *(adat)*, art *(kesenian)*, and—for only those aspects of traditional life which seemed most closely to parallel the concerns of the Christian church—religion.

The relevance of this discussion to scholarly considerations of the definition of religion lies in the light that it sheds on the problem of the articulation of such systems in terms of belief or practices. In effect, the historical changes described here detail a gradual shift from a focus on ritual action and standards of correctness to one on religious dogma and belief. But it is useful to bear in mind Rodney Needham's injunction that the notion of belief is much too slippery to be relied upon for comparative analysis. After an extended discussion of the term in ordinary English usage and ethnographic reports, he concludes that "belief is not a discernible experience, it does not constitute a natural resemblance among men, and it does not belong to the common behavior of mankind" (Needham 1972:188). Although I tend to agree with him on this point, it is my conviction that the conditions which create and define systems of belief can be more rigorously specified.

Needham is correct in stating that when other peoples are said to "believe" in spirits or more general religious principles, it is not at all clear what kind of idea or state of mind is being ascribed to them. In fact, the terms used to translate the concept of belief into other languages often define a very different semantic field. As Needham himself notes, the Kodinese term *waingo*, for instance, refers to the general sense of use (as of a tool or weapon) or wear (as a loincloth or sarong), but does not designate an emotional or existential commitment to worship. Instead, it reflects a pragmatic evaluation of which deities or spirits can be "of use" in a given context—and is thus oriented toward ritual practice rather than the formulation of an abstract creed. Most peoples, it would seem, do not feel a need to express their own system of worship in terms of abstract principles as long as they can practice them more or less in isolation. Thus, the traditional Sumbanese, although aware of regional variations in ritual practice, did not feel that it was necessary to formulate these continuities and differences in more general terms. It was only in the historical situation of religious pluralism—specifically, the encounter with the Christian church and, later, the Indonesian government concept of monotheistic religion— that they began to move toward greater conceptual generalization, tighter formal integration of the system, and a more explicit sense of doctrine.

This process has, of course, had its analogues all over the world. Within Indonesia, it has been eloquently documented by Clifford Geertz in his writings on "internal conversion" in Bali (Geertz 1964). An increased awareness of cultural differences leads to the "rationalization" of religious concepts, as they are gradually lifted "above" or "outside" the concrete details of ordinary life and integrated into systems which at least aim at more logical coherence. As Geertz himself has noted, traditional religions are characterized by "a multitude of very concretely defined and only loosely ordered sacred entities, an untidy collection of fussy ritual acts and vivid animistic images, which are able to involve themselves in an independent, segmental, and immediate manner with almost any sort of actual event" (Geertz 1973:172). Their resolutions of the problem of meaning attack each instance piecemeal and opportunistically, "employing one or another weapon chosen, on grounds of symbolic appropriateness, from their cluttered arsenal of myth and magic" (Geertz 1973:172). It is obvious that the indigenous system of spirit worship of the Sumbanese operated within what Max Weber would have called the still "enchanted world" of magical realism and had not yet come to terms with formulations concerning the universal and inherent qualities of human existence.

The transformation of Sumbanese conceptual systems which led them to focus more on belief and less on practice was also directly related to the introduction of the new domain of "religion" within social life. These terms only emerged in the course of the dialogue carried on with these outside forces, as they were established by colonial contact and the problem of the translation of cultures. Wilfred Cantwell Smith (1962) has shown how the notions of "religion" and "belief" did not become fully demarcated in the Western tradition until after the Enlightenment, when the clash of religious wars and the intellectual ideal of "natural reason" provided an appropriate environment to begin labeling systems of ideas in terms of "isms." He argues that the early Roman concept of *religio* entailed notions of piety and obligation in many ways similar to Sumbanese concepts of ceremonial obligation but did not yet present the notion of religion as an object of speculative interest. The labeling of world religions such as Buddhism and Hinduism did not begin until these systems were seen as ideologies shaped by historical factors, whose coherence as a system had to be interpreted to a Western audience.

It is my argument that "belief" itself is a category of rationalized religions, and it is only after ritual practices and many of their underlying principles have been fully articulated in terms of belief that conversion is possible. Nock (1933) distinguished between "conversion" and "adhesion" in his study of religious change. Conversion, in his use of the term, requires "a re-orientation of the soul...a turning which implies a consciousness that a great change is involved," whereas adhesion proposes "no definite crossing of religious frontiers" and "the acceptance of new worships as useful supplements and not substitutes" (Nock 1933:7). Conversion is usually limited to the prophetic religions which are exclusive and require unqualified commitment. Adhesion, on the other hand, is typical of traditions which more pragmatically seek "to satisfy a number of natural needs, to set a seal on the stages by which a life is marked, and to ensure the proper working of the natural processes and sources of supply on which its continuance depends" (Nock 1933:8). Since, traditionally, Sumbanese villagers were born into the cult of the ancestors and did not ever consciously choose it or examine its basic tenets, they could be described as adherents of the earlier system of spirit worship. When the Christian church was first introduced, it was often interpreted as simply operating in a different sphere from the traditional cult, and as a result many prominent Sumbanese seem to have wanted to "adhere" to its prestige and power, without ever consciously "converting" in the full sense of the term. As long as the two systems were seen as complementary modes of ritual action, one attuned to ancestral villages, the other to the world of education and government service, there was no full articulation of their religious content or doctrine. It was only in the period after independence, when conflict over ritual procedure (such as the reburial of the dead) led to the realization of differences in belief, that the church began to insist on actual conversion or else exclusion from the Christian community. So the dialogue that we have been discussing produced first an awareness of logical inconsistencies and abstract principles, and only later the potential for a fully conscious conversion. It was a dialogue conducted initially in terms of notions of ritual correctness and contrasting practices and only later reformulated in the "religious" vocabulary of doctrine and belief.

7. Mortuary Tourism in Tana Toraja

Toby Alice Volkman

*J*N 1906, FOLLOWING SEVERAL CENTURIES OF NEGLECT, Dutch troops invaded the highlands of southern Sulawesi, the southwestern petal of the orchid-shaped island that lies northeast of Bali. After months of resistance led by a highland big-man named Pong Tiku, local defenses finally crumbled before the superior military forces of the Dutch. This marked a turning point in the history of the mountain province, later to be known as Tana Toraja, and its inhabitants, who, several decades later, were to call themselves Toraja.[1]

Although Dutch moves were but part of a larger shift in policy aimed at establishing control in the remotest enclaves of the archipelago, the Sulawesi highlanders held an added interest for the colonizers. Unlike the Bugis and the Makassarese, the two major ethnic groups that lived along the coasts and throughout the fertile lowlands, the highlanders had not adopted Islam when it penetrated the island in the seventeenth century. The Dutch, recently embittered by a protracted war with the Islamic Acehnese of northern Sumatra, saw in the highland heathens a potential Christian island in a widening sea of Islam (Bigalke 1981:138).

The task of winning native hearts and minds to Christianity fell to the Calvinist Dutch Reformed Mission. The first missionaries, well-trained in the Netherlands in linguistics and ethnography, were soon impressed by the strength of indigenous ritual. That this ritual might be an obstacle to success became clear in the early stages of Mission activity. That it might be a vehicle, if carefully manipulated, through which the Mission could achieve its goals became clear only later. After ten years in the highlands, the Mission devised a strategy whereby at least some forms of ritual could be tolerated and slowly Christianized. Ironically, the Mission's own solution allowed ritual form to flourish regardless of religious conversion. Indeed, ritual did persist throughout the colonial and post-colonial eras. By the 1970s, stimulated by out-migration and widespread economic and social changes, ritual began to undergo expansion, coinciding with and fueled in part by the rise of international tourism. Through a curious reversal, Western Europeans began to come to Tana Toraja in search of rituals and animist religion. The reversal, however, is far from total. Here, by focusing on several key interactions between Toraja and the West, I would like to suggest that Toraja ritual is, as it has been historically, an arena for competing claims to power, not only within the culture but also in relation to the outsider. Today, relationships with the outsider take more subtle forms than in colonial days, as modern tourists seek certain kinds of ritual, in exchange for cash and the honor of their presence. The Toraja reciprocate by creating representations, or signs of Toraja culture.

Ritual and the Mission

The Dutch became embroiled in ritual politics almost immediately. Indeed, this would have been difficult to avoid, for ritual in the highlands pervaded all activities and structured all seasons of the year. Rituals of the east, the rising run, the rising smoke, were celebrations of planting, of fertility, of abundance. Following the rice harvest were rituals of the west, the setting sun, descending smoke—these were the funerals. Whatever the rituals, all entailed the sacrifice of water buffalo, pigs, and/or chickens, and the offering of some portion to the spirits and ancestors. The remainder of the meat was distributed in complex ways among the living.

Through prestations of live animals and distribution of their meat, an elaborate net of debts was tied and knotted, a net that was passed on to succeeding generations and that shaped each person's social universe. Such debts, of course, also shaped an economic universe, and it frequently happened that precious rice land was pawned in order to obtain buffalo needed for a relative's funeral. In this way, land changed hands and new debts and obligations were created. Funerals were particularly consequential when it came to wealth, for inheritance of land was based on the number of buffalo sacrificed by each heir of the deceased. Thus, within the family, funerals could be fiercely competitive affairs, as siblings fought for land; and beyond the family they were equally competitive, as individuals sought to demonstrate the strength of their respective followings, reflected in the number and status of their guests. For the guests as well, these rituals were competitive, as every gift of meat contained a message about status.

In giving meat to many, a ritual sponsor simultaneously affirmed his wealth and his power; the two were inseparable in traditional Toraja thought. Wealth was regarded as a sign of spiritual blessing which underpinned worldly authority. Rich men, *to sugi'*, were also big-men, *to kapua*. Not surprisingly, the structure of the ritual system itself upheld a hierarchy of wealth and power, in which the type and scale of ritual permitted was strictly limited by a person's inherited status, as noble, commoner, or slave.

That ritual was a field for internal political manipulations (or "the politics of meat," as the Toraja sometimes say) was quickly recognized by A. A. van de Loosdrecht, the first Dutch missionary to arrive in the Toraja highlands in 1913.[2] Reasonably enough, van de Loosdrecht decided that a proper Mission strategy would be to convert the nobility first, in hopes that the waves of conversion from below would follow. To this end, he avoided the question of ritual, upon which the nobility clearly depended. He also avoided all questions of theology. Instead he focused on building schools to educate the children of the elite. Unfortunately, his tactic of rounding up truant schoolchildren and sending their parents off to jail did not endear him to his target converts. Eventually he grew annoyed with the nobility's resistance to his efforts and changed his tune, appealing (or so he thought) to lower status groups. He began to criticize the inequities whereby a few were wealthy and many others owned no land at all, and he began to blame the situation on the death feast, observing (correctly) that people often pawned and lost their land as a result of ritual obligations. But van de Loosdrecht's attacks on death rituals (and, at the same time, on cockfights) touched a vital nerve in Toraja culture. Rumors spread throughout the countryside that he conspired with the Governor to abolish the death feast altogether. This was the last straw, and in 1917 a group of big-men surrounded the missionary's house, ending his short career with a sharpened bamboo spear thrust through his heart.

Van de Loosdrecht's murder marked the end of the Dutch frontal assault on ritual practices in the highlands. By 1923, the Mission had established a "Commission" which held meetings with Christian Toraja and cautiously tackled the thorny question of ritual (Bigalke 1981:221). As a consequence of these meetings, the Mission developed a simple but decisive strategy— namely, the formal separation of custom from religion, as two complementary but distinct domains.

This solution, of course, was not based on an indigenous distinction. To the highlanders, there was but one word that encompassed both realms: the word was *aluk*, and it touched the whole realm of what was believed in, said, or done. *Aluk* was the wisdom of the ancestors; it was a multitude of spirits, on mountaintops or streams or house rafters; it was the words spoken by ritual priests; the number of buffalo slaughtered; the countless prohibitions (actually 7,777) that informed daily life; *aluk* was the proper performance of each ceremony. All this and more was part of *aluk*, until the Dutch succeeded in severing it in two, so that *aluk* came to mean "religion," while the neutral Indonesian word *adat* was adopted to mean "custom." One no longer had to renounce everything traditional in order to convert, since *adat*, being secular and social, was deemed acceptable. Only *aluk*, by definition heathen and religious, was threatening to the church and would be forbidden.

The problem, of course, became to distinguish which was what, and this the missionaries' council did by a series of pronouncements. Almost all smoke-rising or fertility rites were declared heathen and hence banned to Christians. Rites of death, on the other hand, were acceptable with revisions. The slaughter of water buffalo, for example, could be seen as a perfectly secular custom (at least if you were Dutch). It was all right, according to the Mission, for Christian converts to cut buffalo and share the meat among the living, but it was not all right to present the spirits with a portion of the sacrifice. The Mission thus attacked the fundamental premise underlying sacrifice and stated this emphatically in a decree: "You must not think that the dead takes the slaughtered animals with him . . . [since] these animals do not have an eternal soul. What is thus slaughtered is not the provisions . . . of the dead, but is offered merely as a repast to the guests and the family" (quoted in Bigalke 1981:224).

In attempting to regulate what the Toraja "must not think" and to reduce ritual to sociology, the Dutch laid the foundations whereby ritual practices might flourish while the beliefs in which they were once embedded waned. Thanks to the Mission dichotomy which split *aluk*, Toraja could join the Christian church, attend Sunday services, and still do almost everything their neighbors did, as long as they did not believe in the spirit world toward which much of any ritual was directed. In spite of this possibility, only 10 percent of the population did convert in Dutch times. By 1965, however, fifteen years after Indonesian independence, about 40 percent of the Toraja were registered as Christian.

New Possibilities

It was not until after 1965 that several factors converged to make ritual performance a problematic issue for the Toraja. The spread of education since independence had produced a generation of literate, worldly, and restless youth from all social strata: no longer just the elite but also commoners and former slaves had access to schools and the possibilities they suggested. These possibilities went unrealized until the late 1960s, when peace returned to South Sulawesi after years of Islamic rebellion, and when multinational corporations began to invest in oil and timber in neighboring Kalimantan, offering jobs. In this period, unprecedented waves of out-migration occurred from Tana Toraja to Kalimantan. Many migrants were young men and women who saw little future in their home-land, where they were poor, landless, or of low status. Almost all were Christian, or quickly became so in their new context. Yet, because of the compelling power of the traditional symbols of shame and honor, and of "the politics of meat," these migrants returned to Tana Toraja to hold big funerals for their families, converting their wages into symbolic capital on the ritual field. The effect of this ritual rush was to undermine status boundaries, boundaries that in the past had been affirmed and reinforced by ritual. Rituals, both Christian and *aluk*, backed by great infusions of new wealth, underwent "inflation" (*inflasi*).[3]

Because, traditionally, wealth was associated with nobility and spiritual blessing and was inseparable from worldly power, the new migration and consequent ritual expansion from below posed a clear threat to the old elite. This elite responded in a variety of ways. Some held even bigger rituals of their own, upping the ante. Others began to question the pro-priety of lavish sacrifice, arguing that the Toraja could not afford to squan-der their limited resources in the modern, developing world. Others, more steeped in *aluk*, pointed out that nouveaux riches' funerals ignored the fundamental *aluk* tenets that divided humanity into nobles, commoners, and slaves. Both modernist and *aluk* critics often said that ritual was "no longer authentic" or "original" *(tidak asli lagi)* or, in Toraja, that it was no longer "true" *(tongan)*. Usually, this meant that either ritual form was no longer perfect or complete (mistakes were made, sequences or roles omit-ted, ritual speech inadequate) or that the ritual itself no longer corre-sponded to the old social order that it had once legitimized. Hierarchy had been infected by chaos, in both ritual and social life.

Thus, through a quirk of history, tourism was launched in Tana Toraja at precisely the moment when the Toraja, for reasons of their own, had begun to argue over "authenticity" and over the proper place and scale of ritual in the modern world. In 1969, Indonesia's Five Year Plan called for the development of tourism as a major source of foreign exchange. In 1971, the first fifty foreign tourists visited the highlands and attended an *aluk* ritual in honor of the ancestors. Five years later, in 1976, 12,000 tourists visited the regency (Crystal 1977:111). By 1984 the figure had stabilized at about 10,000. The majority of tourists were from Western Europe: France, Germany, Switzerland, the Netherlands. To the Toraja, however, all are called by the same name: *Balanda,* or Dutchmen.

The return of the *Balanda,* oddly, is motivated by the desire to see funerals, which is usually what tourists do on their one-day visits to the area. The irony that Europeans are now fascinated with what their colonial forebears not long ago condemned is compounded by the fact that tourists often see Christian ceremonies, although they may not know it. Guides and travel agencies understand quite well that tourists prefer the old religion; after all, it would be hard to entice travelers with the lure of "authentic Dutch Calvinist" funerals. So the media have billed Toraja as a more pristine alternative to Bali, "far from the tourist path" (*Boston Globe* 1981), the "land of the heavenly kings" (Discovery Tours, 1981 – 82). One newspaper even offered tips on how to behave respectfully at funerals (*San Francisco Chronicle* 1981). In television documentaries, travel writing, and cruise brochures, Toraja inevitably appears as a haven for an ancient tribal religion and a unique, flourishing cult of the dead (Adams 1984).

Although the tourist concern for "unspoiled" or "authentic" religion has not affected remote villages, where tourism has not yet penetrated, the tourists' goals have had an impact on more urban Toraja, particularly those involved with the church or politics. Among the more vocal critics of ritual that cater to tourist audiences are some leading members of the Toraja Church (Gereja Toraja), the direct descendant of the original Mission. Their opposition crystallized in 1978 around a much-publicized Christian death feast, which cost US $225,000 and drew high government officials from Jakarta as well as tourists (*Tempo* 1978, *Kompas* 1978). Christian critics charged that this and other funerals, fundamentally religious events, were being turned into spectacles. In insisting on the religious nature of the death feast, these Christians are attempting to reverse the Mission process of neutralizing and secularizing ritual.

The tourist concern with authenticity has also played a role in a recent movement to revitalize and rationalize *aluk,* the supporters of which argue that a revived *aluk* must go hand in hand with tourism and cultural pride. It is probably not sheer coincidence that in 1969, the year of the Five Year Plan promoting tourism, Jakarta's Ministry of Religion granted legitimate status to Toraja religion. *Aluk* now has an official name, *aluk to dolo,* or "the *aluk* of the ancestors," and an official status as a sect of Hindu Dharma (a category that includes Balinese religion as well). A leading figure in this movement is a prominent politician who once headed the regency's tourism office and who now lobbies to have *aluk* taught in local schools, to publish theological texts, and to send wood-carvers and ritual priests for further study in Bali.

The *Balanda* connection has thus come full circle. Originally thwarted in their efforts to convert the Toraja, the Dutch learned how to subvert ritual and maintain their Mission by disengaging custom from conviction. They also learned how not to tamper with existing hierarchies of power, although the schools they built set the stage for dramatic transformations after their departure. Once the Dutch left the scene, both Christianity and mass education mushroomed. The social upheavals predicted by observers such as Raymond Kennedy (1953) did not, however, occur until the 1970s, when new wealth came pouring into the highlands. Into these upheavals returned the generic Dutch—the Western tourists—now delighting in the very paganism the colonial Dutch had tried to squelch.

The Toraja might seem at last to hold the center stage, honored by the presence of their former colonizers' descendants, guests from distant lands. As in Java, guests signify a host's superior status, and the great distances traveled reflect a great drawing power. But the balance of power is ambiguous. For, although the Toraja are flattered hosts, what their wealthy and leisured guests wish to receive is often not the same as what the Toraja have or wish to give. Toraja who have tried for years to make their rituals acceptably modern, modest, or Christian now find that success entails the re-creation of the appearance of the old. This is not known to the *Balanda*, however, who seek ritual reflections of an ancient cult that is truly "other," events in which belief and action are truly joined.

Toraja rituals are not usually staged for tourists, but neither are they without self-consciousness. Roadside markers point to ancestral effigy and grave sites, declaiming boldly in a language that is no language OBYEK TURIS (tourist object), neither English, nor Indonesian, nor Toraja. Even the new airstrip, built to accommodate the influx of flying Dutchmen and other foreigners, echoes the slightly mocking, illusory quality of the Toraja-tourist relation. Surely those who christened it Pong Tiku Airport must have remembered that Pong Tiku, Toraja's greatest hero, fiercely fought off the Dutch invaders in 1906, squirting hot pepper juice and firing cannonballs from his mountain fortress. With this ambivalent welcome, cameras and cash in hand, the tourists come.

Part Two
The Politics
of *Agama*

8. Religions in Dialogue: The Construction of an Indonesian Minority Religion

Jane Monnig Atkinson

EFINING RELIGION HAS LONG BEEN A FASHIONABLE EXERCISE for anthropologists, but recently there has been a lull in this endeavor.[1] No comparable ennui had set in among pagans, Muslims, and Christians in eastern Sulawesi, Indonesia, when I did fieldwork in the mid-1970s. The Wana, an upland swidden population, have been engaged in a debate among themselves, with their neighbors, and with government authorities over what constitutes a religion. Their ongoing dialogue not only illuminates issues of culture and politics in contemporary Indonesia but also suggests some ways to refocus the anthropological study of religion.

"The invention of culture" is the label Wagner (1981[1975]:8 – 9ff.) applies to the ethnographic enterprise to argue that the "culture" that emerges in anthropological investigation is a creation or artifice of the interpretive encounter. Wagner's point is that anthropologists necessarily draw on their own past understandings and experience to interpret the understandings and experience of their informants. If this process applies to the study of culture in general, it is certainly even more applicable to the study of topical subfields that anthropologists carve out in the course of research. We duly "invent" dimensions of a society to study—economic, political, legal, and religious—based on analogies with familiar constructs in our own experience. The anthropological study of religion is conducted in this fashion. Drawing on models of religion in Western society, anthropologists have proceeded to invent religious systems for people who claim to have a religion, as well as for people who do not. Liberal "inventiveness" in this regard has allowed anthropologists to establish insightful comparisons between cultural systems that seem to be quite different.

The "invention of religion" involves at least three strands of discourse. Most obvious is the exchange between field researcher and informants. But each side to this exchange is informed, in turn, by prior understandings and experience. For the anthropologist, constructs of religion derive not only from the academic subculture but from Western culture more generally. Indeed, anthropological understandings of religion are predicated on, and are part of, a series of ideologically charged debates involving Western theology, science, morality, and much more. For this reason, the anthropologist's extension of the label of religion to populations that some in Western society view as pagans in need of conversion is hardly a neutral application of value-free terminology.[2] From the nineteenth-century evolutionist who imagined religion would be superseded eventually by science, to the twentieth-century cultural relativist combating Western ethnocentrism, to the politically sensitive researcher of recent years who opposes cultural hegemony—all speak to their own society when they speak about other societies.

Just as the anthropologist's understandings of religion are embedded in an ongoing discourse, so too the informants' side of the exchange is shaped by prior understandings. In the case of a population familiar with world religions, informants will bring an articulated concept of religion to that exchange. Among peoples who may traditionally lack a cultural category matching Western notions of religion, anthropologists are prepared to tap an abundant literature on "traditional," "primitive," or (worse) "natural religions" to organize *our* understandings of *their* experience with the "sacred," the "numinous," or the "superhuman." But among the prior understandings informants bring to the ethnographic encounter may very well be historical experience with religion as an attribute of other social groups. To cite Wagner (1981:10), the "invention of culture" is not the privilege of anthropologists alone; it transpires "whenever and wherever some 'alien' or 'foreign' set of conventions is brought into relation with one's own." Historically, the introduction of new sets of religious conventions has prompted precisely the kind of cultural inventiveness Wagner describes in most of the world's societies. The spread of proselyting world faiths across the globe has meant that even among the unconverted a self-conscious definition of religion is likely to have emerged.

The case I present here illustrates a process of this kind at work among one Indonesian ethnic minority. I entered the field prepared to study religion, defined in the broadest sense as a cultural system through which fundamental problems of existence are expressed and managed (C. Geertz 1966b). Given what I knew about cultures of the area and the type of society I intended to study, it seemed likely that religion in this case would focus heavily on illness and healing. What startled me was the discovery that my informants held a fairly elaborate notion of religion quite unlike the one I had attributed to them. Whereas for me Wana shamanism represented religion par excellence, religion for my informants was most clearly phrased in talk of diet and government. The disparity seemed curious. Certainly there is anthropological precedent for proceeding according to analytical categories different from the folk categories of one's informants. But it seemed important to pursue just what my informants meant by *agama*, a term that they used for "religion" (in the national language Bahasa Indonesia) and that they had clearly borrowed from their Muslim and Christian neighbors. To do so entailed both an examination of Indonesian assumptions about *agama* and a consideration of Wana relations to the dominant society. What I found among the Wana was an innovative response to a set of conventions that I gloss here as Indonesia's "civil religion." By creating for themselves a sense of what a "religion" is, based on their transactions with the dominant society, they have constructed for themselves a "religion" distinct from that of their Muslim and Christian neighbors. Although the use of religion as an ethnic marker is well documented in the literature, the Wana Case calls for recognition of the fact that the significance of "religion" for the ethnic groups on either side of a cultural boundary may not be self-evident or the same. It is essential to go beyond a functional explanation of religion's intra-ethnic use and ask how religion is culturally constituted in an inter-ethnic exchange.

The Ethnographic Setting

The Wana are a population of swidden farmers, numbering about 5,000, who inhabit a mountainous interior region of eastern Sulawesi Tengah (Central Sulawesi). They are related most closely to the Pamona-speaking peoples of the Poso area, best known as the Bare'e-speaking Toraja, studied by the missionary-ethnographers N. Adriani and A. C. Kruyt (1950[1912]). In a pattern familiar in other parts of insular Southeast Asia (H. Geertz 1963, Koentjaraningrat 1975), the upland population has remained largely pagan with only recent Christian incursions, whereas the coastal and foothill population is heavily Islamic. That characterization is, however, a trifle too static, given the Wana's mobility. Many have moved back and forth between interior and foothill settlements, shifting both residence and religious affiliation. My own work was done primarily in pagan communities in the interior. Among my informants were some individuals who had at one time or another converted to Islam or Christianity but had let that affiliation lapse. Wana have lived in a religiously pluralistic setting for well over a century. Their familiarity with Islam goes back many generations (Kruyt 1930, Atkinson 1979:30–35); by contrast, Christianity is a newer import, the arrival of which my informants dated at World War II.

The Dutch administration that ruled the area from the first decade of the twentieth century until its ouster after World War II did not enact a policy of religious conversion in the area. One Dutch missionary was briefly in residence near the southern coast of the Wana area in a settlement called Lemo, but my older informants asserted that the Dutch must have had a religion like their own, namely, traditional practices that they did not force on others. Since Indonesian independence, a new element has been added to the religious picture not only in the Wana area but in the nation at large. Borrowing a phrase from Bellah (1970), I term this new element Indonesia's "civil religion," a theistic doctrine that legitimates the country's nationalist enterprise.

Indonesian Civil Religion

To understand how Wana ideas about religion have been formulated in response to nationalist Indonesian religious principles, it is necessary to examine Indonesian civil religion itself as the outcome of a series of intercultural exchanges. *Agama*, or a variant thereof, is the word for "religion" in most if not all Indonesian languages, including the national language Bahasa Indonesia. This word, and I dare say the concept itself, is a comparatively recent addition to cultures of the archipelago. The Bahasa Indonesian word *agama* derives from the Sanskrit term *agama* which itself connotes something quite different from the current meanings of *agama* for Indonesians or "religion" for Westerners. As Chaudhuri (1979:19) notes, Indian civilization traditionally lacked a word for "religion" as understood in the West today.

The Sanskrit word *agama* has two meanings significant to the discussion here. First, it refers to " 'a traditional precept, doctrine, body of precepts, collection of such doctrines'; in short, 'anything handed down and fixed by tradition' " (Gonda 1973[1952]:499). Second, it is a name given to the scriptures associated with the sectarian worship of Siva, Sakti, and Vishnu (Sarma 1953:7–10). The word entered the Indonesian archipelago some-time during the early centuries of this millennium when the western islands of what is now Indonesia came to serve as critical nodes of a trade network that linked China, India, and the Near East. It was once assumed by Western scholars that the early kingdoms that developed in the western part of the archipelago were simply Indian colonies, but scholars now argue convincingly that these polities arose as indigenous communities prospered through their active participation in overseas trade[3] As local elites arose in coastal kingdoms such as Srivijaya in Sumatera and in interior kingdoms such as Mataram in Java, they adopted Indian symbols of power and prestige to express their preeminence. Thus, such features as an Indic model of divine kingship, Sanskrit literature, Hindu-Buddhist philosophy, and Indian scholars and administrators became royal trappings of these early Indonesian kingdoms. In contrast to analysts who have focused primarily on the manipulation of Indic symbols for purposes of political legitimation, McKinley (1979:317) argues that Hindu-Buddhist symbolism in this period had significance beyond the power-driven statesmanship of individual leaders. Indeed, he argues, it involved a fundamental transformation of cosmology and world view for the populations of the early kingdoms.

Determining just what *agama* meant for the early kingdoms generally and for different social strata in particular is beyond the scope of this essay. What I underscore here is the fact that during this period an awareness of something called *agama*, an attribute of a rich and foreign civilization, took hold in insular Southeast Asia. *Agama*, one may speculate, had associations with literacy—a new and probably impressive introduction. It was associated as well with power, wealth, sophistication, and a tradition beyond the experience of local peoples.

The use of the word *agama* in Old Javanese was still general enough "to apply to a body of customary law or a Dharma-book and to religious or moral traditions" (Gonda 1973:499). It had not yet taken on the qualities that Indonesians today associate with that word. The Indonesian discourse of *agama* bears the imprints of at least two more alien "sets of conventions," namely, Islam and Christianity. Proponents of both faiths (and their variants) have adopted the term *agama* and, I suggest, have shaped some new associations for it while reinforcing others. Islam, like Hindu-Buddhist traditions, entered the archipelago along trade routes with the West. Although it had been present in pockets of Sumatra for several centuries before, Islam rapidly spread throughout coastal populations of the island chain from the fifteenth century onward. As "People of the Book," its representatives no doubt reinforced the association of *agama* with learning and literacy. As long-distance traders, they probably consolidated notions of *agama* as an attribute of both the wealthy and the cosmopolitan. The link between *agama* and political authority may have been strengthened as local rulers found conversion to be politically and economically expedient. In addition, I suspect that Middle Eastern monotheism, the imperative of salvation, and the importance of a religious "brotherhood" may also have impressed themselves upon local interpretations of *agama* at the time.

Christianity, introduced in different forms principally by the Portuguese in the sixteenth century and later by the Dutch, probably carried similar associations of *agama* with foreign powers, economic and political privilege, internationalism, and education. Certainly an emphasis on a Supreme Deity and the absolute necessity of conversion to a foreign doctrine were features of both Christianity and Islam in Indonesia. Another association that may trace its roots to the latter period of Dutch rule is a link between *agama* and societal progress. Steeped in Calvinism and Eurocentric notions of advancement, the Dutch fostered a sense of Indonesian "backwardness" that progressive-minded nationalists, in turn, have projected on traditional-minded minorities in the country today. How religion and progress are associated in modern Indonesian culture is explored below. That Islam as well as Christianity can serve as a marker of social progress testifies to the ideological independence maintained by Muslim Indonesians during three centuries of colonial rule.

When Indonesia gained independence from the Netherlands after World War II, most of the ex-colony was at least nominally Muslim. Exceptions were Christian converts in Eastern Indonesia in pro-Dutch pockets, such as the Moluccas and North Sulawesi, and in upland interior areas such as the Batak region of Sumatera and the Toraja area of Central Sulawesi, where Christian missionaries had made inroads among non-Islamic populations. The island of Bali, with its distinctive form of Hinduism, remained a holdout against both Islam and Christianity. And Indonesia's Chinese minority (those who had not or were not later to convert to Christianity), lacking the tidy doctrinal delimiters of the Near Eastern religions, were labeled Confucianists when a label was necessary (and in the post-independence period, as we shall see, it came to be so).

When Indonesian independence was declared, Sukarno, the country's first president, proposed a set of five principles, known as the Pancasila, to serve as the foundation of Indonesian nationhood. These principles include belief in one God *(bertuhan)*, nationalism, humanitarianism, social justice, and democracy. Monotheism is linked here with the central political and social values of the state. The use of the Indonesian term *bertuhan* for "monotheism" is deliberate and revealing. Tuhan is the Indonesian word for God. By specifying belief in Tuhan rather than Allah (the Islamic word for God), the doctrine of monotheism is skillfully phrased to allow for religious diversity in a nation whose population is predominantly Islamic. Symbolically, the appeal of the Pancasila is compelling. Like the Indonesian motto "Unity in diversity" *(bhinneka tunggal ika)* it proposes a consensus—belief in God—that transcends the ethnic and religious differences in a population as large and varied as this one.

The religious charter of Indonesia is a cultural model for inclusiveness; in a profound way, however, its application is exclusive. The policy covers only world religions presumed to be monotheistic, to possess a written scripture, and to transcend ethnic boundaries.[4] The official model of religion reveals its Near Eastern roots. Although Hinduism and Buddhism are officially recognized as religions in Indonesia, it is an open secret that they do so by conforming in public dialogue to a Middle Eastern monotheism. As for the "pagan" customs of Indonesia's ethnic minorities—cultural systems that anthropologists are likely to label as traditional religions—these are pointedly excluded under official policy. In practice, however, two groups, the Toraja of Southern Sulawesi and the Dayak of South Kalimantan, have gained official recognition of their indigenous practices as religions, in part by stressing their Hindu-like elements.[5]

The reason for the omission of traditional pagan ways from the Indonesian roster of legitimate religions is clear. Implicit in the concept of *agama* are notions of progress, modernization, and adherence to nationalist goals. Populations regarded as ignorant, backward, or indifferent to the nationalist vision are people who de facto lack a religion. *Agama* is a dividing line that sets off the mass of peasants and urban dwellers, on the one side, from small traditional communities (weakly integrated into the national economic and political system), on the other. People who lack an officially recognized religion are referred to in Indonesian as *orang yang belum beragama* ("people who do not yet possess a religion"). The negative *belum* is significant here, for it implies that conversion to a recognized religion is inevitable. Whereas one would not assert that someone of one ethnic group was "not yet" a member of another ethnic group or that a member of one recognized religion was "not yet" a member of another religion, there is an imperative for a person who has not converted to an officially approved religion to do so.

Indonesia's policy on religion contains different messages for different sectors of society. To members of world religions it guarantees religious freedom and tolerance under the aegis of national unity and purpose. To those who would hold onto traditional ways, it is highly censorious, linking the absence of a recognized religion to a rejection of nationalism. In his book *The Sacred Canopy*, Berger (1967:39), discussing the use of religion for purposes of political legitimation, observes that "to go against the order of society as religiously legitimated...is to make a compact with the primeval forces of darkness." In line with Berger's observation, I heard assertions by members of world religions in Central Sulawesi that such people as the pagan Wana who fail to convert to a world religion are likely to turn Communist. Their claims are buttressed by cultural logic and national history. Before the purges of the mid-1960s, the Communist movement in Java did align itself with the local folk tradition, or *abangan* (C. Geertz 1960, 1972a 1973a). In Central Sulawesi there is no such link between pagans and Communists, nor has there ever been one. In contrast to the Javanese situation, the Wana are not proletarian; that they should develop on their own into a politically subversive element is exceedingly unlikely. But according to the logic of many nationalists, pagan Wana and atheistic Communists share two features: a rejection of religion and opposition to the government. In an ideological sense, both are out of control from the standpoint of the centralized state.

To sum up the discussion so far, the concept of religion is a central one in Indonesian nationalism. Religious freedom is guaranteed to all Indonesian citizens who subscribe to an officially sanctioned faith. Indigenous systems of ritual and cosmology are, with several notable exceptions, denied the status of a religion. Religion is associated in nationalist culture with education, cosmopolitan orientation, sophistication, and progress. The Wana are largely nonliterate, unable to speak the national language, physically remote from government authority, and live at a subsistence level using swidden agriculture. In short, they represent the antithesis of nationalist goals and aspirations. Wana failings to match the ideal of a progressive citizenry are summed up for nationalist Indonesians in the fact that the Wana lack a religion. In cultural terms, conversion then offers a solution to social "backwardness."

The Construction of Wana Religion

Given the centrality of *agama* in official concerns about populations like the Wana, it is perhaps not surprising that, for Wana, religion carries ominous political overtones, and religious conversion is a highly charged political matter. They recognize that nationalist Indonesians interpret the lack of a religion as a refusal to be governed. For the many Wana who have paid taxes, performed government labor, registered as village residents, and even attended school or held village office during Dutch times and the early years of the Indonesian Republic, to be regarded as ungoverned people because they lack a religion is a source of great consternation.[6] Suspicions as to the import of government religious policy are heightened by historical awareness of bloody conflicts over religion elsewhere in Sulawesi. Muslims and Christians fuel pagan anxieties with predictions of religious wars, impending cataclysm, and a widely anticipated end to the world. Finally, rumors and claims by local proselytes to the effect that unconverted Wana face maiming, bombing, the certain death make *agama* a worrisome matter indeed. All these factors contribute to a general apprehension that there is a menacing agenda behind all the concern of others for Wana religious status. For example, current during the mid-1970s was the widely held suspicion among the Wana that the rationale for holding national elections was to determine the relative strength of the Muslim and Christian followings in Indonesia. When everyone has converted to one religion or the other, some claimed, then a general war would erupt between religious groups in the nation. For the Wana, Indonesian religious policy is viewed not as a strategy for national unification but rather as a divisive instrument promoting social and cosmic upheaval. For a people whose own traditional consensus is threatened by pressures to divide allegiance between two poorly understood foreign doctrines, this impression is not unfounded.

In response to assertions that they lack a religion, Wana who have not converted to a world religion contend that they do, in fact, have a religion—one they label with terms that self-consciously reflect the view of the dominant society such as *agama taawa agama* ("a religion not yet a religion") and *agama kapir* (from the Arabic *kaffir*, or "heathen"). To characterize their religion, they draw on models of world religions familiar to them and construct an image of what religion is supposed to be. On the surface, Wana religion appears to be a catalog of ethnic markers, customs that distinguish pagan Wana from Christian Mori and Muslim Buginese. Diet, burial practices, healing measures, farming rituals, sexual propriety, ritual specialization, and government ties are among the features Wana cite as religious issues.

Only one of these features is considered here as illustration. First and foremost, religion to the Wana connotes dietary practices, no doubt owing to the profound effect of Islamic food prohibitions on a boar-hunting hill population. The Wana term for Muslim is instructive in this regard. Muslims are known as *tau puasa* ("fasting people"), in reference to their practices of abstinence, particularly during the fasting month of Ramadan.[7]

The Islamic ban on pork has spawned a rich assortment of Wana stories that seek to explain the affinity between Muslims and that forbidden animal. For example, one prominent story locates the origin of the pork taboo in a contest between two brothers, one pagan and the other Muslim. The Muslim put his two children in a chest, then challenged his elder brother to guess the contents. The brother guessed that the chest contained two pigs. Because seniority confers authority in Wana thought, when the chest was opened two pigs bounded forth. The event upheld the position of the elder brother and serves as a charter in Wana eyes for the Muslim ban on eating pork, literally the flesh of the Muslim brother's children. [8]

If Islam is the religion that prohibits all manner of foods, it follows in the Wana view that Wana religion is one that expressly declares all food edible, especially pork and rat, which are both viewed as highly unclean by Muslims. Christianity is said to be like the Wana religion in that it prohibits no foods.

The link between food and religion is underscored by the special significance both carry for physical health and well-being. Religions, like the foods they permit or prohibit, are thought to affect the body. A religion can agree or disagree with a person, something indicated by one's state of health. Many who de-convert cite chronic sickness or sores as reasons to return to their traditional ways. Susceptibility to a particular religion's effects on the body is determined largely by one's heredity. Thus, a Bugis whose ancestors scorned pork in generations past is understandably wise to adhere to traditional dietary prohibitions, whereas it is ludicrous and unseemly for a Wana descended from a long line of pork-eaters to do the same.

Since food is such an important issue to Muslims, diet is taken to be both the way in and the way out of Islam. According to Wana, one may de-convert from Islam by wringing the neck of a chicken and then eating its flesh, in violation of Muslim butchering techniques—a procedure referred to as *maluba*. [9] Christianity, which lacks dietary laws, offers no such easy exit. Once one has converted to Christianity, simply resuming pagan ways is regarded as ritually dangerous and a cause of illness. Informants proposed that a sensible course for avoiding risk to one's health would be to convert from Christianity to Islam, then wring the neck of a chicken and eat it in order to return safely to one's original pagan state.

The example of diet illustrates the way in which Wana derive the defining features of religion by identifying those Islamic and Christian practices that contrast sharply with their own traditional ways. It follows that the corresponding Wana practices must be key elements in *agama* Wana. But Wana also go beyond a catalog of customs in their side of the dialogue.

They rework themes of the dominant culture, such as monotheism, rewards in the afterlife, and the historical succession of religions, to uphold their own lifeways and values in the face of a relentless challenge by the encroaching nation-state.

Let us take, for example, the issue of monotheism, which is the sine qua non of Indonesian civil religion. Wana have conformed to this principle nicely. Aspects of their cosmology assign roles to two lords, one above the earth and one below, and certain healing rites involve a vengeful lord of thunder. These dual roles are subsumed by the unmarked Wana term Pue (Owner or Lord), the creator and overseer of the world. It may very well be that Pue has assumed a more central place in Wana discourse as a result of contact with Muslims and Christians.[10] My informants uniformly asserted that there is but one God, the same God for all religions. Although *agama* Wana clearly reinforces Wana ethnic identity, the concept of God is not used to distinguish Wana as unique but rather to unite them with the rest of humankind.

It would appear, then, that *agama* Wana is quite in accord with Indonesian civil religion in making God a symbol of human unity rather than of ethnic division. This stance puts neighboring Muslims and Christians in the position of denying that the Wana God is the same as their own, just as they deny that Wana rituals have the same validity as their own. The sophistication of Wana response to such prejudice is brought out fully in the following account I received from Paja, a wily old Wana shaman:

> On his way home from a coastal market, Paja encountered a Christian minister talking with the head of the village in which Paja paid taxes. The minister took note of the raggedy old Wana and asked the village head who he was. Learning that Paja was a Wana from the hills, the minister exclaimed in Indonesian, "Oh, this man is one of the still ignorant, one not yet possessing a religion, an animist, one who worships at trees, one who worships at stones." Paja, who understands some Indonesian, answered the man in a conciliatory fashion. "Yes indeed, it is true, sir. I am a stupid person, an animist. I don't know anything. I worship at trees, I worship at stones. But sir, if you worship in a house made of wood, you sir, worship also at trees. If you worship inside a church made of stone, sir, you also worship at stones. It is the same if one worships outside in the open, for God is everywhere."

As this story illustrates, the Wana are in a position to apply a far more universalistic and all-embracing notion of God than are their neighbors, for the Wana seek inclusion among others with legitimate forms of belief, whereas their neighbors, using religion as a measure of progress, wish to limit the definition of religion to those who conform to their model of societal advancement.

Wana concepts of an afterlife also bear the marks of a dialogue with world religions. Whatever indigenous notions of an afterlife were once present in Wana culture, they have been radically transformed by the concept of *saruga*, the Wana rendering of the Indonesian *surga*.[11] *Saruga* has become a symbol of Wana visions of social justice and a new world order.

Proselyters—both Muslim and Christian—have presented Wana with visions of heaven to lure them into conversion. Pagan Wana accept the idea that heaven exists but declare their own traditional ways as an appropriate means to attain it. In response to Muslim and Christian scorn of Wana lifeways, pagan Wana assert that they, who live a poor and filthy life on earth, will enjoy a beautiful afterlife of leisure and comfort in heaven as a reward for earthly suffering. By contrast, they claim, Muslims live their heaven here on earth, as demonstrated by their comparative wealth and preoccupation with purity. In the Muslim section of heaven, so the Wana story goes, people live in filth (pointedly portrayed as pig excrement) and they are so hungry that their souls take the form of wild boar that root through Wana gardens in search of food. As for Christian souls, they have only scraps of clouds to eat (an apparent reference to Bible school pictures of Jesus and angels floating about on cumulus banquettes).

The following popular story vividly illustrates the use of the Christian concept of afterlife to validate traditional Wana ways:

> The hero of the tale is a Wana named Pojanggo Wawu, whose name means "one who wears a beard full of pig grease." Pojanggo Wawu is a symbol of unequaled generosity. When people pass by his house, Pojanggo Wawu asks them where they are going. If they answer, "To gather thatch," he insists that they take part of his roof, he'll find more. Likewise he dismantles his floor and disperses his household furnishings to those in need. He is a man generous to a fault.
>
> Now there was a man named Pohaji, literally, a Muslim who had made the pilgrimage to Mecca. Pohaji lived in a well-appointed house at the coast. Pohaji died one day and as his body was being readied for burial, his soul arrived in heaven. Looking around, it saw a beautiful house. "Whose house is that?" it inquired. It belongs to Pojanggo Wawu, he was told. Pohaji asked after his own abode and was shown to a filthy hovel. At that, Pohaji's soul departed quickly from heaven and rejoined its body

on earth. Awakening, Pohaji asked his wife to make him coffee (a treat identified with coastal living). Once revived, Pohaji assembled his family and went off to the mountains to find Pojanggo Wawu. The story details Pojanggo Wawu's amazement at the arrival of the rich haji who treated him like a brother, insisted upon sitting upon Pojanggo Wawu's grease-stained mats, and refused chicken meat in preference to wild boar. Pohaji lived out his life in Wana style, and when he died, he took up residence in Pojanggo Wawu's heavenly home.

A third and final example of religious discourse involves the premise of the dominant culture that Wana animism represents the earliest stage of religious development. Muslims and Christians equate Wana customs with the primitive beliefs of their own forebears, over which their own religions represent an advance. McKinley (1979) offers a fine analysis of such thinking among modernist Malays in Kuala Lumpur. [12] The equation allows a contrast between former, animist ignorance and present, high-God enlightenment. Wana accept the premise that *agama* Wana is the earliest religion, but for them priority does not connote primitiveness but rather special claims to validity. Like other pagans of the insular Southeast Asian highlands (Ileto 1971:24), Wana conceive the relation among religions in terms of siblingship. They regard Islam as the younger sibling of the Wana religion. Christianity, a recent introduction to the area, has been grafted onto the family tree as the youngest member of the sibling set. For Wana, seniority bestows privilege and authority; just as children should defer to parents, so younger siblings should defer to elder ones. Wana, in millennial fashion, foresee a time when their now-despised religion will be accorded proper honors. If history is to be a succession of eras, as the dominant culture asserts, then it is only right that, like a shaman's journey, history should end where it began—the first, who are now last, shall be first again.

The Wana case offers a glimpse into religious consciousness in the making. In a succinct summary of Weber on religion, C. Geertz (1964:285) observes "that the process of religious rationalization seems everywhere to have been provoked by a thorough shaking of the foundations of social order." For the geographically isolated Wana, the jolt comes from their perimeters as Indonesians attempt to herd hitherto isolated ethnic minorities into the nationalist fold. Given that religion is a principle idiom in which Indonesian politics are couched, it is not surprising that the Wana response is similarly phrased. To date, *agama* figures prominently in the discourse of inter-ethnic relations.

Discussion

Although they disagree about the usefulness of particular definitions of religion, anthropologists usually favor an inclusive rather than an exclusive use of the term. Most anthropologists regard religion as a general, if not universal, cultural phenomenon (for a more restrictive view, see Spiro 1966). An inclusive definition of religion permits insightful parallels to be drawn between cultural systems that are superficially dissimilar. Thus, nineteenth-century evolutionary theorists identified germs of civilized religion among contemporary peoples whom they equated with their own primitive forebears. Structural-functionalists, eschewing developmental models, have found equivalents for Western religion in institutionally undifferentiated, small-scale societies. American cultural anthropologists have recognized dispositions common to both world religions and traditional religions, despite obvious institutional differences.

In his pioneering article entitled "Religion as a Cultural System," C. Geertz (1966b:4) proposes a general definition of religion that spells out the potential effect of cultural symbols on a generalized cultural subject. Taking exception to analyses that treat social function at the expense of meaning, he emphasizes the symbolic rather than the institutional qualities of religious experience. His definition of religion cuts through such distinctions as "primitive" versus "world" religions and sweeps aside quibbles over definitional criteria such as theism and belief in spirits. Geertz circumvents issues of content, institutional structure, and history in order to identify religions as cultural systems that offer particular solutions to universal human problems of meaning. Despite humorous hedges about the transcendental shortcomings of golf and adolescent love (C. Geertz 1966b:13), his definition is flexible enough to accommodate such claims as Peacock's (1978:12) declaration to reformist Muslim informants that anthropology is his religion.

Although it collapses distinctions of world versus traditional, rationalized versus non-rationalized religion, Geertz's formulation has different implications for research on either side of that historical and institutional divide. For the study of world religions, his formulation has proved liberating because it invites scholars to look beyond the confines of formal religious institutions to examine wider cultural patterns.[13] For the study of traditional religions, Geertz's approach suggests that, in the absence of rationalized religious institutions and dogma, anthropologists can locate a religious system by examining cultural formulations addressed to problems of meaning. For a Western audience, his model of religion lends a degree of legitimacy to alien notions such as witchcraft and magic by portraying them as other ways of addressing general existential human concerns. Geertz (1966b:39) favors the term "religion" over what he terms "such desiccated types as 'animism', 'animatism', 'totemism', 'shamanism', 'ancestor worship' "; yet "religion," like those terms, is an analytical category that serves to organize cultural phenomena. What is different about the term "religion" is that it renders familiar to Westerners what the other terms tend to distance.

Geertz's argument has met with success as a general theory of symbolic process. This success has eclipsed somewhat his ostensible aim of revitalizing the anthropology of religion. One reason for this may be the fact that his discussion renders the concept of religion somewhat redundant by equating it with all those aspects of a culture that address ultimate problems of meaning. In Geertz's formulation, religion becomes "deep culture" and "deep culture" becomes religion. Ironically, his interpretive model offers an approach to the study of symbolic processes that can circumvent entirely the use of Western religious analogies. Indeed, one finds less discussion of religion and more discussion of symbolism in contemporary studies of peoples who have not converted to world religions.

By defining religion as the symbolic rendering of existential dilemmas, Geertz has spanned the division between world religions and traditional cultures by treating religion as a symbolic system and suspending concern for its institutional dimensions. Actually, he has never been blind to the institutional dimensions of religion, but, in an effort to counter social reductionism in the study of religion, he proposes a "two-stage operation": first, a symbolic analysis of meaning, then an examination of religious systems as they relate to "social-structural and psychological processes" (1966b:42). The difficulty with this proposal is that the existential dilemmas he finds at the heart of religion— "bafflement, pain, and moral paradox" (1966b:25)—are constructed within the context of specific social systems.[14] Thus, problems of meaning and their solutions are inseparable from social processes. The systematic properties of a religion result not from the fact that a religion addresses existential issues but instead from the fact that those issues are at once social and cultural.

Significantly, in Geertz's (1964) own analysis of religious rationalization in Bali (to choose an example that parallels that Wana case in many respects), he does not treat religion as a formulation of ultimate meanings acting on a passive existential subject in the manner of his 1966 article. Instead, he places Balinese religious creativity in a social context by exploring its economic and political dimensions. It is evident from his analysis that Balinese religion in the 1950s was taking shape through actors' efforts to grapple not so much with ultimate problems of existence as with proximate issues of cultural hegemony in the context of the Muslim-dominated Indonesian nation-state. The fact that their struggle was constituted in religious terms has cultural, institutional, and historical significance. Just as the symbolic dimensions of that struggle cannot be collapsed to its social ones, so too institutional considerations are critical to the study of religious meaning in that case. Similarly, my consideration of *agama* Wana demonstrates how a culturally defined religious system owes its shape simultaneously to the cultural constructs and the institutional context in which it is embedded.

What the Balinese and Wana examples suggest is that an inclusive definition of religion as a cultural system must not obscure the significance of religion as a historically grounded institution with profound implications for cultural formulations of religion. Wana religion and, for that matter, Balinese religion are neither world religions nor isolated traditional ones. They represent a third possibility, namely, local cultural traditions in dialogue with world religious systems.[15] That culturally defined religions should pattern themselves so sensitively to the wider social and cultural systems in which they are embedded invites further reflection about cases of religious development elsewhere.

Geertz intended his 1966 paper to be a needed corrective to a "vulgar Durkheimianism" that treated institutional dimensions of religion at the expense of meaning. That his effort met with success is demonstrated by widespread concern with symbolic process in anthropology today. But a lingering risk of this endeavor is the analytical divorce of symbolic and social processes. If religions are cultural systems, as most certainly they are, their systemic qualities are at once a product of culture, institutions, and history.

9. A Rhetoric of Centers in a Religion of the Periphery

Anna Lowenhaupt Tsing

O N FRIDAY JUNE 21,1974, AT 6:00 IN THE EVENING, a Dayak woman named Uma Adang first heard voices from the ancient Indonesian empire of Majapahit.[1] Before that time, people said, she was just an ordinary person, with no special interest in either religion or politics. But voices continued to come to her, telling her truths of history that were to transform her community and her role within it. By the time I knew her in 1980 and 1981 during my anthropological fieldwork, Uma Adang had succeeded in attracting a group of devoted kin and neighbors from her small Kalawan community, and she was widely known and respected as a religious leader among a large sector of the Dayak group of southeastern Kalimantan that I call the Meratus.[2]

Uma Adang's voices speak of rulers and rituals of past times and of the still powerful structure of the past, which she calls *sejarah*, History.[3] The voices have revealed, too, a range of esoteric knowledge that enters her religious teachings: the languages of the forty-one prophets who represent the diverse peoples of the world, as well as religious chants with the sound of Koran readings, which she offers as the true texts of a Meratus Dayak religion. Her voices also have taught the correct forms of *adat* community law, abandoned or distorted, she claims, since their original introduction by royalty. Drawing on this law, she has introduced a number of community innovations in Kalawan, and her reputation as an *adat* expert has spread to other Meratus areas. Her personal charisma, combining idiosyncratic inspiration and familiar aspects of Meratus leadership style, has added much to her attraction, but I was equally struck by her success in articulating a version of Meratus "tradition" which, while unconventional, has gained appeal through its relevance to current Meratus concerns about ethnicity and national politics.

My understanding of Uma Adang's religion required a divergence from the prevalent direction of research on Borneo. Until recently, the most interesting questions of Borneo anthropology have seemed to lie in the study of independent local systems that can provide examples of cross-cultural variation. Religious beliefs in particular have been studied as the internal concerns of social groups. While Dayak rhetorical bows to "Majapahit" and "Mecca" have long been noted (e.g., Scharer 1963: 14, 214), most analysis has focused on questions of internal consistency and function. Despite their introductions specifying region, location, and colonial or national developments, researchers have conventionally depicted the influence of government policy and ethnic interaction as a superficial frosting on the well-established cake of local custom.[4] Here, however, I explore how the local "cakes" we may posit or be presented with are themselves made with national and regional ingredients. Uma Adang's religion is only comprehensible viewed within a wider political context. My analysis thus moves back and forth among local, regional, and national perspectives to present a case study of religious politics in southeastern Borneo. My aim is to suggest an approach to the study of peripheral peoples in Indonesia that promotes an understanding of local conditions and concerns while at the same time demonstrating how they are generated within a wider state and regional system.

Familiar themes of ancient kingdoms and spiritual power tie Uma Adang's movement to wider currents of Indonesian culture. The literature on Indonesian culture has often emphasized indigenous notions of powerful, elite centers ruling over outlying followers (e.g., Geertz 1980), yet the relationship between such notions and an existing order of domination has not been fully explored. Even in studies that focus on relations between "peripheral" peoples and centers of power, the precise nature of ties between rural communities and elites remains unclear as long as considerations of ideology are divorced from the treatment of political relations.

Cultural ties between elites and peasants have been a common topic for Indonesianists, as in studies of the use of Hindu, Arabic, and high Javanese terms and traditions in village cultural expression. Village communities have been shown to share cultural imagery with elite centers, although in localized, "rough" forms: Scott (1977), for example, has described Javanese peasant culture as a "little tradition," while Lansing (1979) has argued for a much more direct "court-village axis" in the case of the Balinese arts. But as long as they fail to analyze the specific ways that rural communities are enbedded in a system of power relations, not just a system of cultural assumptions, these approaches are forced to overgeneralize about the relationship between elite and peasant culture. The specific form of political integration is what makes sense of ideological integration.

Studies of Indonesian peasant movements, on the other hand, have demonstrated the importance of historically specific local social and economic conditions in understanding spiritual revivals in rural areas (e.g., Sartono Kartoderdjo 1973). Yet, although many stress the relevance of current *social* changes, their depiction of culture and ideology tends to be static; they conjure a timeless escape into "tradition" or frustrated irrationality. In contrast, my analysis of Uma Adang's movement shows how religious ideologies develop together with social and economic changes. My approach demonstrates the complex interdependence of culture and politics in the integration of local communities within the Indonesian nation.

Uma Adang's movement has developed in her area in the context of a blossoming of concern for ethnic identity and local rights.[5] In order to make sense of her combination of theological discussion, History, and state symbolism, we must look at the context of her movement in a wide field of power relations. Thus, I begin with an examination of state policy on religion to establish how Meratus claims to have a legitimate "religion" are important for their political standing as an Indonesian minority group. Viewed in the light of the national discourse on "religion," Meratus relations with their Muslim Banjar neighbors are then shown to mediate Meratus relations with the state. In this context, I suggest, Banjar-influenced notions of "religion" have become central in Meratus formulations of ethnic identity. Finally, examining local conditions of leadership and community organization clarifies Meratus accommodations and claims for autonomy vis-à-vis both the state and the Banjar.

Before moving into this analysis, I return to my more immediate experience of the Uma Adang and her religious rhetoric.

Majapahit in the Wilderness

A chain of mountains called the Meratus Range bisects the province of South Kalimantan in a north-south direction. The Meratus Dayaks are

Anna Lowenhaupt Tsing

swidden rice cultivators who, unlike their Muslim Banjar neighbors both
east and west of the mountains, practice shamanistic ritual and curing.
Meratus friends in the central mountains first told me of Uma Adang,
saying she was a woman of authority and vision and suggesting I look for
her. Uma Adang lives on the Meratus-Banjar border to the east side of the
mountains, only a few hours upstream from the nearest district administrative seat. So, hiking down the east side of the mountains on my way to
check in with regional officials, I decided to stop overnight at her place.

Accustomed to a relaxed Meratus hospitality, I was awestruck by the
formality of the welcome Uma Adang mustered for me. Within an hour of
my arrival a small crowd of local people had gathered, bending to shake my
hand reverentially and muttering Arabic greetings: "Wassalam." A huge
assortment of food and drinks somehow appeared, from the sweet tea of
"civilized" Indonesian hospitality, which I hadn't experienced since leaving
the cities, to local treats of smoked dear and durian fruit. Topping that,
Uma Adang announced that her voices had told us to eat a specially sacrificed chicken, quite an honor in an area where people slaughter domestic
animals only on ritually significant occasions.

An air of secrecy and seriousness was pervasive, as Uma Adang and her
close associates told me of her inspired knowledge of ritual and History.
Throughout the night we talked of the glorious ceremonial forms of royal
times, the practice of which will return only with the restoration of royalty.
Intrigued, I returned for several long stays with Uma Adang, and each time
I found myself astonished and inspired by the atmosphere of serious devotion to fantasy, formality, and spirituality that I found in Kalawan. Uma
Adang's most solemn presentations of inspiration were yet tinged with a
theatrical, improvisational style. In an earnest parody of articulate knowledge, Uma Adang mimicked Indonesian officials, Islamic prayers, songs on
the radio, and the speech of foreigners. Even the grave looks of her audiences seemed part of the performance.

I too was unwittingly cast into the pageantry. My route to her place had,
it seems, traced the steps of a figure from History, the Diamond Queen,
fetched from a more glorious Banjar court to establish a kingdom in the
wilderness in days of old. My coming was clearly fraught with significance
to Uma Adang and her followers—thus the royal welcome. Even when
I had convinced them, with my ignorant questions, that I was not the
new queen, Uma Adang was able to find a meaning to my visit. Having accepted my self-designation, elevated by the grand and unheard of title,
mahasiswa ('university student' in Indonesian, but *maha* means 'great').
Uma Adang concluded that I, like herself, sought the true History, the
once and future order.

Our mutual respect and affinity grew with my appreciation of her unusual movement and her enthusiasm for my tasks as an anthropologist. Uma Adang loved the grandeur that my serious pursuit of note-taking and tape-recording gave to her religious leadership. Sometimes she would ask me to record speeches when we were alone and then have me play them back to visiting neighbors and friends. As we thrived on these mutual but non-"standard" contributions to each other's work, I gained a distinctive and privileged vantage point on the building of Uma Adang's personal charisma and the devotion of her followers.[6]

The respect and enthusiasm with which neighbors and Meratus visitors approached Uma Adang contrasted strikingly with both the informality and distrust of leaders I had grown used to in other Meratus areas. Of the thirty-five family groups that affiliated loosely in her Kalawan neighborhood, less than a dozen were her constant devotees, bringing gifts of meat and vegetables and asking her advice on small matters; however, these loyal followers formed a cohesive and influential group. Crucial to her leadership was the presence in this group of the Village Head (*Pambakal*), an uncle of Uma Adang. Unable as a woman to obtain a government position for herself, Uma Adang had also been instrumental in having a devoted nephew appointed as *Kepala Adat*, 'Head of Customary Law.'[7] He acted as her indispensable assistant, intoning in serious dramatic tones that her value was like that of a diamond as big as a banana blossom. At the same time, other neighbors, as well as both real and fictive kin from other areas, showed their allegiance to Uma Adang's leadership by consulting her on matters of marriage and divorce, relocation, or ritual, and her voice was central to the planning of community events. Meratus from the mountains often stopped by her place to ask for advice, and her periodic trips to other Meratus areas, where she would preside over an audience with courtly dignity, helped spread her fame and influence.

Uma Adang claims to be a shaman (*balian*), and her activities include curing, rice blessings, and performance in community rituals. However, she rarely uses conventional ritual chants invoking the familiar Meratus array of spiritual powers. Her religious leadership depends instead on a new style of oratory and a rhetoric reminiscent of Muslim theology, national politics, or radio shows. As a woman in an area in which almost all shamans are men, she has not had access to apprenticeship, the conventional route for aspiring shamans. Instead, she has constructed her own ritual texts, which combine snatches of traditional ritual poetry with phrases she must have heard in speeches at the district seat, in her travels to other areas, on the radio, from visitors, and from other Meratus aspiring to "foreign" knowledge. Uma Adang breaks into such oratory on diverse occasions: entertaining visitors in her home, blessing a work party, convoking a formal ritual. Her oratory is distinctive in its contexts as well as content, but she has integrated her innovations into a recognizable system of religious knowledge and leadership.

Playing With Words

We can see the integration of innovative elements into a familiar framework in one of Uma Adang's short speeches. The occasion for this speech, typical of her formal oratory, was the preparation of offering cakes for a traditional ritual. Uma Adang suggested I record her comments on the *adat* of making these cakes, and this is the speech she produced for me and the half-dozen other women present.

1	The date the seventh,	Tanggal tujuh
	The year 1800.	tahun seribu delapan ratus
	Peace be with you.	wassalam
	Including:	bermasuk
5	To the honorable	kepada yang terhormat
	to speak about the History of the World.	mengatakan dalam sejarah dunia
	Which contains the *adat*	terisi adat
	of the Prophet Lahat	Nabi Lahat
	beginning	dimulai
10	to be	untuk
	broadened	dilebarkan
	by History	oleh sejarah
	that is the most famous,	yang termuka
	or the highest,	ataupun yang teratas
15	each day	setiap hari
	or each	ataupun setiap
	of us to actualize	kami untuk mengadakan
	Peace and Perfection.	selamat dan sempurna
	Including a beginning from	mengisi dimulai dari
20	the origin of History,	asal sejarah
	adat from Majapahit	adat dari Majapahit
	including	terisi
	verily	sungguh
	the greatest	yang terbesar
25	ritual tools of shamans,	alat-alat balian
	from the Prophet Lahat.	dari Nabi Lahat
	Until being raised,	sampai dinaikkan
	or being brought down,	ataupun diturunkan
	to the Prophet David.	kepada Nabi Daud

30 Containing
the History
of the era of our *adat*,
Majapahit,
and then
35 the ritual tools of Majapahit.
Our *adat* that has already been
put forward,
or made highly respected,

to praise the Prophets,

40 or pray to Heaven,

    God the Supreme One.
All of us ask for Peace,
or Perfection,
and surrender to
and I quote: huas ter
45 al ai se na el ha
one kun hes ai der hai
ai kun sai
one.

It has already been actualized for You.

50 The true contents have been given,
the contents of History are
brought forward or handed out as prizes—

the era of words of *adat*,
the History of the World,
55 including from
Majapahit, descending to
the contents of the era of kingdoms,
then raised
or revealed
60 to—
Peace be with you.

berisikan
sejarah
jaman adat kami
Majapahit
selalu
alat-alat di Majapahit
adat kami yang sudah
dimukakan
ataupun dibesarkan
tertinggi
untuk menadarkan kepada
nabi
ataupun berdoa kepada
surga
    Tuhan yang Maha Esa
semua kami minta selamat
ataupun sempurna
menyerahkan kepada
pertek dari kata: huas ter
al ai se na el ha
satu kun hes ai der hai
ai kun sai
satu

sudah diadakan kepada
saudara
isi sungguh yang diberikan
isi sejarah atas
bermuka ataupun
berhadiah
jaman kata adat
sejarah dunia
terisi dari
Majapahit turun kepada
isi jaman kerajaan
selalu diataskan
ataupun dari mukakan
kepada
wassalam alaikum

The speech itself says little about cakes or even shamanism and its rituals. However, by speaking at a ritual event, Uma Adang tied her comments to ritual and, in doing so, placed this ritual in the new light of her special knowledge of History.[8] A Meratus shaman leads a religious community by guiding and providing ritual, and Uma Adang's effectiveness as a religious leader is enhanced through placing her message in the context of long-established ritual.

The speech is meant to be in Indonesian, and not in either Meratus or Banjar. Sometimes the Indonesian and the message are less than coherent, but coherence isn't the point. Neither Uma Adang nor her audience ordinarily use Indonesian in informal contexts, although Kalawan people are familiar with a good number of words and phrases. Many of the words Uma Adang chooses are likely to be familiar from the formal speech of officials or from theological discussions with visiting Banjar.[9] Despite familiar phrases, however, the speech is meant, I believe, to be somewhat incomprehensible; Uma Adang is enlightening her audience through their very mystification. This she admits: at one point (lines 44–48) she presents a series of unintelligible sounds and then claims that these are the true contents of History.

Traditional Meratus shamanism likewise gains its authority through unfamiliar language and associated claims of esoteric knowledge. Banjar and Indonesian words are also sometimes used in conventional shamans' chants, and, although most Meratus know phrases from shamans' chants, they don't listen for the coherence of the chant during rituals and are content to recognize odd phrases. Uma Adang's use of a strange but formal-sounding text scattered with familiar phrases thus seems quite standard. Her use of parallel constructions, although linked awkwardly in a prose-like oratorical style rather than a chant, also gives the text a familiar ritual ring (e.g., lines 13–14, 15–16, 27–28). The only phrase I find here, however, that might be found in conventional shamans' prayers is *selamat dan sempurna*, 'peace and perfection,' and her decision to use this phrase may reflect its acceptability in Islamic and Christian as well as shamanistic blessings. Uma Adang's speech draws only slightly on the content and style of ordinary shamans' chants, leaning more heavily on "official" sounding speech.

Lack of coherence in the text is made up for by a dependence on heavy words, such as History, *adat*, and Majapahit. The text pulls together words with "Power," in Anderson's (1972) Javanese sense; Uma Adang thus implies that knowledge is embodied in words which themselves create power.[10] The date she begins with, an arbitrary one, reflects the importance of numbers as words with authority. Another example makes this clearer. After a different ritual, Uma Adang asked me what percentage of the proceedings I had understood. I replied that I had caught perhaps 25 percent. She encouraged me: "I'll add another 20 percent and that will make 45 percent, which is appropriate given the Constitution of '45." The Indonesian Constitution of 1945 has become part of a national rhetoric of patriotism, and

Uma Adang finds in this rhetoric a source of formal authority overriding everyday standards of practical reference.

Much of Uma Adang's speech directs itself to Islam. She has invented a prophet, the Prophet Lahat, as the Dayak counterpart of Islam's Moham-med. Thus Dayak religion, she claims, is separate but equal to Islam. The "words" she quotes in lines 44–48 mimic Koranic verses; their untranslat-able nature (as spontaneously inspired syllables with an Arabic ring) is the source of their power and no detraction from it. In other contexts Uma Adang sings Koran-like chants, claiming to have received the distinctive text of Meratus religion in this Islamicized form. In this speech, her references to praising and praying to Heaven (lines 39–40) similarly cast Meratus religion as equivalent to Islam.

Uma Adang cites the authority of both History and the state to claim an encompassing, syncretic type of knowledge that surpasses religious plural-ism and equality. Her reference to *Tuhan Yang Maha Esa*, 'God the Supreme One,' is drawn from the Pancasila national code, which sets out the principles of Indonesian patriotism and state-centered unity above re-ligious and ethnic diversity. In capturing the phrase Uma Adang suggests that her knowledge, since it connects to state power, overshadows religious divisions. Similarly, Uma Adang claims to speak, through inspiration, the diverse languages of all the world's prophets, not just the Dayak prophet. Pieces of Christian prayers, popular songs, or even the language of advertis-ing and radio shows (cf. line 52 *berhadiah*, with its possible implications of a special giveaway 'prize') add to her aura of encompassing many foreign strains.

Ordinary Meratus shamans may call kings and heros of old to help them lead and protect their communities. Uma Adang, however, uniquely elabo-rates upon the concept of History, using the Indonesian word *sejarah*, which has little everyday use in most Meratus communities. *Sejarah* for Uma Adang combines ritual order and the power of the past into a paradig-matic structure empowering and ordering not just the past, but the present and the future. We see a chain of History momentarily in the speech (lines 27–28, 56–58); it goes both up and down, alternately, as befits a structural transformation, not a sequence of past events. Like many a Dutch struc-turalist, Uma Adang sees the past as embodying a timeless order that is inadequately followed in the present. In her message, present dispersion and conflict can be overcome only through a re-emergence of the orderly and syncretic power of origins found in History; thus, for Uma Adang, knowledge of History unites the contradictory and unintelligible elements of national culture through a more powerful original synthesis, a single esoteric knowledge made accessible to her Meratus community.

A number of aspects of Uma Adang's oratory are especially important for a discussion of her leadership and the development of her movement. First, the incomprehensibility of her message, its formal language, and the potent if obscure catch phrases suggest to Uma Adang's audiences that she is in touch with high sources of knowledge outside of practical familiarity. Such esoteric knowledge underlies her claims to local authority, and particularly the authority to impose and enforce "higher" concepts of order, law, and respect in community social life. Second, Uma Adang's message seems significant and powerful to her followers because of the particular sources of knowledge to which she appeals. She borrows heavily from Islam, as she also contrasts it with Meratus religion. She draws from government rhetoric, such as in references to the Pancasila and the Constitution of 1945. Appeals to the glory of pre-colonial kingdoms are particularly effective because these also form a part of contemporary government rhetoric. "Majapahit" invokes the power of the contemporary state at the same time that it establishes a theme of "traditional" authority.

Uma Adang's speeches were so detached from everyday practical signification that sometimes I was confused about whether she was being serious. Indeed, she was serious, but with all her imagination. If her abstract word play makes theology and patriotism loom larger than life, it is perhaps because she observes Islam and the state from the awe-inspiring distance of the peripheries—close enough to know the power of bureaucrats and armies, but far enough to be detached from their everyday control. This position has led her to a parodic oversimplification—with both its absurd grandiosity and its clarity of political vision.

Religion and the State

Uma Adang's vision of the importance of Islam as well as the Pancasila can only be understood with reference to national issues of "religion" in Indonesia. The importance of religion in Indonesian politics is often oversimplified as a matter of divergent "primordial" loyalties (e.g., Kahane 1973). In fact, however, this importance becomes clear only with a consideration of the specific role of Islam in defining a debate on what constitutes "religion" and the relationship between the state and "religion." As Atkinson (this volume) demonstrates, Indonesian minority "religions" have been defined through a discourse created by people and organizations who think they have religion. Here I will examine the political dynamics that motivate this discourse, and particularly the role of the state in this process. The ambivalent relationship between organized Islam and the state is central to an understanding of the significance of "religion" in Meratus local politics.

Islam became a key idiom for political mobilization during the colonial period, especially in the late nineteenth and early twentieth century when Indonesian nationalism and reformist Islam grew up together (Kahane 1980; Peacock 1978).[11] During the Japanese occupation, both Islamic and nationalist organizations flourished (Boland 1971). The Japanese supported the formation of Masyumi, which continued after Indonesian independence as a major political party organized around Islam. The influence of Muslim political leaders arguing for an "Islamic state" and for state support for Islamic law made such issues central in national political debates in the early period of independence. Religion became increasingly important in defining opposing political positions, as political parties spoke either for or against state support of Islamic programs. Thus, Christian parties were formed and secular nationalist parties mobilized followings in the name of Javanese-syncretist orientations. Organized Islam never won control in this competition,[12] and a compromise was adopted which included state endorsement of "religious" goals combined with an attempt to guarantee that no single religious force would gain exclusive dominance.

Muslim leaders succeeded in establishing a Ministry of Religion in the cabinet, but, in response to wider pluralistic interests, the ministry also included other organized religious forces. In 1952 the ministry established a policy recognizing six official 'religions' (*agama*), with the prerequisite elements of a prophet, a holy book, and international recognition (Islam, Catholicism, Protestantism, Buddhism, Hinduism, and Confucianism) (Mulder 1978). All other belief systems were labeled *kepercayaan*, 'beliefs'; the 'religion'/ belief' differentiation never challenged the truth value of 'beliefs' but merely established that they should not receive state support. At that period, organized Islam was able to push the notion that organized expressions of *kepercayaan*, such as Javanese mystical sects, were potentially subversive, and the Ministry of Religion set up a branch to keep watch over these groups (Mulder 1978).

The differentiation between 'religion' and 'belief' structured the dynamics through which both Islam and other belief systems were used to organize followings. Those Javanese who had come to identify with a syncretic set of beliefs and practices usually labeled *abangan* (Geertz 1960) deferred to official policy on 'religion' by registration as Muslims; however, attempts to organize groups on the basis of *abangan* beliefs also continued. As

Mulder (1978) documents, these groups were led by government support of the *agama/kepercayaan* differentiation to enter the discourse on 'religion.' They tried to promote the equality of 'belief' and 'religion' in a bid for state financial and organizational support.

In the outer islands, numbers of people were left by state policy without an official 'religion' at all. Officials, Muslims, and Christians cited this lack of 'religion' in elaborating their notions of the 'backward' and 'primitive' nature of these peoples' cultural orientations. Aware of the derogatory implications of this discourse as well as its effects in supporting policies of ethnic domination and government control in the name of "progress," many pagans turned either to Christianity[13] or to struggles to gain state recognition of traditional 'beliefs.' In Central Kalimantan, the struggle to gain official religious recognition resulted finally in a 1980 policy declaring *Kaharingan*, a designation for a traditional Kalimantan belief system, to be a form of Hinduism, and thus an official 'religion' (Weinstock 1981). The *Kaharingan* recognition movement demonstrates how a local discourse on what constituted 'religion' was motivated by government policy. In Uma Adang's area, too, 'religion' has become the key element in a dialogue on ethnic relations and political standing, as Muslim Banjar maintain that Meratus have no religion, while "pagan" Meratus hope to show that their ceremonies and beliefs are as religious as is Islam.[14]

Ambivalent state policies toward non-Islamic groups have developed in response to change and complexity in the relationship between organized Islam and the state. With the introduction of Guided Democracy, Sukarno curbed the influence of Muslim political parties, foregrounding a state syncretism and a theism "higher" than competing religious factions. In this period, Sukarno successfully built up loyalties to the Pancasila declaration of 'Belief in God' as an overarching principle of state theism. Some Muslim leaders were able to support this policy, but others saw it as a demonstration of their failure to establish Islam as state ideology. This division, along with state encouragement of religiously inspired political competition, made Islam an appropriate tool to oppose state authority as well as to uphold it. Particularly significant was the role of Islam in mobilizing regional rebellions in the 1950s and '60s, such as the Darul Islam movement in West Java and various uprisings against "Jakarta" policies in Sumatra, Sulawesi, and Kalimantan (Boland 1971). The identification of Islam as the opposition encouraged state support of the *kepercayaan* groups in their attempts to defy the dominance of Islam. This trend was temporarily reversed in the 1965 alliance between organized Islam and the army in opposition to the Indonesian Communist Party. But with the consolidation of the army's position as the strongest element in state power after 1965, organized Islam was pushed back into opposition politics (Utrecht 1979), maintaining its strongest government influence in the Ministry of Religion.

Political conditions in southern Kalimantan have been much affected by national religious alignments. In the 1950s and '60s, a guerrilla force, led by a Banjar Muslim named Ibnu Hadjar, opposed the central government in the name of Islam. The rebels were able to mobilize support among Banjar villagers through Islam, and many Dayaks claimed that local Banjar military authorities, officials, and villagers tacitly supported the rebels in terrorizing non-Islamic peoples. Dayak mobilization against Islam grew during this period, augmented by support from Javanese army officers anxious to squelch the Banjar rebellion (Miles 1976). Dayak mobilization and petitions to the central government resulted in the 1957 creation of a new province, Central Kalimantan, originally intended to be a Dayak province free from Banjar control.

Ibnu Hadjar's rebels found the Meratus Mountains in ideal refuge, particularly the sparsely populated and densely forested east side. In the rebel stronghold, a number of Meratus families abandoned their homes and fled to the forest. Elsewhere, most Meratus gave food and shelter to both government and rebel forces as each passed through. The Meratus were too far to the east to be included in the new "Dayak" province, and a broad Banjar area separated them from the Central Kalimantan movement for Dayak rights. In the western foothills, however, a number of Meratus joined Central Kalimantan Dayaks in a government-sponsored 'head scarf militia' that opposed Ibnu Hadjar's rebels.

The events of this period encouraged a set of political alignments that have continued to shape regional politics long after the suppression of armed rebellion. In particular, Meratus continue to take an ambiguous stance toward the Banjar, reflecting ethnic competition for political standing in relation to the state. On the one hand, the rebellion heightened Meratus respect for the power of the Banjar and reinforced Meratus attempts to play down their ethnic distinctiveness and otherwise to accommodate to Banjar standards and demands. Rumors of local government support for the rebels promoted a Meratus sense of powerlessness toward the intertwined authority of the Banjar and the state. On the other hand, the struggles of this period strengthened Meratus identifications with other Dayaks, as mutually opposed to the Banjar. Dayak successes in Central Kalimantan encouraged Meratus to use, for their own self-defense, the tensions dividing the syncretist-Javanese orientations of central government policy from local Islamic-Banjar officials, traders and villagers. Uma Adang's rhetorical appeals to the state thus draw inspiration from earlier Dayak appeals for protection from the central government in reconstructing

Dayak-Muslim relationships. Her heavy reliance on Islam, on the other hand, reflects Meratus recognition of Banjar authority.

Religion and Ethnicity

As the Meratus response to Ibnu Hadjar's rebellion illustrates, national issues of religion have become relevant to the Meratus in the context of their interaction with neighboring Muslims. In response to state expansion and renewed Banjar immigration into the relatively isolated Meratus area, questions of religious legitimacy, with its implications for ethnic relations and state support of local leaders and programs, have become increasingly important. Particularly in Meratus border areas, Banjar and Meratus negotiate questions of Meratus ethnic identity, status, and relations to the state through the idiom of religion.

The Meratus area in some senses has been defined by its inaccessibility. Vehicular travel—both by river and road—stops at the boundaries of the Meratus Mountains, giving way to difficult foot travel over rough terrain which has discouraged the entry of outsiders. In the central mountains, only occasional Banjar traders and military patrols pass through, representing non-Meratus interests; in the foothills, there is more mixing between Banjar and Meratus people, but, outside of government-sponsored resettlement areas, Meratus communities experience a good deal of autonomy.

At the same time, however, the Meratus have long participated in a regional economy and administrative system. Since Dutch colonial times, regency and district boundaries have been drawn along the ridges of the Meratus Range, breaking the Meratus area into "tail"-like segments of administrative districts radiating out of the hills. Thus the Meratus have been administered not as a single "ethnic" unit but as the border regions of many predominantly Banjar units with their centers in the plains. Meratus orientations to markets similarly follow routes out of the hills and discourage pan-Meratus unity. Decentralization, fragmented loyalties, and Meratus stress on their cultural continuity with the surrounding Banjar population have been supported by such an administrative and economic organization. Citing the higher knowledge and "order" of regional centers, Meratus often imply that they have no independent cultural ideals but only enact general Banjar or Indonesian ideals with less success than their more cosmopolitan neighbors.

Nevertheless, Banjar-Meratus ethnic contrasts have also developed out of this same regional integration. Islam was a successful tool in mobilizing support among Banjar villagers for Ibnu Hadjar's rebels because it was already well-established as a major element in Banjar political and cultural identity. For the Banjar, Meratus identity appears to be based on their refusal of Islam.

Unwilling to convert to Islam, Meratus have developed a response to Banjar views that stresses religious contrast. Conventional Meratus shamanism, with its focus on rice cultivation, health, and building communities, seems little like a 'religion' from the perspective of Islamic theology. Thus, Meratus have adopted a mode of "theological" discussion that incorporates elements Banjar recognize as "religious": belief in God, respect for text and tradition, knowledge of the true and secret "names" of things and their magical power, et cetera. Outside of Uma Adang's movement, such theological discussion has only filtered gradually into Meratus ritual practice. Particularly in the western foothills, however, a parallel interethnic concern with sorcery and magic has transformed the interpretation of Meratus ritual. Banjar are convinced that Meratus are great sorcerers and, anxious to maintain that Meratus have no religion, interpret Meratus ritual as a form of sorcery. Meratus, benefiting from fees for spells and cures and even from the negative respect of Banjar fears, have elaborated on the sorcery theme. Thus, contrasting but simultaneous Meratus claims of theological equality and the "black magic" powers of ritual have developed in this ethnic discourse.

Recent events have intensified ethnic tensions and raised the stakes for claims and counterclaims about the status of Meratus religion. The central government in 1971 classified the Meratus as *suku terasing* ("isolated ethnic group"), a category of ethnic groups considered to be seminomadic and in need of resettlement and cultural modernization (Kantor Wilayah Departemen Sosial 1978; Hamda 1979). The *suku terasing* resettlement program has raised Banjar expectations for ethnic dominance over the Meratus in a number of ways. First, by categorizing the Meratus as a backward ethnic group in contrast to the Banjar, the program has lent ideological advantage to Banjar claims that the Meratus are "primitive." Second, the extension of bureaucratic administration and police jurisdiction has encouraged rapid new waves of Banjar immigration in the foothill areas. Poor rural Banjar of the western plains, particularly those without rights in irrigated rice lands, have jumped at the opportunity for resettlement in Meratus border areas under government protection of "free" land. Immigrant Banjar adopt swidden techniques similar to those of the Meratus but frequently combine these with trading, middleman buying of forest products, and other entrepreneurial concerns. As traders, Banjar depend on their superior connections to market centers to guarantee profits from Meratus clients, and the importance of such connections encourages the stress on Islam as separating Banjar and Meratus networks. The government has also provided support, both administrative and financial, to augmented attempts to convert the Meratus to Islam. Particularly on the east side, the Ministry of Religion has been active in conversion programs, and Meratus claim that potential converts are offered financial rewards and the advantages of government connections in exchange for espousing Islam.

Simultaneously, however, Meratus have tried to use recent government attention to their own "ethnic" advantage, requesting and sometimes receiving government monies for building elaborate new ritual halls and for sending major shamans to conferences of the Ministry of Religion. As early as 1968 a local government-sponsored conference of shamans in the western foothills declared *Balian* (lit. 'shaman') to be the traditional Meratus religion (Team Research Mahasiswa Fakultas Sjari'ah 1969). Debates about the status of Meratus religion, however, still continue.

The *suku terasing* program has also stimulated government and university support of social science research in the Meratus area (e.g., Babas 1978; Hamda 1979; Proyek Pembinaan Perguruan Tinggi Agama 1978). Such research has contributed a reified version of Meratus "tradition" to regional debates on Meratus ethnic status. Following well-established conventions in studies of rural and peripheral peoples in Indonesia, most reports attempt to identify local cultural forms that have been little influenced by Meratus integration within the wider Indonesian system. In extracting and codifying local "traditions," however, they in fact create a new form itself shaped by Meratus accommodations, as researchers both appeal to and direct Meratus interests in building an ethnic distinctiveness that is intelligible by regional and national standards.

Deference to outside authority is important not only in molding Meratus notions of ethnic identity but also in shaping social relations in Meratus communities. Meratus leaders draw heavily on a rhetoric that stresses not only Banjar concerns but also other "foreign" knowledge, and particularly the powerful symbolism of the state. Uma Adang's ritual oratory is distinctive in its elaboration of History, government rhetoric, and Islam, yet her use of estoric knowledge to build personal authority follows a conventional Meratus leadership pattern.

Great Shamans and Small Bureaucrats

Themes of the perfection and unity of ancient kingdoms are not unique to Uma Adang's oratory or to the Meratus. Such imagery is a central feature of the political ideology of the Indonesian state, as discussed particularly by Anderson (1972). Anderson is joined by authors such as Moertono (1968) and Geertz (1980) in showing how similar themes pervaded state symbolism in pre-colonial Java and Bali. The state, in these political views, should ideally be constructed in the present according to principles of cosmic order found in their paradigmatic realization only in ancient kingdoms. The powerful symbolism of court centers should encourage harmony and unity and ensure both social and cosmic order.

All of these authors, however, view such conceptions from the perspective of centers and take for granted the hegemony of these ideologies at all levels of society. Geertz in particular contrasts, for nineteenth-century Bali, a central state ideology stressing unity with the divisive organization of local political interests; thus, he slights the problem of how and why local leaders, and the communities they lead, endorse state symbolism. In Bali the question perhaps fades from prominence, given the multifaceted dominance of social and cultural life exerted by court centers, and what Geertz calls the Balinese "obsession" with hierarchy. In more peripheral areas, farther from kings and state centers, varied local orientations may contrast with dominant conceptions of power, and the influence of state ideology seems more problematic. Anderson, in a footnote, addresses this problem more directly, suggesting (for pre-colonial Java) that in the "distant regions" of the periphery, "formal submission" was combined with "practical autonomy" (1972a:32).

I develop Anderson's suggestion here to illuminate a Meratus leadership style in which state rhetoric is used to build authority in relatively autonomous local communities. Local conditions, including rugged terrain, swidden farming, and the instability of community affiliation and leadership, encourage both the independence of Meratus leaders and their use of a spiritual and political rhetoric stressing exogenous authority. The "peripheral" position of the Meratus is constituted in the simultaneous independence of local communities and their dependence on the power of outsiders.

In most Meratus areas,[15] family swiddening units affiliate loosely into neighborhoods, and one or more central figures tend to play an important role in coordinating neighborhood cooperation, settling disputes, and organizing community ritual. Land is comparatively plentiful, and in most areas families need not appeal to any formal set of jural rights to establish a farm site of their own choosing. The ability of family groups to claim independent responsibility for a farm, as well as the possibilities for mobility, nourish ideals of family autonomy and an ambivalence toward permanent community affiliations and allegiance to specific leaders. Without sanctions of "property" or force, leaders find it necessary to constantly negotiate and renegotiate the political community in which their influence is felt. Yet leadership is thought ideally good, and leaders are expected to guarantee community welfare and encourage neighborhood unity. The effectiveness of their leadership is measured by whether people stay with their leadership or move away—physically or socially—to establish an independent community focus or to join another group.

Ambitious men try to create a community around their leadership by judicious social networking, using kinship ties and the power of their personal reputations to maintain the loyalty of neighbors and other allies. A man's reputation as an attractive community focus is generally built through two routes: shamanism and ties to the government bureaucracy.

Many men claim knowledge of spells; quite a number feel competent to hold curing rituals. But only successful shamans take a central role in sponsoring the great community festivals that draw guests from miles around. Big community rituals usually involve dispute settlement and planning for agricultural cooperation, as well as curing and the honoring of spirits; in areas where settlement is scattered, large groups rarely assemble except for ritual occasions. Thus, a central involvement in community ritual is essential for Meratus leaders. Many leaders are successful shamans, and those who would build a political following without claim to shamanistic excellence at least develop a close working relationship with key local shamans.

Some knowledge of government affairs is similarly claimed by many men, but most effective as a route to leadership is government position. Since the later years of the colonial era, the Meratus have been linked to the state through government-appointed local officials; currently, these are referred to as *Pambakal*, 'Village Head,' responsible in theory for a wide area often requiring several days hiking from one side to the other, and *RT*, 'Neighborhood Head,' whose jurisdiction involves a smaller group of some twenty to fifty more closely settled family groups. Local officials are expected to transmit statements of government policy to their communities and to encourage local law and order. Meratus officials may attempt to facilitate dispute settlement or community plans by threatening to report offenders to the police or district officer (*camat*); in fact, however, the interference of higher levels of government in local affairs is rare and its outcome unpredictable. Local officials receive no regular remuneration and communicate only sporadically with higher-level authorities. Like other Meratus, they depend on family farming and gathering forest products; occasional gifts from higher bureaucrats may cement their loyalty to the government but do little to augment their local authority.

In this context, Meratus leaders may use government position, like shamanism, to augment respect for their authority as men of knowledge, linked to a higher "order" and able to wield frightening threats as well as promises of protection. Spiritual and political claims to power reinforce each other. Not only do individuals combine various sources of authority, but leaders depict the bases of spiritual and political power as similar. Both are identified as exogenous to community social structure; just as community social life provides little basis for authority, the might of forces outside practical daily control—from the state and the Banjar to capricious turns of health and the seasons—has shown itself to be fearsome. In casting power as based on knowledge of outside, unfamiliar domains, Meratus leaders are drawn to local versions of foreign knowledge as an idiom for both spiritual and political authority.

Thus, both shamans and local officials bring to their discussions of community social life images of regional political integration, inspired by Banjar and Indonesian portrayals of "order." To the east of the Meratus Mountains, people speak of the pre-colonial court centers that once flourished sporadically along major east-flowing rivers as the legitimate holders of regional authority. Meratus suggest that these kingdoms once united Muslim Banjar and pagan Meratus in a common devotion to courtly ritual, and the phrase *jaman raja*, 'the era of kings,' connotes the origin time of regional integration. In *dewa* shamanism (the ritual style dominant in Uma Adang's area on the east side of the Meratus Mountains), shamans call on the spiritual assistance of these pre-colonial Banjar kings and their courts, 'borrowing' their power. Such rulers also figure strongly in non-shamanistic appeals to the power of regional authority.

To the extent that colonial and national bureaucracies have also inspired a Meratus sense of integration into the larger region, Meratus may discuss them as drawing power from a source similar to the Banjar kingdoms; Dutch and Javanese royalty are readily collapsed into the Banjar model. The political rhetoric of higher-level regional officials, educated in a related elite model in which ancient kings and modern rulers share a common legitimacy, encourages such an interpretation of the basis of power of the contemporary state. Uma Adang and her small movement thus did not invent the use of a glorified past to speak to the legitimate form of regional integration and state power. Rather, such rhetoric forms a respectable current of thought about spiritual and political authority, familiar from both local and regional sources.

It is ironic that Meratus attempts to harness the knowledge of outsiders, particularly in shamanism, may be denounced by Banjar and other Indonesians as the distinctive signs of a backward or primitive culture, not yet assimilated into modern Indonesian civilization. In fact, the political contours of Meratus links to national centers encourage this local distortion of "foreign" knowledge. Like other Indonesian bureaucrats, Meratus officials are encouraged to indulge in the rhetoric of state power as the sign of their formal submission to distant centers; furthermore, they seem to prefer this loyalty to words and symbols rather than to specific regional leaders or policies, as an appropriate accompaniment of practical local autonomy.[16] Submission to powerful symbols allows each leader to speak of his "absolute" allegiance to as many varied authorities as are available instead of choosing only one. In the Meratus area, multiple higher authorities have always been available in the regional administrative centers of the plains that surround the mountain "border region."[17] Particularly in periods of military struggle, Meratus have found that declaring allegiance to all groups that pass through armed (and then fleeing to more inaccessible spots) presents the best alternative for an "autonomous" neutrality. Rhetorical appeals to multiple sources of exogenous authority have thus developed along with the practical autonomy of Meratus leaders to form and guide independent communities.

Uma Adang and the Definition of Community

Uma Adang has drawn from familiar elements of "religion": She espouses a religious dogma self-consciously gleaned from multiple sources of foreign knowledge, and she simultaneously shapes Meratus "religion" to Banjar standards. Her personal innovations are also significant. Merging rhetoric familiar from theological discussion meant to satisfy Islamic religious requirements with ritual forms of conventional shamanism, she creates a new liturgical form that "modernizes" shamanism in the context of Banjar-Meratus religious discourse. Her own neighborhood, situated in a Banjar-Meratus border area recently experiencing increased Banjar immigration, has been especially sensitive to the intensification of Banjar-Meratus tensions, and the attractiveness of her innovations must be seen in this context. Challenging Banjar views that Meratus have no religion, she endorses a religious practice that cannot be put down as sorcery. Such a religious innovation, however, requires a seriously convincing leadership style. Thus, she turns to ancient kingdoms that evoke both a traditional legitimacy and an imagined state support—and that simultaneously encourage a new basis of authority and community allegiance.

The development of new notions about leadership and "community" can be seen in Uma Adang's elaboration of *adat*. *Adat* developed its national political importance in the colonial period, as Dutch administrators sought to divorce local "custom," left in the hands of local authorities, from religion and from national law. Since this period, *adat* has become, in national discourse, the distinctive mark of an ethnic unit and the definition of its local rights. Meratus use the term *adat* (or *hadat*), but its elaboration has not been so great as in many Dayak groups in which "jural" authority is stronger and more stable. For Meratus, rules about ritual are a central element of *adat*, and shamans have conventionally been *adat* experts to the extent that such exist. But diverging from the national Indonesian definition of *adat* as the most distinctive feature of local ethnicity, Meratus have been ambivalent about the ethnic implications of *adat*. Although, like other forms of knowledge and order, it is said to originate from more powerful regional centers outside the Meratus region, Meratus *adat* may be said to contrast with Banjar traditions, forming distinctive ethnic features. Uma Adang incorporates this tension into her message, claiming Majapahit as the source of *adat* yet developing *adat* as a separate Meratus tradition.

Uma Adang has introduced a new emphasis on *adat* as both etiquette and community law. She administers fines for defaults such as disrespect and has proclaimed new regulations for marriage and divorce. Some of her rules contrast with Banjar codes—such as her insistence on monogamy— while others copy the latter—such as the regulation that babies must not be cradled in the ritual hall, which should be a sacred space comparable to a mosque. Most interesting perhaps are her attempts to use *adat* to define community unity and boundedness. She has instituted a community swidden, which is worked collectively; its produce is used for festivals, for important guests, and for families in need. She has also proclaimed the *adat* importance of neighborhood boundaries, asking families who wish to move in or out of the neighborhood to ask her permission first.

Uma Adang's *adat* innovations have a number of important consequences. First, they challenge conventional Meratus assumptions about charismatic attractiveness and threats as a mainstay of leadership, with the claim that authority based on law and proper conduct is more important. As a woman leader, unable to conjure up images of potential violence upon which many male leaders depend, she has leaned particularly heavily on knowledge of proper etiquette as a basis of authority.[18] Second, her focus on rules and boundaries moves away from conventional notions of the "open" nature of communities, in which charismatic leaders draw followers from all directions, toward an emphasis on a "closed" community in which rights and limits are more clearly codified. In an area in which

Banjar immigrants threaten traditionally assumed but never codified Meratus rights to land use and forest products, notions of community rights become attractive. Because of the national significance of *adat*, Uma Adang's emphasis on *adat* law builds an image of the "community" as a bureaucratic unit under state protection. Third, Uma Adang's *adat* innovations have become a basis for Meratus ethnic mobilization. *Adat* develops a foundation for Meratus identity as Meratus. Uma Adang's travels to other Meratus areas have helped establish her reputation as an *adat* authority, and mountain Meratus on a number of occasions have consulted with her about disputes in their neighborhoods.

Uma Adang's rhetorical focus on History allows a formal submission to a theoretical and timeless state authority, which may go hand in hand with a practical local autonomy. Her close relationship with the Village Head in Kalawan encourages her loyalty to government authority, yet she uses this loyalty to claim local Meratus rights in the face of Banjar expansion. Connecting traditional legitimacy and the contemporary state in her version of History, Uma Adang lays claim to ideological support from a state syncretism that overrides the local interests of Islam. This formal submission to the state, however, is useful in building community autonomy only as long as the real government administration chooses not to interfere, and here Uma Adang faces the dilemma of all Meratus leaders. When central government planners arrived to develop the area as a transmigration site for Javanese, the difficulties inherent in her stance toward the government became more apparent. On the one hand, she shared the fears rampant all over Kalawan about the project, fears that the proposed importation of several thousand Javanese families would only make the Meratus poorer and more peripheral. Certainly, anxiety about change was only fuel for Uma Adang's movement. On the other hand, her leadership stance pushed her toward a conventionally Meratus solution: that only unquestioned loyalty to the state would improve the Meratus position. Thus, when a Javanese transmigration engineer, visiting me, asked her what she thought of the project, she could only assure him of her full support for whatever might come through the wisdom of the government.

Discussion

Despite her innovative rhetoric and its use in building a new interpretation of local identity, Uma Adang's position is not unlike that of many Meratus leaders. Uma Adang draws most heavily for support on close kin, and the community in which she holds any regular influence is quite small—perhaps typical of that of other major shamans. She has developed an extensive network of fictive kin who respect her teachings, but most of them see her rarely, and people in the area adjoining her neighborhood are, in a typical Meratus fashion, suspicious of her leadership. I do not expect Uma Adang to be successful at single-handedly bringing the Meratus to national or regional prominence. Her case, however, is useful in illustrating the significance of national and regional issues, as well as local patterns of political and religious leadership, as factors in the development of a local movement.

Uma Adang' references to the coming of a new age of royalty and the success of her rhetoric in mobilizing a popular spiritual movement recall descriptions of Javanese peasant cults and rebellions. Messianic prophesies of the coming of the Just King, combined with nativism, religious revival, and millenarianism, have been so common in Javanese peasant movements that most studies concentrate on the particular economic and social stimuli that provoke unrest and take it for granted that peasant movements utilize various versions of well-established themes of spiritual power in their rhetoric (e.g., Sartono Kartodirdjo 1966; Korver 1976; Benda and Castles 1969).[19]

The classic study of peasant movements in Java, Sartono Kartodirdjo's *Peasant Movements in Rural Java* (1973), follows a standard approach in rooting peasant orientations, and particularly religious orientations, in "traditional" values. "The religious character of traditional protest movements," he states, "resulted naturally from the fact that traditional society generally reacts against social change in a religious way..."(p. 67). To the extent that peasant movements self-consciously incorporated nontraditional beliefs, Sartono suggests that they were undergoing transformations from "traditional" peasant revitalization to "modern" political protest. Yet this traditional-modern continuum obscures the common ways that "old" and "new" values were molded to speak to political causes: "nativism," like concepts of "reform" and "modernization," must be actively constructed as an ideology. Placing religiously oriented peasant movements in the "traditional" end of this continuum also obscures the importance of what George Rude (1980) calls "derived" as well as "inherent" elements in the ideologies of peasant protest. In looking at Uma Adang's movement it is possible to see how ideas drawn from elites and outsiders may form an essential component in redefining local interests and creating a newly relevant sense of tradition in defense of those interests.

In a study of anti-colonial movements in a number of areas including Java, Adas (1979) criticizes tautological elements evident in the assumption that millenarian movements arise out of "tradition"; he points instead to the importance of prophetic leadership in articulating millenarian ideologies (whether derived from local or outside sources) to speak to historically specific local discontent. In the context of anti-colonial discontent, millenarian ideologies both supported the authority of local leaders and made possible the identification of leader-follower relationships with the defense of local political rights. Thus, prophetic leaders stimulated peasant mobilization through visions promising new and larger communities, which their adherents hoped would augment security and solidarity in times of accelerated change.

My analysis of Uma Adang's movement similarly points to the role of her prophetic leadership in encouraging new ideas of how the community is constituted and, thus, what its "interests" are. Her inspirational History, uniting themes of religion, state authority, and ethnic competition, supports new standards of ethnic unity and leadership as it simultaneously depends on conventional modes of authority. Her leadership has thus inspired a popular movement by capturing Meratus concerns for religious legitimacy and ethnic standing vis-à-vis the Banjar and the state.

IO. *Islam and Law in Indonesia*

Mahadi

*I*SLAM IS A RELIGION WITH AN UNUSUAL INTEREST in law and legal codes. Indonesia is a country with a multitude of unwritten customary legal systems in the various ethnic groups and a long history of contact with European legal systems, codes, courts, and legal personnel. In this article, the focus will be on the shifting relationships between all these diverse legal traditions as they have been combined and mutually redefined to yield Indonesia's unique national legal situation today. Islamic law shapes national consciousness; in fact, it helped give diverse Indonesian ethnic groups a language of unity during the Dutch colonial period before political unity was a social reality. Importantly, the Ministry of Religion is considered an integral part of the national government today. Local ethnic culture in most parts of Indonesia bears the imprint of Islam and Islamic law, in such areas as marriage contracts, child-rearing, inheritance, and village civil law.

The principles adopted at a 1981 National Law Development Center symposium on national private law demonstrate the impact of Islam and the continued importance of the other legal traditions. The principles were as follows:

1. In codifying national civil law, European law, Islamic law and customary law shall be the components.

2. The Government should take into consideration the equi-
librium between the interests of secular life and those of the
life hereafter.
3. The spiritual consciousness of the population should be taken
into consideration.
4. Matters related to religious areas should be treated very pru-
dently to avoid social unrest.

In this essay, I will provide a brief historical overview of legal developments leading to an Indonesia that could produce such a set of guiding
principles. This will entail a look at the Dutch colonial period as well as at
the years of Independence. Of particular interest are recent changes in the
national marriage laws, modifying such familiar concerns of Islamic law as
the practice of polygamy.

The Dutch Period

The colonial era can be seen as a series of confrontations—symbolic and
institutional—among European law, local ethnic *adat* law, and Islamic
law. The Dutch attempted to control these confrontations to their benefit,
seeking to effect strategic redefinitions of local *adat* systems to help secure
the loyalties of the various ethnic populations. For this reason, *adat* and
Islamic law were often conceptualized as antagonistic opposites, with Islam
allied to interethnic unity and *adat* allied to a combination of local ethnic
loyalties and Dutch sympathies.

Hooker is thus partly right in saying that "the relationship between adat
and Islam in Indonesia can, in some cases, be considered as an opposition
of legal systems" (1978:92). In fact, the Dutch authorities considered both
the relationship between traditional customs *(adat)* and Islam, and the
relationship between the Dutch religion/law and Islam as opposed legal
systems. The unfriendly attitude of the Dutch to Islam was apparent in the
seventeenth century. In December 1643, the Municipality of Batavia (now
Jakarta) ordered that Moorish circumcision and schools be forbidden. In
1767 Batavia prohibited the ships of the United East-Indian Company from
transporting pilgrims who had visited the holy places in Mekka and Medina
(Hooker 1978:93). In the nineteenth century the opposition of Dutch re-
ligion/law and Islam appeared in article 15 of the Transitional Regulation
of 1848:

> The Indonesian persons who want to conclude marriage with
> European persons have previously to submit themselves to the
> European civil and business law.

The question of polygamy was probably the main impetus for this regulation. Clause 97 of the Regulation for Commissaries General stipulated, however, "the prayer meetings of all religions in the Netherlands Indies have the protection of the High Government, provided that this prayer meeting is of no danger for the public order" (Gazette 1818:no.87).

The year 1848 is known as the year of codification in Indonesia. For Europeans, a Civil Code (almost like-worded with the Dutch Civil Code) was written. A Code of Commerce also came into being at this time. Another legal product of the codification year was the so-called General Rules of Legislation (De Algemene Bepalingen van Wetgeving). Relevant here is article 11 of these rules, stipulating that the courts apply, among others, religious laws (godsdienstige wetten). Closely related to this stipulation is also article 7 of the Regulation on Court Organization and the Administration of Justice (Reglement op de Rechterlijke Organisatie en het Beleid der Justitie), also a product of 1848, which provided that an Islamic clergyman should attend sessions of the native courts as an adviser when Muslims were litigants. Thus the Dutch Government of the nineteenth century evidently had the intention of applying Islamic law for the adherents of Islam. The Dutch scholar Lodewijk Willem Christiaan van den Berg (1845–1927) advocated the application of Islamic law to the Muslim inhabitants of Indonesia, arguing that embracing Islam meant *receptio in complexu* (Habibah Daud 1982:2).

The father of the Codification of 1848, Paul Scholten van Oud Haarlem, adopted another attitude. He wrote an advice-letter to his Government arguing that imposing foreign law systems on the natives would provoke strong reaction. He advocated a policy of noninterference in the legal systems of the natives and urged that all remain subject to the rules of their religion or customs (Habibah Daud 1982:3). It was perhaps from the influence of Scholten van Oud Haarlem that article 75, paragraph 3, of the Constitutional Regulation of 1854 provided an instruction to native courts to apply both religious and customary law. Considering this provision, Daniel S. Lev wrote, "Until the late nineteenth century the predominant Dutch view of Indonesian law was that it was basically Islamic" (1972:9).

According to Lev, religious courts in Java "existed in all Kabupaten from about the sixteenth century." The judges were the "Penghulus," chief administrators of the local mosque. Their competence was limited to the areas of marriage, divorce, and inheritance (Mahadi 1969;5–7). For instance, the Governor General issued a resolution (no. 12) on June 3, 1823, establishing a religious court for the town of Palembang (Mahadi 1969:7–8). Its competence was extended in 1825 to include marriage, divorce, inheritance, child custody, guardianships, and other cases related to religion.[1] Similarly, the Decree of the Commissaries General (no. 17) of

March 12, 1828, for Jakarta stated in articles 20 and 23 that a district court should be established in each district. Members should consist of the district head as chairman, the chief administrator of the district mosque, and the heads of the quarters in Jakarta. The Courts' competence covered religious disputes, marriage, and inheritance.

The evolving relationship between *adat* law and Islamic law in various parts of the archipelago in this period is interesting. Gazette 1820, no. 22, in its article 13, instructed the "Bupatis" to give attention to religious matters and to watch that the Islamic clergymen in Java could execute their duties according to Javanese customs on marriage, inheritance, and the like. This article 13 was a source of difference in interpretation between the Landraad (native court) in Pekalongan and the Appellate Court in Semarang (Raad van Justitie). On July 30, 1833, the Landraad issued a verdict commanding a certain Singodirono to transfer inheritance goods to the Head-Administrator of the local mosque in order to divide them among the heirs. Singodirono was not satisfied and appealed to the Appellate Court in Semarang. This Appellate Court was of the opinion that the case should have been treated by the religious court (article 13 of Gazette 1820, no. 22). The local religious court in its turn gave the same decision as the Landraad. Singodirono then petitioned the Governor General, who asked the advice of the Supreme Court. In 1835 in article 13 of Gazette 1820, the Dutch Government issued an explanatory memorandum. This memorandum said that disputes among the Javanese people on marriage, inheritance, and the like, wherein Islamic law had to be applied, belonged to the competence of the religious court, but that claims of payment emerging from these decisions should be brought up to the usual court (v.d. Velde 1928:134; Lev 1972:11). The Islamic courts could not try claims for money or goods.

An important milestone in the history of the religious court was the Constitutional Regulation of 1854. Clause 78, section 2, of this Regulation provided that disputes among the natives, where application of religious law was required, remained in the competence of the "priest." There was no formulation of the Court's competence because this regulation aimed merely to maintain the previous regulation, i.e., the explanatory memorandum of 1835. Such was the situation when the Regulation of 1882 was enacted, a regulation called Priests' Courts in Java and Madura (Gazette no. 152). This regulation, too, like the Constitutional Regulation of 1854 did not elaborate the question of competence. Its articles regulated the composition of the religious court: the Penghulu of the local Landraad as chairman, three to eight Islamic clergymen as members. This regulation also stipulated that a decision is legitimate if the session concerned has been attended by three members including the chairman.

Margadant informs us that the religious courts in the Outer Regions operated as one-man courts. The Penghulu as judge gave his decision without the aid of others. In the West Coast Province of Sumatra the religious courts flourished in spite of not being approved by the Dutch Government (v.d. Velde 1928:36). They were called "Sidang Jamahat" (Friday Session). Imitating the reality in a number of villages in Lampung, the most southern Province of Sumatra, the people of the subdistrict Kalianda in 1925 constituted a "Dewan Penghulu" (a Council of Penghulus). This Council had competence to give decisions in matters of religious character. Pontianak had a religious court beginning in 1863 (v.d. Velde 1928:42).

In the twentieth century up to the outbreak of World War II, the prevailing doctrine was the so-called "Reception Theory," adopted by the Dutch Government and promulgated at the Law School in Jakarta. V. Vollenhoven and ter Haar had a major part in supporting this approach. The two *adat* law scholars wanted to preserve the purity of the *adat*. The Reception Theory meant that Islamic law could be applied by the court only on the condition that Islamic law had been adopted as part of the local customary law. Not surprisingly, in the struggle between Islam and *adat*, the Dutch took the side of the local *adat* (Lev 1972:10). All later developments in defining the competence of the religious court must be seen in the light of the Reception Theory. It was probably this theory that moved the Dutch Government in 1922 to create a special Commission to "look again into the question of the *priesterraden*." Professor ter Haar, the most influential proponent, was one of its members. In this context, Lev wrote that the Commission "proposed to remove all Islamic court competence over property affairs to the *landraden*. This included *wakaf*—religious property, usually in the form of land—and, most critically, inheritance" (Lev 1976:17–19). The report of the Commission, submitted to the Governor General in 1926, was partly incorporated in a new legislation in 1931 (Gazette 1931, no. 53). This regulation went into effect in 1937.[2] The legislation of 1937 has been maintained since independence through one of the transitional articles of the 1945 Constitution. This legislation created an Islamic Appeals Court. It also removed inheritance disputes and *wakaf* from the competence of the religious court to the Landraad.

The Post-Independence Period

In the Dutch era, religious matters had been entrusted to the Departments of Home Affairs and Justice. The Japanese occupational authority created a "Syumubu" (Department of Religion): similarly, the Republic of

Indonesia established a Ministry of Religion on January 3, 1946. From the beginning of the Republic, the nation asserted firm allegiance to a monotheistic, "all-embracing God." This concept was invoked at frequent intervals in various documents of the new Republic from 1945 to 1949. For example, the Preamble to the Indonesian Constitution of 1945 includes the following typical phrases:

> With God's blessing and moved by the high ideal of a free national life the Indonesian people declared their independence on August 17, 1945.
> We believe in an all-embracing God.

In addition to such general statements, the religious component of Indonesian nationhood is also made more concrete in the Constitution. Article 29 of the Constitution runs as follows:

> Section 1: The State shall be based upon belief in the all-embracing God.
> Section 2: The State shall guarantee the freedom of the people to profess and to exercise their own religion.

The phrase "belief in an all-embracing God" merits our full attention before an adequate account of the question of Islam and law in modern Indonesia can be attempted.

What is the meaning of the phrase? The report of the Council of Experts constituted by the National Law Development Center (Badan Pembinaan Hukum Nasional) included the following comments. (pp. 4–5):

> The whole universe and the human existence therein is not a mere historical phenomenon or accidental product of the universe itself. This universe has been created with a certain aim, managed by a certain Law and is the creation of God, the Benevolent, the Merciful, the Almighty, the Greatest Creator. Indonesia as a State, which according to human organs of sense has been constituted by the people, should not exist without God's blessing. . . .Most important in the conception of God is the recognition of His being all embracing. God manages everything, great and small. The universe is a single diagram managed prudently by one Creator/Mover in such a way that all creations complete each other, influence each other, and there is mutual interdependency between them. Life has an aim. For that reason, in the Universe there exists a moral structure and a moral rule governing interaction and mutual interdependency between everything. The pur-

port of the moral structure is that everything exists in terms of take and give.[3]

Let us now turn to the ways the phrase "belief in all-embracing God" was implemented through legislation.

Owing to one of the transitional clauses of the 1945 Constitution, the Dutch rules on the organization and procedure of civil courts remained valid. Emergency Law no. 1 of 1951 aimed to unify the civil judiciary and gradually abolish the *adat* courts, recognizing at the same time the separate existence of religious courts. Article 1, section 4, of this law declared that the Government was entitled to regulate the continuation of religious courts; consequently, the Government Regulation (Peraturan Pemerintah) no. 45/1957 came into force. This Regulation has validity in the Outer Regions outside of Java and Madura, excluding the Banjarmasin district. It provides the name of Mahkamah Syariah (Islamic Law Court) for the first instance court. The appeals court is called Mahkamah Syariah Propinsi. There is no court of cassation.[4] The competence of the religious courts according to the Government Regulation of 1957 covers *nikah* (marriage disputes), *talak* (repudiation), *rujuk* (reconciliation), *fasach* (judicial dissolution of marriage), *nafakah* (food), *mahar* (dower), *tempat kediaman* (domicile), *mut'ah* (divorce gift), *hadhanah* (custody and support of the children), *waris-malwaris* (inheritance), *wakaf* (religious foundation), *hibah* (gift), *sadakah* (charity), *baitalmal* (religious treasury), and *taklik* (conditional repudiation). Several of these areas are also subject to *adat* control in many ethnic areas. Gift exchange associated with marriages and funerals are central to *adat*. Land law, especially matters of inheritance, was a particularly important area of *adat* control.

Prior to the Basic Agrarian Law (BAL) there was no unification (Undang2 Pokok Agraria, Gazette 1960, no. 104). In fact, there were two entirely separate systems of land law. On the one side was land law based on Western law, the principles of which were to be found in the Civil Code. This Code, introduced in the middle of the nineteenth century as one of the products of the Codification Year 1848, was similar to the Netherlands Civil Code. On the other side, there was land law based on the customary law. This customary law was known as *Adat* Law, or in the Indonesian language, as *Hukum Adat*. Thus, there were two kinds of land, i.e., land subject to Western codified law (Civil Code) and land subject to unwritten Indonesian customary law. This prevailing dualism in matters of private law resulted in interpersonal legal problems in relation to land. There were, however, conflict rules to deal with these problems.

Soon after independence day, preparations were made to change the pre-war land law. These preparations were finalized on September 24, 1960, the day of the enactment of the BAL. Several articles of the BAL relate to religion:

1. *Article 1, section 2*: All lands, water and air in Indonesia, including the natural richness therein, are a blessing of the all embracing God and form national richness.
2. *Article 5*: Agrarian law should take into consideration the rules of religious law.
3. *Article 14*: The Government should initiate a general plan of the supply, distribution and use of land, water and air among others for the benefit of religious purposes.
4. The right of ownership of religious bodies is recognized and protected.
5. *Article 49, section 3*: *Wakaf* (religious foundation) is protected and regulated by Government Regulation.

Also, Government Regulation no. 28, 1977, gives provisions on registering and supervising *wakaf.*

It is perhaps matters of marriage, however, in which the connections between law and religion are most elaborate. The Civil Code of 1848 contained codified rules on marriage for Europeans and foreign Orientals of Chinese origin. For Christian Indonesians there was the Marriage Ordinance of 1933, having validity in Java, Madura, and other areas of the Outer Regions. The Christian Indonesians in Sumatra and other regions were subject to unwritten customary law, while the majority of the Indonesian population, professing Islam, submitted to the rules of Islam. These Islamic rules on marriage were regarded as having been accepted by the *Adat* Law (Reception theory). By late 1946 the Ministry initiated the enactment of Law 22/1946 replacing three colonial laws on the administration of marriage and related matters. The new law was intended to unify the administration of marriage and related matters and simultaneously to adapt to the new conditions of national independence. A booklet published in 1975 by the Indonesian Department of Information states in its introduction that "the basic issues affecting the position of women and children were child marriage, forced marriage, polygamy without meeting the requirements of Islamic law, easy arbitrary divorce with the right of repudiation by the husband, no proper alimony for the divorced wife, etc." Owing to one of the transitional articles in the Constitution of 1945, however, the colonial regulations remained valid. Thus, women's position in marriage matters continued to be unsatisfactory, "in spite of efforts by the Government and women's organizations to improve the situation" (Department of Information 1975:6).

Prior to the enactment of the Marriage Law of 1974, two drafts of Marriage Bills were discussed in the House of People's Representatives. One draft was based on unification, the other on diversity of laws, but no result was reached. New efforts were undertaken. In 1967 the Government submitted a draft applying to Muslims, in 1968 another, applicable to all religious groups. The debates in Parliament did not produce any results. The main problem was the question of whether there would be one Marriage Law for all layers of the population, or a diversity of laws. In 1973 there were new attempts based on the ideal of unification. After adoption of several amendments, the new law was promulgated on January 2, 1974. Law no. 1, 1974, on marriage (Article 2, section 1) states that a marriage is legitimate if it has been performed according to the laws of the respective religions and beliefs of the parties concerned. This law, applicable to all Indonesians, regardless of religion and ethnic group, went into effect on October 1, 1975. It must be regarded as an important step in codification and in the effort to unify Indonesia's legal system. The law reads in part:

1. A marriage is legitimate if it has been performed according to the laws of the respective religions and beliefs of the parties concerned.
2. Every marriage will be registered according to the regulations of the legislation in force.
3. In principle a male person shall be allowed to have one wife only. A female person shall be allowed to have one husband only.
4. The Court shall be entitled to grant permission to a husband to have more than one wife, if the wife concerned so wishes.
5. The Court shall grant permission to a husband to have more than one wife if:
   a. the wife is unable to perform her duties as wife.
   b. the wife suffers from physical defects or an incurable disease.
   c. the wife is incapable of having descendants.
6. The husband shall submit to the Court:
   a. approval of the wife.
   b. the assurance that he will guarantee the necessities of life for his wife and children.
   c. the guarantee that he shall act justly in regard to his wife and children.
7. An agreement between both the aspirant bride and bridegroom is required for a marriage.
8. A person who has not attained the age of 21 years shall obtain the consent of both parents.

9. Marriage shall be permitted only if the male aspirant has reached the age of 19 years and the female aspirant the age of 16.
10. For a woman whose marriage has been dissolved there shall be applicable a waiting period, the length of which shall be regulated in a Government Regulation.
11. A marriage may be prevented in case any party does not meet the prerequisites for the performance of the marriage.
12. A marriage can be dissolved.
13. A husband or a wife may submit a request for the dissolution of a marriage if it was performed under illegal threat.
14. Both parties by mutual consent may enter into a written marriage-contract.
15. That marriage-contract shall not be capable of being legalized if it is in violation of legal, religious and moral limits.
16. The husband is the head of the family and the wife the mother of the household.
17. The husband shall have the responsibility of protecting his wife and provide her with all the necessities of life.
18. Property acquired during marriage shall become joint property.
19. In case a marriage has been dissolved on account of a divorce, the joint property shall be dealt with according to the respective laws.
20. A marriage may be dissolved for the following reasons:
    a. death
    b. divorce
    c. by virtue of a judgment of the Court
21. In this Law a mixed marriage shall be understood to be a marriage between two persons who in Indonesia are subject to different laws owing to the difference in nationality and one of the parties is a foreign national, while the other party is an Indonesian national.
22. In this Law a Court shall be understood to mean:
    a. the religious Court for those embracing Islam
    b. the General Court for all others

This marriage law represents both a deeply Indonesian, national statement (in its general non-ethnic character) and an Islamic statement, in its attention to "appropriate" Islamic features of marriage. I take this law as a harbinger of future developments in Indonesian legal culture: Islam is a necessary part of national life, and the Islam practiced is a thoroughly Indonesian one. I am deeply convinced that Islamic law in the Republic of Indonesia will be honored and appreciated by our Government.

II. Islam and Adat Among South Tapanuli Migrants in Three Indonesian Cities

Basyral Hamidy Harahap

A PERENNIAL TOPIC OF RESEARCH among students of Sumatran cultures is the shifting relationship between local *adat* and Islam. In his studies of Minangkabau social history, Taufik Abdullah (1966) has described a number of delicate adjustive mechanisms that allow that culture to reconcile creatively two overtly opposed symbolic and social institutional systems: Minangkabau *adat*, with its strong matrilineal cast and its undeniable "local custom" character, and Islam, with its patrilineal inheritance norms and its universalistic religious outlook. James Siegel (1969) has examined the interplay of Islamic symbols, local political developments, and *adat* in Aceh in his study of the changing folk definitions of selfhood there.

These works examine *adat* and Islam largely as an ethnic homeland phenomenon. This short paper, on the Muslim Batak from South Tapanuli, North Sumatra, examines the relationship between *adat* and Islam for a population of migrants who have moved to Medan, Jakarta, and Bandung, all ethnically mixed large cities shaped by the developing national Indonesian culture. My findings, based on survey research in June and July of 1982, are in contrast to the findings of Susan Rodgers on the Angkola and Sipirok Batak societies. Rodgers often stresses the social mechanisms which Batak Muslims in that area have developed to reconcile their *adat* and Islam into a locally defined "compatible" whole (Rodgers-Siregar 1979,

1981). My findings also differ from those of A.K. Pulungan, a leading *adat* master of ceremony in Jakarta, who also explains that Islam has strengthened *adat* among Batak Muslims (Pulungan 1973:35–50). My research differs also from that of Sormin, a Protestant minister, who claims that Christian Batak believe that *adat* and Christianity cannot be separated as basic philosophy for a Christian Batak way of life (Sormin 1961:4, 46).

In my questionnaire research, interviews, and observations of South Tapanuli Muslim migrants, I found that Islam and *adat* are often conceptualized as antagonistic, not mutually supportive as is the case in Angkola and Sipirok. Among the South Tapanuli Muslim migrants I contacted, *adat* is best seen as a system in retreat from Islam, a case similar to that in Barumun (Pulungan, 1974). In fact, South Tapanuli *adat* has been reduced to a ceremonial system. The South Tapanuli people I studied refer to both *adat* and Islam in solving problems of everyday life, but the institutions of their *dalihan na tolu*[1] *adat* have been weakened in the process. *Adat* functions in *adat* ceremonies and some aspects of inheritance law, marriage arrangement, conflict settlement, and in the discussion of family problems. Islam, however, shapes all these spheres and, in fact, defines them. To take a telling illustration of the whole process, 55 percent of my respondents asserted that *kawin semarga* (marriage within the named patrilineal clan) conforms to Islamic rules and is acceptable in the abstract on those grounds. This idea is in direct contradiction to Batak *adat*, which explicitly forbids clan endogamy in its system of asymmetrical marriage alliance.

The South Tapanuli migrant communities thus offer an intriguing case of one particular Indonesian solution to questions of Islam and *adat*. Here, as in other areas of Indonesia today, Islam does not simply adjust to local *adat*—Islam defines *adat*.

This paper has several sections: a brief social history of the South Tapanuli migration from the ethnic homeland to the cities; a consideration of the general processes of modernization at work in the society; and a report on my survey and interview findings in the areas of marriage, community integration, and *adat* ceremonialism. This last topic led to a short examination of the special stand toward *adat* taken by the Muhammadiyah sect of modernist Muslims in Batak migrant communities.

My methods followed standard survey research approaches (Babbie 1973). I disseminated eight hundred questionnaires to married adult migrants living in the three cities. Two hundred of these questionnaires have been returned at the time of this writing. Respondents, both male and female, ranged in age from twenty-nine to seventy-seven years. Sample questions and several reasons for the low return rate are set out in the Notes.[2] I have supplemented the survey research with interviews over the course of several years and through personal involvement in migrant society and culture. I have interviewed some sixty people ranging from former local chiefs to three former *bupatis* (sub-province administrators) to the present *bupati* of South Tapanuli. Also included in my interviews are many *ulamas* (religious teachers), local leaders, *adat* orators, politicians, teachers, reporters, and the General Secretary of the HKBPA (the Huria Kristen Batak Protestan Angkola, the local, ethnically based denomination of the Batak Protestant church). These interviews included people from both the South Tapanuli homeland and the migrant cities.[3]

Migration From the Ethnic Homeland to Urban Areas

A number of factors have motivated South Tapanuli people to leave their homelands. The Padri War (1821–37) was one of the early shocks which motivated people to migrate (Tugby 1979:17–18). Forced labor, introduced by Dutch colonial authorities in cooperation with local chiefs, also stimulated people to leave, as did wars among local chiefs which sometimes resulted in slavery. Castles (1973:20) reports that as many as one-third of the population may have been slaves or debtors of varying degrees of subordination. These conditions led to the first waves of South Tapanuli migration in the regency. Some migrants fled to nearby areas. For example, some Mandailing migrants crossed the Bukit Barisan, the mountain range dividing South Tapanuli from north to south, and settled in Barumun, Sosa, Barumun Tengah, and even Saipar Dolok Hole districts. They named their new settlements after their original *huta* (village), so that even today we find many Mandailing *hutas* in these areas.[4] About ninety households or 425 persons still live in this very isolated mountainous area. They say that their ancestors reached these places about 125 years or five generations ago. They settled in Tanjung Ale, Sigalagala, and Simangambat in the Sosa district and lived under poor conditions without formal education facilities. People of Tanjung Ale say their ancestors hid in these hills to escape from tyrannic local chiefs. Although avowed Muslims, those who live in this area are nevertheless still strongly influenced by animism and the traditional culture. The Department of Social Affairs has classified the region as one in special need of development *(masyarakat terasing)* (Laporan 1982). Other early migrants, however, moved via the east and west coasts to distant places. The harbor of Natal on the west coast became the gate to West Sumatra or Java, and the east coast became the gate to the Malay Peninsula.

In the second half of the nineteenth century, the Dutch government introduced formal education in South Tapanuli in the form of two-year elementary schools. The Rheinishce Missionsgesellschaft (RMG) also opened such schools in the Sipirok district (Castles 1973:27). William Iskander followed later with his *Kweekschool voor Inlandsch Onderwijzers* (Native Teacher's Training School) in Tanobato, Mandailing (1862–1974) (Harahap 1979). Education, an open door to new horizons, was an important influence on migration. Migrants now left not to escape tyrannic chiefs but to study, as well as to trade or search for work. South Tapanuli migrants became teachers in Deli, Aceh, Central and South Sumatra, and Riau. These teachers also became models, success stories for the young to emulate. Books written by South Tapanuli authors, and magazines and books in general, were other sources of new ideas and inspiration for those who would leave home. Education, however, was only one avenue out of the homeland.

South Tapanuli people also moved to open new rice fields in the northern parts of West Sumatra and in the Malay Peninsula; many young people left their villages for the east coast (Heyting 1897:23). Some worked for Dutch companies in Deli (Sumatra's east coast) or in the tin mines in the Malay Peninsula (Tugby 1979:18). In the beginning of the twentieth century, rubber and coffee exports created a brief golden age in South Tapanuli, but, when this changed sharply with the worldwide economic depression, migration out of the region again swelled. Most migrants of this recent period have settled in Medan, especially in Sungai Mati around the Palace of the Sultan of Deli (Castles 1973:186; Ihutan 1926:5, 70–71). Gradually, migration became one of the traditions of South Tapanuli. *Merantau*, as it is called, is now seen as an informal means of education, a way to accumulate the experiences and knowledge for a successful life.

Today people migrate from South Tapanuli to escape the poverty of this rural area. Population growth is a continuous pressure on limited agricultural lands. Rice production does not cover daily needs, and coffee and rubber, still the main export crops, are no longer a source of prosperity. Poor highway access hinders the sub-province's development. Trunk roads from Padang Sidimpuan (the capital and main trade center) are poor, as is the main road running through the sub-province, although that road is part of the Trans-Sumatra Highway. There are, of course, hundreds of *huta* which lie far from even these main roads. In recent years, some migrants have moved to other rural agricultural areas such as the Pasaman region of West Sumatra (Naim 1976) or the south and southeastern areas of Aceh.

Some fifty households have moved to the national transmigration site in Sinunukan, Natal district, and twenty-eight of these came from the Panyabungan district, supposedly one of the most fertile parts of South Tapanuli. According to the Regional Bureau of Statistics, two villages have recently been erased from the map of this regency. South Tapanuli parents frequently tell their children that they will not inherit anything; they must make their way on their own. This advice plays an important role in motivating people to leave their village and go to the big cities to study and build their careers. Five principal motives account for migration nowadays: to study (28.89 percent), to search for better living conditions (25.56 percent), to work in the government or military service (12.78 percent), to secure better education for their children (11.11 percent), or to combine study and work (8.55 percent).

Adat, *Modernization, and the Influence of Islam*

The urban migrants' way of life, as well as that in the homeland, is undeniably based on both Islam and *adat* traditions. It is to these sources that people turn in meeting their problems. Islam is ascendant in South Tapanuli migrant life, as noted. Islam, stressing each person's relationship to Allah, encourages greater individualism than does *adat*. *Adat* primarily regulates social life and defines the ways people should interact, although Islam is also an authority on these matters.

Modern education and administration have encouraged a certain disintegration of traditional social structure and have changed people's attitudes toward traditional social forms. In 1946 and 1947, the Tapanuli Resident, Dr. Ferdinand Lumban Tobing, replaced local chiefs with winners of democratic village elections. The traditional chiefs had drawn their legitimacy from *adat*; the elected officials now draw their legitimacy from participation in a national power structure. Representatives of the traditional type of *huta* chiefs grow ever smaller in number. Those still alive are seventy to eighty years of age and live in the cities as well as the *huta*. Frequently, they have also made the pilgrimage to Mecca, and yet, like many other South Tapanuli people, even the traditional chiefs protest that they are not rich enough to sponsor big *adat* ceremonies. Although there are still men respected for their knowledge of *adat*, their significance as leaders has diminished relative to religious leaders and the new secular system of leadership. Other forms of traditional social life have also disappeared. *Marsialap ari* is the custom of reciprocal labor exchange for the planting and harvesting of rice. This tradition has gradually diminished during the last twenty-five years, and nowadays, most people simply hire wage laborers to help at these busy times. Perhaps the most central feature of South Tapanuli traditional social life, however, the *dalihan na tolu*, still has contemporary importance. It must be noted, though, that Islam strongly sculpts this centerpiece of *adat*.

Dalihan na tolu is a phrase which, to the South Tapanuli mind, sums up the whole of the traditional social structure built on a threefold division of kin into *kahanggi* (ego's patrilineal group, i.e., of the same *marga* or patrilineal clan), *mora* or *hula-hula* (wife-giver groups), and *anak boru* (wife-taker groups). The interaction of these three dominated village life, giving shape to economic relations such as inheritance, exchange, and labor relations. These divisions of kin also structured relationships of sacred power and deference to superiors. In times of family crises or conflicts, this structure, rather than a system of courts, came into play in the arbitration of disputes and in the discussions and decisions about family rights and obligations. This social triad was the organizational form through which families sponsored life-crisis events such as funerals and weddings, and it provided much of the content, the "meaning" of those events as well.

Let us turn to the research findings on the fate of this *dalihan na tolu—*based kinship system in the migrant communities.

Islam, Adat, *and Kinship*

Migrant *adat* belies any comfortable assumption that Indonesian *adat* systems are unchanged bequests from the ancestors. Migrant *adat* in this society also demonstrates that the relationship between *adat* and Islam need not be one of peaceful coexistence. We shall consider clanship, the resolution of family conflicts, marriage, and the role of parental advice-giving in turn.

One of the first questions migrants ask when meeting somebody else from South Tapanuli for the first time is about each other's *marga* membership (55 percent). They may also ask for the *huta* of the new friend (30.56 percent). These questions are important for finding out what *tutur* (kinship terms) have to be used on the basis of the *dalihan na tolu* relationship system. Most respondents considered documents concerning the history of their ancestors very important. These documents are the principal sources for drawing up family trees. The migrants feel that the story of their ancestors has to be told to the younger generation; 39.44

percent said that they already owned family genealogies, and 36.67 percent said that they were looking for the documents. Only 3.89 percent did not consider family trees as important. According to some of these latter persons, Islam, not kinship, should be the basis of brotherhood.

Although a national system of police and courts, including also official Muslim courts *(pengadilan syari'ah)*, has replaced some of the legal functions of the *dalihan na tolu,* the latter remains strong as a way of resolving family conflicts. The migrants solve most of their family conflicts by an appeal to members of their *dalihan na tolu* (36.11 percent). Sometimes they abandon the conflicts because they believe that sooner or later both parties will reach reconciliation in a natural way (17.78 percent). There were only two respondents who had applied to the courts about their family conflicts.

As noted, some 55 percent of the respondents agreed that marriage within a named patrilineal clan was acceptable in the ideal, citing as a reason that it "conformed to Islamic rules." Forty-five percent objected to clan endogamy, asserting that it is forbidden by *adat.* My interviews indicate that this mixed pattern of responses is characteristic of both migrant communities and homeland communities. The practice of *kawin semarga* is more general among Mandailing Batak than among Batak living in Angkola, Sipirok, Padang Bolak, and homelands to the north. This supports the idea that *adat* influence is stronger in these last-named regions, even though Angkola and Sipirok are approximately 90 percent Muslim.

How does the Batak marriage pattern of preferred matrilateral cross-cousin marriage fare in the Muslim migrant communities? Marriage arrangements of migrants' sons and daughters are strongly influenced by Islam, it happens. A migrant's child should marry somebody who is also Muslim. This is indicated by the following answers: the respondents agree to their sons marrying non-South Tapanuli girls, but these must be Muslims (51.11 percent); their daughters, too, may choose to marry non-South Tapanuli men, but they must also be Muslim (48.33 percent). Marriages between children with different regional backgrounds in fact frequently occur. The second preference is marriage with somebody also of South Tapanuli origin. Of the respondents, 21.67 percent said that they wanted their sons to marry South Tapanuli girls, and 30.56 percent said that they wanted their daughters to marry South Tapanuli men. The third preference is matrilateral cross-cousin marriage. Cross-cousin marriage (marriage of a son with a daughter of wife's brother, or marriage of a daughter with the son of a sister) is the ideal *adat* marriage. The percentages in this case are 3.33 percent for sons and 2.78 percent for daughters. These observations indicate that Islam is stronger than *adat* with regard to preferred marriage choice among the migrants. Interestingly, among the groups surveyed, an emphasis on Islam appears to increase after a couple has children. Migrants answered that most of their children's names were derived from *Al Quran* or from famous Muslim leaders or historical figures such as prophets. Of the respondents, 47.78 percent said that their children's names derived from Islamic sources, 30 percent gave their father's name to their sons, 18.89 percent said that their children's names were taken from parts of their own names (husband and wife names), 18.89 percent gave South Tapanuli names, and 6.11 percent of the respondents said that they named their children after well-known figures. When I asked my informants to mention three names of persons whom they accepted as their models, Prophet Muhammad got the highest percentage, with 66.67 percent choosing him as their model.[5]

Batak are enthusiastic advice-givers—how has this practice fared in a Muslim urban world? Islam frames all advice-giving, Muslim or otherwise.

Migrants feel that education of their children is not complete without religious education. They send their children to Islamic courses *(madrasah)* before or after school days, or to evening courses held at religious teachers' homes. They also pay private teachers to come to their home and teach their children at least to learn to read *Al Quran*. They believe that religious education is as important as secular education. Muslim advice also is considered crucial to the whole endeavor of advice-giving. As noted in Table 11.1, counsel on Muslim religious loyalty precedes in importance other types of advice.

Parents in South Tapanuli have many hopes and plans for their sons and daughters who choose to migrate. They typically give advice to those who *merantau*, advice which reveals something of these hopes and of the ways the "success" of the migrants will be measured by their society. The kinds of advice parents give to their children who plan to leave their village and resettle in faraway places outside South Tapanuli can be seen in Table 11.1. The parents hope that their children will become religious people and good members of their urban societies; they ask their children to find new "parents" in the strange place but not to forget their real parents in the home village; they emphasize the importance of studying and hard work. These are the five most prominent kinds of advice. My informants claimed to have followed their parents' advice (Table 11.2), although their priorities and the percentages on these two tables are not exactly parallel. For example, while only 21 percent said that their parents had advised them to find new parents, 45 percent had in fact eased their urban adjustment in that way. Conversely, while the predominant parental advice was "to be a good

Table 11.1.
Parental Advice, according to South Tapanuli Migrants, Which They Received
From Their Parents When They Left Their Village for Large Cities

Advice	Percentage of 180 Migrants Receiving the Advice
To be a real Muslim	53.89
To be a good member of society	47.67
Do not forget us	22.22
You must study hard	21.67
For your safety, find your "new parent" in the strange place	21.11
You must be honest	17.78
Be polite	15.00
Diligent	13.33
Economical	10.55
Optimistic	6.66
Helpful	4.44
Love worldly life but do not forget to prepare for life in the world hereafter	3.89
Patience and firmness	3.89
Find your good friends	3.33
Be careful	2.22
Find South Tapanuli Muslim as your marriage partner	1.67
Be on your own	1.11
Read books	0.55
Do not waste time	0.55
You may ask our family—migrants in the city— to help you in difficulties	0.55

Muslim," only 17 percent felt that they had fully carried out the duties of Islam. Although less than 2 percent reported that their parents had advised marrying a South Tapanuli Muslim, this is indeed the general rule; 74.63 percent of my respondents had married with South Tapanuli Muslims. Others married North Sumatra Muslims from other ethnic backgrounds (6.11 percent), Central Javanese (3.89 percent), East Javanese, Jakartans, Buginese, and Indonesian-born Chinese.

Table 11.2.
Activities of the New Migrants After They Arrived in the City

Activities	Percentage of 180 Migrants
They found "new parent" and South Tapanuli families and stayed with one of the families.	45.00
They adjusted to the new environment.	27.78
They continued their study.	21.67
They searched for work.	18.33
They did their duties as Muslim.	17.22
They made friends with good persons.	12.22
They were honest, patient, and firm, and worked diligently.	11.67
They did not forget their parent in the village. They sent letters to their parent to tell them about their conditions.	8.89

The second most predominant advice from parents is to be a good member of their new society. Migrants achieve this through participation in migrant associations, as well as through participation in religious and other multi-ethnic associations.

Christian migrants usually set up *marga* associations. The Muslim migrants, however, set up *huta, luat* (district), or even Tapanuli or South Tapanuli associations: for example, *Keluarga Sayurmaincat dan Anak Boru* (KESAN), *Ikatan Keluarga Barumun Raya* (IKABAYA), *Persatuan Wanita Muslim Tapanuli* (PERWAMTA), *Keluarga Muslim Tapanuli* (KMT), or (with names in the Batak language) *Pardomuanta* (our union) and *Pengajian Sahata*.

The migrants who responded to the questionnaire appear to be educated and successful persons. Of the respondents, 50 percent live in their own house, 10.56 percent in a rented house, 6.11 percent in a government official house, and 6.66 percent in houses bought in installments from government building companies. Many have traveled internationally; 18.89 percent of them have made the pilgrimage to Mecca, and 30 percent planned to make the pilgrimage between 1982 and 1985. Some have visited foreign countries for official visits (20.56 percent), tours (12.78 percent), study (10.56 percent), business (5 percent), seminars (5 percent), and medical treatment and family visits. They attribute their successful careers to hard work (40 percent), God's benevolence (21.11 percent), family assistance (17.22 percent), and personal connections (9.44 percent). Many had achieved higher education: 43.89 percent had graduated in the various

Table 11.3.
Education Level of the Migrants

Name of Schools	Percentage of 180 Migrants
University, IKIP, ITB, IAIN	43.89
Senior High School (SMA)	21.67
Academy	14.44
Junior High School (SMP)	5.56
Hollandsch Inlandsche School (HIS)	5.00
Meer Uitgebereid Lager Onderwijs (MULO)	4.44
Religious School (Pesantren)	3.89
Elementary School (Sekolah Rakyat)	1.11

universities, and 14.44 percent had completed bachelor's level study (Table 11.3). Some of them—the older respondents—had completed their preliminary and secondary school education in South Tapanuli during the colonial period before their departure to their new destinies. They have good jobs in almost all kinds of professions (Table 11.4). Many of them are now prominent members of the heterogeneous pan-Indonesian society. Of the 180 migrants, 20.55 percent were elected as chairmen of *kampung* associations or neighborhood organizations *(rukun warga* and *rukun tetangga)*, 15.55 percent as members of the board of mosques, 4.44 percent as chairmen of mutual help associations, and 3.33 percent as chairmen of sport clubs. They also become members of migrant associations and of religious meeting associations *(pengajian* and *majelis taklim)*. Some are members of the board of professional associations. Moreover, successful migrants influence their relatives to leave their village and resettle in Indonesian cities. The 180 respondents had 774 siblings, most of whom have also migrated to many places within Indonesia (71.83 percent), and abroad (5 percent).

Although those in the home village view the successes of those who leave with pride and satisfaction, it is perhaps inevitable that the great distances between family members sometimes strain migrant-home relationships. City dwellers comment that the home villagers are lazy and always ask for material help. On the other side, many people in South Tapanuli feel that migrants no longer care for their original villages. They sometimes complain that those who leave do not pay enough attention to the development needs of the home village. Migrants, however, claim that they do contribute to the building and restoration of village mosques (77.22 percent), school buildings (39.44 percent), or their parents' graves (17.78 percent).

Table 11.4.
Migrants' Jobs and Professions

Jobs and Professions	Percentage of 180 Migrants
Civil servant	18.33
Teacher	12.22
Lecturer (University, IKIP* or IAIN)	11.11
Employee of state entrepreneur	8.89
Retired civil servant	7.78
Policeman or military	7.78
Entrepreneur	7.78
Employee of private entrepreneur	5.56
Businessman	3.89
Lawyer	1.67
Journalist	1.67
Hydrologist	1.11
Engineer	1.11
Member of parliament	0.56
Author	0.56
Public prosecutor	0.56
Diplomat	0.56
Nurse	0.56
Preacher	0.56
Housewife	2.22

*Teacher Training Institute.

The migrants report that they make return visits to their villages (Table 11.5) in order to see their parents (65 percent), or parents' grave (56.11 percent), to attend parents' funerals (22.22 percent), or the wedding of a sibling (16.67 percent), or other ritual gatherings (8.89 percent), specifically, to attend the departure of their parents for Mecca (7.78 percent). Others said they had sometimes returned home to resolve family conflicts (8.33 percent).

In summary, both Islam and *adat* regulate social life among South Tapanuli migrants. Migrants use *marga* clan identities and *dahlihan na tolu* relationships as a partial basis for structuring social life in the cities, but, as followers of Islam, they also see religion as a source of brotherhood and commonality. Islam teaches Muslims to forge a brotherhood based on

Table 11.5.
Frequency of Visits to the Village

Frequency	Number of Migrants		
	Medan	Jakarta	Bandung
Monthly	1	...	...
Twice a year	3	...	...
Once a year	28	5	...
Once in two years	14	10	1
Once in three years	12	7	3
Once in four years	7	6	2
Once in five years	4	13	1
Once in more than five years	9	39	13
Never	1	1	...

common faith and practices *(ukhuwwah Islamiyah)*, and in many ways the urban environment encourages this basis of social unity over traditional bases. The prominent *ulama* live in the big cities; mosques in the cities have routine religious meetings which bring people together on a regular basis; and many migrants hold positions in the mosque management. Religious meetings and organizations link South Tapanuli to Muslims in other ethnic groups, but religious commonality also links migrants to each other. The religious symbolism of the Hilal Bi Hilal is one example of this. It is not easy always to separate Islam and *adat* in South Tapanuli traditions. So-called *adat* ceremonies contain prayers to Allah, Arabic greetings, and other Arabic phrases and blessings. Even the distinction between NU supporters and Muhammadiyah supporters is not a simple *adat* versus Islam distinction.

Let us turn now to consider the survey results in the area of community cohesion and then *adat* ceremonialism. The role of the Muhammadiyah will be discussed in relation to *adat* ceremonialism.

Islam and Community Integration

The spirit of *gotong-royong* or everyone-pulling-together for mutual self-support is a familiar idea in Indonesian studies. Among Mandailing South Tapanuli people, the social reality of this concept varies between the city and the homeland village. While my general observations from 1976 to 1982 indicate that some *gotong-royong* acts are still carried out in the farm villages, even there the practice can hardly be said to be flourishing. In the migrant cities, there is a trend toward the use of hired labor, or, if Batak-based groups are used for community projects, these are often constituted on a transformed, urban basis.

Migrants appear to have a jaundiced view of the homeland village, seeing it as a haven for the lazy. South Tapanuli's economic modernization has been relatively slow when compared with other regions of Sumatra. This general impression is not only felt by South Tapanuli people themselves from inside and outside the sub-province but is also voiced by travelers who cross the region on their way from North and West Sumatra. Importantly, people are often not wealthy enough to repair their houses, a prime local sign of economic and national development. Some city migrants blame this relative lack of homeland development on the villagers themselves. My interviews and observations indicate, however, that homeland villagers sometimes complain about city migrants who "forget" the villages they have left behind, visiting them only for lavish *adat* ceremonies—which city folk stage for their own social status purposes (this, again, in the view of migrants).

Islam and Adat Ritual

Most South Tapanuli people still feel that their family's social status depends on sponsoring *adat* ceremonies, and the continuing practice of these ceremonies in the cities is one measure of the strength of *adat*. Urban migrants *select* the traditions to which they will adhere and then make them conform to the requirements of life in the busy and crowded cities. If a family lacks close relatives in one or more of the three categories of kin, it will ask other people to act as its *kahanggi, mora,* and *anak boru* in its ceremonies. In the cities, a family may hire a restaurant or caterer to prepare the meal for a ceremony, and they hire an *Adat* Master of Ceremony to direct the event. Most of the migrants cannot fully participate in *adat* ceremonies because they have not mastered any *adat* proverbs. If forced to speak during such a ceremony, they usually speak in Indonesian, and most of the migrants' children no longer speak the Mandailing or Angkola dialects at all. The role of a professional *adat* speaker has thus become very important. The Masters of Ceremonies are usually older men—fifty to seventy years old. Some professionals such as Zakaria Dalimunte (a member of local parliament), Akil Lubis, and Pangeran Ritonga (a musician from Medan) have been invited several times to act as Masters of Ceremonies in South Tapanuli. Thus, this figure is not just an artifact of city life.

The significance of the *adat* ceremonies has diminished for South Tapanuli people everywhere. This is due both to the influence of Islam and to economic difficulties. People say that *adat* ceremonies—including funeral ceremonies—have animistic and feudalistic elements. The appreciation of *adat* ceremonies among the younger generation of migrants appears to be diminishing. To 57.22 percent of the respondents, the South Tapanuli younger generation does not appear to be interested in *adat* ceremonies; 34.44 percent, however, responded that the younger people are still interested in participation in these ceremonies. The modernization of *adat* ceremonies was suggested by 68.89 percent of the respondents; 13.89 percent wanted to maintain the *adat* ceremonies as they are; 15 percent rejected these ceremonies altogether because so many words and attitudes at these events are forbidden by Islam. Only 18.33 percent of the respondents said they would organize an *adat* ceremony during their son's or daughter's wedding; 20 percent were against any *adat* marriage ceremony; and 49.44 percent would invite an *ulama* to deliver a religious speech on this occasion without any *adat* ceremony.

Several items on the questionnaire sought opinions about specific ceremonial practices. The attitudes toward these practices gauge people's views about Islam and *adat* and how these may or may not be combined. In general these opinions conform to an ideological split between those who support Nahdatul Ulama (NU) and those who follow Muhammadiyah teachings. The former, who might be called orthodox Muslims, accept more *adat* practices than do the latter so-called modernist Muslims. Muhammadiyah supporters thus tend to replace *adat* ceremonial practices with those they find more compatible with Islam. Instead of a traditional *adat* wedding, they would sponsor a *walimah* or *manjumu*, where family members and *ulamas* give the new couple advice according to Islamic teachings and then share a meal together. In particular, the questionnaire asked four questions about funeral practices and remembering the dead:

If a friend or family member dies, the Muslim migrants organize either a *tahlilan* or a *takziyah*. The *tahlilan* consists of reciting a chapter from the Holy *Quran (Surah Yasin)* and praying for the deceased family member in the hope that Allah forgives all of his or her sins and allows him or her a place in Heaven. The *takziyah* (the preference of Muhammadiyah supporters) is an event at which the mourning family hears religious advice to make them feel determined in facing the misfortune. The percentage who responded they would sponsor *tahlilan* was 57.72 percent, and *takziyah*, 42.28 percent.

A mourning family may serve a meal after the *tahlilan* or *takziyah*. The NU supporters usually consume these meals within the house of the mourning family; the Muhammadiyah supporters do not eat and drink on such occasions. Muhammadiyah followers believe that it is not right to indulge in such pleasure meals in the house of a mourning family. Moreover, the meals may reduce the inheritance of the orphans. It is considered a big sin to eat or use anything belonging to orphans or considered to be orphan property. Those who said they would provide meals numbered 47.22 percent; 51.11 percent said they would not.

Visits to a sacred place form another indicator for characterizing people as Orthodox Muslims versus Modernist Muslims. The Orthodox Muslims visit family graves to pray for the late family members. By contrast, Modernists do not pay such visits for they believe that there are not time and space boundaries in praying for the deceased. Of the respondents, 68.89 precent said they pray at graves; 24.44 percent said they would not.

Another indication concerns ritual commemoration of late family members: 61.67 percent of the respondents refuse to take part in such ritual gatherings; 25.56 percent of the respondents said they might organize such ritual gatherings.

In sum, Muhammadiyah followers profess an *"agama"* (monotheistic, "true" religion) free of any comprises with possibly blasphemous local ritual practices and spirit beliefs.

Conclusions

My research indicates that religious loyalties, locally conceptualized as somewhat antagonistic to local ethnic customs, are stronger than *adat* conscience. I predict that in the long term South Tapanuli *adat* will retreat further and that *adat* ceremonies (the "badge" of *adat* in modernizing Indonesia) will come to occupy a smaller and more constricted sphere. The advice of religious teachers, family, and close friends will increasingly supplant verse-form *adat* advice sayings. I also predict that traditional music will be played on modern musical instruments and will be transformed in the process.

Why is Islam ascendant in this way? Perhaps part of the answer lies in the fact that *adat* is losing its formal educational institutions just as Islamic educational outlets become stronger. Ceremonies such as weddings are declining in educational significance. By contrast, Southern Batak Islam in the homeland and in the migrant cities has an abundance of educational forms, from schools with distinctive dress to tape cassettes of Arabic music to the national printed media and telecommunications. This social fact about the institutional carriers of Islam and *adat* should not be forgotten in studies of Indonesian religions and cultures.

12. Sundanese Islam and the Value of Hormat: Control, Obedience, and Social Location in West Java

Jessica Glicken

$\mathcal{R}$ELIGION PROVIDES A VOCABULARY through which other kinds of events can be understood; it provides a context for social life (Geertz 1966b:20–21). Emile Durkheim's discussion of the interdependence between religion and society proposed that religion both "reflects" society and is an integral part of it (Durkheim 1961:470). Clifford Geertz argued that not only is religion itself a system but it is integrated in a systemic way with other cultural domains, providing an idealized conception of society which also functions as a model or guide for social action (Geertz 1966b). An analysis of religion, coupled with a cultural investigation, will provide an additional perspective on cultural phenomena.

Lévi-Strauss (1963b) offers a masterful demonstration of this on the psychological level in his analysis of South American myth. Geertz also suggests a psychological dimension of religion when he writes that religious symbols "induce in the worshiper a certain distinctive set of dispositions" (1966b:9), tendencies toward certain kinds of activities. Participants couch these tendencies or predilections in the language of religion.

This discussion is an analysis of the interaction of a religion and a cultural system. I will examine the interface between Islam as experienced by the Sundanese in western Java[1] and the key Sundanese cultural value of *hormat*.[2] I will gloss *hormat* as the recognition of social location and argue

that its cultural power is best understood in terms of the Sundanese definitions of the Islamic community and the structure of religious education.
Elementary religious instruction among the Sundanese inculcates highly
valued social attitudes in children, focusing on the moral rules and obligations that define the child's place within the community and bind him to
that community.

Functioning as the key institution of Islam (Abdullah 1971:54), formal
religious instruction in Pasundan (the Sundanese area of the Indonesian
province of West Java) also provides a means for transmitting and reinforcing some of the most important values of Sundanese culture. The notion
of obedience and the demonstration of respect are fundamental to West
Javanese Islam and are refracted in the Sundanese value of *hormat*. These
Islamic and Sundanese values develop primarily through a special use
of language—Arabic and Sundanese, respectively—that focuses attention
less on the semantic content of language than on its performance—the
nondenotative, often extraverbal, aspects of the speech event. Learning
social location and appropriate (Sundanese) behavior is also expressed as
a religious struggle—the triumph of *akal*[3] over *hawa nafsu*.[4] Mastery of
the rules defining social location and the corresponding correct behavior
(the rules defining the Sundanese community) is exhibited by demonstrating *hormat* through the appropriate use of language levels. Students
demonstrate the development of *akal* within the religious context by controlling the language of the Qur'an through memorization of the text, and
they recognize the rules defining the religious community by obeying the
teacher.

The special use of language in Islamic religious instruction has been
treated in previous studies. Wagner and Lofti (1980a,b) and Miller (1977)
discuss the cognitive and psychological effects of an intensive program of
"rote" learning in the Islamic areas of Yemen, Senegal, and Morocco.
Eickelman discusses the relationship between the "cognitive style" (1978:
491) associated with Islamic instruction and other, nonreligious spheres of
knowledge. Jones (1981a) also addresses the question of the sociological
consequences of language use in her discussion of the role of the Arabic
language in religious instruction in traditional Muslim schools in Java.
Several of the points Jones raises concerning restricted literacy, the role of
the literate individual, and the symbolic aspects of literacy in a nonliterate
society are also treated in the collection of essays edited by Goody (1968),
most of which deal with non-Islamic areas.

The Sundanese experience the Arabic-language Qur'an as an oral text;
it is usually performed rather than read. The Sundanese focus attention
on the form, arrangement, and performance of the language rather than on

the content of the text. Elementary religious lessons in West Java "teach" the Qur'an. The content of lessons is assumed since the Qur'an and the religious laws it embodies are not and cannot be problematic or challenge-able: religious knowledge comes to a student not through an examination of content but by acceptance of its source. Lessons focus implicitly upon recognition of the relationship between teacher and pupil. The oral form of the text also makes the student-teacher relationship imperative for trans-mission of those texts and creates a context within which that relationship is defined and the texts rendered intelligible.

Sundanese express social relationships and the obligations they entail with *hormat*. Usually translated as "respect," *hormat* should be glossed as knowing one's social location and acting in accordance with its attendant rights and obligations. One demonstrates *hormat* by correctly using the formalized levels of politeness of the Sundanese language and by producing politeness phrases appropriate to a given situation. Correct use of these two aspects of language indicates that a person has internalized the criteria upon which Sundanese society is organized and has accepted the Sun-danese way of life.

West Javanese Islam and the Language of the Qur'an

West Java, as a whole, is the most strongly Islamic province on the island of Java and, indeed, one of the strongest Islamic areas in Indonesia. Of the 3,872 *pesantren* (Islamic religious schools) in Indonesia in 1975–76, 1,696 of them—almost half—were located in West Java (Departemen Agama 1975:188–89). Islam is a visible and audible presence in the life of Ban-dung, West Java's largest city. The calls to the five daily prayers, broadcast over loudspeakers from each of the many mosques in the city, punctuate each day. On Friday at noon, sarong-clad men and boys fill the streets on their way to the mosques to join the midday prayer known as the *Juma'atan* which provides the visible definition of the religious community (*ummat*) in the Sundanese community. West Java's history of involvement with militant Islam is also important to the Sundanese. As I traveled around the province in 1981, people would point with pride to areas of particularly heavy military activity during the Dar'ul Islam period.[5] The Dar'ul Islam movement technically ended in 1962 with the capture and execution of its leader, Kartosoewirjo, but as late as 1972 an anthropologist doing research in a *pesantren* located near Garut (about 50 km southeast of Bandung) was provided with an armed escort as she traveled through the hills to visit other *pesantren* in remote areas; her hosts said Dar'ul Islam made such travel dangerous (personal communication). In 1981, there were rumors in Bandung of an extant and viable Islamic separatist movement in western Java. Finally, over the last four years, West Java has consistently sent far more pilgrims to Mecca to make the *haj* than any other province in Indonesia (Biro Pusat Statistik 1981:100), and Sundanese men and women bear the title *haji* with pride.

Formal religious instruction for Sundanese children begins as it has for centuries with instruction in Qur'anic recitation (*mengaji* [Ind.], *ngaji* [Sund.]). *Ngaji* lessons for small boys (and usually but less importantly for young girls) generally take place in the *langgar* (a small room, usually in the mosque or the home of the religious teacher) or in the child's home. These lessons teach the children how to pronounce the Arabic letters of the Islamic religious texts. The children begin to memorize the Qur'an, reciting the letters and words without understanding the content. The emphasis is on correct pronunciation and copious memorization. Most children do not continue their formal religious education beyond these elementary lessons.

Anderson (1966:92) suggests that the power of Qur'anic recitation lies in a special use of language:

> The 'domestication' of Islam and Arabic by the Javanese cultural impulse was done through the transformation of the Koran into a hermetic textbook of riddles and paradoxes. Arabic was maintained as the language of 'initiation' precisely because Arabic was *not* understood . . . the whole point of a spiritual ritual in an uncomprehended language is that it manifests power, limitless power, and implies a deliberately non-rational mode of cognition. Islam had forbidden the continued use of Shivaitic and Tantric mantra; Java answered by turning the Koran into a book of mantra.[6]

As in other situations of strongly restricted literacy, language in Pasundan becomes a means to certain types of extralinguistic knowledge and power (cf. Meggitt 1968, Goody 1968):

> The use of Arabic also serves to strengthen the *kiyayi's* claim to power through knowledge. As a man of learning, the *kiyayi* was to the *santri* community what the dalang or shadowpuppeteer and guru or mystic teachers were to *abangan* and *priyayi* culture. In each case, *ilmu* was associated with a language and a book to which few had access: Arabic and the Qur'an in the case of the

kiyayi, Kawi or old Javanese and the Mahabharata-Ramayana stories in the case of the dalang, mystic manuals in the case of the
guru. (Jones 1981:76)

The Islamic holy book, the Qur'an, is a written rendition of a text
"orally delivered to mankind by the Prophet exactly as it had orally been
delivered to him by the Angel . . ." (as-Said 1975:56). The Qur'an thus is
the Word of God (contrary, for example, to the Bible which consists of
recountings by various individuals of the words of God—a secondary
source, as it were). This Word of God was told to Muhammad in Arabic
and so must be rendered in that language in order to be fully, religiously
experienced.

Since the Qur'an is considered to be God's words (note that the Qur'an
is written in the first person), the language itself takes on a sacred quality:
"The letters of Arabic . . . are the vessels of revelation: the divine attributes
can be expressed only by means of these letters" (Schimmel 1975: 411). The
oral nature of the text is emphasized; to read the Qur'an is to speak God.
An incorrect reading suggests a violation of God (Rasjidi 1956:69). Sundanese say that to mispronounce the Qur'an is to commit a sin *(dosa).*

The Arabic letters have a peculiar characteristic. Written Arabic uses
only consonants. The vowels (which are also grammatical markers as
word-final vowels mark case) appear only as superscripts. However, the
Qur'an as it was initially written did not contain these vowel markings.
Thus the reader could extract only about two-thirds of the meaning from
the written text. The reader's own knowledge of Arabic grammar allowed
him to infer where and how the vowel marks should be placed, the text
pronounced, and grammatical case indicated. Given the sacred nature of
the language itself, the possibility of mispronunciation is particularly
threatening. To avoid this, vowel markings were added to the Qur'an some
centuries after it was written (Prasodjo 1974:52). There are, however, still
many arguments over pronunciation which are essentially arguments over
syntax and ultimately arguments over interpretation and significance
(cf. Rippin 1980), underscoring the importance of the oral transmission of
the text.

To speak the Qur'an is, in and of itself, a religious act; by memorizing
the complete Qur'an, one acquires much religious merit (Jones 1981:77,
Dhofier 1980:V 39). The efficacy of Qur'anic recitation lies in exercising
the discipline and control required to memorize and perfectly reproduce
the text in its entirety. This self-control allows the development of *akal,*
which is one of the primary paths to God.[7]

It is important to recognize that, in this context, efficacy inheres in the performance of the text (or, rather, in the acquisition of the skills and discipline that allow a performance to happen), not in the text itself. Since the *language* of the Qur'an is itself religiously charged, the memorization and subsequent reproduction of the phrases in their correct order with the proper intonation, pronunciation and rhythm is a religious act; it creates the conditions for the development of *akal*. The denotative aspects of the Arabic language text, its contents, are discounted and attention focused on form. Anderson used the term "mantra" in his discussion of Javanese Islam to refer to a conception of power located not in the content of the speech, but in its order, shape, and use. Access to the power of the Qur'an is collapsed into the production of language. I was told by different individuals on several occasions that they did not know the Qur'an because they could not read it in Arabic (e.g., "Saya belum tahu al-Qur'an karena bacanya itu belum bisa dalam bahasa Arab" [Ind.]) although they possessed—and read—Indonesian language translations. To "know" the Qur'an in West Java *means* to be able to produce it.

The "knowing" manifested through the production or recitation of the Qur'an is the result of exercises to acquire control. Control, achieved through Qur'anic recitation, the five daily prayers, and the practice of other disciplines of Islam, allows the triumph of *akal* (which I will roughly gloss as reason) over *hawa nafsu* (roughly, desires or instinct) (cf. Siegel 1969). *Hawa nafsu* or indulgence of the self through lack of control takes one away from God; *akal* or control of desires in obedience to the religious laws allows one to approach God. *Hawa nafsu* should be contained through the exercise of the order of Islamic law and through the performance of its accompanying obligations as explicated and enforced by the religious teacher.

The tale of the conversion of Sunan Kalijaga, one of the nine saints *(wali)* reputed to have brought Islam to the island of Java in the fifteenth century, suggests the importance of obedience in Islam in Pasundan and establishes the importance of the student-teacher relationship. Kalijaga, called Raden Jaka Sahid before his conversion, was a dissolute man who spent his time whoring and gambling. Having used up his mother's money in pursuit of his diversions, he left her destitute and set out upon the road. He became a highway robber to support his pastimes, traveling until he came to the port city of Japara. There he met a richly dressed Arab. Seeing an easy mark, R. Jaka Sahid stopped the Arab and demanded his money. The Arab asked why R. Jaka Sahid acquired his riches in such a difficult manner when it was all there for the taking. He pointed behind R.

Jaka Sahid, who turned and saw a tree whose leaves had turned to gold. Realizing that the Arab had some great power, R. Jaka Sahid asked what he must do in order that he also might have that power. The Arab told him to wait for him by the side of the river. R. Jaka Sahid waited. He waited by the river for forty years, covered by floods, swallowed by cities that appeared and disappeared, engulfed by crowds. And as he waited, he meditated. At the end of forty years, the Arab returned. As a result of R. Jaka Sahid's steadfast obedience to the Arab's orders and to the rigors of the forty-year meditation, he now had a new name (Kalijaga) and a new creed—Islam.[8] Kalijaga thus became a Muslim

> through an inner change of heart brought on by the same sort of yoga-like psychic discipline that was the core religious act of the Indic tradition from which he came. His conversion was not a matter of spiritual or moral change following upon a decisive change in belief . . . but a willed spiritual and moral change which eventuated in an almost accessorial change in belief. (Geertz 1968:29)

The Source of the Teacher's Authority

In West Java, the relationship between the teacher and his students is the fundamental relationship of Islam. Goody notes that situations of restricted literacy can transform the nature of knowledge and its transmission: in such situations, the acquisition of knowledge *requires* a mediator between the student and the texts (Goody 1968:13).

The teacher of *ngaji* lessons is usually an "ordinary" religious teacher called an *ajengan*, although he may occasionally be an individual of extraordinary religious knowledge and commitment known as a *kyai*.[9] The relationship of the *ajengan* to his students is simply a paler reflection of the more structured and religiously more powerful relationship between a *kyai* and his student-disciples known as *santri*. Both the *ajengan* and the *kyai* occupy a mediating position between the student and the texts he must learn.

Ideally, the authority of the teacher is absolute. Respect shown to the teacher constitutes an obligation for every individual and is of the same order as the respect shown to parents, parents-in-law, and the king (Noer 1973:15).[10] The teacher is a religious mediator and guide, both through his own personal example (as his life exemplifies the religious laws) and as an adept in a system of restricted knowledge, particularly the Arabic language. If the student should forget his tie to his teacher, his knowledge may lose its efficacy (Dhofier 1980:IV 34). Thus a large part of religious lessons must consist of the recognition of that relationship (which is made functionally imperative by the oral nature of the transmission of texts) through the practice of obedience and the demonstration of respect (Chirzin 1974:84).

The authority of the teacher derives from his position in the religious community (the *ummat*) defined both diachronically and synchronically. *Kyai* and, to a lesser extent, *ajengan* are titles given by the community: they are not self-assumed appellations. Such titles mark public recognition of an individual's religiosity: recognition of his holiness, his supernatural abilities *(karamat)* (Prasodjo 1974:13), affirmation of his greater knowledge and wisdom (Anderson 1966:91), and acceptance of his prominent role in the community (Chirzin 1974:92).

In a diachronically defined *ummat*, the position of the teacher depends largely upon intellectual descent (Prasodjo 1974:83):

> . . . a religious teacher [in Islam] has no status in his own right. He represents the impress made upon him by the school to which he belonged. His authenticity and the guarantee of his competence as a member of that school is provided by the line of transmission he can produce, depending on the authority of his teacher, that of the teacher of his teacher, and so on. (Johns, quoted in Dhofier 1980:IV 30)

In the synchronically defined *ummat*, the teacher's position is at once religious and secular; the education he gives is neither civil nor religious but both (van Nieuwenhuijze 1958:72). Since the teacher, by virtue of his religiosity, embodies the patterns and values of the Islamic community, and since he acts in the name of that religiosity when he teaches, he acts on behalf of the *ummat*. Pupils' respect and obedience to the teacher are a manifestation of their respect and obedience to the community and to Islamic (social) laws and demonstrate the possession of the control necessary to submit to those laws.

The consequences of disobedience to the *ummat* (and so to the religious law) are also the consequences of lack of control as manifested by the indulgence of the *hawa nafsu*. The story of Adam and Eve and their expulsion from Paradise teaches this lesson. According to Islamic belief, humans are endowed with two parts to their nature: *hawa nafsu* and *akal*. It is *akal* that makes humans superior to the angels—the angels do good because it is their nature, but humans know the difference between good and evil and must struggle to do good. Control of human desires, which allows the exercise of *akal,* is a triumph, a victory. Thus, human nature is neither good nor evil: it is human acts that are judged (Siegel 1969:102). Adam and Eve were expelled from Paradise because they were disobedient. They ate what they were forbidden to eat: they indulged the *hawa nafsu.* This is not like the Christian conception of Original Sin, for the Islamic burden of sin is not transmitted through the generations (Anawati 1974:351). Each individual begins anew the struggle to control desire.

Akal is a capacity and so cannot, in a strict sense, be taught or learned. The best that can be done is to provide an atmosphere in which it can develop. This atmosphere is created by valuing obedience to the teacher above all else, and by teaching control through mastery of the rituals and disciplines of Islam, beginning with the memorization of the Qur'an.

Akal is not the only mode of knowing in Islam and is not the primary mode in Sundanese Islam. The source of most religious knowledge in Pasundan is tradition. Because Islamic doctrine from the eleventh through the nineteenth centuries did not recognize the right of individual interpretation of the Islamic texts through the exercise of *akal (ijtihad),* scholars taught an unquestioning acceptance of established practice *(taqlid)* as doctrine (Noer 1973:9–10). Indonesian Muslim reformists, returning from the Middle East in the early twentieth century, introduced *ijtihad* to Indonesia, but for the vast majority of the Sundanese today, the Qur'an and its early interpretations embodied in *taqlid* are still unquestionable and must be valued more highly than knowledge acquired through the exercise of *akal.*

A religious teacher, demanding absolute obedience on the basis of his recognized position as a transmitter of divine law, guides the development of the various modes of knowing in his students. The teacher controls a type of knowledge that gives him extraordinary power. The knowledge is based on his command of the Qur'anic text and its commentaries, and the power is located in the Arabic language itself and the Islamic law which regulates all relationships and activities. The teacher teaches through the power of tradition *(taqlid)* which is religiously interpreted as the power of the source; the proximate source for the student is his teacher.

In summary, the teacher's legitimacy derives from his position vis-à-vis the religious community, a community defined both diachronically (by a recitation of intellectual genealogies) synchronically (as a collection of individuals who adhere to the Islamic law). To question the information taught by the teacher is to challenge the community which recognizes him as qualified to occupy his position. Challenging the *ummat* means questioning the Qur'an which provides the definition for the (religious) community and is the ultimate source for all knowledge. Thus, the power of religious lessons—also part of what it means to "know"—inheres in the relationship of the student to the teacher and the teacher to the community and, ultimately, the relationship of all to the Qur'an.

Sundanese Values: Hormat *and Social Location*

Hormat, as noted above, should be glossed as the recognition of social location. The criteria that govern social intercourse and define social location in the community are internalized by all Sundanese; to *be* Sundanese means submitting to these strictures and fulfilling their requirements, just as part of being Muslim means recognizing the *ummat* as it is defined by the Qur'an and religious law.

The Sundanese language highlights social location. All utterances require that the speaker choose among three formalized levels of politeness (*lemes, sedeng, kasar* in decreasing order of politeness)[11] which overtly mark the participants' relative social location. To be able to communicate meaningfully in Sundanese requires not just linguistic but social competence. Speakers must demonstrate *hormat* with each utterance.

Wessing (1974:6) describes level selection in Sundanese as governed by social distance, as expressing "asymmetrical relationships." In Bandung, however, I observed that, although level use may *express* social distance, level selection varied along two axes: intimacy and formality. English collapses these two axes; formal speech is not usually appropriate in intimate situations. However, formality in speech in Bandung indicates respect *(hormat)* and an acceptance of social obligations. Sundanese require formal speech to one's grandmother, for example, as an expression of respect and a recognition of the obligations of a relationship elsewhere defined as intimate (cf. Dewey 1978).

Sundanese speakers select language levels that express the relative social status, defined in terms of shared criteria, of speaker and listener. Participants in a given conversation use the same criteria for assessing social location, although the location assigned may differ. These criteria, in traditional Sundanese (i.e., non-Indonesian) society, depend primarily upon ascriptive features—descent, sex, and relative age. All these criteria (plus a few others of secondary importance such as occupation and wealth, which tend to be a function of descent) come into play in any conversation, but participants may assign them different relative weights, resulting in different decisions about level selection. For example, in a conversation between two same-sex individuals of relatively the same descent status but of different ages, the speaker(s) may choose to accentuate either their similarities of gender and descent, or their differences of age. Speakers can also shift levels in the course of a single conversation. I observed a mother and daughter-in-law (two women of different age but approximately the same descent status) initiate conversation in the speech level reserved for peer interaction when their relationship was harmonious. When, in the course of that conversation, the situation grew strained and the mother-in-law wished to indicate disapproval with her daughter-in-law, she switched to talking "down" to the younger woman. More frequently, the daughter-in-law would initiate the change by speaking "up" to her mother-in-law, indicating that, although she acquiesced, she was submitting primarily to her mother-in-law's higher social status as defined by age and kin relationship rather than to the content of the discussion. The primary message of a speech event thus may be the expression or manipulation of a relationship through the extraverbal aspects of language, rather than the denotative content of the utterance.

The Sundanese themselves define language in terms of the appropriate use of levels. Inappropriate use of levels renders an utterance, according to native speakers, not just incorrect but NOT-Sundanese *(sanes basa Sunda* [Sund., *lemes]).* In contrast, speakers label grammatically incorrect Indonesian utterances as incorrect *(tidak betul* [Ind.]). (Indonesian does not have levels.) Native speakers who were fluent in the middle *(sedeng)* and lower *(kasar)* levels of Sundanese would claim that they could not speak the language *(teu tiasa Sunda* [Sund., *lemes])* because they could not use the polite form properly. A speaker incapable of manipulating Indonesian fluently would be labeled (or would label himself) "not yet fluent"—but he would say that he could speak Indonesian (e.g., *bisa bahasa Indonesia, tapi belum lancar* [Ind.]). For Sundanese speakers, the "how" of speaking takes precedence over the "what"; the emic definition of Sundanese depends upon the speaker's appropriate demonstration of *hormat.*

Ascribed characteristics—i.e., characteristics that are perceived to be relatively immutable by the actions of individuals—have traditionally defined the parameters of *hormat.* One could *achieve* higher status in Pasundan only by making the *haj* or acquiring a great deal of religious knowledge. Higher status in the religious sphere, however, indicates increased subservience to the (immutable and unchallengeable) religious laws located in the Qur'an which regulate behavior in the *ummat.* The demonstration of *hormat* marks social location and guides social behavior in the secular community according to unchangeable and unchallengeable social "rules" as the divine law found in the Qur'an defines and regulates behavior in the religious community, the *ummat.* Both sets of constraints are an integral part of what it means to *be* Sundanese and are perceived as unchallengeable.

Sundanese participation in the Indonesian nation-state has added new criteria to the definitions of social location. These new criteria—most particularly education level—are usually achieved rather than ascribed and frequently conflict with the traditional ascribed criteria, creating potentially paradoxical situations. For example, the head of a government office may be a relatively young woman of non-aristocratic descent who has acquired her position primarily by virtue of her education level. Beneath her in the office, is an older man of aristocratic descent. By virtue of age, sex, and descent, the woman should use polite Sundanese to the man, should defer to him. However, by virtue of her position in the office, acquired through a higher level of education, she should speak "down" to him. In such a situation, Sundanese speakers will generally choose to speak Indonesian (if fluent in the language), the national (not-Sundanese) language which has no levels. The social categories of the Sundanese community are thus rendered irrelevant (as the situation is perceived as taking place within the national, Indonesian community), and the level selection problem is avoided without violating the integrity of the Sundanese criteria of social location. The order of Sundanese society, refracting into another form the order of the *ummat,* remains unproblematic.

The large repertoire of politeness phrases highlights the formal dimension of Sundanese. Politeness phrases are ones such as "how are you?" in which the content is fixed and non-referential (Ferguson 1976). The selection and utterance of such phrases are required by context; the cues to which the sender and receiver respond are located in the social situation. We have already seen that in order to meaningfully send and receive any message in Sundanese, one must be aware of the social relationship of the speaker and listener and sensitive to the social situation. The high incidence of politeness phrases highlights the importance of context.

The initial determining criterion of the appropriateness of an utterance in Sundanese is the (in)correct use of language levels. Verifiability is secondary: lying does not have a strong negative value. It is more important to produce a communication appropriate to a given situation (to show *hormat*) than it is to impart "true" information. To be called a liar *(tukang ngabohong)* is less harsh than to be labeled "rude" or "socially coarse" *(kasar).*

A *Lesson in* Hormat *and Social Location*

The language of most households in Bandung is middle- or low-level Sundanese. As children begin to understand high-level Sundanese, elders expect them to use it increasingly in appropriate situations in the household. As children get older, all relationships of respect will be couched in polite language. Parents in Bandung feel strongly that correct behavior and correct language use are one and the same (Widjajakusuma 1980:322). A socially mature individual must use language correctly.[12] Utterances in Sundanese derive their efficacy not from content but from the form and context of the utterance. Information is located as much in the social "who" of the speaker and listener and the "how" of the communication as it is in the "what" of the utterance. I had several rather disorienting experiences in which I conducted some transaction (such as a purchase) in recognizable Sundanese, only to have the respondent (who also spoke Sundanese during the transaction) compliment me on my Indonesian. He did not hear the Sundanese because, by definition, white foreigners did not speak Sundanese.

Language levels can (and do) constrain the content of utterances. Words of anger, for example, are impolite by Sundanese definition. Informants said that anger and similar uncontrolled emotions could only be expressed in *kasar* or low-level Sundanese. Polite or *halus* Sundanese is smooth and controlled. The description of *halus* language and, by extension, the description of a speaker of *halus* Sundanese was couched in the same vocabulary that was used to discuss the attributes of *akal*.

To express anger in polite Sundanese is—as the Sundanese say—funny *(lucu)* and not effective as an expression of negative feelings; the demonstration of proper *hormat* precludes the expression of anger toward a social superior. By the same token, it requires sophisticated linguistic and social manipulation to ask a "why" question in polite Sundanese without appearing simultaneously to violate *hormat*. Such questions appear to challenge or examine the knowledge of the superior. As inferiors do not (by Sundanese definition) examine superiors, such questions cannot be asked.

West Javanese Islam places great emphasis on appropriate production of oral religious texts, discounting the denotative aspects of the Arabic language and emphasizing the oral or performance aspects of the texts. The content of the texts (religious laws and strictures) is assumed and, in fact, is nonverifiable. Children taking *ngaji* lessons are usually quite young and just beginning to learn to use polite Sundanese; since religious teachers must be addressed in polite Sundanese by virtue of their social location, the language precludes certain kinds of questions regarding the content of the lessons. Following is a brief excerpt from a *ngaji* lesson given to a seven-year-old Sundanese boy. The lesson contains material the child is seeing for the first time.

Teacher	[*says, Sundanese*]	:	Nah, dangukeun... [Now, listen...]
	[*chants, Arabic*]	:	Bismillah hirochman nirochim...
	[*says, Sundanese*]	:	Nah, ulangi. [Now, repeat after me.]
	[*chants, Arabic*]	:	Bismillah...
Child	[*chants, Arabic*]	:	Bismillah...
Teacher	[*chants, Arabic*]	:	Hirochman...
Child	[*chants, Arabic*]	:	Hirochman...
Teacher	[*chants, Arabic*]	:	Nirochim...
Child	[*chants, Arabic*]	:	Nirochim . . .
Teacher	[*chants, Arabic*]	:	Bismillah hirochman nirochim . . .
Child	[*chants, Arabic*]	:	Bismillah nirochim—
Teacher	[*chants, Arabic*]	:	Bismillah hirochman nirochim . . .
Child	[*chants, Arabic*]	:	Bismillah hirochman nirochman . . .
Teacher	[*chants, Arabic*]	:	Bismillah hirochman nirochim . . .

The lesson continues in this fashion until the child correctly reproduces the text. When he chants the Arabic to the teacher's satisfaction, the lesson is over. As the child does not "understand" the Arabic language, he has no access to the texts except through his teacher and cannot challenge the text itself. Since the rules of *hormat* require that he use polite Sundanese to this teacher, the pupil cannot challenge the texts through his teacher.

A historical note would be useful as a concluding point, to indicate the resilience of oral conceptualizations of religious knowledge in Sunda. The Islamic reformist movement in Indonesia in the early years of the twentieth century was concerned with the nature of religious knowledge and the mode of its transmission. Individual rationality *(ijtihad)* was "energetically cultivated" (Abdullah 1971:59). "Understanding" the Qur'an became very important. The text itself became primary; the reformists "have made so bold as to say that the Qur'an means what it says!" (Anderson 1966:94). This leads to an increased interest in the denotative aspects of language and downplays the student-teacher relationship. In western Java,[13] however, this reform movement was not very successful, even among advanced Islamic scholars. Lessons in the *pesantren* Islamic religious schools for advanced students today still consist of translations by *kyai* from Arabic into semi-archaic Javanese or Malay, with explications in Sundanese. A study done by the Indonesian government in the early 1970s of eight well-known and respected *pesantren* in Bogor, West Java, reports a lesson which proceeded as follows:

Text [read by *kyai* in Arabic]	: Alhamdu
Translation	
[by *kyai* into semi-archaic Javanese]	: Utawi sekabehane puji
Text	: Lillahi
Translation	: Iku tetap keduwe Gusti Allah
Text	: Rabbil 'alamin
Translation	: Kang mengerani wong alam kabeh

The text is then explained (not translated) in Sundanese (Prasodjo 1974: 50–51); the students usually memorize both the translation and the explanation (Janus 1960: 48). According to the study, the *kyai* said that the translation of the holy books into semi-archaic Javanese is necessary for grammatical purposes. With a translation into Javanese, they said, the place of the word in the sentence becomes clear so we know better how to pronounce it and so how to understand it (Dhofier 1980:III 14, Prasodjo 1974:51). However, there seems to be nothing inherent in the structure of semi-archaic Javanese that would make it better suited than Sundanese to the task of explicating Arabic grammar. I suggest that the *translation* into semi-archaic Javanese and the subsequent *explication* in Sundanese allows the *kyai* to resist the demystification of Arabic that would occur with direct translation into the local language, keeps him in control of a form of esoteric knowledge, and maintains the strength of the student-teacher relationship.

Reference Material

Notes to the Chapters

Introduction: Indonesian Religions in Society

1. Basic studies on the recent political history of Indonesia include George McT. Kahin's *Nationalism and Revolution in Indonesia* (1952), Herbert Feith's *The Decline of Constitutional Democracy in Indonesia* (1962), Daniel Lev's *The Transition to Guided Democracy: Indonesian Politics, 1957–1959* (1966), Benedict Anderson's *Java in a Time of Revolution* (1972), Feith and Castles's *Indonesian Political Thinking 1945–1965* (1970) and Karl Jackson and Lucien Pye's *Political Power and Communications in Indonesia* (1978).

2. See Soedjatmoko's *An Approach to Indonesian History: Toward an Open Future* (1960) and Soedjatmoko et al., *Introduction to Indonesian Historiography* (1965) for critical discussions of the historical literature.

3. See Clifford Geertz's *Agricultural Involution* (1963), chapter 2, for a concise summary of this division.

4. See McKinley's "Zaman dan Masa" (1979) and the essays in Reid and Marr's *Perceptions of the Past in Southeast Asia* (1979) for examples of this approach.

5. Basic works on the Dayak peoples include Scharer (1963), Appell (1976), and Hose and McDougall (1966).

6. Sources on Nias include Kleiweg de Zwann (1913), Modigliani (1890), Suzuki (1959), Feldman (1977; 1979), and Marschall (1976).

7. See Boon's *The Anthropological Romance of Bali* (1977) and Geertz's *Negara* (1980).

1. *Space, Motion, and Symbol in Tetum Religion*

1. I thank the Portuguese Government and the Junta de Investigacoes do Ultra-mar for permitting my work on Timor. I wish to express appreciation, also, to the London Committee of the London-Cornell Project for East and South East Asian Studies and the Nuffield Foundation for providing a grant which enabled me to undertake the field research upon which this study is based. An award by the Frederick Soddy Trust contributed to the productivity of my research, and I thank its members. Maribeth Erb suggested improvements upon an earlier draft of this paper, and I wish to convey my gratitude to her, too. Further improvements were gratefully incorporated from suggestions made by Susan Rodgers and Rita Kipp.

2. *Ui* is the usual term for this female organ, but the more generic term for "hole" or "opening" *(fono)* is sometimes employed—as it is in the English language.

3. See Hicks, 1984.

4. Transcribed by Marcal Andrade, and published in Sá (1961:24—33). This narrative specifically pertains to the corpus of oral literature belonging to the Tetum peoples of the Samoro region.

5. I am indebted to Needham (1978:30) for reference to this remark.

6. The Tetum social classes were as follows: royalty, aristocrats, commoners, slaves (Hicks 1983).

7. To my knowledge the Tetum have no Orpheus-like tales of a descent made into the Underworld. In the Eel myth of origin (Hicks 1976:77—78) the youngest of *seven brothers,* Ali-iku, is transformed at *sunset* into an eel, a transformation occurring in the middle of a stream (the Wé Klobor). Midday and sunset are agents of transformation in various narratives. In another tale, the youngest of *seven sisters,* also called *Ali-iku,* transforms a dead hero into a live one as she is helping transport him over the *sea.*

8. The crocodile is itself a liminal creature in some stories and local beliefs, being credited, for example, with the capacity to transform itself into a girl (Hicks 1984).

9. As an alien, rather like the spirits of the sacred world, a wife is considered especially appropriate to act as mediator between the secular world of her husband's hamlet and the sacred world's inhabitants. Just as wives come from outside, so do immigrants, of course, and these are thought to be associated with the sacred side of life. They usually arrive from the west, and in the diarchy that is the princedom of Caraubalo they are granted sacred authority in contrast to the autochthones, who hold the reins of secular authority (Hicks 1978a).

10. It would be interesting to find out if other Indonesians make a lexical distinction between narratives which deliver their respective "messages" vertically and those which do so horizontally.

2. Power of Gods: Ma'bugi' Ritual of the Sa'dan Toraja

1. Both authors of this paper worked on the same *adat* area termed Tallu Lembangna (The Three Petty-Kingdoms), which covers the southern part of the Tana Toraja Regency—that is, the present districts *(kecamatan)* of Makale Sangalla' and Mengkendek. The characteristic of the area is that hierarchical relations dominate village society and center on the endogamous aristocrats termed *puang*. In this respect, the region contrasts quite sharply with the more democratic northern districts. Crystal conducted his fieldwork in the Makale district during 1968–69 and 1971 with additional short trips in 1974 and 1976. His research was facilitated by grants from The Southeast Asia Development Advisory of The Asia Society (1971) and USPHS Training Grant in Anthropology GM-1224 (1968–69). Yamashita's fieldwork, sponsored by the Ministry of Education, Japan, was carried out in the Mengkendek district between 1976 and 1978. Crystal observed the *ma'bugi'* ritual in Makale in 1971 and shot the film (Crystal 1974). Yamashita's observations of the ritual were made in Mengkendek in 1977, and the result was published in Japanese (Yamashita 1980). The joint work was accomplished by the exchange of information, opinions, and drafts between the authors during Yamashita's stay in the United States (made possible by the Nitobe Fellowship Program of The International House of Japan) in 1981–83. Both authors are responsible for the present paper. Lastly, the authors acknowledge the help of Professors James Boon and James Siegel of Cornell University, who read the earlier draft of this paper, and also thank Susan Rodgers and Rita Kipp for their editorial work.

2. On the recent development of international tourism in Tana Toraja, see Crystal (1977) and Volkman (this volume).

3. The figures are from the local government census in 1976. Christianity was introduced to Tana Toraja in 1913 soon after the Dutch entered in 1906. Since then the Toraja have been Christianized, but this process went very slowly. By 1950 less than 10 percent of the population were Christian. Mass conversion to Christianity occurred in the 1950s in relation to the Darul Islam rebellion in South Sulawesi. In this period, *Aluk To Dolo*, the traditional Toraja religion, "fell victim to the Muslim concept which restricts religious legitimacy to religions of the Books" (Crystal 1970:140), and the people were forced to choose either Islam or Christianity. The choice of Christianity, which was clearly the major trend as shown in the census figures, seems to have been their response to, or even reaction against, the dominant Islamic coastal peoples; in the circumstance, Christianity offered a minority like the Toraja a better chance to keep their own identity. Since 1969, *Aluk To Dolo* has been recognized by the national government as a "sect" of *Hindu Dharma* and thus granted official status as a religion.

4. In the context of recent tourist development, the Christian Toraja have adopted the traditional style of ritual performance, claiming that their religion *(agama)* is Christianity but the custom *(adat)* should be shared with all the Toraja people. In extreme cases some of the Christians converted back again to the

traditional religion. During Yamashita's stay in Toraja one leading figure of the reconverted asked him to get financial help from Japanese *Shinto* organizations for developing the *Aluk To Dolo.* The Christians do (or did) get such help from the Dutch church organizations. Another reconverted made a prayer to the ancestral gods before and after sleeping, in the traditional style of prayer, after he came back to the traditional faith (this regular prayer, of course, never happened in the traditional *Aluk To Dolo*). Thus, one may say that the "religious renaissance" of Toraja in the 1970s, brought forth mainly by the development of international tourism, is not a reversion to "olden times" but a process of "cultural involution" in the contemporary circumstances (to borrow McKean's [1977] term from his discussion of tourism in Bali).

5. With the introduction of Christianity, however, it seems that the traditional whole *aluk* as a cultural system has been differentiated: there is a separation between the religious belief *(kepercayaan)* and the practice *(adat),* and between ritual *(upacara)* and art *(kesenian).* The modern Christian Toraja often comment on their involvement in the traditional *aluk* as the "custom" or "art."

6. In relation to the adherents of Christianity, the traditionalist informants suggested that the Christians who doubted the reality of the *deata* spirits were hard pressed to counter the dangerous "games" *(paningoan)* undertaken by the possessed during the *ma'bugi'* ritual. The word *paningoan* here is derived from *manigo,* meaning "to play." For comparative purposes, it might be interesting to note that the essence of the Japanese rituals is considered as *kamiasobi,* "playing with deities."

7. In his "Fieldnotes" R. Kennedy writes: "There is no shamanism here [in Tana Toraja] at all" (1953:171). The problem, however, is how to define shamanism.

8. Fox suggested that complementary dual opposition in Rotinese ritual language reflects certain cosmological patterns shared by many peoples of the archipelago (1971:247). This is also the case with the Torajan categorization of rituals.

9. Prior to Nobele's observation, Grubauer witnessed a *ma'bugi'* ritual in his expedition to this area in 1911 (1913:242–45). As far as we know, this is the first report on *ma'bugi'* by a Western observer.

10. The *ma'bugi' ma'gandang* ritual can be considered as the final stage of the "cleansing" process of the deceased (cf. Yamashita 1981). By this ceremony the Toraja ritual cycle returns to the side of life from death. For this reason this ritual is also termed *dibalikan to mate,* "reversing the dead." Zerner (1981) has reported the *maro* ritual at the Sesean district which was carried out at the final stage of death ritual like the *ma'bugi' ma'gandang* in the Tallu Lembangna. The *maro* ritual in the northern districts is regarded as a parallel to the *ma'bugi'* in the southern districts (cf. Veen 1979:163).

11. The first settler of the land who founded the village is termed *to piara tondok,* "the one who takes care of the village," or *pangala tondok,* "the forest of the village." The direct descendant of this figure occupies the office of the *to bara',* the chief.

12. The *ma'bugi'* ritual is planned and carried out on the basis of the village council which consists of the *to parenge',* the representatives of each *adat* house *(tongkonan)* in the community, headed by the *to bara',* the chief of the village.

13. That is: (1) a black-legged hen *(karurung)* is offered to the *to dolo* or ancestor spirits, (2) a red-necked hen *(kollong rae')* to *ampu' padang*, the "owner of the land" or "master of the earth," (3) a yellow-legged cock *(lentek riri')* to the *to randa langi'*, "spirit at the edge of the heaven" (which is the same as the *Puang Maruruk* in Makale), and (4) a white-legged cock *(sella')* to the *deata* spirits and the high god, *Puang Matua*. These are set, one to four, from the south to north (or the left to right) as the sacrifice is made facing east. In the Toraja folk taxonomy there are more than twenty terms for the varieties of chickens. The fundamental criteria of classification are, as suggested, the color—of feather and legs—and gender. In the verse text, eleven or fourteen varieties of chickens are mentioned as the decendants from the ancestor of chickens termed *Puang Maro* (cf. Veen 1965:94−95; 1976; 419−20).

14. It must be noted that the food offered to the evil spirits (to *randa langi'*) is raw: uncooked chicken meat and uncooked (and also yellow-colored) rice.

15. In some cases two *kampungs* form one *penanian* (or *bua'*) ritual community, while in the other one *kampung* is divided into two *penanian* (or *bua'*) communities. The present *desa* organization is a local administrative formation introduced in the late 1960s in connection with the governmental *Desa Gaya Baru* system.

16. One may interpret this as the centralization of the ritual. In Mengkendek the dualism is observed between the rice priest and the political chief, and also between the rice barn and the *pa'bugiran* as the ritual spaces. On the other hand, in Makale, so far as the *ma'bugi'* we have observed is concerned, both are integrated into the chieftainship in the village contexts. Whatever the local "eccentricity" might be, structurally this example is close to the Buginese model in the sense that the rice ceremonies there are incorporated into the kingship. That is, in the ceremony of the official inauguration of sawah tilling among the Bugis, the king symbolically ploughs the first furrows in the field (cf. Holt 1939:29), whereas in Toraja it is the priest of rice, not the chief, that inaugurates the sawah tilling at the beginning of the rice cultivation cycle.

17. The word *puang*, which signifies the high nobles in the Tallu Lembangna region, is used in ritual verses interchangeably with the word *deata* (for instance, Veen 1965: text B; strophes 46−65, 69−72, 82−84, 90−93, 142−67, 172−76, and 209−82, etc.). As we have seen, the high god is called *Puang Matua*, the "Old Lord." The aristocratic *puang* class is said to be descended from the *to manurun*, the "one who descended from the heaven."

18. The bamboo tree termed *tallang* serves as the particular metaphor for this purpose as there is a customary expression, *to ma'rapu tallang*, meaning "the large family like the *tallang* bamboo." In the funeral, pieces of the bamboo sticks are used in the genealogy counting of the family of the deceased.

19. At the end of the folktale called *Bulu Pala'*, Bulu Pala', the revived hero, and his cock go up to sky and become the stars: the hero becomes the star termed *Ma'dika*, "the Noble" (the Orion Belt), while the cock becomes the star termed *Manuk*, "the Cock" (the Southern Cross). The observations of the stars *(pentiro taunan*, literally "to see the year") is carried out especially at the beginning of the rainy season when the new agricultural year begins. Thus, the hero and the cock in the stars give the fundamental guidance to their basic life activity, the rice cultivation.

20. The word *kurre sumanga'* which means "to thank you" in everyday contexts originally signified "to call a soul."

21. If one faces toward the north, the direction of promoting life, the east is to the right and the west is to the left. Therefore, the concept of the cardinal directions in Toraja is generated by the combination of two dual oppositions: the north and south and the east and west axes. Thus, to be precise, the fundamental opposition between life and death, the *deata* and the ancestors, is expressed as the opposition between the northeast and the southwest as observed before. In these contexts, the "country of the dead," *puya*, is believed to be located somewhere in the south. The Toraja term for the south is *lo'* which corresponds to the Indonesian *laut* ("sea"). However, *lo'* in Toraja does not mean explicitly a "sea" but implies a "downstream" of river. On the other hand, the high god, *Puang Matua*, is conceived to abide at the center of, or literally at the "north-head" of the heaven *(daa ulunna langi')*. *Daa* is the Toraja term for the north, connoting also an "upstream" of river. Therefore, the opposition of the north and south in Toraja seems to be related, at the deeper level of unconsciousness, to that of the "mountain" and "sea" as found in Bali, for instance (cf. Swellengrebel 1960:37–38).

22. In the sixty-minute tape we have recorded from the live performance of the *ma'bugi'* song, we find only a few strophes of the verse text. This is also the case with the *ma'badong* dance performance which is held in the funeral ceremonies.

23. Belo considers the trance in Bali in the perspective of the "puppet complex" (1960:11–13). In this view the entranced are compared with the puppets. Of course, the Toraja have no tradition of the *wayang* puppet, but the underlying concept, the control by someone else, seems to be very similar in both cultures.

24. In the ritual verse, the Bugis—especially *to Bone* (the people of the former Buginese kingdom of Bone)—as well as the Dutch *(to Balanda)* signify "strangers" in general. In the ambivalent attitudes toward strangers, the Bugis in the poetical language are, contrary to the image of the "evil invader," positively valued: see, for example, the strophes such as "having a stalwart appearance like the people of Bone, robust like the Dutch," "that which is made by the people of Bone smells the agreeable perfume of it; that which is minted by the Dutch receives its wafted sweet-smelling fragrance," etc. (Veen 1965:18–19, n. 5).

25. An interesting parallel is found, again in Java, about which B. Anderson writes: "The best guide for sensing the contours of the conception [of power for the Javanese] is perhaps the image of the burning-glass or the laser-beam, where an extraordinary concentration of light creates an extraordinary outpouring of heat" (1972:8).

3. *Kaharingan: Life and Death in Southern Borneo*

1. The material presented here is primarily based upon the Luangan (Lawangan) Dayaks, among whom I undertook research between late 1979 and mid-1981. On the basis of the material which I gathered among the Luangan, and published materials on the Ngaui, Ot Danum, and Maanyan, I believe the

basic principles of Kaharingan to be the same, or nearly so, across southern Borneo.

2. The concept of a tribe as used here is based upon Steward's (1951) operational definition of tribal level of sociocultural integration. In brief, the concept of tribal culture (1) emphasizes shared behavior, (2) has a pattern or configuration expressing some underlying consistency and unity, and (3) is essentially relativistic, that is, in contrast to cultures of other traditions.

3. Other names include *Tempon Telon*, *Agama Tantaulang*, *Agama Dayak*, and the word *agama* (religion) attached to the names of various ethnic groups practicing it—i.e., *Agama Taboyan*.

4. The parallel between *Kenharingan* being the Supreme Deity/Creator of the Tempasuk Dusun and *kaharingan* as the "source of life" among the peoples of southern Borneo is apparent.

5. Hardeland, A. (1859), *Dajaksch-Deutsches Worterbuch*, Amsterdam.

6. Although there are certain spirits known by all shamans, no two individuals would ever agree on them all since each shaman includes the spirits of his deceased teachers and ancestors among his spiritual coterie.

7. Among the Tunjung the spirit of a living human soul is known as *merega'*. Kertodipoero (1963:30) encountered the term *merue'* along the middle Barito River. *Amirue* is used by the Maanyan (Hudson 1966:362) and *hambaruan* is the Ngaju term for the living soul.

8. Sickness is conceived of as a miasma floating in the air. Interestingly, late night, after about 10 P.M., it is considered safe to be outside since it is "too cold" for sickness to be in the air. Contrarily, water is not believed to be a bearer of sickness, and thus often little effort is made to secure clean drinking water.

9. *Kelalongan* is the cognizant essence of man which is perceived of as located in the brain or the head.

10. Among the Ngaju, the "refined" soul of the head is known as *Salumpok Liau* and the "coarse" soul of the body is known as *Liau Krahang* (Hertz 1960:34). For all Kaharingans except the Tunjung, the "coarse" soul of the body is *liau*. The Tunjung alone use the term *pedara*.

11. Among the Ngaju the journey of the soul is slightly different. They believe that bifurcation of the soul occurs at death producing a "refined"soul, *Salumpok Liau*, and a "coarse" soul, *Liau Krahang*. The abstract heaven to which the "refined" soul goes is referred to as *Lewu Tatau* by the Ngaju. But, unlike the Luangan, the Ngaju believe that the "coarse" soul goes to *Lewu Liau* (literally, village(s) of *Liau*) which is also an abstract place, and not a concrete location such as Gunung Lumut. After secondary mortuary rites have been held, they believe that the "coarse" soul leaves *Lewu Liau* and travels to *Lewu Tatau* where it joins the "refined" soul.

Among the Maanyan, Hudson (1966:360) reported that at death the living soul, *amirue*, turns into *adiau*, but only until it reaches heaven, which is known as *Datu Tunjung*, where it again becomes *amirue*. Hudson later (personal communication, 1979) stated that both the Maanyan and the Luangan looked to Gunung Lumut as the site of the afterworld. My Luangan and Maanyan informants alike agreed with the latter, that both groups believe Gunung Lumut to be the home of the dead.

12. Dayak soldiers fighting in East Timor did not suffer a single fatality, it is believed, since they had *naiyu* supporting them.

13. That is, *Juwata* or *Dewata*.

14. Although shamanism has its origins in the religious practices of the aboriginal peoples of northern Asia, as an anthropological concept it has taken on wider useage. *The American College Dictionary* (1967:1112) defines a shaman as "a medicine man; a worker with the supernatural," and shamanism as "1. the primitive religion of northern Asia embracing a belief in controlling spirits who can be influenced only by shamans, 2. any similar religion." Use of the terms shaman and shamanism here will follow the more general definition of the concept.

15. Exceptions to this are certain life-process rituals, particularly those of agriculture, performed by nonspecialists, in which case the term *balian* is generally not used.

16. Since the terms *balian* and *wara* refer both to the type of ritual and to the type of shaman, I shall always affix "shaman(s)" to the terms when indicating the person(s) rather than the event. Among the Benuaq and Tunjung subgroups of the Luangan there is an alternate set of death ritual known as *setanggi*, although *wara* death ritual is also used by these people. *Setanggi* appears to be a simplified version of *wara* ritual using fewer "ingredients" and less elaborate ritual.

17. This is the same dialect used for ritual by the Maanyan, which is referred to as *Bahasa Pangandraun* (Mallinckrodt [1925] 1974:14 noted the same). It may also be the same as the Ngaju ritual language of *Bahasa Sangiang*. *Sangiang*, or *seniang*, in the Luangan dialect of the upper Tweh River refers to the world of the spirits.

18. A *Penghulu* may, or may not, be a *balian* and/or a *wara* shaman.

19. *Cordyline Terminalis* used as a ritual plant is encountered across insular Southeast Asia. Conklin (1980) reports its use among the Ifugao of the Northern Philippines, Yamashita (1981) encountered it among the Toraja of Sulawesi, and Welsch and Heider (personal communication, 1982) report the ritual use of *Cordyline terminalis* among New Guinea peoples. Actual meanings vary, but the plant always carries the ritual connotation of life and/or death.

20. Other names for secondary mortuary rites, and the groups using them are: *Kwangkai* (Benuaq and Tunjung subgroups of the Luangan), *Mbia* and *Kedaton* (Maanyan), *Ijambe* (Padju Epat subgroup of the Maanyan), and *Tiwah* (Ngaju and Ot Danum).

21. This has also been reported for the Ngaju (Miles, 1965:172; Hardeland and Grabowsky, in Hertz 1960:39).

22. Miles (1965:172) reported the same situation among the Ngaju.

23. Luangan death shamans say that in the olden times slaves of rich individuals were also sacrificed at secondary mortuary rites so that they could serve their master's *Liau* in the afterworld. Some individuals say that sacrifice of a carabao has symbolically replaced slave sacrifice. Schwaner (1853:4) translated in Roth (1968 [1896]: clxxiv) also noted the same.

24. The exception to this is the restriction placed on females becoming death shamans.

25. Prior to eating of ritual meals at Kaharingan ceremonies, Christians in attendance will be invited to say a prayer should they so desire.

26. In some areas it is increasingly common for there to be village-wide sponsorship of longer, more expensive, ceremonies such as a full eight-day *Bantang* thanksgiving ceremony. Miles (1966:4) also noted among the Ngaju that, although participation in ceremonies may include all members of the community, it is the component households that are responsible for the expense of ceremonies.

4. The Religion of Balance: Evidence From an Eleventh-Century Javanese Poem

Much of my work on the translation and analysis of the *Arjuna Wiwāha* was performed in 1974–76, under the sponsorship of the Ford Foundation's Michigan-Malang Exchange Program. I owe a great debt to the scholars in Java who translated Old Javanese poetry with me during this time: I Gusti Ngurah Oka, Imam Hanafi, and the late Soewojo Wojowasito. I am especially indebted to Ki J. Padmanpuspita, both for his assistance in translating the *Arjuna Wiwāha* and for his kindness and patience in teaching me the philosophy behind it. My thanks also to my teacher and adviser, A. L. Becker, for his help and counsel. Several colleagues have offered suggestions on earlier drafts of this paper, in particular Allen Balaz and Robert Wessing; Susan Rodgers and Rita Kipp have been most helpful as editors. My thanks to them all and to the participants in the tenth annual Indonesial Studies Summer Institute Conference for their comments. All errors in translation and interpretation are, of course, my sole responsibility.

5. Islamic Transformations: From Sufi Doctrine to Ritual Practice in Gayo Culture

1. Kirk Endicott, for example, distinguishes "the popular or folk religion of the Malay," which he calls Malay magic, from "orthodox Islam." "I am interested in Islam," he continues, "only to the extent that it has become embedded in this generally held body of ideas" (Endicott 1970:7).

2. Compare, for example, the transformation of the relation of ruler and priest in Buddhist Thailand (Tambiah 1976) and the historical interplay between Confucian Chinese and local models of the Vietnamese polity (Woodside 1971).

3. Villages are usually clusters of houses owned by matrilaterally related women. *Ulama*, or persons learned in Islam, were and still are produced by local religious schools or *pesantrens* in Aceh. Chieftains or *uleebelang* were local rulers, whereas the sultan ruled primarily over Banda Aceh, a multi-ethnic trading port. One might add to Siegel's overview that in the western part of Aceh there appears to have been a much tighter fit between village structure and religious hierarchy. In this century, a religious-political "shadow government" extended over much of West Aceh, focused on a line of *habib* (persons claiming descent from Muhammad).

4. On seals, see Siegel 1979:1–31; on the political ideology and literary culture of seventeenth-century Aceh, see Lombard 1967. Snouck Hurgronje 1906, vol. 1:58–80, is still the best description of the Acehnese village.

5. Aceh proper (Aceh Besar) and Pidie are the areas around the city of Banda Aceh and immediately to the east of the city; they have been the basis for almost all the writing in English concerning Aceh. It was, however, farther to the east along the northern coast that the most important literary and religious developments took place, and this area is still considered the one in which the "best Acehnese" is spoken. See Siegel 1969:98–133 for a description of the reformist movement in Aceh.

6. Polo 1958:252–57. The description of Ferlec (page 253) reads:

> You must know that the people of Ferlec used all to be idolaters, but owing to contact with Saracen merchants, who continually resort here in their ships, they have all been converted to the law of Mahomet. This applies only to the inhabitants of the city. The people of the mountains live like beasts.

7. See Ricklefs 1979 on the Islamization of Java, and Lombard 1967:30–35 for a summary of the evidence for early conversion in Aceh.

8. Schrieke 1955:15–48.

9. See Johns 1957 for a discussion of these forms of knowledge, and Johns 1961.

10. Snouck Hurgronje 1906, vol. 2:1–65; Lombard 1967:159–64.

11. Johns would attribute to these Sufi missionaries the initial conversions in Aceh, whereas al-Attas argues that Sufis came into the picture rather later in Aceh, perhaps in the late fifteenth century. John's view is supported by the peculiarly Sufi tone of the accounts of conversion to Islam that appear in the fourteenth-century *Hikayat Raja-Raja Pasai* and the sixteenth-century *Sejarah Melayu* (see Jones 1979). Elsewhere, too, conversion to Islam appears to have been largely the work of wandering Sufi scholars. Both the *fuqarā* of the eastern Sudan and the *baba* of Anatolia are described in recent articles as the major bearers of Islam into their respective regions (O'Fahey 1979, Ménage 1979).

12. Brakel (1969,1979) and al-Attas (1970:3–30) disagree in their interpretations of all of these matters. Since we have little material to work from other than the internal evidence of Ḥamzah's texts I find the words "likely" and "probably" necessary qualifications on these points.

13. Cod. Or. 2016, Library, University of Leiden, cited in al-Attas (1970:18). Unless stated otherwise, I have followed al-Attas in his translations of Ḥamzah's

passages. The majority of quotations will be from two of Ḥamzah's works, which will be referred to as follows:

Asrār: Asrāru'l-Ārafīn fī batyā Ilm al-Sulūk wa'l-Tawhid. (Cod. Or. 7291(I), Library, University of Leiden, reproduced in al-Attas 1970:233–96.)

Sharāb: Sharābu'l-Āshiqīn. (Cod. Or. 2016, Library, University of Leiden, reproduced in al-Attas 1970:297–328.)

14. Cod. Or. 2016.
15. Cod. Or. 3374, Library, University of Leiden, cited in al-Attas (1970:22). I have somewhat altered the translation of this passage.
16. Ibn Arabī (1165–1240) was born in Murcia, Spain, and spent most of his life in Damascus. Schimmel (1975:263–74) provides a summary of his treachings, while Corbin (1969) explores in great detain Ibn Arabī's theory of being and creation, which is of central importance to this paper. Johns (1957) analyzes the intellectual filiation of Ḥamzah to Ibn Arabī.
17. The complete passage, describing the successive stages of maifestation in liquid terms, is to be found in Sharāb:16–17.
18. Brakel (1979) brought this to my attention.
19. This passage is cited in al-Attas (1970:271). I have altered the translation slightly.
20. I have found a few printed books of spells in circulation among Gayo, most notably the nineteenth-century Taj ul-Mulk. The interpretation of the latter text, however, demands orally transmitted conventions of lucky and unlucky days, meteorological cycles, etc.
21. My fieldwork in Gayo took place from March 1978 through June 1980, sponsored by the Universitas Syiah Kuala in Banda Aceh and funded by the Social Science Research Council and by a grant administered under the Fulbright-Hays program. I am deeply grateful to all three institutions for their assistance.
22. The letter *lam-alif* is two letters joined to become one and is the vehicle in Sufi poetry for descriptions of lovers embracing and for mystical union with God. It is also linked to the initial *lā* of the confession of faith (Schimmel 1975: 419).
23. Corbin (1978) discusses the image of the "man of light" in Iranian Sufism. Al-Attas (1970:83–85) presents the image of the double mirror in Ḥamzah.
24. Ḥamzah consistently distinguishes in Malay between *mengenal*, "know, connaître," and forms of the word *ilmu*. "knowledge, verbal sense of *savoir*." The former is a translation of *'arafa* and is often linked to *menghampiri*, "to draw near to." Interestingly, Eickelman reports that the fields of knowledge referred to by these two terms in Arabic is elsewhere reversed. In Moroccan usage, *ma'rifa* refers to knowledge outside of religion while *'ilm* is glossed as "the religious sciences" (Eickelman 1978: 489–92).
25. Repeated throughout Ḥamzah e.g. in *Sharāb*:10.
26. *Asrār:* 65, 67; Sharāb:11. The passage from *Muntahī* cited above is in al-Attas (1970:349).

27. The term *seduei* is derived from the Gayo pronunciation of the Acehnese words "sa, dua" (one, two).

28. The Gayo text for this spell and the spell performed on the following day are as follows:

> (I) Hé limo si reje limo. Aku tahu asalmu jadi. Nur ollah nama nyawamu, nur Muhammad nama tubuhmu, ruh batin sebenar-benar nyawamu.
>
> Hé limo jelenmu tulu perkara. Kesa penjuci kedue jahat ketige kin pemulih. Reje Rengkan menurun ko ari langit. Peteri Rengkan menuripen ko ari bumi. Reje Rengkan, Peteri Renkan, Tengku Jumal-ul Hamkim, malékat putih.
>
> Hartamu ni maléh kugunei kin tawar serta pemulih, kati (name of patient) pulih dari penyakit (name of sickness). Si bise tawar, si mugah magéh, si bĕret ringen . . .
>
> (filled in by ordinary speech repetitions of this command)
>
> . . . karena ko seger turun orum wé dan tenironmu nge sawah serloni, dan turah ignunei.
>
> (II) He malékat Jibra'il, Mika'il, Izrapil, Isra'il, ikunul ko kuini jin si berilet denki chianat, kerna ko jema benar, ko jema suci, kati kuèngon jema iso si berilet dengki chianat, kerna ko betéh, aku gere betéh. Enti iosah ko pé bloh ku kuen, enti osah ko pé bloh ku kiri, enti iosah ko pé bloh ku atas, enti osah ko pé bloh ku tuyuh.
>
> Hé reje Malekal Maut. Datangmu tiada waktu, datangmu tiada berketike. Datangmu gerak item bujang sebet suderenku menyebut namaku. Kole kusuruh seraya sekejep seketike memukul jin iblis sétan si didalam limo ini.
>
> Hé limo, bukan engko yang kupukul, malénkan iblis sétan si berilet dengki. Bukan aku memukul ko, pi'ilmu memukul dirimu. Babu item tungel, bujang item tungel, tumpah derejet.

A proper linguistic analysis of these and other Gayo spell texts would focus on, among other things, the frequent use of Malay in the more formulaic parts of the text, followed by a movement into, and then back out of, Gayo.

6. Entering the Bitter House: Spirit Worship and Conversion in West Sumba

1. This paper is based on twenty-two months of field research in the Kodi district of West Sumba, Nusa Tenggara Timur, Indonesia. The research was sponsored by Universitas Nusa Cendana, Kupang, and the Lembaga Ilmu Pengatahuan,

Jakarta, and supported by grants from the Social Science Research Council, the Fulbright Commission and the National Science Foundation. I would like to acknowledge all of them here, and thank them—as well as the many people in Kodi who have also proven invaluable to this study—for their help.

2. The term that he uses for "religion" here is a borrowing from the Indonesian, which has been incorporated into the Kodi language in recent years, especially for polemical discussions concerning the religious status of local spirit worship.

3. This is the Kodinese double name for the single divinity, which combines both male and female aspects: the male activity of metal smelting is seen as creating the hard skull at the crown; the female activity of binding the hairs (just as women bind the threads of *ikat* cloth) is seen as securing the forelock or seat of the soul.

4. This is the double name of the region of Balaghar, whose ancestors were said to have traveled to this southern river valley on a large boat which was then turned into stone at the source of Lyali, near the site of their traditional villages. The rock formations which are said to be the petrified remains of this ship are still found near the bay at Nyapu.

7. Mortuary Tourism in Tana Toraja

This paper was originally presented at the American Anthropological Association meetings in Washington, D.C., December 1982. It is based on research in Tana Toraja carried out from 1976 to 1978, supported by a Fulbright-Hays Doctoral Dissertation Research Fellowship and by the National Science Foundation and Cornell University's Southeast Asia Program.

1. For an ethnography of "traditional" Toraja society, see Nooy-Palm (1979); see Volkman (1985) for a contemporary account.

2. The early history of the Mission and its interaction with indigenous ritual are superbly documented by Bigalke (1981:138–92).

3. See Volkman (1984) for discussion of these processes and construction of cultural identity; and Volkman (1979) for an account of one particularly striking nouveaux riches' funeral.

8. Religions in Dialogue: The Construction of an Indonesian Minority Religion

The fieldwork on which this paper is based was conducted in Indonesia from June 1974 until December 1976 under the auspices of the Lembaga Ilmu Pengetahuan Indonesia. Support was provided by an NSF predoctoral fellowship, and NIGMS training grant administered by the Stanford University Department of Anthropology, and the Gertrude Slaughter Award from Bryn Mawr College. The precursors to this article are a paper on Wana ethnicity and religion presented at the 1980 Annual Meeting of the American Anthropological Association and a discussion of Indonesian religion prepared for an Indonesian audience (Atkinson in press). The argument presented here was developed initially in a paper delivered at the Tenth Annual Indonesian Studies Conference held in Athens, Ohio, in August 1982. I am indebted to many people for helpful discussions on the subject of Wana religion, but I owe special thanks to Tim Babcock, Elizabeth Coville, Virginia Dominguez, Michael Dove, Van Dusenbery, Patricia Henry, Ward Keeler, Daniel Maltz, Richard Rohrbaugh, Michelle Rosaldo, and Renato Rosaldo. I am particularly grateful to Anna Lowenhaupt Tsing for her critical insights and editorial advice.

This article is reproduced by permission of the American Ethnological Society from *American Ethnologist* 10(4), 1983.

1. Perhaps this pause is due to recent developments in symbolic and medical approaches that provide alternative frameworks for treating problems of both meaning and suffering.

2. Spiro (1966:88–89) notes this problem but nevertheless hold out the hope of establishing an anthropological definition of religion that is free of value-laden implications. I realize that my argument here faces the same implications, but as long as anthropologists communicate with the public, that problem remains.

3. The argument can be traced through the work of Coedès (1968), Van Leur (1955), and Wertheim (1959[1956]). Useful summaries are provided by Hall (1968[1955]:12–24) and Cady (1964: 41–48).

4. The issue of whether or not *agama* must have a prophet has also surfaced in official deliberations. (Mulder 1978: 4, 6). Inclusion of that criterion would further tighten Indonesian religious policy.

5. In fact, after independence, the highly restrictive qualifications for *agama* excluded the Balinese. C. Geertz (1964:299–302) discusses the struggles within the Ministry of Religion over the legitimacy of Balinese Hinduism. In the final years of his presidency, Sukarno declared Islam, Protestantism, Catholicism, Buddhism, Confucianism, *and* Hinduism to be officially sanctioned religions (Mulder 1978:6). *Aluk to dolo*, the traditional ways of the Toraja of South Sulawesi, attained the status of a religion in 1969 (Crystal 1974:144). (Not incidentally, the Toraja area is billed as the "new Bali" by the Indonesian tourist industry. See Volkman, this volume.) *Kaharingan*, the traditional "belief system" of the peoples of Central Kalimantan, was deemed "belief system" of the peoples of Central Kalimantan, was deemed an official religion in 1980 (Weinstock 1981). Significantly, both populations have influential contacts in government, in contrast to groups like the Wana.

6. Great, too, is the consternation of some Wana converts when they find that government policies regarding the resettlement of pagan hill tribes also apply to them. Despite the prominence of religion in defining who is and is not backward, officials do not always distinguish the converted from the unconverted among people who, in all other respects, live the same kind of life as upland swidden cultivators far from administrative access or control.

7. *Puasa* derives ultimately from the Sanskrit *upavāsa*, "a religious attitude comprising abstinence from all sensual gratification, the use of ornaments, per-

fumes, etc. included." Like other words from the Hindu-Buddhist period, it was used in later times to apply to Islamic fasting and Ramadan, as well as to Roman Catholic practice (Gonda 1973:500).

8. In a similar story presented by Kruyt (1930: 418), the Muslim brother's distaste for the pagan way of life is expressed through his repugnance toward pork. The Muslim will not enter his pagan brother's house, the walls of which consist of layers of pig fat. In their audience before God, the Muslim brother refers to the pagan's heaven as that of a swine. Later in the paper I present a contemporary pagan response to that claim.

9. I have not been able to determine whether or not his procedure is unique to the Wana. The derivation of the term *maluba* is unclear. Sjamsir Sjarif, Sumarsam, and Alton Becker have all suggested to me that it may derive from the Indonesian word *malupa* (to forget). In Indonesia one speaks of "forgetting a religion." This may well be the source, although the sound shift from /p/ to /b/ is not typical of Wana borrowings.

10. My impression, based on a comparison of Kruyt's (1930) account and my own data, is that my informants in the 1970s were more inclusive and consistent in their use of the unmarked term Pue, or God, than were Kruyt's informants in the 1920s.

11. Like the words *agama* and *puasa* mentioned so far, this word derives from the Sanskrit *svarga*.

12. McKinley's analysis examines religious systems in dialogue. He explores the contrasts drawn by modern urban dwellers in Kuala Lumpur between their present and their past.

13. Ortner's (1978) monograph *Sherpas Through Their Rituals* illustrates this point. Although focusing on Buddhism in Sherpa society, she does not confine herself to Buddhist rituals per se but traces elements in secular ritual as well to construct a sense of what rituals do in Sherpa life.

14. Whereas C. Geertz's (1966b) existential treatment of religion leaves problems of meaning sociologically ungrounded, Ortner (1978:152) locates them largely within the social order.

15. Boon's treatment of Balinese religion illuminates the dynamic interplay between Balinese ritual and Javanese Islam (see especially pp. 206–18).

9. A Rhetoric of Centers in a Religion of the Periphery

Research in South Kalimantan was conducted from September 1979 to September 1981 under the auspices of the Lembaga Ilmu Pengetahuan Indonesia and the sponsorship of Dr. Masri Singarimbun of Gadjah Mada University. Support was furnished by National Institute for Mental Health Fellowship No. F31-MH0784 and by the Social Science Research Council. This paper would never have been written without the advice and encouragement of Gaylord Neely and Jane Atkinson. I also received many helpful comments from Sylvia Yanagisako, Renato Rosaldo, Sarah Stapleton, Mark Handler, and Elizabeth Coville.

1. "Uma Adang" and "Kalawan" are pseudonyms. "Dayak" refers to the non-Moslem indigenous peoples of Borneo.
2. The name Meratus was chosen from the geographical designation of the area in consultation with a Meratus university student, Bingan Sabda. The term *Bukit* is used by Banjar, as well as in earlier reports by social scientists and journalists, but has derogatory implications to most Meratus, who therefore rarely use the term as an ethnic label. (I heard it used as a swear word, as a description of even more "primitive" people elsewhere, and in defensive reactions to Banjar designations.) Meratus sometimes call themselves *Dayak* or *Kaharingan*—terms used in the literature on Kalimantan with wider meanings—or they may use local designations, including names of neighborhoods, administrative villages, or rivers.
3. Throughout the paper, History refers specifically to Uma Adang's concept of "history," for which she uses the Indonesian term *sejarah*. Elsewhere, I use single quotation marks to indicate glosses for Indonesian or Meratus terms; double quotation marks either highlight the ambiguity of English words or indicate direct quotations from an author or speaker.
4. One outstanding exception to this generalization is Douglas Miles's *Cutlass and Crescent Moon* (1976). Dayak ethnic relations are also discussed in King (1979). Moving beyond Kalimantan, the issues here have been usefully considered in the collection of essays edited by G.W. Skinner, *Local, Ethnic, and National Loyalties in Village Indonesia* (1959).
5. A religious movement among the Karen of upland Thailand, discussed by Hinton (1979), shows some striking parallels to the case presented here. In 1968–69 an ex-Buddhist known as The White Monk organized a large following among a non-Buddhist hill people, the Pwo Karen. Hinton demonstrates that this movement drew on an ideology of power from the lowland states to build a broad-based upland movement mobilizing Karen ethnic identity. Arguing convincingly against explanatory frameworks stressing frustration as the motivation for religious mobilization, Hinton (p.91) suggests that Karen millenarian movements gain their significance by uniting a peripheral and scattered ethnic group under "a common banner against an external threat."

    Van der Kroef's analysis (1962) of a millenerian movement among the Lawangan of south-central Kalimantan in the 1920s also seems relevant. He stresses the importance of new taxation policies and an intensification of Dutch control, as well as a locally "changing appreciation of leadership" in building the Lawangan *njuli* movement. Muslim-influenced mystic word play was combined with transformed Lawangan themes of the power of the ancestors in the *njuli* message.
6. In 1980, Uma Adang was thirty-five years old and had been widowed for five years; she lived with her sixteen-year-old son. Her voices have told her that she may not eat rice, the staple food of the Meratus, and thus in 1980–81 she did not farm a rice swidden, concentrating on growing beans and peanuts as cash crops. Her ability to survive on meat, vegetables, root crops, and foods bought at market, such as dried noodles, amazes other Meratus who think of rice as necessary for human health.
7. This position does not exist in other Meratus areas but is common in other

Dayak areas of Kalimantan. The "nephew" referred to here is actually Uma Adang's ex-husband's son-in-law.

8. She does once mention "ritual tools of shamans" (line 25), tying them through a parallel construction to "ritual tools of Majapahit" (line 35).

9. Her use of this foreign and official language emphasizes her concern with formality. Thus, she not only begins with the Arabic greeting "Wassalam" (line 3), never used in my experience in other Meratus areas, but also follows it with the formal letter opening *Kepada yang terhormat*, 'to the honorable' (line 5), which I heard nowhere else in speaking contexts.

10. In line 53 she implies that "words" are the essence of *adat*.

11. As Worsley (1968) has pointed out, religion is inherently political because it involves not just belief but the organization of people in religious practice. Islam has certainly had political uses since its introduction in Indonesia (Kahane 1980). However, in this discussion I am concerned with the political importance of Islam in highlighting the definition of "religion" for the Meratus, as a concept contrasting those with "religion" and those without; this definition only became central to Indonesian politics after nationalist struggles, reformist Islam, and state policy established its priority.

12. Sukarno's 1945 speech, "The Birth of the Pancasila," illustrates his support for a religiously oriented political competition. Speaking of parliamentary representation, he said, "For Muslims this is the best place to promote religion. . . . If we really are an Islamic people, let us work as hard as we can to see that the greatest number of seats in the Parliament which we shall form will be held by Islamic representatives. . . . If, for instance, the Christians want every letter of the regulations of the state of Indonesia to be in agreement with the Bible, let them work as if their lives depended on it, so that a large proportion of the representatives who are members of Parliament will be Christians. That is reasonable— 'fair play' " (quoted in Boland 1971:22–23).

13. Whittier (1973:146) documents a case in which East Kalimantan Dayaks endorsed Christianity so as not to be pejoratively labeled "Communist."

14. The Indonesian government requires that every citizen declare an official religion to be displayed on an individual's identity card. Many Meratus asked for *Kaharingan* on their identity cards, although at the time of my research they did not know of its success in achieving official recognition. Others claim to be Buddhists, following an earlier Dayak movement from the north to have Dayak religion considered Buddhism. Still others encourage local efforts for Meratus religious recognition by picking the name *Balian* ('shaman') as their religious designation.

15. This discussion mainly applies to the east and central sectors of the Meratus area. In the western foothills, a number of kinds of more permanent, more centralized settlement have been adopted, and leadership conditions differ accordingly.

16. Other Indonesian bureaucrats presumably may have *different* reasons to support state rhetoric.

17. Similarly, in Meratus conceptions, spiritual beings are not ranked, but shamans declare their equally "total" allegiance to each.

18. Uma Adang's leadership is highly exceptional in the Meratus area because she is a woman; almost all shamans and community leaders are men. Uma Adang takes advantage of conventional Meratus arrangements in which women and men socialize in common conversations and women are not limited by formally articulated sex-role stereotypes from leadership positions. However, she also actively transforms the gender system: She stresses gender etiquette, the formal spatial separation of men and women, and a philosophical dualism with an uncanny resemblance to published accounts of "Indonesian dualism" but which I never heard elsewhere in the Meratus area. She posits a Meratus "tradition" of 'female shamanism' in contrast to 'male shamanism,' and she has tried, although not with much success, to train other women in this "tradition." Her stress on gender etiquette supports her leadership stance and simultaneously responds to Banjar conventions that emphasize gender separation and women's separate "domestic" orientations. Uma Adang's etiquette posits instead a "separate but equal in every sphere" gender model. But she treads a fine line between power and oppression in creating a more rigid gender classification for Meratus women. Her own hesitancy to do both household chores and swidden work, and her ability to get her son, neighbors, and kin to help out, clearly helps to free her energies for ritual and *adat* leadership. Other women cannot easily follow her example.

19. Van der Kroef's (1959) discussion of Javanese messianic expectations does highlight the construction of ideology. However, his focus on Javanese culture and its ability to incorporate new and foreign elements without essential changes in turn neglects the specific political context of messianic movements.

10. Islam and Law in Indonesia

1. The name of the Regulation was "Regulation on the administration of police, of criminal and civil justice and of dealing with little cases for the capital of Palembang."

2. Gazette 1937, no. 116. The area of jurisdiction of this Gazette was Java and Madura. The law of December 21, 1937, was enacted for the Banjarmasin district. Gazette here refers to the Staatsblad van Nederlansch-Indie (Batavia, a series starting in 1816).

3. "bahwa seluruh alam semesta ini beserta eksistensi manusia di dalamnya, bukanlah sekedar insiden sejarah atau hasil dari alam sendiri secara kebetulan. Alam semesta ini diciptakan dengan suatu tujuan, dikendalikan oleh suatu hukum dan merupakan ciptaan dari zat Yang Maha Pemurah, Maha Pengampun, Maha Kuasa, Maha Pencipta, yaitu Tuhan. Demikian juga dengan negara, yang menurut inderaan manusia adalah lembaga buatan manusid, iatak akan pernah ada bila tak men dapat perkenan Tuhan" (p. 4). "Dalam pengertian Ketuhanan, yang paling pokok yalah pengakuan akan Keesaan Tuhan. Tuhan mengendalikan segala hal, besar dan kecil. Alam semesta ini merupakan skema tunggal, dikelola oleh kekihakan dari satu Pencipta dan Penggerak demikian rupa sehingga segala hal dalam alam semesta ini mengisi

satu sama lain, saling berpengaruh, saling tergantung. Kehidupan ini mem-punyai tujuan. Karena itu, dalam alam semesta ini terdapat tata moral dan hukum moral yank menguasai antar aksi dan saling keter-antungan dari segala yang ada" (Report, Badan Pembinaan Hukum Nasional, April 1981:4 – 5).

4. The Basic Law for Justice (1970) created a three-tiered system of courts. Having to deal with many petitions of litigants from the regions in 1977, the Supreme Court issued a temporary regulation on cassation of religious court verdicts.

11. Islam and Adat Among South Tapanuli Migrants in Three Indonesian Cities

1. Literally, the phrase *dalihan na tolu* means the arrangement of three stones on a hearth for balancing a cookpot. Figuratively, the three stones are a man's close lineage mates, this wife-receiving lineage, and his wife-providing lineage. Each must ideally work together for their mutual benefit. The Batak cultures have patrilineal clans, and asymmetrical marriage alliances involving preferential MBD marriages.

2. Some potential respondents thought the questionnaire contained too many questions. Others did not regard the research as important, while others felt they could not answer some of the questions. Some accused me of being an agent of Christianization.

3. Material on 33 percent of the returned questionnaires indicates whether the respondents are *Mandailing* or *Angkola-Sipirok Batak* (sub-ethnic groupings). Of my respondents, 39.44 percent are *Mandailing*, while 53.89 percent are *Angkola, Sipirok, Padang Bolak, Barumun, Dolok* and *Saipar Dolok Hole*. The rest of the informants cannot be identified (6.67 percent).

4. Some Angkola, Padang Bolak, Barumun and other northern and eastern area migrants also crossed the natural walls of the mountain range and settled in Angkola Jae and in Mandailing valleys. They also named their new settlements after their original *hutas* as the Mandailing migrants did.

5. This conforms with Hart's assertion that Prophet Muhammad heads the list of the world's most influential persons, as the only man in history who was su-premely successful on both the religious and secular levels (Hart 1978:33).

12. Sundanese Islam and the Value of Hormat: Control, Obedience, and Social Location in West Java

Research for this paper was carried out in Bandung, West Java, in 1980–81. Fulbright Grant #G00-8002450 provided financial support for the research, for which I am grateful. I would also like to thank Sidney Jones and Susan Millar for their comments and criticisms on early drafts of this paper.

1. The Sundanese, numbering about fifteen million, are the second largest ethnic group in Indonesia. They are the dominant ethnic group in the western end of the island of Java.

2. Rigg's Sundanese-English dictionary (one of the most complete extant) defines *hormat* as "honour, reverence, respect. Compliments of ceremony" and notes that the word is of Arabic derivation (Rigg 1862:150). The Sundanese-Sundanese dictionary issued by the Indonesian government defines *hormat* as "civility, politeness" (Lembaga Basa dan Sastra Sunda 1976:172 [my translation]).

3. *Akal* is also of Arabic derivation and means "device, cunning contrivance, judgment" (Rigg 1862:8) or "thought, the faculty of thought; way, path" (Lembaga Basa dan Sastra Sunda 1976:7 [my translation]).

4. *Hawa nafsu* is defined as follows: *hawa*: "affection, desire, lust; inclination, will, wish" (Rigg 1862:145) and *nafsu*: "the energy of life; the passions; . . . sensual desires, lust" (Rigg 1862:294). The newer Sundanese-Sundanese dictionary defines the phrase as 'desire' (Lembaga Basa dan Sastra Sunda 1976:325 [my translation]).

5. Dar'ul Islam was a militant Islamic movement that began in the early years of Indonesian independence. Its purpose was to establish Indonesia as an Islamic religious state.

6. A suggestive etymological point: the root word of the Sundanese term for Qur'anic recitation is *aji*. *Aji* means *elmu gaib*, or spirit knowledge. The root word of the Indonesian term is also *aji*—which means spell or charm.

7. See Geertz (1980) for an elaborate discussion of the notion of theater and performance in the political domain.

8. The word "Islam" is derived from the Arabic *aslama* which can be glossed as "to obey" or "to surrender" (Smith 1962:112).

9. The difference between a *kyai* and an *ajengan* is analogous to that between a priest and a pastor or religious teacher.

10. Evidence for this in western Java is in patterns of language use, as discussed below.

11. Information on the number of levels in Sundanese varies (see Wessing 1974 for a description of Sundanese as a language with more than three levels). However, informants in Bandung during the period of this research generally agreed that the language currently had three levels.

12. One of the Sundanese words for "socially mature" is *cumarita*, an adjective derived from *carita*, to speak.

13. By 1981, the Muhammadiyah organization (the organization which institutionalized Indonesian Islamic reformism) had succeeded in establishing only six elementary schools in the strongly Islamic city of Bandung.

Bibliography

Abdulgani, H. Roeslan
1983   Kekacauan Semantiak tentang Sekularisme dan Negara Pancasila. *Waspada*.
Abdullah, Taufik
1966   Adat and Islam: An Examination of Conflict in Minangkabau. *Indonesia* (Cornell University) 2:1–24.
1971   *Schools and Politics: The Kaum Muda Movement in West Sumatra (1927 – 1933)*. Ithaca: Cornell University Modern Indonesia Project.
1972   Modernization in the Minangkabau World: West Sumatra in the Early Decades of the Twentieth Century. In *Culture and Politics in Indonesia*, ed. Claire Holt, et al., 179–245. Ithaca: Cornell University Press.
Adams, Kathleen M.
1984   Come to Tana Toraja, "Land of the Heavenly Kings": Travel Agents as Brokers in Ethnicity. *Tourism and Ethnicity, Annals of Tourism Research* 2:3.
Adas, Michael
1979   *Prophets of Rebellion: Millenarian Protest Movements against the European Colonial Order*. Chapel Hill: University of North Carolina Press.

Adriani, N., and C. Kruyt
1950   *De Bare'e-sprekende Toradjas van Midden-Celebes.* Amsterdam: Noord-Hoijandsche Uitgevers Maatschappij. [Orig. 1912]
al-Attas, Syed M. N.
1970   *The Mysticism of Hamzah Fansuri.* Kuala Lumpur: University of Malaya Press.
Anawati, Georges C.
1974   Philosophy, Theology and Mysticism. In *The Legacy of Islam,* 2d ed., ed. Joseph Schacht and C. Bosworth, 350–92. Oxford: Clarendon Press.
Anderson, Benedict R.
1966   The Languages of Indonesian Politics. *Indonesia* (Cornell University) 1:89–116.
1972a   The Idea of Power in Javanese Culture. In *Culture and Politics in Indonesia,* ed. Claire Holt, et al., 1–69. Ithaca: Cornell University Press.
1972b   *Java in a Time of Revolution: Occupation and Resistance, 1944 – 1946.* Ithaca: Cornell University Press.
Anwar, Chadir
1968   *Beberapa Masalah Pendidikan Islam.* Bandung: IKIP Bandung.
Appell, G. N.
1976   *The Societies of Borneo: Explorations in the Theory of Cognatic Structure.* Amercian Anthropological Association Special Publication no. 6. Washington, D.C.: American Anthropological Association.
Arberry, A. J.
1953   *The Holy Koran: An Introduction with Selections.* London: Allen and Unwin, Ltd.
Asad, Talal
        Anthropological Conceptions of Religion: Reflections on Geertz. *Man* 18:237–59.
as-Said, Labib
1975   *The Recited Koran: A History of the First Recorded Version.* Trans. Weiss, Rauf and Berger. Princeton: Darwin Press.
Atkinson, J. M.
1979   Paths of Spirit Familiars: A Study of Wana Shamanism. Ph.D. diss. Stanford University.
In press Religion and the Wana of Sulawesi Tengah. In *Peranan Kebudayaan Tradisional Indonesian Dalam Modernisasi,* ed. M. Dove. Yogyakarta, Indonesia: Obor Foundation.
Babas, Djajamadi
1978   *Pembinaan Pendidikan Agama di Masyarakat Terasing Cantung Kota Baru Pulau Laut.* Banjarmasin: IAIN Antasari.
Babbie, Earl R.
1973   *Survey Research Methods.* Belmont, Calif: Wadsworth.

Becker, A. L.
    1979a   The Figure a Sentence Makes. In *Syntax and Semantics*. Vol.
            12 of *Discourse and Syntax*, ed. Talmy Givón, 243 – 59. New
            York: Academic Press.
    1979b   Text-Building, Epistemology, and Aesthetics in Javanese
            Shadow Theater. In *The Imagination of Reality: Essays in
            Southeast Asian Coherence Systems*, ed. A. L. Becker and
            Aram A. Yengoyan, 211–43. Norwood, N.J.: Ablex Publishing
            Corporation.
Becker, A. L., and Aram A. Yengoyan, eds.
    1979   *The Imagination of Reality: Essays in Southeast Asian Co-
            herence Systems. Norwood, N.J.: Ablex Publishing Corporation.*
Becker, Judith
    1979   Time and Time in Java. In *The Imagination of Reality: Essays
            in Southeast Asian Coherence Systems*, ed. A.L. Becker and
            Aram A. Yengoyan, 197 – 210. Norwood, N.J.: Ablex Publish-
            ing Corporation.
Bellah, Robert
    1970   Civil Religion in America. In *Beyond Belief: Essays on Re-
            ligion in a Post-Traditional World*, 168 – 89. New York: Harper
            & Row.
    1964   Religious Evolution. *The American Sociological Review* 29:
            358–74.
Belo, Jane
    1960   *Trance in Bali*. New York: Columbia University Press.
Benda, Harry J., and Lance Castles
    1969   The Samin Movement. *Bijdragen tot de Taal-, Land- en Volk-
            enkunde* 125:207 – 40.
Berg, C. C.
    1938   De Arjunawiwaaha, Er-langga's Levensloop en Bruilofslied?
            Bijdragen tot de Taal-, Land- en Volkenkunde 97:19–94.
Berger, Peter L.
    1967   *The Sacred Canopy: Elements of a Sociological Theory of Re-
            ligion*. New York: Doubleday.
Bigalke, Terance
    1981   A Social History of Tana Toraja: 1881–1965. Ph.D. diss., Uni-
            versity of Wisconsin, Madison.
Biro Pusat Statistik
    1981   *Buku Saku Statistik Indonesian 1979/1980*. Jakarta: Biro Pusat
            Statistik.
Boland, B. J.
    1971   *The Struggle of Islam in Modern Indonesia*. The Hague: Mar-
            tinus Nijhoff.
    1974   Discussion on Islam in Indonesia Today. In *Studies on Islam*,
            Koninklijke Nederlandsie Akademie van Wetenschappen, 37–
            50. Amsterdam: North Holland Publishing Company.

Boon, James A.
    1977   *The Anthropological Romance of Bali 1597–1972: Dynamic Perspectives in Marriage and Caste, Politics and Religion.* New York: Cambridge University Press.

Boston Globe
    1981   Sulawesi: Far From the Tourist Path (March 29).

Brakel, L. F.
    1969   The Birthplace of Hamza Pansuri. *Journal of the Malaysian Branch of the Royal Asiatic Society* 42 (no. 2):206 – 13.
    1979   Notes on: Yoga Practices, Lahir dan Zahir, the "Taxallos," Punning, a Difficult Passage in the Kitab al-Muntahi, Hamza's Likely Place of Birth, and Hamza's Imagery. *Journal of the Malaysian Branch of the Royal Asiatic Society* 52 (no.1):73 – 98.

Buku Saku Statistik Indonesia
    1982   *Statistical Pocketbook of Indonesia.* Jakarta: Biro Pusat Statistik.

Cady, J. F.
    1964   *Southeast Asia: Its Historical Development.* New York: McGraw Hill.

Castles, Lance
    1973   *The Political Life of a Sumatran Residency: Tapanuli 1915 – 1940.* Ph.D. Diss., Yale University, New Haven.

Cederoth, Sven
    1981   *The Spell of the Ancestors and the Power of Mekkah: A Sasak Community on Lombok.* Goteborg, Sweden: Acta Universitatis Gothoburgensis.

Chaudhuri, N. C.
    1979   *Hinduism: A Religion to Live By.* New York: Oxford University Press.

Chirzin, M. Habib
    1974   Agama dan Ilmu dalam Pesantren. In *Pesantren dan Pembaharuan,* ed. M. Dawam Rahardjo, 77–94. Jakarta: LP3ES.

Clamagirand, Brigitte
    1980   The Social Organization of the Ema of Timor. In *The Flow of Life: Essays on Eastern Indonesia,* ed. James J. Fox, 134 – 51. Cambridge: Harvard University Press.

Coedes, G.
    1968   *Indianized States of Southeast Asia.* Honolulu: East-West Center Press.

Conklin, H. C.
    1980   *Ethnographic Atlas of Ifugao.* New Haven: Yale University Press.

Conley, William
    1976   *The Kalimantan Kenyah: A Study of Tribal Conversion in Terms of Dynamic Cultural Themes.* Nutley, N.J.: Presbyterian and Reformed Publishing Company.

Corbin, Henry
1969   *Creative Imagination in the Sufism of Ibn Arabi.* Princeton:
          Princeton University Press. [orig. 1958]
1978   *The Man of Light in Iranian Sufism.* Boulder and London:
          Shambhala. [orig. 1971]
Crystal, Eric
1970   Toraja Town. Ph.D. diss., University of California, Berkeley.
1974   Cooking Pot Politics: A Toraja Village Study. *Indonesia*
          (Cornell University) 18:119–51.
1977   Tourism in Tana Toraja (Sulawesi, Indonesia). In *Hosts and
          Guests: The Anthropology of Tourism.* ed. Valene L. Smith,
          100–125. Philadelphia: University of Pennsylvania Press.
Crystal, Eric, and Catherine Crystal
1973   *Ma'bugi' Trance of the Toraja.* 16mm; 21 min. Berkley: Exten-
          sion Media Center, University of California.
Dapawole, L. D.
1969   Kedudukan Tanah Suku di Pulau Sumba (The basis for tradi-
          tional land tenure on the island of Sumba). report of the 1969
          Conference on Custom and Land Ownership, Waikabubak,
          West Sumba.
Daud, Habibah, SH.
1982   *Working Paper for the Seminar on Islamic Inheritance Law,
          Cisarua Bogor, April 1982.* Jakarta: Indonesia Department of
          Religious Affairs.
de Josselin de Jong, P.E.
          The Concept of the Field of Ethnological Study. In *The Flow
          of Life: Essays on Eastern Indonesia,* ed. James J. Fox,
          317–26. Cambridge: Harvard University Press.
Dempwolf, Otto
1938   *Austronesisches Worterverzeichnis.* Vergleichende Lautlehre
          des Austronesischen Wortschatzes, Vol. 3. Beihefte zur Zeit-
          schrift fur Eingeborenen-Sprachen, no. 19, Berlin: Dietrich
          Reimer.
Departemen Agama
1975   *Almanak 1975.* Jakarta: Direktorat Pendidikan Islam.
Departemen Pendidikan dan Kebudayaan
n.d.   *Pendidikan Moral Pancasila.* Jakarta: Bali Pustaka.
Department of Information, Republic of Indonesia
1975   *The Indonesian Marriage Law.* Jakarta: Department of Infor-
          mation.
Dewan Kemakmuran Masjid Indonesia
n.d.   *Islam in Indonesia Today.*
Dewey, Alice G.
1978   Deference Behavior in Java: Duty or Privilege. In *Spectrum:
          Essays Presented to St. Takdir Alisjahbana.* ed. S. Udin,
          420–28. Jakarta: Dian Rakyat.

Dhofier, Zamaksyariyah
1980   The Pesantren Tradition: A Study of the Role of the Kyai in
         the Maintenance of the Traditional Ideology of Islam in Java.
         Ph.D. diss., Australian National University.
Discovery Tours
1981 – 82 Indonesian Odyssey. New York: American Museum of Natural
         History.
Dobbin, Christine
1977   Economic Change in Minangkabau as a Factor in the Rise of
         the Padri Movement, 1784–1830. *Indonesia* (Cornell Univer-
         sity) 23:1–38.
Douglas, Mary
1966   *Purity and Danger: An Analysis of the Concepts of Pollution
         and Taboo.* London: Routledge and Kegan Paul.
Durkheim, Emile
1954   *The Elementary Forms of the Religious Life.* Glencoe, Ill.: The
         Free Press. [orig. 1915]
1961   *The Elementary Forms of the Religious Life.* New York: Collier
         Books. [orig. 1915]
1965   *The Elementary Forms of Religious Life.* Trans. Joseph Swain.
         New York: The Free Press. [orig. 1915]
Dyson, L.
1979   *Sistim Dan Motivasi Gotong Royong Pada Sukubangsa Dayak
         Tunjung Di Desa Juhan Asa Kabupaten Kutai—Kalimantan
         Timur.* Jakarta: Skripsi Sarjana Sastra, Fakultas Sastra, Univer-
         sitas Indonesia.
Echols, John M., and Hassan Shadily
1963   *An Indonesian-English Dictionary.* 2d ed. Ithaca: Cornell
         University Press.
Eickelman, Dale F.
1978   The Art of Memory: Islamic Education and Its Social Repro-
         duction. *Comparative Studies in Society and History* 20
         (no. 4): 495–516.
Eliade, Mircea
1957   *The Sacred and the Profane.* New York: Harcourt.
Emmerson, Donald K.
1976   *Indonesia's Elite: Political Culture and Cultural Politics.*
         Ithaca: Cornell University Press.
1981   Islam in Modern Indonesia: Political Impasse, Cultural Op-
         portunity. In *Change and the Muslim World,* ed. Philip H.
         Stoddard, et al., 156 – 68. Syracuse: Syracuse University Press.
Endicott, Kirk
1970   *An Analysis of Malay Magic.* Oxford: Clarendon Press.
Evans, I. H. N.
1922   *Among Primitive Peoples in Borneo.* London: Seeley, Service
         & Co., Ltd.

1953   *The Religion of the Tempasuk Dunsun of North Borneo.* London: Cambridge University Press.

Evans-Pritchard, E. E.
1965   *Theories of Primitive Religion.* London: Oxford University Press.

Feith, H., and L. Castles, eds.
1970   *Indonesian Political Thinking 1945–1965.* Ithaca: Cornell University Press.

Feith, Herbert
1962   *The Decline of Constitutional Democracy in Indonesia.* Ithaca: Cornell University Press.

Feldman, Jerome
1977   The Architecture of Nias, Indonesia, with Special Reference to Bawomataluo Village. Ph.D. diss., Columbia University.
1979   The House as World in Bawomataluo, South Nias. In *Art, Ritual, and Society in Indonesia,* eds. E. Bruner and J. Becker, 127–89. Athens, Ohio: Ohio University Papers in International Studies.

Ferguson, Charles A.
1976   The Structure and Use of Politeness Formulas. *Language in Society* 5:137–51.

Fox, James
1971   Semantic Parallelism in Rotinese Ritual Language. *Bijdragen tot de Taal-, Land- en Volkenkunde* 127:215–55.
1980   *The Flow of Life: Essays on Eastern Indonesia.* Cambridge: Harvard University Press.

Franken, H. J.
1984   The Festival of Jayaprana at Kalianget. In *Bali: Life, Thought and Ritual.* Koninklijke Instituut voor Taal-, Land- en Volkenkunde Reprints on Indonesia. Dordrecht Holland 2nd Cinnaminson, N.J.: Foris Publications. (Originally published 1951. Het feest van Djajaprana te Kalianget. *Bijdragen tot de Taal-, Land- en Volkenkunde* 107 (1951): 1–30.)

Fuller, C. J.
1982   The Attempted Reform of South Indian Temple Hinduism. In *Religious Organization and Religious Experience,* ed. J. Davis, 153–67. ASA Monograph no. 21. London: Academic Press.

Geertz, Clifford
1956   Religious Belief and Economic Behavior in a Central Javanese Town. *Economic Development and Culture Change* 4:134–58.
1957   Ritual and Social Change: A Javanese Example. *American Anthropologist* 59:32–54.
1960   *The Religion of Java.* Glencoe, Ill.: The Free Press.
1963   *Agricultural Involution: The Processes of Ecological Change in Indonesia.* Berkeley: University of California Press.
1964   Internal Conversion in Contemporary Bali. In *Malayan and*

Geertz, Clifford *(continued)*

          Indonesian Studies Presented to Sir Richard Winstedt, ed. J. Bastin and R. Roolvink, 282–302. Oxford: Oxford University Press. (Reprinted in *The Interpretation of Cultures.*)

1966a   Person, Time, and Conduct in Bali: An Essay in Cultural Analysis. Southeast Asia Program, Cultural Report Series, no. 4. New Haven: Yale University. (Reprinted in *The Interpretation of Cultures.*)

1966b   Religion as a Cultural System. In *Anthropological Approaches to the Study of Religion*, ed. M. Banton, 1–46. New York: I. A. Praeger. (Reprinted in *The Interpretation of Cultures.*)

1968   *Islam Observed: Religious Development in Morocco and Indonesia.* Chicago: University of Chicago Press.

1972a   Religious Change and Social Order in Soeharto's Indonesia. *Asia* 27:62–84.

1972b   Deep Play: Notes on the Balinese Cockfight. *Daedalus* 101 (1972):1–37. (Reprinted in *The Interpretation of Cultures.*)

1973a   *The Interpretation of Cultures.* New York: Basic Books.

1973b   Thick Description: Toward an Interpretive Theory of Culture. In *The Interpretation of Cultures.*

1977   "From the Native's Point of View": On the Nature of Anthropological Understanding. In *Symbolic Anthropology; A Reader in the Study of Symbols and Meanings*, ed. Janet L. Dolgin, David S. Kemnitzer, and David M. Schneider, 480–92. New York: Columbia University Press.

1980   *Negara, the Theatre State in Nineteenth Century Bali.* Princeton: Princeton University Press.

Geertz, H.

1963   *Indonesian Cultures and Communities.* New Haven: HRAF Press.

Gennep, Arnold van

1960   *The Rites of Passage.* London: Routledge.

Ginting-Suka, Pdt. A., Chairperson, Gereja Batak Karo Protestan

1983   Personal communication with R. S. Kipp.

Goody, Jack, ed.

1968   *Literacy in Traditional Societies.* Cambridge: Cambridge University Press.

Gonda, J.

1973   *Sanskrit in Indonesia.* New Delhi: International Academy of Indian Culture. [orig. 1952]

Grabowsky, F.

1889   Die "Olon Lowangan" in Sudost Borneo. *Ausland* 61:581–84.

Grothaus, Werner

1970   80 Jahre Karobatakkirche. In *Die Welt for die Welt: Berichte der Reinischen Mission* 6:1–11.

Grubauer, A. von
1913   *Unter Kopfjarern in Central-Celebes.* Leipzig: R. Voigtlanders
         Verlag.
Hadjiwijono
1967   *Man in the Present Javanese Mysticism.* Baarn: Bosch and
         Kenning.
Hall, D. G. F.
1968   *A History of South-East Asia.* London: Macmillan. [orig.
         1955]
Hall, Kenneth
1976   *State and Statecraft in Early Srivijaya.* In *Explorations in
         Early Southeast Asian Statecraft,* ed. Kenneth Hall and John
         Whitmore, 61−105. Michigan Papers in South and Southeast
         Asia. Ann Arbor: University of Michigan Press.
Hamda, M. J.
1979   Pembangunan Masarakat Pedesaan Malalui Proyek Pem-
         bangunan Kesejahteraan Masarakat Terasing. Paper presented
         at the Seminar. Pembinaan Kehidupan Beragama Masarakat
         Pengunungan Meratus di Kalimantan Selatan, IAIN Antasari,
         Banjarmasin.
Harahap, Basyral Hamidy
1979   *103 tahun wafatnya Willem Iskander: tokoh pendidikan dan
         sastrawan Indonesia.* Jakarta: Panitia Peringatan 103 Tahun
         Wafatnya Willem Iskander.
1981   The Political Trends of South Tapanuli and Its Reflections in
         the General Elections (1955, 1971 and 1977). Paper presented
         at the Symposium on Cultures and Societies of North Suma-
         tra, 25−27 November at Universitat Hamburg, Hamburg.
Hardeland, August
1859   *Dajacksch-Deutsches Worterbuch.* Amsterdam: F. Muller.
Harrison, Jane E.
1951   *Ancient Arts and Ritual.* New York: Oxford University Press.
         [orig. 1913]
Hart, Michael H.
1978   *The 100: A Ranking of the Most Influential Persons in History.*
         New York: A & W Visual Library.
Heckeren, H. R. van
1958   *The Bronze-Iron Age of Indonesia.* The Hague: Martinus
         Nijhoff.
Heider, Karl
1982   Personal communication.
Heine-Gerdern, Robert
1966   Some Tribal Arts Styles of Southeast Asia. In *The Many Faces
         of Primitive Art,* ed. Douglas Frazer, 165−214. Englewood
         Cliffs, N. J.: Prentice-Hall.

Henry, Patricia B.
  1981   *Text Analysis of an Old Javanese Poem: An Annotated Transla-
            tion of Mpu Kanwa's Arjuna Wiwaha "The Marriage of
            Arjuna,"* Sargas I–XII. Ph.D. Diss., University of Michigan,
            Ann Arbor.
Hertz, R.
  1960   *Death and the Right Hand.* Trans. Rodney and Claudia
            Needham. Glencoe, Ill.: The Free Press. [orig. 1907]
Heyting, Th. A. L.
  1897   *Beschrijving der Onder-Afdeeling Groot Mandeling en Batang
            Natal.* Leiden: E. J. Brill.
Hicks, David
  1973   Tetum Narratives: An Indigenous Taxonomy. *Ethos* 1 (no. 4):
            93–100.
  1976   *Tetum Ghosts and Kin: Fieldwork in an Indonesian Com-
            munity.* Palo Alto, Calif.: Mayfield Publishing Company.
  1978a   *Structural Analysis in Anthropology: Case Studies from Indo-
            nesia and Brazil.* Bonn: Studia Instituti Anthropos 30, Verlag
            des Anthropos Institut bei Bonn.
  1978b   *Mata* in Tetum. *Oceania* 48 (no. 4): 299–300.
  1983   Unachieved Syncretism: The Local Level Political System in
            Portuguese Timor, 1966–1967. *Anthropos* 78:17–40.
  1984   A *Maternal Religion: The Role of Women in Tetum Myth and
            Ritual.* DeKalb, Ill.: Northern Illinois University Center for
            Southeast Asian Studies.
  n.d.   Tetum Sacred Space. Typescript.
Hinton, Peter
  1979   The Karen, Millenarianism, and the Politics of Accommoda-
            tion to Lowland States. In *Ethnic Adaptation and Identity:
            The Karen on the Thai Frontier with Burma,* ed. Charles
            Keyes, 81–94. Philadelphia: Institute for the Study of Human
            Issues.
Hocart, A. M.
  1936   *Kings and Councillors: An Essay in the Comparative Anatomy
            of Human Society.* Cairo: Printing Office Paul Barbey (Re-
            printed 1970. Chicago: University of Chicago Press.)
  1954   *Social Origins.* London: Watts & Co.
Holt, Claire
  1939   *Dance Quest in Celebes.* Paris: Archives Internationales de la
            Dance.
Hooker, M. B.
  1978   *Adat Law in Modern Indonesia.* Kuala Lumpur and New
            York: Oxford University Press.
Hose, Charles, and William McDougall, eds.
  1966   *The Pagan Tribes of Borneo.* 2 vols. London: Frank Cass.

Hudson, A. B.
  1966   Death Ceremonies of the Maanyan Dayaks. *Sarawak Museum Journal* 13 (no. 27): 341–416.
  1967   *The Barito Isolects.* Southeast Asia Program, Department of Asian Studies, Data Paper no. 68. Ithaca: Cornell University.

Ihutan, Mangaradja
  1926   *Riwayat tanah wakaf bangsa Mandailing di Sungai Mati— Medan: terkarang dan di-impoen õentoek peringatan bagi mereka jang tjinta akan bangsanja.* Medan: Sjarikat Tapanoeli.

Ileto, R. C.
  1971   *Magindanao 1860–1888: The Career of Datu Uto of Buavan.* Southeast Asia Program, Department of Asian Studies, Data Paper no. 82. Ithaca: Cornell University.

Iskander, Willem
  1976   *Si Bulus-Bulus Si Rumbuk-Rumbuk: sebuah buku bacaan.* Trans. Basyral Hamidy Harahap. Jakarta: Campusiana.

Jackson, Karl
  1980   *Traditional Authority, Islam and Rebellion: A Study of Indonesian Political Behavior.* Berkeley: University of California Press.

Jackson, Karl, and Lucien Pye, eds.
  1978   *Political Power and Communications in Indonesia.* Berkeley: University of California Press.

Janus, Mahmud
  1960   *Sedjarah Pendidkitan Islam di Indonesia.* Jakarta: Pustaka Mahmudiah Djakarta.

Johns, A. H.
  1957   Malay Sufism as Illustrated in an Anonymous Collection of 17th Century Tracts. *Journal of the Malaysian Branch of the Royal Asiatic Society* 30 (no. 2): 1–111.
  1961   Sufism as a Category in Indonesian Literature and History. *Journal of Southeast Asian History* 2 (no. 2): 10–23.

Jones, Leslie
  1980   It Can't Happen Here: A Post-Khomeini Look at Indonesian Islam. *Asian Survey* 20 (no. 3): 311–23.

Jones, Russell
  1979   Ten Conversion Myths from Indonesia. In *Conversion to Islam,* ed. Nehemia Levtzion, 129–58. New York: Holmes and Meier.

Jones, Sidney
  1981a   Arabic Instruction and Literacy in Javanese Muslim Schools. *Prisma* 21:71–80.
  1981b   What Indonesia's Islamic Revival Means. *Asia* (New York) 4 (no. 3): 18–19, 46–49.

Joustra, M.
1896   Vervolg van de Aanteekening der Minahassische Onder-
            wijzers: van den Goeroe van Pernangenen, R. Tampena-
            was. *Mededeelingen* (Nederlandse Zendeling Genootschap)
            40:289–96.
Kahane, Reuven
1973   *The Problem of Political Legitimacy in an Antagonistic So-
            ciety: The Indonesian Case.* Beverly Hills, Calif.: Sage
            Publications.
1980   Religious Diffusion and Modernization: A Preliminary Reflec-
            tion on the Spread of Islam in Indonesia and Its Impact on
            Social Change. *Arch. Europ. Sociol.* 21:116–38.
Kahin, George McT.
1952   *Nationalism and Revolution in Indonesia.* Ithaca: Cornell
            University Press.
Kantor Wilayah Departemen Sosial, Propinsi Kalimantan Selatan
1978   *Proyek Pengambangan Kesejahteraan Masyarakat Terasing
            (PKMT Atiran).* Banjarmasin.
Kapita, Oembu Hina
1976a   *Masyarakat Sumba dan Adat Istiadatnya* (Sumbanese society
            and its customs). Waingapu: penerbit Gereja Kristen Sumba.
1976b   *Sumba di dalam Jangkauan Jaman* (Sumba throughout the
            ages). Waingapu: Penerbit Gereja Kristen Sumba.
Kennedy, Raymond
1953   *Fieldnotes on Indonesia: South Celebes 1949–50.* Ed. H. C.
            Conklin. New Haven, Conn.: Human Relations Area Files.
Kern, H.
1917   De Steen van den Berg Penarggungan (Surabaya), thans in 't
            Indian Museum te Calcutta (1885). In *Verspreide Geschriften*
            7. The Hague: Martinus Nijhoff.
Kertodipoero, Sarwoto
1963   *Kaharingan: Religi dan Penghidupan di Pehuluan Kaliman-
            tan.* Bandung, Indonesia: Penerbitan Sumur Bandung.
Kleiweg de Zwann, J. P.
1913   *Die Insel Nias bei Sumatra.* The Hague: Martinus Nijhoff.
King, Victor
1979   *Ethnic Classifications and Ethnic Relations: A Borneo Case
            Study.* Centre for South-east Asian Studies, Occasional Paper
            no. 2. Hull, England: University of Hull.
Koentjaraningrat, R. M.
1975   *Introduction to the Peoples and Cultures of Indonesia and
            Malaysia.* Menlo Park, Calif.: Cummings Publishing.
Kompas
1978   Pesta Kematian di Tana Toraja (The Death Feast in Tana
            Toraja). October 18–20.

Korver, A. Pieter E.
1976   The Samin Movement and Millenarianism. *Bijdragen tot de Taal-, Land- en Volkenkunde* 132:249–66.
Kruyt, A. C.
1923 – 24 De Toradja's van de Sa'dan, Masoepoe en Mamasa Rivieren. *Tijdschrift voor Indische Taal-, Land- en Volkenkunde* 63:81 – 176, 256 – 402.
1930   De To Wana op Oost-Celebes. *Tijdschrift voor Indische Taal-, Land- en Volkenkunde* 70:398 – 625.
Lambooy, P. J.
1937   Het Begrip "Marapu" in den godsdienst van Oost Soemba (The concept "Marapu" in the worship of East Sumba). *Bijdragen tot de Taal-, Land- en Volkenkunde* 95:425 – 39.
              Laporan survai kemasyarakatan suku Batak Mandailing (Tapanuli Selatan) di
1982   *Desa Tanjung Ale, Kecamatan Sosa, Kabupaten Tapanuli Selatan.* Medan: Kanwil Departemen Sosial Propinsi Sumatera Utara.
Leach, E. R.
1954   *Political Systems of Highland Burma: A Study of Kachin Social Structure.* Boston: Beacon Press.
1961a   *Rethinking Anthropology.* London: The Athlone Press.
1961b   Two Essays Concerning the Symbolic Representation of Time. In *Rethinking Anthropology.*
1968   Ritual. In Vol. 13, *International Encyclopedia of the Social Sciences.* New York: Macmillan and The Free Press.
Leach, Edmund R.
1972   Ritualization in Man in Relation to Conceptual and Social Development. In *Reader in Comparative Religion: An Anthropological Approach.* 3d ed., ed. William Lessa and Evon Vogt, 333 – 37. New York: Harper and Row.
Legge, J. D.
1961   *Central Authority and Regional Autonomy in Indonesia: A Study in Local Administration 1950–1960.* Ithaca: Cornell University Press.
1966   *Indonesia.* Englewood Cliffs, N. J.: Prentice-Hall.
Lembaga Basa dan Sastra Sunda
1976   *Kamus Umum Basa Sunda.* Bandung: Penerbit Tarate.
Lev, Daniel
1966   *The Transition to Guided Democracy: Indonesian Politics, 1957–1959.* Ithaca: Cornell University Press.
Lev, Daniel S.
1972   *Islamic Courts in Indonesia.* Berkeley: University of California Press.

Lévi-Strauss, Claude
  1955   The Structural Study of Myth. In Myth, a Symposium, *Journal of American Folklore* 78 (Oct.–Dec. 1955): 428–44. (Reprinted in *Structural Anthropology.*)
  1958   *Anthropologie structurale.* Paris: Plon.
  1963a   *Structural Anthropology.* Trans. C. Jacobson and B. G. Schoepf. New York: Basic Books.
  1963b   The Effectiveness of Symbols. In *Structural Anthropology.*
Lewis, I. M.
  1971   *Ecstatic Religion: An Anthropological Study of Spirit Possession and Shamanism.* Middlesex: Penguin Books.
Lombard, Denys
  1967   *Le Sultanat d'Atjeh au Temps d'Iskandar Muda, 1607–1636.* Paris: Ecole Francaise d'Extreme-Orient.
Luckas, Y.
  n.d.   Sejarah Gereja Katolik di Sumba dan Sumbawa (The history of the Catholic church in Sumba and Sumbawa). Off-set print. Waitabula: Sumbanese Catholic Church.
Mahadi
  1969   *Beberapa Tjatatan tentang Peradilan Agama* (Some notes on religious justice). Medan: Law Faculty of U.S.U., North Sumatra University.
Majid, Nurcolish
  1979   The Issue of Modernization among Muslims in Indonesia: From a Participant's Point of View. In *What is Modern Indonesian Culture?* ed. Gloria Davis, 143–55. Athens, Ohio: Ohio University Papers in International Studies.
Malinowski, Bronislaw
  1961   *Argonauts of the Western Pacific.* New York: Dutton.
Mallinckrodt, J.
  1974   *Gerakan Nyuli Kalangan Suku Dayak Lawangan.* Jakarta, Indonesia: Bhratra. [orig. 1925]
Marakub M., Baginda
  1969   *Djop ni roha pardomuan (paradaton Tapanuli Selatan).* Padangsidimpuan: Pustaka Timur.
Margadant, Leonard
  n.d.   *Het Regeeringsreglement* (The Constitutional Regulations).
Marschall, Wolfgang
  1976   *Der Berg des Hern der Erde.* Munich: Deutsche Taschenbucher.
McKean, Philip F.
  1977   Toward Theoretical Analysis of Tourism: Economic Dualism and Cultural Involution in Bali. In *Hosts and Guests: The Anthropology of Tourism,* ed. Valene L. Smith, 93–107. Philadelphia: University of Pennsylvania Press.

McKinley, R.
1979   Zaman and Masa, Eras and Periods, Religious Evolution and
        the Permanence of Epistemological Ages in Malay Culture.
        In *The Imagination of Reality: Essays in Southeast Asian
        Coherence Systems*, ed. A. L. Becker and Aram A. Yenogyan,
        303–24. Norwood, N. J.: Ablex Publishing Corporation.
McVey, Ruth
1981   Islam Explained. *Pacific Affairs* 54:260–87.
Meggitt, M.
1968   Uses of Literacy in New Guinea and Melanesia. In *Literacy in
        Traditional Societies*, ed. J. Goody, 298–310. Cambridge:
        Cambridge University Press.
Menage, V. L.
1979   The Islamization of Anatolia. In *Conversion to Islam*, ed.
        Nehemia Levtzion, 52 – 67. New York: Holmes and Meier.
Miles, Douglas
1965   Socio-economic Aspects of Secondary Burial. *Oceania*
        (Sydney) 35 (no. 3): 161–74.
1966   Shamanism and the Conversion of Ngaju Dayaks. *Oceania*
        (Sydney) 37 (no. 1): 1–12.
1976   *Cutlass and Crescent Moon*. Sydney, Australia: Centre for
        Asian Studies, University of Sydney.
Miller, Gerald D.
1977   Classroom 19: A Study of Behavior in a Classroom of a
        Moroccan Primary School. In *Psychological Dimensions of
        Near Eastern Studies* ed. L. Carl Brown and Norman
        Itzkowitz, 142–52. Princeton: Darwin Press.
Modigliani, E.
1890   *Un Viaggio a Nias*. Milan: Trves.
Moertono, Soemarsaid
1968   *State and Statecraft in Old Java*. Ithaca: Cornell University
        Modern Indonesia Project.
Mulder, Niels
1978   *Mysticism and Everyday Life in Contemporary Java*. Singa-
        pore: Singapore University Press.
Naim, Mochtar
1976   Segi-segi kehidupan budaya di Pasaman Barat. *Panji Mas-
        yarakat* (nos. 200, 202).
Needham, Rodney
1972   *Belief, Language and Experience*. Chicago: University of Chi-
        cago Press.
1978   *Essential Perplexities*. Oxford: Clarendon Press.
Nobele, E. A. J.
1926   Makale. *Tijdschrift voor Indische Taal-, Land- en Volkenkunde*
        65:1–143.

Nock, A. D.
1933   *Conversion: The Old and the New in Religion from Alexander the Great to Augustine of Hippo.* Oxford: Oxford University Press.

Noer, Deliar
1973   *The Modernist Muslim Movement in Indonesia (1900 – 1942).* Oxford: Oxford University Press.

Nooy-Palm, C. H. M.
1979   *The Sa'dan Toraja: A Study of Their Social Life and Religion.* Vol. 1. The Hague: Martinus Nijhoff.

O'Fahey, R. S.
1979   Islam, State and Society in Dar Fur. In *Conversion to Islam,* ed. Nehemia Levtzion, 189–206. New York: Holmes and Meier.

Onvlee, L.
1938   Over de Weergave van "Heilig" in het Soembaasch (Concerning the translation of "holy" into Sumbanese). *Tijdschrift voor Indische Taal-, Land- en Volkenkunde* 78:124–36.

Ortner, S. R.
1978   *Sherpas through Their Rituals.* Cambridge: Cambridge University Press.

Peacock, James
1978   *Purifying the Faith: The Muhammadijah Movement in Indonesian Islam.* Menlo, Calif.: Benjamin/Cummings.

Poerbatjaraka, R. Ng.
1926   Arjuna-Wiwaaha, Tekst en Vertaling. *Bijdragen tot de Taal-, Land- en Volkenkunde* 82:181–305.

Polo, Marco
1958   *The Travels.* Trans. R. Latham. Middlesex: Penguin Books.

Prasodjo, Sudjoko, et al.
1974   *Profil Pesantren: Laporan Hasil Penelitian Pesantren Al-Falak dan Delapan Pesantren Lain di Bogor.* Bogor.

Proyek Pembinaan Perguruan Tinggi Agama
1978   *Upacara Religi dan Beberapa Adat Istiadat Masyarakat Pegunungan Meratus di Kalimantan Selatan.* Banjarmasin: IAIN Antasari.

Pulungan, A. K.
1973   *Mangupa dengan aqidah agama.* Padangsidimpuan: Pustaka Timur.

Pulungan, A. K., and A. P. Parlindungan Lubis
1974   *Panuturan turtur di Tapanuli Selatan.* Medan: Toko Buku Deli.

Pulungan, Haspan
1974   *Masalah santan pamorgo-morgoi di Kecamatan Barumun ditinjau dari sudeut hukum Islam.* Padangsidimpuan: Universitas Nahdlatul Ulama Sumatera Utara.

Rabinowtiz, Isaac
1966   Toward a Valid Theory of Biblical Hebrew Literature In *The Classical Tradition: Literacy and Historical Studies in Honor of Harry Caplan*, ed. Luitpold Wallach, 315 – 28. Ithaca: Cornell University Press.

Radjab, Muhamad
1952   *Toradja Sa'dan (Kepelikan Satu Suku-Bangsa).* Djakarta: Balai Pustaka.

Random House
1967   *The American College Dictionary.* New York: Random House.

Ras, J. J.
1976   The Historical Development of the Javanese Shadow Theatre. *Review of Indonesian and Malaysian Affairs* 10 (no. 2): 50–76.

Rasjidi, Mohammad
1956   L'évolution de l'Islam en Indonesie (Java): Consideration Critique du Livre Tjentini (lière partie), Traduction du Livre Pati Tjentini (2ième partie). Manuscript. Wason Collection, Cornell University, Ithaca.

Rassers, W. H.
1959   Panyji, the Culture Hero: A Structural Study of Religion in Java. *Koninklijk Instituut vooar Taal-, Land- en Volkenkunde.* Translation Series, no. 3. The Hague: Martinus Nijhoff.

Reid, Anthony
1979   The Nationalist Quest for an Indonesian Past. In *Perceptions of the Past in Southeast Asia*, ed. Anthony Reid and David Marr, 281–98. Asian Studies Association of Australia, Southeast Asia Publication Series, no. 4. Singapore: Heinemann Educational Books (Asia) Ltd.

Reid, Anthony, and D. Marra, eds.
1979   *Perceptions of the Past in Southeast Asia.* Asian Studies Association of Australia, Southeast Asia Publication Series, no. 4. Singapore: Heinemann Educational Books (Asia) Ltd.

Ricklefs, M. C.
1979   Six Centuries of Islamization in Java. In *Conversion to Islam*, ed. Nehemia Levtzion, 100–128. New York: Holmes and Meier.

Rigg, Jonathan
1862   A Dictionary of the Sunda Language of Java. In *Verhandelingen van het Bataviaasch Genootschap van Kunsten en Wetenschappen.* Vol. 29. Batavia: Lange & Co.

Rippin, Andrew
1980   Qur'an 7.40: "Until the Camel Passes Through the Eye of the Needle." *Arabica* 27 (no. 2): 107–13.

Riwut, T.
1958   *Kalimantan Memanggil.* Jakarata: N. V. Pustaka.

Robson, S. O.
1983   Kakawin Reconsidered: Toward a Theory of Old Javanese Po-
         etics. Paper presented at the 3d European Colloquium on
         Malay and Indonesian Studies, 2–4 June, at the Instituto
         Universitario Orientale, Naples.
Rodgers-Siregar, Susan
1979   A Modern Batak *Horja*: Innovation in Sipirok Adat Cere-
         monial. *Indonesia* (Cornell University), no. 27 (April 1979):
         103–28.
1981   *Adat, Islam, and Christianity in a Batak Homeland.* Ohio
         University Papers in International Studies Series, no. 57.
         Athens, Ohio: Ohio University.
Rosaldo, Michelle
1980   *Knowledge and Passion, Ilongot Notions of Self and Social
         Life.* Cambridge Studies in Cultural Systems. Cambridge:
         Cambridge University Press.
Roth, H. L.
1968   *The Natives of Sarawak and British North Borneo,* 2 vols.
         Kuala Lumpur and Singapore: University of Malaya Press.
         [orig. 1898]
Rude, George
1980   *Ideology and Popular Protest.* New York: Pantheon.
Sa, Artur Basilio de
1961   *Textos em Teto Literature Oral Timorense.* Lisbon: Junta de
         Investigacoes do Ultramar.
San Francisco Chronicle & Examiner
1981   In Indonesia's Toraja, There's Life after Death (November 29).
Santoso, Soewito
1975   *Sutasoma: Study in Javanese Wajrayana.* New Delhi: Interna-
         tional Academy of Indian Culture.
Sarma, D. S.
1953   The Nature and History of Hinduism. In *The Religion of the
         Hindus Interpreted by Hindus,* ed. K. W. Morgan, 3–47. New
         York: Ronald Press.
Sartono Kartodirdjo
1966   *The Peasants' Revolt of Banten in 1888.* The Hague: Martinus
         Nijhoff.
1973   *Protest Movements in Rural Java.* Singapore: Oxford Univer-
         sity Press.
Schärer, Hans
1963   *Ngaju Religion: Conception of God among a South Borneo
         People.* Trans. Rodney Needham. The Hague: Martinus
         Nijhoff. [orig. 1948]
Schimmel, Anne Marie
1975   *Mystical Dimensions of Islam.* Chapel Hill: University of
         North Carolina Press.

Schrieke, B.
1955   *Indonesian Sociological Studies.* The Hague: W. van Hoeve.
Schwaner, C. A. L. M.
        Ethnographic Notes Translated from Dr. Schwaner's "Borneo." In *The Natives of Sarawak and British North Borneo,* ed. H. L. Roth, 2:clxi–ccvii. Kuala Lumpur and Singapore: University of Malaya Press.
Scott, James C.
1977   Protest and Profanation: Agrarian Revolt and the Little Tradition. *Theory and Society* 4.1 – 38, 211 – 46.
Siegel, James T.
1969   *The Rope of God.* Berkeley: University of California Press.
1979   *Shadow and Sound.* Chicago: University of Chicago Press.
Siregar, Palti Radja
1958   *Hukum warisan adat Batak di Angkola/Sipirok—Mandailing dan Padang Lawas.*
Skeat, W. W.
1900   *Malay Magic.* London: Macmillan.
Skinner, G. William
1959   *Local, Ethnic, and National Loyalties in Village Indonesia: A Symposium.* Southeast Asia Studies Cultural Report Series, no. 8. New Haven: Yale University.
Smith, Wilfred Cantwell
1957   *Islam in Modern History.* Princeton: Princeton University Press.
1962   *The Meaning and End of Religion: A New Approach to the Religious Traditions of Mankind.* New York: The Macmillan Company.
Snouck Hurgronje, C.
1906   *The Acehnese.* Leyden: E. J. Brill. [orig. 1894]
Soedjatmoko
1960   *An Approach to Indonesian History: Toward an Open Future.* Ithaca: Cornell University Modern Indonesia Project.
Soedjatmoko, et al.
1965   *Introduction to Indonesian Historiography.* Ithaca: Cornell University Press.
Soeharto
1981   *Agama dalam Pembangunan Nasional (Himpunan Sambutan Presiden Soeharto).* Jakarta: Pustaka Biru.
Sormin, P.
1961   *Adat Batak dohot hakristenon.* Pematang Siantar: Parda.
Spiro, M. F.
1966   Religion, Problems of Definition and Explanation. In *Anthropological Approaches to the Study of Religion,* ed. M. Banton, 85–126. London: Tavistock.

Bibliography

Statistik Indonesia
   1982   *Statistical Yearbook of Indonesia.* Bagian Statistik Tahunan
           dan Penerbitan, Jalan Dr. Sutomo No. 8. Jakarta: Biro Pusat
           Statistik.
Steward, J. H.
   1951   Levels of Sociocultural Integration: An Operational Concept.
           Southwestern Journal of Anthropology 7 (no. 4): 374–90.
Stoddard, Philip, et al., eds.
   1981   *Change and the Muslim World.* Syracuse: Syracuse University
           Press.
Suharso, Alden Speare, Jr., Yulfita Raharjo, et al.
   1981   *Migration and Education in Jakarta.* Jakarta: National In-
           stitute of Economic and Social Research (LEKNAS-LIPI).
Supomo, S.
   1979   "The Image of Majapahit in Later Javanese and Indonesian
           Writing." In *Perceptions of the Past in Southeast Asia,* ed.
           Anthony Reid and David Marr, 171–86. Asian Studies Asso-
           ciation of Australia, Southeast Asia Publication Series, no. 4.
           Singapore: Heinemann Educational Books (Asia) Ltd.
Suzuki, Peter
   1959   The Religious System and Culture of Nias, Indonesia. Ph.D.
           diss., Leiden, The Hague.
Swellengrebel, J. L.
   1960   Introduction to *Bali: Studies in Life, Thought and Ritual,* ed.
           W. F. Wertheim. The Hague: W. van Hoeve.
Tambiah, S. J.
   1976   *World Conqueror and World Renouncer.* Cambridge:
           Cambridge University Press.
Tampenawas, R.
   1894   Een en Ander uit de Aanteekening van R. Tampenawas, te
           Pernangenen. *Mededeelingen* (Nederlandse Zendeling
           Genootschap) 38:227–49.
Tanner, Nancy
   1970   Disputing and the Genesis of Legal Principles: Examples from
           Minangkabau. *Southwestern Journal of Anthroplogy* 26 (no. 4):
           375–401.
Team Research Mahasiswa Fakultas Sjari'ah
   1969   *Adat Istiadat dan Kepertjajaan Suku Dayak Pembakulan dan
           Hinas Kiri.* Banjarmasin: IAIN Antasari.
Temple, Gordon Paul
   1974   Migration to Jakarta: Empirical Search for Theory. Ph.D.
           diss., University of Wisconsin, Madison.
Tempo
   1978   Mangtrapai Nek Atta' (Ne' Atta''s Death Ceremony). 35 (no.
           8): 26–27.

Tugby, Donald
  1979   *Cultural Change and Identity: Mandailing Immigrants in West Malaysia*. Queensland: University of Queensland Press.
Turner, Victor
  1969   *The Ritual Process.* Chicago: Aldine Publishing Co.
UNESCO
Usop, Kma M., and Teras Mihing
  1979   *Adat Istiadat Daerah Kalimantan Tengah.* Palangkaraya, Indonesia: Departmen Pendidikan dan Kebudayaan, Propinsi Kalimantan Tengah.
Utrecht, Ernst
  1979   Army and Islamic Opposition in Indonesia. *Journal of Contemporary Asia* 9 (no. 2): 175 – 86.
vad der Kroef, Justus M.
  1959   Javanese Messianic Expectations: Their Origin and Cultural Context. *Comparative Studies in Society and History* 1 (no. 4): 299 – 323.
  1962   Messianic Movements in the Celebes, Sumatra, and Borneo. In *Millenial Dreams in Action,* ed. Sylvia Thrupp, 80–121. The Hague: Mouton and Co.
Van Leur, J. C.
  1955   *Indonesian Trade and Society: Essays in Asian Social and Economic History.* The Hague: W. van Hoeve.
van Nieuwenhuijze, C. A. O.
  1958   *Aspects of Islam in Post-colonial Indonesia: Five Essays.* The Hague: W. van Hoeve.
Veen, H. van der
  1965   *The Merok Feast of The Sa'dan Toradja.* The Hague: Martinus Nijhoff.
  1976   Ossoran Tempon Daomai Langi'. *Bijdragen tot de Taal-, Land- en Volkenkunde* 132: 418 – 38.
  1979   *Overleveringen en Zangen der Zuid-toradja's.* The Hague: Martinus Nijhoff.
Velde, J. J. v. d.
  1928   *Godsdienstige Rechtspraak in Ned. Indie.* (Religious justice in Indonesia). Leiden.
Volkman, Toby A.
  1979   The Riches of the Undertaker, *Indonesia* (Cornell University) 28:
  1984   Great Performances: Toraja Cultural Identity in the 1970s. *American Ethnologist* 11 (no. 1): 152 – 69.
  1985   *Feast of Honor: Ritual and Change in the Toraja Highlands.* Urbana: University of Illinois Press.
Wagner, Daniel A., and Adelhamid Lotfi
  1980a   Learning to Read by "Rote" in the Quranic Schools of Yeman and Senegal. Typescript.

Wagner, Daniel A., and Adelhamid Lotfi *(continued)*
1980b   Traditional Islamic Education in Morocco: Sociohistorical and Psychological Perspectives. *Comparative Education Review* 24 (no. 2, part 1): 238 – 51.

Wagner, Roy
1981   *The Invention of Culture.* Chicago: University of Chicago Press. [orig. 1975]

Weinstock, Joseph A.
1981   Kaharingan: Borneo's "Oldest Religion" Becomes Indonesia's Newest Relgion. *Borneo Research Bulletin* 13 (no. 1): 47 – 48.

Welsch, R.
1982   Personal communication.

Wertheim, W. F.
1959   *Indonesian Society in Transition: A Study of Social Change.* The Hague: W. van Hoeve. [orig. 1956]

Wessing, Robert
1974   Language Levels in Sundanese. *Man* 9 (n.s.): 5 – 22.

Whittier, Herbert L.
1973   Social Organization and Symbols of Social Differentiation: An Ethnographic Study of the Kenyah Dayak of East Kalimantan. Ph.D. diss., Michigan State University.

Widjajakusuma, Husein
1980   Perolehan Bahasa Indonesia Oleh Murie-murid SD yang Berbahasa Pertama Bahasa Sunda di Kotamadya Bandung (Studi Sociolinguistik). Jakarta: Pusat Pembinaan dan Pengembangan Bahasa.

Wielenga, D. K.
1909   Soemba: Slavenhandel, Annimsme en Spiritisme (Sumba: The slave trade and animism and spirit beliefs). *De Macedonier* 13:300 – 306, 369 – 73.
1923   Doodencultus op Soemba (Death ritual on Sumba). *De Macedonier* 27:297–310.

Woodside, Alexander
1971   *Vietnam and the Chinese Model: A Comparative Study of Nguyen and Ch'ing Civil Government in the First Half of the Nineteenth Century.* Cambridge: Harvard University Press.

Worsley, Peter
1968   *The Trumpet Shall Sound.* New York: Schocken Books.

Wouden, F. A. E. van
1968   *Types of Social Structure in Eastern Indonesia.* Trans. Rodney Needham. The Hague: Martinus Nijhoff.

Yamashita, Shinji
1980   The Ma'bugi' Feast in the Sa'dan Toraja (in Japanese). *Nanpo-Bunka* (Tenri Bulletin of South Asia Studies) 7:1–29.

1981   From Death to Life: A Ritual Process of Death in the Sa'dan Toraja. Paper presented at the South Sulawesi Conference, 9–11 December, at the Centre for Southeast Asian Studies, Monash University, Australia.

Zerner, Charles

1981   Signs of the Spirits, Signature of the Smith: Iron Forging in Tana Toraja. *Indonesia* (Cornell University) 31:89 – 112.

Zoetmulder, P. J.

1974   *Kalangwan: A Survey of Old Javanese Literature.* The Hague: Martinus Nijhoff.

1982   *Old Javanese-English Dictionary.* The Hague: Martinus Nijhoff.

Index